ISSUES OF REGIONAL IDENTITY

MANCHESTER
UNIVERSITY PRESS

John Marshall

edited by Edward Royle

ISSUES OF REGIONAL IDENTITY

In honour of John Marshall

MANCHESTER
UNIVERSITY PRESS
MANCHESTER AND NEW YORK

distributed exclusively in the USA by St. Martin's Press

Published by Manchester University Press
Oxford Road, Manchester M13 9NR, UK
and Room 400, 175 Fifth Avenue, New York, NY 10010, USA

Distributed exclusively in the USA by
St. Martin's Press, Inc., 175 Fifth Avenue, New York, NY 10010, USA

Distributed exclusively in Canada by
UBC Press, University of British Columbia, 6344, Memorial Road, Vancouver, BC, Canada V6T 1Z2

British Library Cataloguing-in-Publication Data
A catalogue record is available from the British Library

Library of Congress Cataloging-in-Publication Data applied for

ISBN 0 7190 5028 6 *hardback*

First published 1998

05 04 03 02 01 00 99 98 10 9 8 7 6 5 4 3 2 1

Typeset by
Servis Filmsetting Limited, Manchester

Printed in Great Britain by
Bookcraft (Bath) Ltd, Midsomer Norton

CONTENTS

Figures and tables

Figures

Tables

Notes on contributors

Robin Butlin is Principal and Professor of Historical Geography at the University College of Ripon and York St John, and was previously Professor of Geography at Loughborough University. His main field of research is historical geography and includes works on the changing character of rural England, *c.*1600–1900, historical geography and British imperialism, and the historical geography of the Holy Land.

Neil Evans is Tutor in History and Co-ordinator of the Centre for Welsh Studies at Coleg Harlech and Honorary Lecturer in the School of History and Welsh History at the University of Wales, Bangor. He has published extensively on urbanisation, ethnic minorities, labour and women's history in Wales, and on the national identities and historiography of Britain and Wales. He is joint editor of *Llafur: the Journal of Welsh Labour History* and a member of the committee of CORAL.

Luis Castells Arteche is Professor of Contemporary History at the University of the Basque Country. He is a specialist in social history and is the author of many books, including *Modernización y dinámica política en la sociedad guipuzcoana de la Restauración 1876–1915* (Madrid, 1987). He is a member of the executive committee of the Spanish Association for Contemporary History.

John Langton is Fellow in Geography at St John's College, Oxford. Born into a coalmining family in Standish, Lancashire, he was educated at the University College of Wales in Aberystwyth where he researched coalmining in south-west Lancashire in the seventeenth and eighteenth centuries. He has lectured in Human Geography at, successively, the Universities of Manchester, Cambridge, Liverpool and now Oxford. His continuing research is on the regional dimensions of English industrialisation and their relationship to cultural changes and differences, though he spent ten years working with Gören Hoppe on the effects of increased production for market exchange on the Swedish peasantry in the nineteenth century.

Norman McCord is Emeritus Professor of Social History in the University of Newcastle upon Tyne. Born at Boldon, County Durham, he was educated at Tynemouth High School, King's College, Newcastle (now the University of Newcastle upon Tyne), and Trinity College, Cambridge. He returned to Newcastle in 1960 as Lecturer in Modern History and remained there until his retirement in 1988. His work falls into three main sectors, mainstream modern British history, publications including *The Anti-Corn Law League* (Cambridge, 1958) and *British*

History, 1815–1906 (Oxford, 1991); local and regional history of north-east England, publications including *North East England: The Region's Development 1760–1960* London (Batsford, 1979); and archaeological aerial photography, publications including *North East History from the Air* (Chichester, 1991).

David Neave is Senior Lecturer in Regional and Local History in the Department of History at the University of Hull. He was one of John Marshall's first students at the University of Lancaster, and has since written extensively on aspects of the social, architectural and landscape history of the East Riding and Lincolnshire. Amongst his recent publications is the revised edition of Nikolaus Pevsner, *The Buildings of England. Yorkshire: York and the East Riding* (London, 1995).

Sidney Pollard is a graduate of the London School of Economics. From 1950–1980 he was successively Knoop Fellow, Lecturer, Senior Lecturer and Professor of Economic History at the University of Sheffield, and from 1980–90 Professor of Economic History at the University of Bielefeld, Germany. His main interests are the economic development of the British economy and the economic history of Europe in the modern period.

Elizabeth Roberts is Director of the Centre for North-West Regional Studies (CNWRS) in Lancaster University. She is interested in regional and women's history and her special research interest is oral history. She is honorary vice-president of the Oral History Society. She has published *A Woman's Place* (Oxford, 1984 and 1995), *Women and Families* (Oxford, 1995) and *Women's Work 1840–1940* (London, 1988 and Cambridge, 1995). She is editor of the *Regional Bulletin* (published by CNWRS) and is on the editorial board for the Centre's growing list of publications.

Edward Royle is Reader in History at the University of York. Born in Yorkshire, he was educated at Cambridge where he was a Fellow of Selwyn College before returning to Yorkshire in 1972. His main interests are in nineteenth-century radical political, religious and social history, with a developing interest in the local and regional history of religion in Yorkshire. His publications include *Victorian Infidels* (Manchester, 1974), *Radicals, Secularists and Republicans* (Manchester, 1980), *Modern Britain, a Social History 1750–1997* (London, 1997) and *Chartism* (Harlow, 3rd edn. 1996), as well as pamphlets, articles and chapters on aspects of Yorkshire religion, especially Methodism. He is chairman of CORAL and a member of the editorial board of the *Journal of Regional and Local Studies (JORALS)*.

Winifred Stokes was brought up in south-west Durham and educated at the University of London where she undertook for her doctoral research a local economic study of France during the Revolution. This converted her into an economic historian and she then directed her attention to the history of the north-east coal trade. After teaching cultural studies, family history and comparative local history at the University of East London, she retired back to Durham in 1989 and is now an Associate Lecturer with the Open University northern region. She is treasurer of CORAL and a member of the editorial board of *JORALS*.

JOHN K. WALTON is Professor of Modern Social History at Lancaster University. His books include *The English Seaside Resort: A Social History, 1750–1914* (Leicester, 1983); *Lancashire: A social history, 1558–1939* (Manchester, 1987); and *Fish and Chips and the British working class, 1870–1940* (Leicester, 1992). John Marshall supervised his Ph.D. thesis on the social history of Blackpool. Professor Walton is currently working on the comparative social history of seaside resorts in Britain and Spain.

OLIVER M. WESTALL is Senior Lecturer in Economics in the Management School at Lancaster University and Chair of CNWRS, whose publications series he founded and edited. He has published *The Provincial Insurance Company 1903–1939: Family, Markets and Competitive Growth* (Manchester, 1992) and edited *Windermere in the Nineteenth Century* (Lancaster, 1976), *The Historian and the Business of Insurance* (Manchester, 1984) and *Business History and Business Culture* (Manchester, 1996), along with papers investigating cartels, regulation, marketing and business culture in insurance, winning the Wadsworth Prize for Business History in 1992 and the Cass Prize for Business History in 1994. He is treasurer of the Economic History Society. He is currently working on a history of competition and collusion in British general insurance.

MICHAEL WINSTANLEY is Senior Lecturer in History at the University of Lancaster. He studied under John Marshall in 1972–73, was Research Fellow in Oral History at the University of Kent between 1974 and 1977 and has taught at Lancaster University since 1978. He is a member of CNWRS and has published on a variety of aspects of nineteenth-century Lancashire history including the cotton factory workforce, child labour, retailing, rural society, Oldham radicalism and the history of Lancaster.

Acknowledgements

The editor and publishers acknowledge the following for permission to use copyright material:

Thomas Nelson and Sons Ltd, for permission to reproduce a map as Figure 6.1 from A. E. Smailes, *North England* (London and Edinburgh, 1960), p. 165.

The University of Wales Press, for permission to reproduce a map as Figure 10.1 from A. H. Dodd, *The Industrial Revolution in North Wales* (Cardiff, 1971), p. 130.

Financial assistance for this publication has been gratefully received from the Conference of Regional and Local Historians (CORAL) and the Marc Fitch Fund which has generously met the costs of producing the maps for this volume.

The editor and contributors are very grateful to Unity Lawler of the University of Lancaster for her invaluable work in helping to compile the section, 'John D. Marshall: a bibliography'. Finally, as editor I should like to thank the contributors for their support in this project, and John Marshall himself for inspiring it.

Edward Royle
University of York

Abbreviations

[C]RO	[County] Record Office
EcHR	*Economic History Review*, second series
EU	European Union
JORALS	*Journal of Regional and Local Studies*
PRO	Public Record Office
CNWRS	Centre for North-West Regional Studies
CORAL	Conference of Regional and Local Historians

Figure 1.1 **The ancient counties and modern standard regions of Britain**
Sources: *Ordnance Survey Atlas of Great Britain* (Ordnance Survey and County Life Books, London, 1982), p. 178; *Social Trends* (Stationery Office, London, 1997), p. 229; *Britain 1997. An Official Handbook* (Stationery Office, London, 1997), inside front cover

1 *Edward Royle*

Introduction: regions and identities

The historical concept of the 'region' is frequently used but difficult to define. Its etymology suggests a link with administration, an area under common rule,[1] but this creates as many problems as it answers, for, conversely, region is today a convenient word to describe an area of territory not necessarily under one government. The building blocks of administration in Britain and the western world have been the manor, the parish or township, the borough or city, the county and, increasingly over the past five hundred or so years, the nation-state. Regions can transcend these, larger perhaps than the borough, smaller perhaps than the county or nation, though sometimes cutting across county or national boundaries and even embracing large parts of a continent or group of continents. Thus, Pirenne and Braudel could each focus on the Mediterranean as a region, and Palmer could think of a North Atlantic world of democratic revolution.[2] In the late twentieth century, 'Pacific rim' countries have become a 'region' and, as measured by transport times even by sea, the Pacific is smaller now than the Mediterranean was a millennium ago.

Such historical regions are unstable, which was the point of Pirenne's thesis about the break-up of the ancient world centred on the middle sea, so when religious divisions cut across what had formerly looked like a coherent region, it ceased to be such. The region, therefore, is for the historian a term of convenience, located specifically in time as well as space, with no promise of more than temporary existence. In this sense it differs from the geographical region which begins with a fixed definition in physical characteristics and with identifiable boundaries. The Himalayas, the Pyrenees and the Alps have within human history been relatively stable facts of life. Yet even the significance of physical barriers, such as might delineate geographical regions, is historically determined. A sea or a river, which might be a barrier in one era, can form a communications link in another – the Mediterranean again being a case to exemplify this. When land communications are slow and difficult, water unites, as with the North Sea in Viking times or the Baltic then and now. As land communications become more rapid and convenient, water can present a relative barrier. Much depends on the availability of suitable bridge points on rivers, or the presence of rapids. The Rhine in Europe, it could be argued, has both defined a region along its banks – the Rhineland – and has divided that region into different political units – the Rhine frontier. Similarly of mountains. The Eifel/Ardennes in one sense form a unified region of high moorland and deep valleys across three countries and languages, but it has also provided an impenetrable barrier as secure as the Rhine – or did so until the *Blitzkrieg* of 1940.

The geographical region then, might appear to have more permanence than the administrative unit, but this does not mean it is immutably fixed in the 'reality' of the physical landscape. It is how human beings have reacted to, and in some cases modified or evaded, the physical environment that has shaped the changing concept of the physical 'region'. The East, for example, may be a geographical expression but it is culturally determined. The Near East, the Middle East and the Far East are all used as descriptions of regions, relative to the West and conventions of European map-making. Whether Turkey belongs to the Near East or the Middle East depends on the criteria and the historical period. In the 1870s, Britain saw the Ottoman Empire as very much a part of the Near Eastern 'question', even though the disputed territories of 1878, in Serbia and Bosnia, are now seeking to join 'the West', while Turkey, although part of the North Atlantic Treaty Organisation, is consigned to the Middle East. The Near East, in its former sense, has now been abolished, but it is the political not the geographical map of the eastern Mediterranean that has changed in this process of redefinition.

Such variations in usage over time might suggest that the regional concept should be abandoned. Yet this would be unrealistic in a world which speaks of regional powers, and in a European Union with a regional policy, in which regional government is becoming more the norm than the exception. Regions are assumed to exist, and the historian must therefore seek out their meaning and identity, unstable, fluctuating and ambiguous though these meanings and identities are. To the bureaucrat and planner, though, this is not good enough. Regions need to be fixed. Who is to receive regional aid and who is not? Which area do these statistics refer to, as opposed to those? Boundaries must be drawn. Regions can therefore be defined in two ways beyond their mere physical characteristics – important and sometimes decisive though these have been and are. They can be taken as administrative units, or they can be regarded more loosely as zones of human activity.

The first is the simplest, because data is usually collected within administrative boundaries. This is a major reason why regional historians, unlike physical geographers, are seldom tempted to study regions across national frontiers, desirable though this might be in theory. The legislative writ stops even when the geological strata continue beneath man-made borders. Within

Britain, the natural unit for regional studies has therefore often been the county, or group of counties, more because they are 'there' than because they necessarily have any 'objective' meaning. The county boundaries of Britain, with perhaps rare and important exceptions like the Tamar between Cornwall and Devon, are not natural, and even a river such as the Tamar is more a convenience for the map-maker than a serious barrier to human activity. The custom was to use rivers and streams to mark administrative boundaries because they were easy to locate on the ground and relatively fixed, but there has been no consistency. The Dee and the Severn do not offer an invariable boundary between England and Wales, nor until recently did the lower Wye. These boundaries have, partly for historical reasons, been drawn elsewhere.[3] Similarly with estuaries. Most have divided counties in the past, though not Morecambe Bay until 1974. In 1974, the Furness District was taken out of Lancashire and into Cumbria, but at the same time the decision in other cases was to make estuaries the centres of new counties rather than the divisions they formerly were. Thus the area around the Tyne and Wear was carved out of Northumberland and Durham; Cleveland around the Tees was formed from Durham and Yorkshire; Humberside took its name and identity from the River Humber, incorporating parts of Yorkshire (East Riding) and Lincolnshire; Merseyside similarly was created from parts of Cheshire and Lancashire; and Avon was fashioned from parts of Somerset and Gloucester around the river Avon. By April 1997, though, none survived intact as administrative units. Unpopular though these estuary counties were, it is interesting that the attempt was made in the 1970s to forge new county identities based on rivers, and it is also significant that no attempt was made at that time to create others based on the Thames estuary, or the lower Severn across the Wales/England border, or across the Solway Firth from Cumbria to Dumfries and Galloway. In Scotland, the Forth with its bridges, continued and continues to divide, whereas the Clyde, without a bridge downstream of Erskine, was made the rationale behind the single county of Strathclyde until again fragmented twenty years later. Strangest of all, in matters of county identity, is the re-emergence of Rutland out of Leicestershire in 1997.

The existence of counties, old or new, and reasons for their survival or not in changed forms, is not therefore simply a matter of physical geography. As with the nations of Europe or the former European colonies in Africa, boundaries are frequently the product of historical accident, past military truces, administrative vested interests, and much human sentiment. These do not in themselves create regions, though historically the areas within traditional boundaries may become regions, just as they may become nations. Boundaries may be drawn from above, by appeal to physical or statistical characteristics, but their validity will depend upon their acceptance from below. The geographer, planner and political scientist frequently approach the delineation of a region from the top – the view, in Britain, from Whitehall or Westminster, or in the European Union, from Brussels/Bruxelles – though the human geographer is also concerned with human activities on the ground. The historian and historical geographer is – or should be – concerned primarily with the view from the bottom, what a region means (if anything) to the person who lives there and how this is expressed in human activities. Region historically, therefore, is not a fixed concept, but a feeling, a sentimental attachment to territory shared by like-minded people, beyond the local administrative unit but possibly not – or not always – extending so far as the boundaries of a more distant administrative unit. It is an imagined community no less than the nation is, though frequently it lacks the confirmation of a government and boundaries defended if necessary by force, characteristic of the nation-state.

The relationship between the top-down and bottom-up views of a region is an intriguing one, for they do not exist in isolation from each other. As Sidney Pollard shows in his wide-ranging essay (chapter 2), the starting point for a regional study can be the geographical 'given' – the uplands of Cumbria, the Pennines, the 'high fen' of the Eifel/Ardennes; or the waterlogged low ground of the English Fens, and of the Rhine or Po deltas. These geographical features do not determine the activities of the people but they do condition them so that the economic activities and culture of a people may reflect the 'natural' features of their environment. Though many a mountainous region might appear to generate a William Tell or, indeed, a Peer Gynt, and the lowland might produce its Tyl Ulenspiegl, similar regions do not always produce the same characters and culture. The historian's task is to discern the general in the unique and the unique in the general and to use the one to help explain the other. Physical geography might prompt certain cultural forms but human beings then enact – or fail to enact – them, just as in turn human activities may reshape or redefine the physical geography of an area by building tunnels through mountains, damming streams, bridging rivers and draining fens. As Pollard points out, physical features might define a potential region and help shape human activity, but ultimately it is what human beings make of that environment which shapes the nature of the region.

This is clearly illustrated in the study of the Fens provided by Robin Butlin (chapter 3) who shows how a region that is relatively clearly defined in geographical terms has prompted in the past different perceptions in the outside world and generated attitudes and institutions peculiar to itself. On the one hand there was an image of 'waste' and isolation, and on the part of Fenlanders a suspicion of the wider world and deep poverty. On the other, the Fens presented a challenge to 'improvers' and called for Crown and parliamentary interventions which imposed a faltering and hesitant but progressively regional approach to improvement in the form of drainage commissions and corporations, sometimes in conflict with local interests and inertia. In this way a geographical region cutting across administrative boundaries could generate its own images, character and institutions.

But the correspondences between the geographical region, and the perceptions and institutions developed in and for it, are not always so clear. In their comparative essay, John Walton and Luis Castells take the Basque Country of northern Spain and the north-west of England as case studies and demonstrate the limits of environmental determinism (chapter 4). Here two superficially similar regions, apparently similarly subdivided, appear to their inhabitants in quite different ways despite many parallels in history as well as geography. Regional identity is thereby seen to be a difficult and elusive entity, as much the product of external forces, such as the differing policies and traditions of the central administrative state, as of internal factors such as language and culture.

Yet such cultural matters are basic to identity and their roots can be understood only historically. Across Catholic Europe, for example, surprising correspondences can be found between twentieth-century patterns of religious – and indeed political – behaviour on the one hand, and on the other the size of parishes and level of spiritual provision or neglect in the seventeenth and eighteenth centuries, reflecting in turn economic organisation and the wealth of the land.[4] Such persistence of cultural and religious patterns can also be seen, as John Langton shows in chapter 5, in south Lancashire where the supposed impact made on the identity of the area by Irish Catholicism in the nineteenth century is seen to rest on deeper traditions of English Catholicism from two or more centuries earlier. The patchwork of different allegiances in that part of Lancashire between the Mersey and the Ribble, the Pennines and the sea, raises again the question posed by Walton and Castells about when is a region not a region?

The same question is raised by Norman McCord in chapter 6. As he shows, the north-east of England has been a very flexible idea over many centuries, extending for some purposes from the Humber to the Tweed. As a historical concept it must be made time specific if it is to have any useful meaning in historical analysis: not what makes the north-east a region, but what gives it regional identity at a particular time? In the nineteenth century, it was the dominance of coal – its mining, transporting and shipping – which shaped the economy, the outlook and the culture of sufficient of the people to make it the defining characteristic of the north-east as a region at that time. Winifred Stokes shows, in closer detail in chapter 7, how other networks of activity might establish separate identities within such larger regions, as she examines the financing of the railways, docks and mines of south Durham, where local connections and rivalries proved stronger than links with London in defining a financial and business community of a distinctively regional nature. None of this can be given a precise boundary to satisfy the statistically inclined, for the regionality of Stokes's study lies in the relationships of people and institutions with territorial links rather than in territory itself.

The idea that England, and indeed Britain, is a country of regions shaped by dominant industries and forms of employment is explored by Michael Winstanley in chapter 8 with reference to the variegated pattern of female employment in grocery and general shopkeeping. Here he starts not with a region seeking justification and definition, but with intriguing differences in the female participation ratio in the retail labour force which call for a regional understanding and interpretation of national statistics, opening up views on the rich diversity of working-class lives which expressed themselves in styles of housing, attitudes to employment, consumption patterns and gender relations. The different identities which this study discloses in different parts of Edwardian Britain reinforce the importance of regional studies in the construction of national histories.

Nevertheless, the quest for the identity of a region can often seem analogous to the pursuit of the meaning of class, about which McCord has written elsewhere.[5] Both have that property of the Cheshire cat. Penetrating and critical historical analysis can make the physical form disappear, and yet something still remains, a reality beyond reality: not what a region is or how it is to be explained, but what it means, how it was understood in a specific context, and how it was created in that context. A notoriously difficult case study here concerns the Yorkshire version of the Cheshire cat. The existence of Yorkshire, not merely as an administrative unit – which, as David Neave points out in chapter 9, for many purposes and much of its history it has not been – but as a living region, is more frequently asserted than demonstrated or explained. Yet if Yorkshire folk feel a reality – and the same might be said of north-easterners, Lancastrians if not all north-westerners, Fenlanders or the Welsh – that feeling can become a historical 'fact' as much as any river or mountain range. Yorkshire, as Neave explains, has its boundaries, but they are neither consistent nor logical and certainly do not embrace a single, unified region. Physically, Yorkshire stretches from the Tees in the north, to the high point of Mickle Fell and the crest of the Pennines (but not consistently) in the west, to the sea at Flamborough Head and the tip of Spurn Head in the east and then along the Humber and south to – where? Geography fails to provide an answer. After the marshes of the Isle of Axholme, several minor watercourses form the actual boundary, without any particular logic.[6] In J. B. Priestley's imagination, he knew on his way northwards from Chesterfield that on entering Sheffield he was 'in the true North country' when he saw the people, 'with their stocky figures and broad faces, humorous or pugnacious'.[7] He had reached the 'North of England' when, 'On the road to Barnsley the stone walls began'. Though, as a Yorkshireman, Priestley thought he knew instinctively when he was in Yorkshire, in fact his tell-tales were unreal, but no more so than the criteria used in 1965 and again in 1974 to create a region for the Yorkshire and Humberside Economic Planning Council.[8] Initially this included the counties of the West Riding, East Riding, the City of York and the Kesteven division of Lincolnshire. After 1974 it included the counties of West, South and North Yorkshire and Humberside. Neither version had coherence and it was abolished in 1979 along with the other planning councils, although it remains as one of the eight Standard Regions into which England is divided for statistical purposes. Yet Yorkshire as an idea persists like the grin on the face of the cat, in a false identification with the dynastic struggles of the later middle ages, a county cricket club and, as Neave points out, a host of other institutions bearing the name 'Yorkshire', even if some of them have little or nothing to do with the county. The Yorkshire Television transmission region, for example, excludes half the county – including parts of York – but includes the whole of Lincolnshire, with parts of Cambridgeshire and Norfolk; and North Yorkshire takes its electricity not from Yorkshire Electric in Leeds but from Northern Electric in Newcastle.

In his chapter on the East Riding (chapter 9), Neave seeks to unpick the Yorkshire concept, and to discover the reality of one of its Ridings, a place which stubbornly refused to be abolished in 1974 and which achieved a resurrection in name and almost in boundaries in 1996 even though the county of Humberside had much more to commend its existence than the people north of the Humber were ever willing to admit. What Neave shows is that the East Riding had boundaries, despite some fuzziness at the edges, with a heartland centred on the Wolds and the Holderness plain but, more importantly, within these boundaries there was sufficient of a distinctive history, economy and culture to create an identity stronger than economic and commercial links across the Humber.

The same kind of analysis could be applied to other parts of Yorkshire, and other large counties. The plain of York may have been separated from the textile uplands to the west of Leeds by economic structures based on differences in rock, soil and water types, but this regional distinctiveness was reinforced in the consciousness of the inhabitants by political and cultural traditions. For example, in the early nineteenth century, the two areas were differentiated by newspaper circulation zones: to the west, the Leeds press, and in particular the *Leeds Mercury*, established in its readership a set of horizons and a way of looking at the world which were distinctively urban, commercial, industrial, and in religion Nonconformist. The county papers based on York, notably the *Yorkshire Gazette*, did the same for the farmers of the vale and moors, with a content and image related to an older and more hierarchical way of life based on agriculture, large estates and the Church of England. The volume and direction of communications, whether by cart or car, newspaper or television, provide geographers and historians alike with one measurable contribution to the making of a sense of identity. As Neave and Stokes both show, a region is never water-tight, but the flow of ideas and people, gossip and produce, investment and influence, help to establish what might approximate to an identity for the people and their region at any single point in time.

The student of regions in England and Wales is confronted with the problem that this regional sense has rarely been overwhelming or maintained in the same form for long. The tensions between nationhood, regionality and faltering identity are clearly seen in Wales. As Gwyn Williams put it with brutal frankness and a twinkle in his eye: 'Wales is impossible. A country called Wales exists only because the Welsh invented it. The Welsh exist only because they invented themselves.'[9] As with much of Williams's humour, this contains a serious point about the basis, or otherwise, for a Welsh identity. With supreme arrogance, the Standard Regions into which Britain is divided for governmental statistical purposes treat both Wales and Scotland as single 'English' regions. Yet neither is homogeneous in physical structure, language or culture. As Neil Evans shows, the land called Wales can be divided into at least two regions, centred on Chester (later, Liverpool) and Bristol – neither of which is in Wales at all. Cardiff had little to offer Caernarfon in the nineteenth century, and had even less to offer before the surge in demand for coal brought prosperity and population growth to the south Wales coal field during the course of the century. Then, as with the north-east of England, this south-eastern region of Wales gained its own identity from its economy and the social consequences of that economy in mining and heavy industry. Similarly, Evans explores the identity of Wales beyond its southern-most counties at a specific historical moment in relation to particular defining features, and concludes that it subdivides into three regions: the north-east, based on slate; the north-west, based on coal; and the centre as a sort of residual category which achieved no real identity at all (chapter 10).

Nevertheless, Wales and Scotland have aspirations to be or become regions in the original etymological sense of the word. As with the Basque Country, but not the north-west of England, disparate parts of regions can become a single and more or less coherent region under certain – often political – circumstances. Scotland is united by neither language nor religion; it is economically diverse and geographically divided. Yet, with the possible exception of Shetland, nationalism driven by a political agenda has, in the last quarter of the twentieth century, been reinventing Scotland as a distinct European region. The same has been happening, to a lesser extent, in Wales. This in turn raises the problem of the peculiarities of the English who are in danger of becoming what is left over in Britain when the Scots and the Welsh have departed.

The English have a state without a constitution, and a nation without the trappings of nationality.[10] In that context regionalism ought to be strong but what England has lacked is a tradition of regional government. Whereas Germany inherited a pattern of federal regional governments from the patchwork of medieval jurisdictions in the Holy Roman Empire, only partly rationalised by Napoleon, and even went so far as to re-invent *Länder* for the former DDR territories in 1990, England has been a politically united country for a thousand years, with a devolved administration but a central legislature. Countries with centralised Napoleonic constitutions, such as France, Italy, and Spain, have since the 1970s learned to devolve both legislative powers and administrative responsibilities to their regions. In England, the centralist tradition has coexisted with an administration devolved over a period of five hundred years and more to parish, corporate borough and shire county. These have become substitutes for the English regions. As Walton points out with regard to the north-west, it lacks a political identity distinct from the centre, and its involvement in the economy of the Empire subordinated any sense of regional identity to participation in the imperial nation-state as a whole. The same could be said of Wales and Scotland. When Britain was a world power, there was something for its components to feel part of as they participated in the economics and settlement of Empire. Only with the decline of Britain as a major power has that identification with the centre weakened and been replaced by a stronger sense of regional, even national, identities.

What the nineteenth century did see in England was not the growth of regionalism but the rise of provincialism, expressed through political and commercial interest groups, partly but not exclusively involving new and assertive social classes who developed an image of themselves and their importance as a challenge to the dominance of London in English and British affairs. At the beginning of the nineteenth century, the population of London came to over 10 per cent of the population of Great Britain. The equivalent figure for Paris was 2 per cent.[11] London uniquely appeared to gather all things to itself. The rise of the English provinces, with their new economic power, can be seen as a response. 'What Manchester thinks to-day, London thinks tomorrow', was the aphorism asserting provincial pride. Organisations demonstrated the power of the provinces – the Anti-Slavery movement, the Anti-Corn Law League, Chartism, the National Education League and the National Liberal Federation. Donald Read, who has argued this interpretation of nineteenth-century history, sees a decline of this provincial movement in the twentieth century.[12] Yet even in the nineteenth century, it was a movement to reform the electoral system and reshape governmental policy at the centre, not to take political power from the centre, or was so until the Irish forced the issue of political devolution on the rest of the country in the 1880s. And in the twentieth century, even that provincial initiative has been lost, except in the subordinate Celtic fringes of Greater England.

Regional identity in England, therefore, has lacked a political dimension and so for many purposes it is the administrative unit which has served as a substitute – in particular, the county. Regions in other shapes and forms have existed in the mind's eye of the statistician, the planner, and the map-maker of land usage, geological structure or river basins, but these alone do not make history. So what remains for the historian? The first task of the historian is to remind those who approach the subject from a physical or administrative point of view that regions considered from the bottom up exist first in the minds of the people, and if they do not live in the imaginations of the people they are unlikely to inspire loyalty and gain a living identity. True regions must be an expression of regional culture in its broadest sense. Moreover, this is a constantly changing culture, with deep roots in the past and links with the physical environment, yet susceptible to inventions and reinventions of tradition in the present. Like nationalists in the nineteenth century, those who would discover 'natural' regions must be prepared to invent them in the literature, religion, music, leisure, values and outlook of the people. Read's argument in his study of the *English Provinces* is that the forces of centralism in the twentieth century have re-asserted themselves successfully against the contrary forces of provincialism.[13] The development of BBC English, for example, has led to a weakening of distinctive regional dialects, compounded, one might add since the 1960s, by the encroachment of an all-pervasive mid-Atlantic accent, the harbinger of an American culture which Britain, unlike France, has been reluctant to oppose. Another sign of the times might be the loss of the *Manchester Guardian*'s regional title in 1959 and its transference to London in 1964; or, of wider significance, the general demise of an independent provincial press and its subordination to national and international media corporations. Far from promoting regionalism, the coming of BBC radio with its regional home services merely projected a metropolitan image with regional top-dressing, while the coming of local radio in the 1960s has, amid the clamour of many radio stations for the air waves, projected a transatlantic image in a parochial context. Regional television and television companies have done something to redress the balance but beyond regional news programmes they have done more to neutralise than to promote regional identities. Other examples could be added, such as the rise and fall of local football teams, once identified with their home in town or region, but now – in the case of major city-based teams – attracting players and supporters from across the country and beyond.

Though unduly pessimistic, and smacking of nostalgia, there is something in this argument that the regions of England today mean less than they ever have. Regional identity may well be reinforced by the daily objects and symbols that confront the inhabitants of a region – the newspaper, the train or bus company, the radio or television station, the brewery. As McCord suggests, one definition of the north-east in the nineteenth century might be the extent of the North Eastern Railway's operations. Certainly, if a region is an imagined community, then the familiar livery of a railway company could re-enforce a shared self-image as powerfully as the train itself as it transported the inhabitants of the hinterland to and from its regional commercial and cultural capital. Similarly, in the twentieth century, the Midlands were known to a generation not by some hypothetical grouping of counties, but by the coverage of the Midland Red bus company. Like animals, human beings know their territory by their familiar marks, however lacking in authenticity these might be or become. With the disappearance of these familiar marks the identity they conveyed is also weakened. Yet this may be too pessimistic. New signs may emerge to replace the old. With the decline of the north-east's nineteenth-century industries, it has lost that identity associated with those specific forms of economic and social organisation, but the identity of the region may still be recognised in other ways – in its football teams, for example, its distinctive brew of beer and its regional television company, even though the football teams contain players from across the globe, and neither the brewery nor the television company is owned within the region in the sense that the infrastructure of much of south Durham was owned regionally in the mid-nineteenth century. Above all, perhaps, a region such as the north-east is now recognised by its history or 'heritage', as presented in the Scandinavian-style open air folk museum of the north-east at Beamish in County Durham.

The historian is concerned with the richness of human life in all its perversity. He or she may not be able to define what regional identity is, but can warn that it is transient and recognisable for what it is not. The paradox is that identity is often easier to recognise by its absence than for its presence. Even if they are not sure what they have in common with one another, human groups can define themselves in their opposition to those who are not like themselves. This is one perception of the identity of class, and it applies also to the identity of a region. The Welsh and Scots might best be defined as not-English. As Gwyn Williams whimsically suggested, the Welsh were what was left when the rest of Britain had fallen to the English.[14] The businessmen of south Durham in Stokes's chapter were opposed both to London control and the Tyne-Wear coal monopolists. In his novel, *The Day the Queen Flew to Scotland for the Grouse Shooting* (1968), Arthur Wise imagines the rising of the provinces against London. The revolt begins in York, in anger at the choice of a southerner to play Christ in the York Mystery Plays. The people march against London. They cross the Trent, the supposed boundary of the north, but still they find local people joining them against London. They are joined by the Welsh. They enter the Home Counties. Still people join them. When they reach London, still they find yet more supporters, for London too is a province. The opposition against which they march turns out to be as much

in their own heads as the provincial identity that they represent. The irrationality of human sentiment may come as bad news to the tidy-minded administrator, but it is the stuff of history and it is the pleasure of the historian to celebrate it.

One task of the historian is, through the attempt to understand the people of the past, situated specifically in time and place, to inform and to warn those with other skills and purposes of the enigmatic nature of regional identity. But beyond this lie other reasons for studying regional history within the nature of history itself. As John Marshall has reminded us,[15] the region can be a preferred unit of study. Knowledge is so fragmented into academic disciplines which narrow the horizons and limit the questions posed of evidence, and history is so fragmented into sub-disciplines, that the nation-state is often too large a territory within which to attempt to grasp the full range of human experience. But at the other extreme English traditions of local history have been too local – literally parochial and too often tending to the antiquarian. As a number of magisterial French histories have shown, an approach which moves from local to regional, and perhaps thence to national, can still take in the contributions of different disciplines and achieve new insights in the process.[16] The region in this view constitutes an ideal unit for an integrated study. Local studies may grasp the unique and guard against generalisation, but in their uniqueness they frequently lack the broader context to give their uniqueness meaning. The region can provide that context, containing sufficiently similar case studies for comparisons to be meaningful, but sufficiently different for more general interpretations to be checked and qualified. Ideally a comparison of regions such as Winstanley, or Walton and Castells offer in this volume will then take the argument a step further. Also, as Butlin argues, despite inconveniences for the student reliant on conventionally gathered, county-based sources, the geographical region can form a proper alternative unit for study precisely because it does challenge conventional administrative divisions and definitions as it reminds us of the stubborn grandeur of 'natural' regions.

John Marshall has devoted his life to this regional approach, both in practice and in his more theoretical writings. In the part he has played in CNWRS at Lancaster University, he has influenced one of a growing number of Regional Centres in institutions of higher education whose purpose is precisely the bringing together of different disciplines to enrich an understanding of what gives meaning and identity to a region – whatever its boundaries might be. And in his unremitting work for CORAL and support for the *Journal of Local and Regional Studies* (*JORALS*), he has attempted to create the means by which scholars from these Centres – and wherever local and regional history is taken seriously – can come together to forge a comparative understanding of the past. This collection of essays is one attempt to contribute to that vision and we offer it to John Marshall with gratitude and affection.

Notes

1 J. D. Marshall, 'Why study regions? (1)', *JORALS*, 5:1 (Spring 1985), 15.
2 H. Pirenne, *Mohammed and Charlemagne* (1937), trans. B. Miall (London, 1939). F. Braudel, *The Mediterranean and the Mediterranean World in the Time of Philip II* (1949), (London 1972–73 trans. S. Reynolds 2 vols); R. R. Palmer, *The Age of Democratic Revolution*, 2 vols (Princeton, 1959 and 1964).
3 For a discussion of the England/Wales boundary, see W G. East, *The Geography Behind History* (1938), enlarged ed (London, 1965), pp. 103–14.
4 W. J. Callahan and D. Higgs (eds), *Church and Society in Catholic Europe of the Eighteenth Century* (Cambridge, 1979), p. 6.
5 N. McCord, 'Adding a touch of class', *History*, 70 (1985), 410–19.
6 The boundaries of Yorkshire are described in D Hey, *Yorkshire from* AD *1000* (London, 1986), pp. 1–4.
7 J. B. Priestley, *English Journey* (London, 1934), p. 119.
8 D. C. Pearce, 'The Yorkshire and Humberside Economic Planning Council, 1965–1979', in P. L. Garside and M. Hebbert (eds), *British Regionalism, 1900–2000* (London, 1989), pp. 129–41.
9 G. A. Williams, *When Was Wales? A History of the Welsh* (London, 1985), p. 2.
10 See the essays in Garside and Hebbert (eds), *British Regionalism*, especially M. Burgess, 'The roots of British federalism'; M. Keating, 'Regionalism, devolution and the State'; and M. Hebbert, 'Britain in a Europe of regions'.
11 Population of Great Britain in 1801: 10,501,000; London 1,117,000; population of France in 1801: 27,349,000; Paris, 547,000 – see B. R. Mitchell, *European Historical Statistics 1750–1970* (London 1978), Tables A1 and A2.
12 D. Read, *The English Provinces c. 1760–1960. A Study in Influence* (London, 1964).
13 *Ibid*, pp. 243–67.
14 Williams, *When Was Wales?*, p. 3.
15 J. D. Marshall, 'Why study regions? (2)', *JORALS*, 6:1 (Spring, 1986), 1–12.
16 For example, F. Furet and J. Ozouf, *Lire et écrire: L'alphabétisation des Français de Calvin à Jules Ferry*, 2 vols (Paris, 1977) of which volume 1 has been translated as *Reading and Writing. Literacy in France from Calvin to Jules Ferry* (Cambridge, 1982).

Regional character: the economic margins of Europe

Introduction

'Region', it is well known, is a flexible term, and there is no agreement as to what kind of territory may be covered by it. European economic historians have tended to use it for three types of division, which Maarten Prak has named macro-, meso-, and micro-regions, respectively.[1] The first refers to large parts of the continent, such as the 'Atlantic region'; the second refers to substantial parts of countries; while the third would be represented by something like a single town and its hinterland. This essay is concerned with the second of these terms: regions large enough to have a broadly based internal economic life and yet small enough to possess a strong cohesion and an internal homogeneity based on occupational specialisation. For most purposes this would mean measurements of perhaps twenty to fifty miles (thirty to eighty kilometres) across.

In this chapter, particular interest lies in those regions of this kind which have frequently been grouped together as 'marginal': essentially these are mountainous areas, forests and marshlands, or, as Fernand Braudel put it rather more picturesquely, 'the rocky massifs, the foothills of mountains, damp or marshy regions, the wooded *bocages*, or the sea coasts'.[2] Jennet termed them 'deserts': 'The obvious deserts are moors and mountain tops; there are other desert areas, of a different kind, by the sea or the mouths of rivers – saltings, sand dunes and beds of oozy ground'.[3] According to LeGoff, 'the desert [in the middle ages] was the uncultivated and the wild'; most characteristically it was the forest.[4]

It will be evident that the marginality of these contains a strong historical element: mountains are easier to cross or climb, forests are less inaccessible, marshes more effectively drained nowadays than they were, say, two hundred years ago. This may be seen as part of the general development of regional differentiation: before the modern age, regions had little contact with one another and, since they had to be largely self-sufficient, there was a good deal of similarity between them. As we approach the modern age and the linkages between them improve, they are put in a position to specialise in accordance with their competitive advantages. Prak aptly sees this as an example of a Spencerian simultaneous progress of differentiation and specialisation, a development from 'incoherent homogeneity' to 'coherent heterogeneity' since the middle ages.[5] In the European context, the marginal areas in particular stand out as having been more different from the rest in former times than they are today. Moreover, then as now they formed only a small part of the whole, the exception rather than the rule. Yet, possibly, it is precisely this oddness which may lead to a new and perhaps a more profound insight into the nature of an economic region.

Disadvantages of the physical environment

In the extensive literature on European marginal areas from the middle ages onward, there is widespread, though by no means universal, agreement on the characteristics to be found among the societies living in them.[6] Possibly the most commonly noted quality was their poverty. This arose essentially out of the unsuitable nature of their environment in an age when most people were engaged in agrarian pursuits. On mountains, the land was sloping and the humus cover often thin and interspersed with rocks; the climate was harsh, the summers short and the winters long. It was therefore hard to eke out a living given the level of agricultural technology available in the past. On marshes, the ground would be waterlogged and, if near the coast, threatened by repeated inundations. Forests, even when they were not on difficult slopes, needed labour-intensive clearance to become workable at all.

At least as difficult as the nature of the ground was the problem of transport. On mountains, everything, including often even manure, had to be carried uphill on the backs of people or animals, and the produce carried downhill, as wheeled traffic was frequently impossible. Forests were equally difficult, though marshland sometimes was not since water afforded an easy means of moving heavy traffic. With a population thin on the ground, internal communications tended to be costly in time and resources; externally, these regions suffered from the distance to markets located in the richer regions of a country.

To these natural disadvantages was added, in the eyes of contemporaries, a general backwardness in the techniques in use. Innovations such as fertilisers, new rotations, new strains of plants, or steel ploughs, seemed to reach marginal lands later, not least because of fewer contacts with the outside world. People close to the poverty line could not afford to experiment even where practice on more favourable grounds had shown positive results.

Technical backwardness may, according to many observers, be seen as part of a larger problem of ignorance among marginal populations. Few professional men would settle there, while the churches would typically organise these regions into huge parishes, with the main place of worship, together with the residence of the priest, at one extreme point where they touched the lowlands. In any case, only the less educated clergy from less influential families would consent to live there. The people of those lands tended to be more superstitious and more likely to believe in magic, while for outsiders also, mountains, forests and marshes were haunted by evil spirits and inexplicable dangers. Marginal people were seen as being less well-read, and often ignorant on current affairs. Being far from the centre, they possessed little political or social power: decisions came from the centre to them, while they could exert little influence in the opposite direction.

Travellers, visitors and neighbouring populations, observing these hardships, would often express pity for the disadvantaged people living on the margins; others had nothing but contempt for them. People in the fertile lowlands, to which men and women from marginal lands would have to travel to seek seasonal work, would poke fun at their outlandish dialect, their exotic clothing, or their different ways of doing things. 'The mountain dweller is apt to be the laughing stock of the superior inhabitants of the towns and plains. He is suspected, feared and mocked.'[7] Their low wages, of which little was spent in order to take some cash home at the end of the season, and their necessarily shabby or primitive temporary accommodation would confirm the prevailing prejudice about the poverty and backwardness of this migrant labour. On the other hand, people far from these regions would in their ignorance endow their inhabitants with odd qualities: as late as the seventeenth century, Cornish miners were believed to spend all their lives underground, and fen people to have webbed feet.[8]

There was also much permanent emigration out of many marginal areas. Its particular significance lies in the fact that its extent can be ascertained in a more reliable statistical manner, rather than being based merely on the report of, possibly faulty, observation. Emigration was particularly heavy out of bleak uplands, with a tendency for its incidence to be the greater, the higher and the more distant the location of origin.

Challenge and response

Yet, perhaps surprisingly, the views expressed about people in marginal lands were not wholly negative. A minority of observers found much to admire, even to envy. In contrast to the spoilt inhabitants of the comfortable but unhygienic towns, people on the margins were often said to be healthy, as well as being well-built, taller and stronger. Far from the vices of civilisation, they were considered to be morally superior, unspoilt, leading a cleaner life. Some ages, like the eighteenth century, influenced by Rousseau among others and a little later by the Lake Poets, accepted particularly easily the notion of the Noble Primitive of those less advanced areas.

Marginal people were also said to be more resourceful, more able to turn their hands to anything, and more self-confident when thrown back on their own resources. Their societies turned more easily to mutual support and to collaborative effort, be it to maintain paths on mountains, or to build and repair the elaborate dams and dykes, the drainage and irrigation schemes of fens and marshes: these were frequently not merely a tribute to their co-operative talents, but also to their engineering skills.[9] It is part of the same historical picture that the British industrial revolution, a profoundly regional phenomenon, had its original locations almost exclusively in marginal regions.[10]

All these alleged positive qualities, it will be seen, were directly and precisely linked to the adverse natural circumstances facing these societies – a kind of Toynbee effect of challenge and response.[11] The same might also be said of the highly regarded military quality of men from the mountains. The courage, endurance under hardship and fighting spirit of the men from Switzerland, the Scottish Highlands or the Balkan uplands, which made them such sought-after mercenaries between the sixteenth and nineteenth centuries, were to a large extent thought to be the result of their Spartan living conditions at home.

Moreover, although badly equipped for tillage, marginal lands were not without other resources. Uplands generally offered favourable opportunities for stock breeding; the marshes, too, often had rich pasture land as well as easy fishing. It was on the basis of the consumption of their meat and dairy produce that marginal people were often seen to be well nourished. Animals or cheeses taken to distant markets acquainted them with the outside world, and the very need to trade, because their land could not fully feed them, encouraged entrepreneurial skills. The forests afforded nourishment to animals, and their timber was a most valuable commodity as fuel, as building material and as raw material for manufactured products. Deep forests were often hives of activity, housing charcoal burners and highly paid iron and glass makers, as well as makers of wooden articles of all kinds. Fens and marshes yielded reeds and osiers.

Mountains were rich in water power. They were also rich in minerals, or, at the least, the existence of minerals was more easily observed on mountain slopes. Once discovered, mineral ores were more easily worked than in the plains, partly because the water collecting in the pit bottoms could be led off to lower grounds without elaborate pumping apparatus, and partly because, the ground having little value agriculturally, landlords were willing to lease it on easier terms.

Lastly, marginal regions were more easily defended against invaders than open plains, since professional armies could not bring their superior numbers, artillery or cavalry effectively into play in them. Mountain and forest people used their intimate knowledge of the terrain, and people on the marshes their control over the water system, to defeat invaders who might, in any case, doubt if the poor lands were worth the fighting. 'The hills were the refuge of liberty, democracy and peasant republics'.[12] It is no accident that some of the earliest examples of freedom both from local feudal control, and from distant imperial domination, were encountered in such regions as Switzerland, Tyrol and the Netherlands. This, in turn, reduced the draining out of resources by parasitic outsiders, encouraged the search for innovation and made these regions pioneers in economic enterprise in certain periods of history. Given these characteristics, we are led to find reasons why some comparable regions, such as the Balkan uplands, failed to conform to this pattern. The relatively mild rule of the Ottomans in the early centuries of their occupation there offers part of an explanation. Moreover, conforming to their social structure, feudal estates were not found in these mountains: it was a region of peasant (family) proprietors and of freely roaming and frequently rebellious herdsmen.

Clearly, not all these attributes apply to the three types of region classified here, as well as widely in the literature, as 'marginal'. There are obvious differences between mountains, marshes and forests. Yet they have enough in common to be described quite regularly in a similar manner.

Much of this is common coin. Discussions of the way in which marginal conditions helped to shape social characteristics of this kind will be found in innumerable detailed contemporary accounts as well as in the more generalised geographical and historical literature. The implicit assumption which emerges from the widespread, perhaps universal, consensus is one of a substantial, even decisive, effect of the environment on society. Yet there is no agreement on its exact nature, and the mechanism by which it operates is by no means always clear. In fact, little attention has been given to it in the past.

Economic development in marginal areas

Of the direct impact of the environment on economic activity there can be little doubt. Rich, potentially fertile land will induce the dwellers on it to turn to tillage; forests will lead to wood working; fens to fishing and animal breeding; minerals to their mining and, if fuel and water power are available, to their refining. However, the exploitation of these opportunities also depends on the social structures shaped by humans. Thus we know that some social arrangements will react more quickly than others to the gains from specialising in, say, grain, wine or industrial crops when markets change. Some societies will not react to such incentives at all, or only after a long interval. Thus serfdom of the Russian type did not permit the exploitation of certain resources in the eighteenth and nineteenth centuries in a manner which could make it competitive with contemporary European practice.

Moreover, the possibilities for societies to exploit their environmental resources depend directly on the stage of technological development reached. Thus the exploitation of the enormous riches of the central European copper and silver mines in the early modern period depended on pumping, transport and metallurgy technology not available in earlier centuries. By the same token, some three centuries later, the more sophisticated geological techniques and advanced machinery which had then become available neutralised the advantages of upland mining, and allowed the plains to make use of their more favourable transport conditions; similarly, the steam engine allowed the textile mill owners of the industrial revolution period to desert their remote sites on mountain streams and move into the towns to reap the benefits of the more flexible labour supply to be found there, their lower transport costs and their range of external economies.

Coal diminished much of the value of forest location, and railways and canals built over much of Europe in the nineteenth century reduced some of the advantages of regions rich in natural waterways like the Low Countries. While the cottage industry, in textiles, metal work, clocks or musical instruments in their heyday in the eighteenth century favoured marginal regions in which agrarian yields were poor and labour was necessarily idle in certain seasons, the large-scale factory needed flat land and easy access. Pre-history and history, therefore, play a large part in the way in which marginal regions impact on the economic activities in them.[13]

Acculturation and the environment

Once we move away from purely economic activity, the influence of the marginality of regions on the societies living in them becomes more complex and subtle, but by no means any less pervasive. As an example we may revert to the overwhelming testimony to the bravery, pugnacity and martial skills of mountain people, compared with those people from the plains, over many centuries from the Scottish Highlands in the West to the Balkans in the East. Clearly, that is no accident. Herds and flocks grazing on uplands are easily robbed and need constant protection from humans and beasts. To chase rustlers or, for that matter, to engage in some reiving oneself, in difficult conditions over dangerous and often uncharted terrain, requires both courage and skill with arms. Villagers living by stock raising in mountainous areas would hold people who were deficient in these qualities in low esteem. Moreover, in the different yet comparable lives of foresters or fishing people, such conditions require not only rapid decisions, but also reliance on one's own judgement: a very different environment from the settled routine, determined by village agreement or the lord's *fiat*, which typically faced agriculturalists in the arable areas.

Again, there is wide agreement in the accounts on the strong sense of family honour as well as clan loyalty characteristic of such marginal regions. One aspect of this is to be found in the fierce vendettas which are a frequent feature of these societies, in which the overwhelming and inescapable social obligation is placed on all members of an extended family to avenge any harm done to any one of them. Arising out of a tight family system, this tradition is bound to strengthen it further. It is part of a linkage which reaches back into the past and will be projected into the future. In such conditions, history is family history, told, repeated and no doubt embellished, from generation to generation.

It is not difficult to associate this narrow social focus with the broken nature as well as the difficulties of the terrain. Households are dependent on one another within their close neighbourhood in emergencies; the large population centres are a long way away. The writ of the state hardly runs in truly marginal regions. While, as noted above, these exert little power in the major political centres, the reverse also tends to be true: thus these communities have had to develop their own social morals and their own methods of enforcing them. Tough conditions leave little room for mildness, and survival may depend on tough enforcement of the rules.

A similar line of explanation is likely to account for the equally well established tradition of hospitality to strangers reported from regions of this kind. Behind this lies the fact that locals well knew the difficulties of survival in their environment; but it may also be that living fairly isolated lives most of the time, they were glad to see new faces and to learn of the outside world.

Yet another quality of these regions appears frequently in reports of travellers and visitors: the alleged laziness of the menfolk. Most of the work around the house as well as in its immediate surrounding, in garden or fields, was done by women, while the men are reported as lounging around, bestirring themselves only in case of dire necessity, and frequently mocking those who are forever active and worrying about the next move and about accumulating material possessions. Again, it is not too difficult to derive the vision of extremely hectic activity, alternating with phases of apparently contemplative idleness, from the practical needs of herdsmen in inhospitable terrain and often harsh climate. By contrast, the womenfolk, who were not required to ride out in order to fight or rob, worked within a more tranquil routine. Clearly differentiated roles according to gender, and respect and protectiveness towards women, would follow naturally in those societies.

The list of peculiarities of social behaviour in marginal areas, as recorded in past centuries, could easily be extended; but it is clear that there is an important link in the chain of reasoning missing in the identification of the marginal environment with certain social characteristics: people, after all, are born with similar potentialities everywhere, and a baby transferred from marshland or mountain to city or plain would grow up with the characteristics of a burgher or plainsman. How are individuals acculturated to marginal life?

Few were there because they moved deliberately in order to be in an environment which suited their own predisposition, though history knows of a long line of mystics and oddballs, of criminals and those persecuted unjustly by the authorities, of rebels and religious sectarians, who moved into the deepest forests or the less accessible mountainsides as refuges, for security or to find isolation and tranquillity. Most marginal people are not there by choice, but by accident of birth. How do they adapt?

One explanation might be on the lines of the survival of the fittest. Weaklings, those unable to fend or decide for themselves, those born without initiative, would not survive the tough conditions for long; if we make the somewhat dubious assumption that some of these qualities might be inherited, their families would soon die out, leaving the field clear for the better adapted.

More plausible would be an explanation in terms of each generation growing into and accepting the necessary qualities for survival and canons of behaviour learnt from their elders. Some known characteristics, such as co-operativeness in the local context, or hospitality to strangers, could thus be easily accounted for, but courage, endurance and military spirit would be less easily derived on that basis. No doubt even mountain villages or forest settlements needed and could find room for individuals without such endowment in the posts of schoolteacher, clerk or village blacksmith; yet without a large majority of the population possessing the pattern required by the marginal existence, the settlement could hardly survive. Social selection, along that chain of reasoning, would pull out from a wide range of potential qualities at birth those needed by the regional environment, with the requirement that there were sufficient individuals well endowed with the necessary properties in the group to permit the society to flourish.

How did the society itself discover its best survival strategy? To some extent, it could learn from neighbours; new settlements brought with them the practices of their established community when they moved out into new marginal lands. Frequently, however, communications were poor and, more importantly, conditions would differ from mountain to mountain and from fen to fen. We must imagine a process of trial and error on a social scale, in the search for the most suitable variety of grain, the best month for sowing, the most productive time span for replanting of woodland or the most effective means of draining marshy land. What would then be required would be a record of years of complete or partial failure or loss, compared with relative success, associated with the practices used, embedded in a long and accurate memory of what caused either, but at the same time modified by accidental or contingent influences such as a season of drought, an enemy incursion, or an epidemic of man or cattle; and all of this would have to take place in ages innocent of scientific methodology or written records. Even then, moderate success may be fastened on as desirable practice, omitting the search for an even better method. There might also have been a more difficult choice between methods giving optimal results in good years or, as has been argued as an explanation of the adoption of open-field strips, methods which would be less than optimal as a rule, but prevent total catastrophe in bad years.[14] In any case, as conditions, such as the absorptive capacity of markets, changed, the whole process would have to be gone through *de novo*.

Once a 'best practice' – say transhumance, drainage of a certain kind, a crop sequence – had been found, the whole settlement would have to be persuaded to switch to it: the role and prestige of the successful pioneer would play an important part in that process. Contrariwise, if the leading personalities were among the more conservative members of the community, the necessary change could be fatally delayed. This also opens up the thought that 'best' practice might not be best for all, but could conceivably damage the interests of leading members of the community, who would on those grounds block it.

In the writings on cultural adaptation of this kind, an unspoken assumption often appears to be that a process similar to the one which created stripes for zebras or long necks for giraffes was at work. But those processes of natural selection would, as far as present knowledge goes, take an enormous number of generations, in which animals of unusual qualities, or sports, enjoyed superior chances of survival. Such a generous provision of time for experimentation is clearly not available to human communities. These, however, enjoy the advantage of reacting by observation rather than waiting for genetic sports. Nevertheless, it is often assumed far too easily and thoughtlessly that regional communities in pre-modern periods are likely as a matter of course to hit on social practices which fit them best into their environment.

Conclusion

All these considerations would apply to all societies, including those on fertile and blessed plains, and not merely those in marginal regions. It is, however, precisely the additional difficulties encountered by man on the economic margins which prompt the thought that adaptation to one's environment does not occur automatically, and that the region will exert an influence not merely on the character of society as a whole, but also on individuals living in it.

The differential roles which regions play in modern life in this way acquire an added dimension. It is not merely natural resources, location or overriding political and legal traditions which must be drawn on to account for their specific and specialised development, but also the more obscure yet powerful influence which the regional environment has over time exerted on social and individual character.

Thus, to cite the example which springs most frequently to mind, it was neither pure accident nor obvious natural resources, such as water power, mineral riches or cheap labour alone, which located the most dynamic regions of the British industrial revolution in marginal lands, including the uplands of Lancashire, Derbyshire and Yorkshire, north Wales and Cornwall, Clydesdale and the barren heath lands of the west Midlands, while no comparable innovatory activity appeared at the time in London, the other major cities, the old woollen districts of the West Country or the rich farm lands of East Anglia or Lincolnshire. Initiative, pushfulness, the willingness to work hard for low wages, habits of thrift and economising on resources, the ruthlessness of the *nouveau riche*, risk taking, a tendency to ignore authority derived from the long absence of guild power and physical distance from landlord, magistrate and parson, and similar qualities nurtured by the hard but also freer life on the margins, were surely of major importance too. They were precisely the qualities to be found in these regions which struck both contemporaries and today's reader of their accounts. There had taken place here a mutual adaptation of individuals to society, and society to its individual members.

Such specific regional characteristics of behaviour may still be discerned today, but for obvious reasons they have been much weakened by modern technical and cultural conditions. This should not, however, blind us to their significance in the past.

Notes

1 M. Prak, 'Regions in early modern Europe', in 11th International Economic History Conference, *Debates and Controversies in Economic History: A-Sessions* (Milan, 1994), pp. 19–55.

2 F. Braudel, *Civilization and Capitalism 15th-18th Century. Volume 1. The Structure of Everyday Life: The Limits of the Possible* (1979), trans S. Reynolds (London, 1988), p. 118; also S. Pollard, 'Marginal areas: do they have a common history?', in B. Etemad, J. Batou and T. David (eds), *Towards an International Economic and Social History. Essays in Honour of Paul Bairoch* (Geneva, 1995), p. 121.

3 S. Jennet, *Deserts of England* (London, 1964), p. 9.

4 J. LeGoff, 'The town as agent of civilization, c. 1200 – c. 1500', p. 72, in C. Cipolla (ed.), *Fontana Economic History of Europe*, vol. 1 (London, 1972), pp. 71–106.

5 Prak, 'Regions in early modern Europe', p. 27.

6 The literature is reviewed at length in S. Pollard, *Marginal Europe: The Contribution of Marginal Lands since the Middle Ages* (Oxford, 1997).

7 F. Braudel, *The Mediterranean and the Mediterranean World in the Time of Philip II* (1949), trans. S. Reynolds (London, 1972), vol. I, p. 46.

8 For images of the fen people, see below, chapter 3.
9 H. E. Hallam, *The New Lands of Elloe. A Study of Land Reclamation in Lincolnshire* (Leicester, 1954) and *Settlement and Society. A Study of the Early Agrarian History of Lincolnshire* (Cambridge, 1965); H. C. Darby, *The Medieval Fenland* (Cambridge, 1940). See also below, chapter 3.
10 Eg., P. Hudson, 'The regional perspective', in her *Regions and Industries. A Perspective on the Industrial Revolution* (Cambridge, 1989).
11 A. J. Toynbee, *A Study of History*, 12 vols (Oxford, 1934–61), esp. vol. 2.
12 Braudel, *The Mediterranean*, vol. 1, p. 40.
13 J-F. Bergier, 'Régions et histoire économique: quelques interrogations', pp. 106–7, in Etemad, Batou and David (eds), *Towards an International Economic and Social History*, pp. 101–7.
14 D. McCloskey, 'English open fields as behavior towards risk', *Research in Economic History*, 1 (1976), 124–70.

3 Robin A. Butlin

Images of the Fenland region

Introduction

As far as the aesthetics of their landscapes are concerned wetlands are not perhaps among the most obviously attractive places, nor for the most part do they attract instant inquiry about their evolution, the ways in which they have been perceived over historical time, or the social relations which underpin their rather monotonous topography and scenery.

Wetlands, however, including those that have been subject to varied and extensive attempts at drainage and reclamation for more intensive economic activity and human occupation over long periods of time, afford fascinating opportunities to investigate and exemplify the considerable complexities of the ways in which changing societies, through the lenses of belief systems and the opportunities of available technologies, have partly succeeded and partly failed to modify such environments for their own ends.[1]

Such is the case of the history of the Fenland of eastern England, whose evolving physiographic nature derives from the events and aftermath of rising sea levels after the last phase of the Quaternary glaciation, but whose regional historical geography owes much to the parallel processes of resource use by traditional economies and more centralised, or at least institutionally authorised, attempts to extract greater use value via drainage and intensification of land use. One attraction of the investigation of the history of this region is the possibility of uncovering the tensions and contradictions that are posed and effected by these opposing forces. The story of this region, like that of so many others in Britain and elsewhere, is not one of an even progress over time from a primitive to an advanced state, but a complex and at times confusing set of narratives, punctuated with periods of very strong resistance to change and of failure to effect change by reason of technical inadequacy and failure to understand the nature of the Fenland societies.

This essay in regional historical geography will address some of the basic features of the Fenland, with particular reference to the areas south of the

Wash, before moving to consider some of the 'hidden' processes affecting change or lack of it in the past. The chronological focus of the chapter will mainly be from c. 1600 onwards, and comparison from time to time will be made to parallel and contrasting experiences in other regions and countries of Europe.

Wetland environments: the broader context.

Wetlands are for the most part what would be called low energy environments, and many of them have coastal borders and outlets for their drainage systems. Thus water from catchments is conveyed for the most part by slow-moving rivers, with inadequate capacities for the discharge of large quantities of water. This context is compounded by other factors, including blockages at the coastal ends of wetlands variously by silt of higher level, or, in the case of the Netherlands, the Landes and the coasts of western France, by sand-dunes. Add to this the problems from peat shrinkage through drainage over time, through the agency of oxidation, plus the critical question of storm surges (the combination of high tides and very strong onshore winds) usually resulting in catastrophic flooding, especially in the North Sea, and the complexity of the problem is clear.

There are other senses in which wetlands are dynamic rather than static environments, evidenced in changes in climate and changes in natural vegetation sequences. Changes in climate through historic time are still insufficiently documented, notwithstanding the work of historical climatology. It is interesting to note that Lambert in her study of the history of the landscape of the Netherlands attributes the major reclamations of the Dutch Golden Age to ameliorations in the storminess of the late medieval climate when between about 1530 and 1725 there was a marked slackening off in the rate of the rise of sea-level with far fewer storm tides.[2] This was the period of the Little Ice Age, with colder winters, a drier climate and lower sea-level. The history of the storminess of the North Sea and the effect of storm surges on the history of flooding catastrophes around its coasts has been well documented by Gottshalk.[3]

The region on which this chapter focuses – the Fenland – is an area of 3,367 km^2 in eastern England, located within the counties of Cambridgeshire (including the former administrative unit of the Isle of Ely), Huntingdonshire, Lincolnshire, Northamptonshire, and parts of Norfolk and Suffolk (see figure 3.1). Its physiography is that of a basin, into which are fed large volumes of water via the rivers draining from the surrounding uplands (chalk in the north, east and south, and Jurassic clays and limestone to the west). The main drainage arteries of the Fen region include the river called the Great Ouse, the main southern drainage channel of the Fens, which has been frequently and

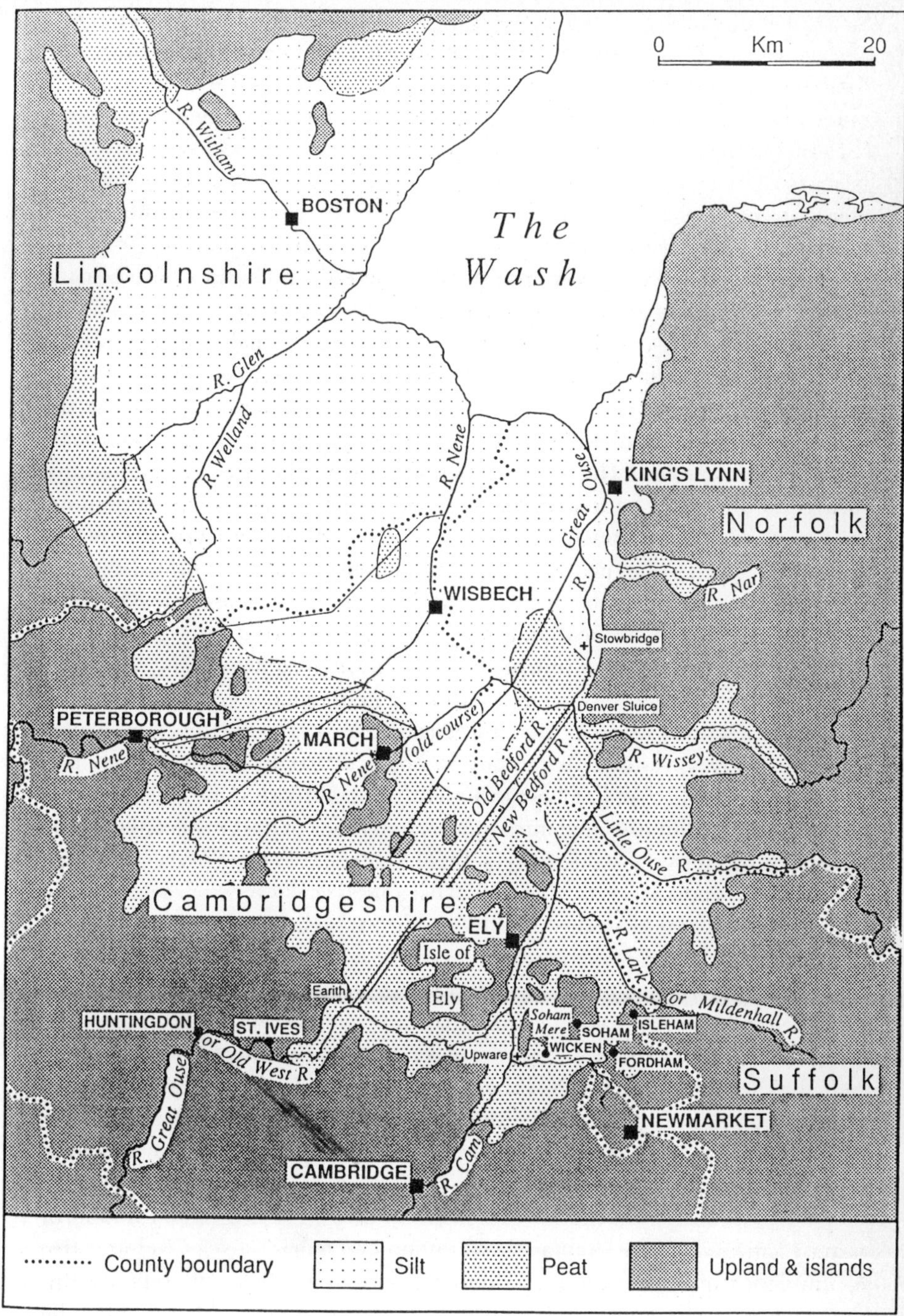

Figure 3.1 **The Fenland region**

extensively modified by the creation of cut channels since the seventeenth century. It rises in Northamptonshire and thence flows, formerly by means of a very tortuous course, to the North Sea at King's Lynn. Its main Fenland tributaries are the Little Ouse, Wissey, Nar, Cam and Lark (or Mildenhall river). The other main Fenland rivers are the Nene, Glen, Welland and Witham. They have a total catchment area of about 6,000 square miles (156,000 km^2), and discharge into a lowland area which is only one fifth of the area of the catchment. Very large amounts of water are thus regularly discharged from the uplands, particularly in winter, into the lowland Fenland basin whose coastal end is barred by silts at heights of about 10–15 feet (3–4.5 m) above sea level, the differential between peat and silt partly reflecting the shrinkage of the inland peats after drainage, especially from the seventeenth century onwards.

The basin itself, it has been suggested, was probably scoured out by glacial action in a Quaternary cold phase, though its physiographic origin goes back to the Tertiary period. The key sedimentary aspects are the accumulations during the Flandrian period of the last 10,000 years in differing sedimentary environments, conspicuously the freshwater environments around the inland edge of the basin, where peat was formed at a time of rising sea-levels, and the marine environments of the coastal region where clays, sands and silts were deposited, though some peatland formation also occurred during sea coast retreat. Hence, as a recent survey of the Fenland explains, 'The resulting Flandrian deposits thus consist of a series of interbedded organic and mineral layers. The accumulation of thick sequences of peat towards the edges of the Fenland and the presence of mineral sediments at the surface towards the Wash allows the Fenland to be conveniently divided into the "peat fen" and the "silt fen"'.[4] Additional and important components of past Fenland environments are the residual calcareous soils of former meres or lakes, including Soham Mere, and a series of gley soils. The soils of the lower slopes of the fen-edge uplands are mainly brown earths and brown calcareous soils.

This chapter will primarily be concerned with the peatland part of the region, notably that part where what is called the Upper Peat is a major feature, deposited it is thought during a marine regression, with a base date of *c.* 2750 BC inland and *c.* 2450 BC at its seaward limit, where further marine incursion had deposited silt over the peat in the Romano-British period.[5] Peat generally developed under eutrophic conditions, raised bog peats being rare. The accumulation was essentially in floodplain mires, with some raised mires along the western edge of the Fens, the Flandrian accumulation being influenced by the location at the lower reaches of major rivers draining mid- and eastern England whose drainage was influenced by rising sea-level and the accumulation of coastal marine sediments.[6] Its depth varies, but originally the Upper Peat, before considerable shrinkage after drainage and through subsequent oxidation, must have been of an average depth of at least 6–9 metres

(20–30 feet). Additional features of the physiography of the Fenland Region include the 'islands' and peninsulas in the Fen, the largest being the 'Isle of Ely' on which stands the famous cathedral. It was from the surrounding uplands and the islands of the Fens that colonisation and settlement took place. The historical economies of the rural areas of the Fens involved for the most part a combination of upland and lowland use systems, with arable and pasture mainly on the uplands, and peat-cutting, extraction of other natural resources, and grazing, usually in the summer, on the low peat wetlands. The hazards of use of the wetlands were extensive, and included frequent catastrophic flooding and the high density of drainage ditches, in which human and animal life was frequently lost.

According to Burton and Hodgson, in 1630, there were between Lincoln and Cambridge 1480 km^2 of peat which reached a height of 3.7 m above sea level between the higher ground and the coastal marine alluvial deposits of the Wash. Between 1630 and 1850 land use for summer grazing, wildfowling, fishing, reed and sedge cutting and turf exploitation gave way to arable cultivation thanks to large arterial drainage schemes. With this change came the destruction of much of the peat so that by 1985 only 240 km^2 of peat soils remained, only 16 per cent of its former extent.[7]

The Fenland and its images through time

The way in which the Fens were viewed varied and changed through time, partly in relation to the perceived economic potential and needs of the region and the nation as a whole, and partly in relation to what loosely might be described as environmental belief systems, that is the way in which various sections of society viewed the relationship between nature and people.

Camden's late sixteenth-century account of the Fens in his *Britannia* perhaps typifies the image of the region which prevailed in Elizabethan times, referring to the Fen inhabitants as 'a sort of people ... of brutish uncivilis'd tempers envious of all others whom they term Upland men, and usually walking aloft upon a sort of stilts: they all keep to the business of grazing, fishing and fowling', and to the abundance of grass, peat turf, sedge reeds, elders, willows and wildfowl.[8] This image of the Fens as wild, remote and untamed territory, inhabited by strange people who made a living from peat-cutting, the taking of wildfowl and fishing, and from grazing cattle on the drier pastures in the summer informed, as we shall see, the developing notions of the region as an area of potential for improvement and development. At this time, therefore, attempts were begun by the state to encourage the improvement of land by drainage, leading, it was hoped, to cultivation and greater profitability. Not surprisingly, there were widely differing views on the subject. Sermons against interference with nature – the work of God – were preached in Ely Cathedral, and dialogues were printed to counter what some regarded as reactionary arguments. One such, reproduced by Thomas Fuller in his *History of the University of Cambridge*, published in 1665, comprised a series of dialogue arguments for and against fen drainage at a time when active proposals were being made and implemented:

> Argument 1. Some objected that God said to the water, 'Hitherto thou shalt come and no further'. It is therefore a trespass on the Divine prerogative, for man to presume to give other bounds to the water than what God hath appointed.
> Answer 1. The argument holdeth in application to the Ocean, which is a wild horse, only to be broked, backed and bridled by him who is the maker thereof; but it is a false and lazy principle if applied to fresh waters, from which human industry may and hath rescued many considerable parcels of ground . . . .
> Argument 7. The Fens afford plenty of sedge, turf, and reed; the want whereof will be found if their nature be altered.[9]

An interesting contemporary argument in favour of preservation of the Fens in their natural state is that the would-be drainers were exaggerating their supposed backward state in order to appropriate large areas of land. Darby supports this with a quotation from a pamphlet of 1606 called *The Anti-projector* which claims that, although the 'Adventurers' (drainage investors) said that the Fen was a quagmire of little value, it provided employment for many thousand smallholders and cottagers through its turf peat, reeds, sedges, and the undrained fen through its wild birds, fish and eels.[10]

In the eighteenth century, a famous commentator, the Rev. William Gilpin, a tourist in effect looking for picturesque rural scenery, bemoaned in his *Tours* (of 1769 and 1773, published in 1809) of the area near Ely, that 'If it had been remote, it might have lost in obscurity its disgusting form. But its disagreeable features were apparent to the utmost verge of its extent.'[11]

These two contrasting images of the Fens – of wilderness beyond economic redemption and as an area of great economic potential – are presented in the introduction to Clarke's essay of 1848 for the Royal Agricultural Society's *Journal*, 'On the Great Level of the Fens'.

> In considering the state of this region as it first attracted the enterprise of man to its improvement, we are to conceive a vast wild morass, with only small detached portions of cultivated soil, or islands, raised above the general inundation; – a most desolate picture, when contrasted with its present state of matchless fertility.[12]

He obviously takes a 'progressive' view of the state of the Fens, but this is not surprising from the author of an essay for the Royal Agricultural Society, whose whole purpose was to encourage the improvement of agriculture and which, in the 1840s, was particularly interested in land drainage.

The contrasting images of the Fens as backward and remote on the one hand and advanced and productive on the other continue into the twentieth century, evidenced in the obvious productivity and prosperity of commercial horticulture, contrasted with the continuing myths about the Fens being a remote and inaccessible region in which social and geographical isolation has resulted in great introspection, fear of strangers, and inbreeding.

Wetland regions as national symbols of progress and achievement

Simon Schama's important book, *The Embarrassment of Riches: An interpretation of Dutch Culture in the Golden Age* [13] gives helpful initial direction to the interesting concept of wetland regions (and their transformation) as symbols of national pride and aspiration. Writing in the context of what he calls the 'moral geography' of the Dutch nation at this time, he speaks of the allegories linking national experience and environmental change at a time of struggle against both flood and their Spanish oppressors:

> Memories of the epic inundations in the late Middle Ages, transmitted to succeeding generations as written and oral folklore – fables, ballads, fairy tales – conditioned the sixteenth-century Dutch to regard themselves as ordained and blessed survivors of the deluge . . . the land was not merely reclaimed but redeemed, and in the process both were morally transformed. So the act of separating dry land from wet was laden with scriptural significance. . . . Compounded in their determination not to yield to foreign tyrants what had been laboriously wrested from the sea were the *historical* title of ancestral reclamation, the *moral* title awarded to those whose work had created the land and the *scriptural* title that survived against the flood was itself a token of divine intervention.[14]

Is it possible to find similar metaphors and symbolism in the landscapes of the Fenland region in, for example, the seventeenth century? I think that it is, but perhaps not on so dramatic a scale. The major attempts to drain the Great Level before and after the Civil War led, among other things, to the debates on the theological implications of fen drainage, as already cited.

During the course of the seventeenth century, a combination of circumstances led to intensive efforts to render the Fens more productive. They included an increased general interest in England in the more intensive (and profitable) use of 'waste' land, with consequent changes in property rights and greater investment of capital in land, and the application of new engineering techniques to achieve more efficient land drainage: a combination, in effect, of necessity with opportunity. Lindley argues that

> the case for internal colonisation [in England] was couched in the same terms as that for external, as coincidently serving the national interest and satisfy-

> ing the profit motive. Successful drainage enterprises brought in effect the addition of a new province to England. National interests were served in a number of ways: drained fenland increased the area of tillage; it accommodated the surplus population of neighbouring regions; it increased the area of the country that could contribute to the taxes of Church and State; it contributed to national pride by freeing the kingdom from the imputation of laxness and want of industry levelled at it by foreigners for allowing large areas of the country to remain nonproductive; and it made a significant contribution to national self-sufficiency.[15]

Wet and apparently unused land was deemed to be symbolic of waste and indolence. This idea might be seen as parallel perhaps to the ideas of the physiocrats in France, writing and advocating land reclamation in the national economic interest at the time of the French Revolution.

The state and regional improvement projects

The relations between region and state in the early modern period in England were in part bound up with both general price and wage trends and also with specific problems of raising moneys to wage war: Charles I, for example, fought wars with Spain from 1624–30 and France from 1626–29, but could not persuade Parliament or his people to lend the necessary money for their conduct.

During the course of the seventeenth century, therefore, James I, Charles I and successive English monarchs and governments looked both to swell the income of the state and to effect what were deemed to be more efficient uses of under-utilised or 'waste' land. The measures adopted for these and other purposes included, in the reign of Charles I, the pawning of the crown jewels, the sale of crown lands on a very large scale, the maximising of income from feudal dues, and the promotion of 'projects and patents', these including commissions to grant licences for the sale of tobacco, proposals to make salt from seawater, to revive copper mining in the South West, and to drain the Fenlands of eastern England.[16]

Historians have suggested that the three main incentives or factors behind the early seventeenth-century attempts by the monarchy to raise money by disafforestation and drainage were: the increase in the population of England from an estimated three million in 1554 to perhaps twice that number a century later; the creation of a new cultural climate, more pragmatic, empirical and realistic, coinciding perhaps with the new science and mechanistic views of nature; and a recognition that money could be made by stimulating and encouraging and then taxing progress, rather than opposing it.[17]

Although the Statutes of Westminster and of Merton (re-enacted in 1549) allowed manorial lords to improve wastes and commons for their own use, the procedures were not clearly defined. The management of significant changes in the use and value of land required changes in the scale of operation and in the powers of the enabling authority but, and in the absence of a Parliament (which met infrequently before 1640) to provide such powers, the process was left in the hands of manorial lords and of local authorities such as the Commissioners of Sewers. Attempts by groups of landowners to effect larger-scale reclamations failed. The main possibility was for the Crown to encourage reclamation on its own estates. The process was administratively effected, it would seem, through the state Exchequer, which appointed commissions to oversee project progress, the commissions being headed by senior officers of government. Surveyors were appointed to evaluate developments in the areas affected.

Drainage required, however, not only the will to transform wetlands, and the implicit *credo* that such common lands were economically only marginal (which view, of course, substantially underestimated the natural human ecology of such regions), but also the technical ability to effect drainage at medium to large scales, and to raise the considerable capital for doing so. These were two additionally important factors.

The pattern which emerges is that of the Crown engaging the expertise of foreign drainage engineers, notably Cornelius Vermuyden, and the capital of local entrepreneurs. It might be argued, therefore, that the Crown risked little, and stood to gain much; but that is not always the way that it turned out. The general picture, therefore, from the late Elizabethan period, as Joan Thirsk has indicated, is that the Fenlands were brought into public debate, with strong arguments in favour of improvement; one focus of attention was wetland, hence

> Private drainers were showing a willingness to employ foreign drainers, and the drainage lobby, led by foreign engineers circulating among courtiers in London, was building up argument in favour of private projects. [There was some private employment of Italian engineers in the 1580s]. The Crown was swept along by these events, to consider its position as the owner of many manors having undrained fenland, around the Wash, in Hatfield Chase and the Isle of Axholme.[18]

The deteriorating climatic conditions of the 1590s which seem to have been leading to greater flooding and loss of life, accelerated interest and urgency. A General Draining Act was passed in 1600, and in 1602 draining began in Deeping and Spalding Fens. The key point of acceleration of interest probably came, as Thirsk has indicated, with the appointment in 1612 of Commissioners 'touching Projects and Improvement of the King's Revenue', who thoroughly examined every opportunity for raising money.

There were many drainage projects following the Act of 1600 projects, some of which have been well documented and studied, others not. The best studied are those of the Cambridgeshire and Lincolnshire Fens, covered in the classic works by Darby and by Thirsk.[19] The history of the technology of reclamation in the Fens, an important feature of their history, has been extensively reviewed by Darby, Hills[20] and others and need not be repeated here. It is necessary to note, however, that in spite of progress from the windmill in the sixteenth century to the steam engine in the eighteenth, and electric and other modern means of pumping out water in the twentieth century, the power of natural hazards and the inadequacies and limitations of these evolving technologies, together with the considerable power of human indifference to the maintenance of drainage ditches, frequently offset any advantages resulting from technological progress. It has been shown that the various schemes for reclamation and settlement of fens and marshlands, including those in Yorkshire and Nottinghamshire, involved a partnership of monarch, government, and individual speculators or 'adventurers', whose reward was to be both financial and territorial – the award of a proportion of the land reclaimed. These early adventures in rural capitalism were not, however, unopposed, and were accompanied by fierce riots and protests, which tested the state's resolve and its sense of justice. Protest against land drainage and the attendant removal of rights of use of the Fens for grazing, wildfowling, and the gathering of reeds, sedge, and the cutting of peat were common from about 1630–60,[21] involving the commoners themselves but with the support of minor gentry and clergy who saw this process as an erosion of the rights of the poor and of an equitable social justice.

The social geography of the Fenland

The inhabitants of the region were not thus passive players in a drama produced by others. The distinctive independence of the smaller freeholders and cottagers of the region was an important feature of its character and evolution, not least the growth of Nonconformist religion from the seventeenth century onwards. The consequences of the social make-up of the region were not, however, always positive, in that the sheer numbers of the less privileged and the continued marginality of their material existence, in a region of great environmental hazard, were often tragic. This marginality of material existence is particularly evident in the nineteenth century from the detailed parliamentary and other surveys of the human condition in areas of known poverty.

The maintenance of traditional systems of cultivation and tenure, in many cases through to the nineteenth century, especially the preservation of the extensive commons, probably owes much to the defence of their use by the cottagers and commoners. This was a region in which the enclosure of the extensive open-field systems of the upland areas was quite late, and where even the extensive re-allocation of lowland peat grazing areas as a result of the drainage schemes of the seventeenth century had not completely alienated the grazing and other resource rights of the poor.[22] Marginal squatting by the poor on the edge of the poor's commons in large settlements such as Soham is evident from records and maps of the nineteenth century, as is the frequency of death by epidemic disease and the necessity to provide for the relief of dire poverty through various processes, including at times of dearth and high population increase, emigration.

The intensity and marginality of the occupation of land is well illustrated by the reports of parliamentary select committees and commissions. Thus, in the *Report from the Select Committee on Allotments, Small Holdings and Peasant Proprietors* for Friday 31 May 1889, evidence from Mr Charles Bidwell, Land Agent and Surveyor, exemplifies the intensity of population pressure on land:

> the parish of Soham is a parish very well known to me . . . It contains 12,526 acres; and there are 195 occupiers of under one acre (these are chiefly small gardens, with which I need not trouble you); there are 77 occupiers of plots under five acres; there are 34 occupiers of plots under 10 acres; there are 43 occupiers of plots under 20 acres; and there are 57 occupiers of plots under 50 acres. There is a considerable quantity of this land occupied by little men who own the fee . . . . These little men where they own the land have not done so well, nor have they stood the bad seasons as well as the men who rent the land . . . . It is very good land, accessible to good roads, and convenient to the railway; the parish is, curiously enough, an uninclosed parish. A great many of these small strips of land under an acre in size, lie in different parts of the parish. It is very extraordinary how these little men have struggled and worked through the bad times we have experienced lately.[23]

Invisible processes: the administration of drainage systems

The management of one of the most important resources – land – in order to achieve optimal and, in certain societies, egalitarian access and use, is an important and common theme in historical geography and economic history. This process and the institutional contexts within which it operates is of particular significance in the case of marginal land, such as wetland, where failure of individual or institutional management can make a difference between success and failure, and even between life and death.

In an econometric and historical analysis of property rights, litigation and French agriculture in the period 1700–1860, Jean Rosenthal has spelled out one of the problems of wetland administration:

> water control is the kind of investment that magnifies the role of institutions, because providing improvements like drainage and irrigation requires that a score of contracting problems be overcome. Drainage is a local public good in that it is extremely costly to drain only part of a marsh. Thus, some mechanism must exist to ensure that all owners of the marsh participate in the draining effort. Otherwise some owners will be tempted to shirk and force the costs of drainage [and maintenance] on the others.[24]

This is an econometric analysis, but there is another perspective: that of human interest, or lack of it, and of human efficiency or inefficiency in initiating, managing and repairing watercourses, drainage ditches and the various mechanisms which facilitate the removal of unwanted water from agricultural and habitable land.

Even this is not a simple and straightforward issue: land rights are inevitably complex, engaging not only very local issues of access, and control of use and condition, but also national issues of coherence of legislation and the membership of the controlling authorities. It is worth noting in passing that, in the context of the management of frequently waterlogged environments, equally complex administrative systems evolved in, for example, France, Germany and the Netherlands in the early modern and modern periods.

Three types of administrative institution evolved to deal with land drainage in the Fenland of eastern England, institutions which not only assisted in the making, but also at times in the hindering of historical geographical change. These were: the Commissions of Sewers (a medieval creation lasting until the nineteenth century); the Bedford Level Corporation (a seventeenth-century institution, operating at a regional level until, in effect, the nineteenth century); and the local drainage boards, originating in the eighteenth century and, in modified form, operating until the early twentieth century (and in changed form under national legislation until the present).

Local juries, known as the Courts of Sewers, were the main local institutions responsible by statute for the maintenance of watercourses in England. The purpose of the Commissions of Sewers (the term applied originally to watercourses and streams, being used in the modern sense only from *c.* 1600) was 'not to inaugurate new administrative methods, but to enforce customs and practices of long standing which had shown a tendency to lapse in the absence of any official machinery of coercion; in a word to superimpose some sort of order on the administrative chaos prevailing in the region'.[25] Summers, in her study of the Great Level of the Fens[26], suggests that they represent formal recognition by central government of the need to overcome the inadequacies of local organisations evolving on an *ad hoc* basis, although the scale of improvement as a result of this legislation is debatable. The process involved was legal institutionalisation of existing best practices in matters of drainage.

Relatively little has been written about these important institutions. They receive quite extensive passing comment in Darby's main works on fenland drainage,[27] but mainly as part of the painting of a larger-scale picture of landscape modification through drainage. One source for their operation is in the fourth volume of Sydney and Beatrice Webb's study of *English Local Government*[28] but, as Owen has pointed out, the usefulness of this work is constrained by their primary interest in the period 1689 to 1835, their preoccupation with the history of the Courts of Sewers in and around London, and their consequent bewilderment at

> those in more rural parts, whose administrative vagaries they seem to have found somewhat bewildering. The metropolitan commissioners of sewers, pre-occupied with the drainage problems of built-up areas and in particular with the disposal of urban sewage – with sewers, that is, in the modern sense – were, however, not typical, the average land drainage authority being concerned first and foremost with the drainage of agricultural land and, in coastal areas, its protection from the sea.[29]

The first Commission of Sewers was established by authority of the Crown in the thirteenth century with the direct authority to implement good maintenance practices, and fine those who were negligent, by means of local Courts of Sewers. In the fifteenth and sixteenth centuries, central legislation clarified and extended their functions and purposes. Their powers were, however, largely confined to overseeing maintenance and periodic improvement of existing watercourses and drainage systems. The basic interest was land drainage, though the interests of navigation were also served.[30]

The main piece of relevant legislation was the Statute of Sewers of 1531 in the reign of Henry VIII, which enabled the *ad hoc* appointment as Commissioners of groups of freeholders. These were local landlords, who were given judicial, executive and legislative powers in respect of matters pertaining to the maintenance of drainage systems, though their authority was for a limited time, initially about three years though extended to ten after 1571.

They were mainly charged with the implementation of regulations concerned with the maintenance of drainage and with the prevention of practices which might cause obstruction to the system. They were responsible for the survey and viewing of the state of drainage, and for the rectification of problems caused by accident or through neglect. They appointed people to implement their policies and the use of hired labour, animals and carts as was necessary. They had the right to appropriate material such as timber and stone for repair work. In the case of exceptional flooding, the cost of the repair work was divided among those whose land benefited. They could fine, punish, and direct in consequence of negligence in such matters as they saw fit. Their composition varied, but mainly comprised landholding residents of the areas over which they had jurisdiction. Their areas of jurisdiction were on the whole quite small and therefore local and parochial, in consequence of which their approach was essentially practical and pragmatic, a kind of crisis management, with little if any element of visionary planning of major drainage works. The short life of the Commissions, together with the requirement of summoning local juries before taking action, a lack of direct authority to enable the construction of new works, and the carelessness of individuals, all seem to have militated against swift, structured and successful action.

The sheer scale of the problem of drainage of the Fenland militated against an aggregate success story of the work of the many Commissions of Sewers. While it is conceivable that for some periods such institutions were partially effective in such regions as the wetlands of Somerset, Kent, Middlesex and Essex, and along the coasts, the Fenland area was too big.

The transfer of the administration of drainage in the southern Fenland (the North, Middle and South Levels) to the Bedford Level Corporation in 1663, marks not only the recognition that the scale of the drainage problem required a larger-scale and legally more powerful authority than the Commissions of Sewers, but also the transition from localised, decentralised, self-governing bodies to the more centralised authority of Parliament.

The minutes and proceedings record the administrative and environmental hazards which the Corporation struggled to control, and give, until the nineteenth century, a detailed series of accounts of the region. They illustrate attempts to maintain and develop the main drainage channels, such as the Old and New Bedford rivers, the conflicts with the Commissions of Sewers, and other vested local interests and prejudices, including those attached to the rights of common grazing over the Fens.

The new Bedford Level Corporation was invested by Act of Parliament of 1663 with powers of taxation for drainage revenue and confiscation of land for arrears of drainage. Its members were the original Adventurers, or their heirs, who had invested in southern Fenland drainage. New officials were appointed, including area drainage superintendents, an engineer, surveyor, treasurer and registrar, and this new body took responsibility for drainage and navigation. The drainage of the Bedford Level was thus placed on a firmer administrative footing, but nonetheless struggled constantly against a chronic shortage of funds.[31]

In addition to protests and destructive actions, the drainage records are full of complaints about the failure to maintain channels and ditches, the erosion of banks, problems with low bridges across watercourses, and conflicting interests over navigation and other river uses (especially as a result of the construction of weirs). The minutes of the Adventurers' Proceedings for April 1663 record a complaint that weirs still existed on the Grant (Cam) River at Wicken, which were impediments to navigation and the passage of flood waters. The minutes of the Commissioners of Sewers for November 1687 state that the drain in Isleham known as Isleham Lode, which conveyed water from the fens at Isleham and Soham to the Mildenhall River was 'defective and grown up', and required ditching and scouring.[32]

One of the ubiquitous features of drainage management in the Fens and indeed elsewhere in England was thus the anachronistic nature of the drainage administrative systems. This is a point which Darby stresses in his major works on the Fens, and with justification:

> Looming above the technical questions of outfall difficulties and their associated internal problems was the legacy of antiquated administrative arrangements. Commissioners of Sewers still continued to look after the drainage of some areas, and they had power to levy rates to sustain their operations. Their ancient rights were codified and their working clarified by the Sewers Act of 1833, but this did nothing to affect the fundamental basis of drainage administration[33]

Conflicts of interest between individual landowners, the limited powers of the Bedford Level Corporation (whose jurisdiction included only the main drainage and navigation channels), the indolence and extravagance of some of the officers of the Corporation, lack of finance, and frequency of land floods, led ultimately to a search for alternative and more expeditious means of effecting better drainage, through the establishment of more local drainage authorities. Applications were thus made by groups of landowners for private Acts of Parliament for the drainage of particular Fenland districts, and the power to levy additional taxes to pay for the costs of drainage initiation and maintenance of private internal drainage districts, administered by their own commissioners. The first such body in the South Level was established in 1727 for Haddenham Level. Similar acts of 1758, 1789 and 1800 created the Soham or Middle Fen district, whose commissioners were charged with the relief of the lower land in Soham, Isleham and Wicken, which 'have for divers years past been, and still are, frequently overflowed, and annoyed with waters, through the defect of their outfalls to sea, and thereby rendered of little value', and thus with the improvement of drainage and navigation, by means of raising and strengthening the banks of the rivers Cam and Ouse, the Mildenhall river, Soham Drain, Barroway Lode, and carrying out improvements to bridges and tunnels.

The drainage commissions for the internal drainage districts were replicated across the Fenland. Summers has indicated that by the end of the eighteenth century there were twenty or more of these private internal drainage districts in the southern Fenland, some of which relieved the Bedford Level Corporation of responsibilities for major river bank maintenance.[34] John Beckett, in his study of the Burnt Fen, recites the familiar history of the consequences and difficulties of the seventeenth-century drainage scheme for the Burnt Fen region of the South Level: shrinkage of the peat after drainage, the limited responsibility of the Bedford Level Corporation (maintenance of the main rivers, with smaller rivers and tributaries outside their control), the drainage activities (or lack of them) of individual landlords, the increase in the number of mills.[35] In 1759 Commissioners for draining the Burnt Fen were established by Act of Parliament in relation to two districts (First Burnt Fen and Second Burnt Fen, the former evolving to the later Burnt Fen Internal Drainage District).

Under the Act the Commissioners were to be the 'Lord Bishop of Ely, the Lord or Lady of the Manor of Littleport, an agent appointed by the Dean and Chapter of Ely, and every person owning 300 acres of taxable land within the District'.[36] Taxable land was mainly land liable to flooding, and the Bedford Level Corporation had rights to appoint Commissioners in relation to vested lands. The Commissioners were to meet twice per year in Ely in June, and they did so in 1760 when they appointed clerks, a receiver and a master of works. They had powers to maintain and construct new drains, to co-ordinate drainage mills (mainly windmills) and to levy drainage rates, which in the event proved unrealistically low. Mills in a poor state of repair were purchased from private owners and repaired, and new mills built. These works and others were not always popular, and workmen and officials – and mills – were attacked.

The budgets were found to be inadequate, and in a second Act of Parliament of 1772 they applied for further powers for levying funds; they were granted this only in respect of paying off debts and for flood emergencies, but were given powers to construct turnpikes and charge tolls on the banks of rivers which were experiencing increasing commercial traffic. A further Act of 1796 levied an additional tax of 7s 6d. per acre. There was a continuing saga of Acts for taxes and drainage funds well into the early nineteenth century. Major advances were made with the installation of a steam engine in 1832, followed by a second in 1842, which, in spite of some technical problems, undoubtedly advanced the drainage of the area, though there was no final solution to these major regional problems of drainage until the 1930s.

The multiplicity of drainage authorities, as Darby has shown,[37] continued until the late nineteenth century, when the Land Drainage Act of 1861 amended the powers of the Commissioners of Sewers and created new Drainage Boards, but there remained the lack of unified control along the length of rivers. Thus, notwithstanding the move from the late seventeenth century towards a more regional type of drainage authority, which was by now widespread and effective in the Netherlands, the Fens in general, including the Southern Fenland, continued to be dominated by local interests.

The drainage commissions were replicated across the Fenland. Taylor has undertaken a study of Burwell Fen and of the work of the Burwell Drainage

Commission.[38] This was created in 1840 by Act of Parliament, in spite of opposition to the idea from some landowners, and in the first five years after its first meeting on 30 June 1841 had to deal with major problems of finance, opposition from landowners for the acquisition of new land for new drains, banks and a pumping station, the high cost of land purchase and of bank and drain construction and maintenance, problems with the pumping engine, and problems with levying and collecting the drainage tax. From 1840–1900 there were problems of peat shrinkage, and difficulties of pumping, but more of the Fen became cultivated, in spite of drainage problems. The Commissioners' activities might, therefore, be judged a partial success.

Conclusion

This chapter has touched upon only a few selected aspects of the historical geography of a complex region. Its identity – or, rather, identities – lie not only in its obvious, though changing, physical characteristics, but also in the ways it has been perceived by different people at various times, and in the challenges it has presented to private and public 'improvers' alike. Sufficient has been said to support the initial thesis that the apparently monotonous appearance of flat wetland landscapes is highly deceptive, and that they offer as much of a challenge to the scholar as any other regional type, demonstrating how a geographical region such as the Fens has meaning and significance for students of many interests, not least in economic, administrative and cultural history.

The challenge of reading the histories of regions is one which John Marshall has long encouraged historians, geographers and others to face, and which he himself has successfully exemplified in his own tuition and writing. An important feature of his own work is that it has engaged with the work of local, amateur, historians, and demonstrated the stimulus that can derive from the collaboration of scholars working on related topics from a wide variety of perspectives and bases. Perhaps one consequence of this pioneering work might be a major attempt to follow up the work of John Marshall, Joan Thirsk, and others in a renewed attempt on a large scale to re-write the histories and geographies of regions in Britain?

Notes

1 M. Williams (ed.), *Wetlands: A Threatened Landscape* (Oxford, 1990).
2 A. Lambert, *The Making of the Dutch Landscape* (London, 1957).
3 M. K. E. Gottshalk, *Stormvloeden en Rivieroverstromingen in Nederland: I, De periode voor 1400* (Amsterdam, 1971); *II, De periode 1400–1600* (Amsterdam, 1975); *III, De periode 1600–1700* (Amsterdam, 1977).
4 D. Hall, and J. Coles (eds), *Fenland Survey. An Essay in Landscape and Persistence*, English Heritage (London, 1994), p. 13.

5 Hall and Coles, *Fenland Survey*, p. 14.
6 R. G. O. Burton and J. M. Hodgson, *Lowland Peat in England and Wales*, Soil Survey of England and Wales, Special Survey No. 15 (Harpenden, 1987), p. 90.
7 Burton and Hodgson, *Lowland Peat*, p. 91.
8 W. Camden, *Britannia* (1586) ed. E. Gibson, facsimile edition, ed. S. Piggott (Newton Abbott, 1971), p. 407.
9 E. Conybeare, *A History of Cambridgeshire* (London, 1897), pp. 249–50.
10 H. C. Darby, *The Changing Fenland* (Cambridge, 1983), p. 60.
11 W. Gilpin, *Observations on Several Parts of the Counties of Cambridge, Norfolk, Suffolk and Essex . . . relative chiefly to picturesque Beauty, in two Tours (1769, 1773)* (London, 1809), p. 28.
12 J. A. Clarke, 'On the Great Level of the Fens, including the Fens of South Lincolnshire', *Journal, Royal Agricultural Society*, 8 (1848), 81.
13 S. Schama, *The Embarrassment of Riches: An Interpretation of Dutch Culture in the Golden Age* (London, 1988).
14 Schama, *Embarrassment of Riches*, pp. 34–5.
15 J. Lindley, *Fenland Riots and the English Revolution* (London, 1982), pp. 4–5.
16 J. Thirsk, 'The Crown as projector in its own estates, from Elizabeth I to Charles I', in R. W. Hoyle (ed.), *The Estates of the English Crown, 1558–1640* (Cambridge, 1992), pp. 297–35.
17 R. W. Hoyle, 'Disafforestation and drainage: the Crown as entrepreneur?', in Hoyle (ed.), *The Estates of the English Crown*, pp. 353–88.
18 Thirsk, 'The Crown as projector', p. 298.
19 H. C. Darby, *The Draining of the Fens* (Cambridge, 1940); Darby, *The Changing Fenland*; J. Thirsk, *Fenland Farming in the Sixteenth Century* (Leicester, 1965); J. Thirsk, *English Peasant Farming:The Agrarian History of Lincolnshire from Tudor to recent times* (London, 1957).
20 Darby, *Draining of the Fens* and *Changing Fenland*; R. L. Hills, *Machines, Mills, and Unaccountable Costly Necessities: A Short History of the Draining of the Fens* (Norwich, 1967).
21 Lindley, *Fenland Riots*.
22 R. A. Butlin, 'Drainage and land use in the Fenlands and Fen-edge region of northeast Cambridgeshire in the seventeenth and eighteenth centuries', in D. Cosgrove and G. Petts (eds), *Water, Engineering and Landscape* (London, 1990), pp. 54–76; R. A. Butlin, 'Social, economic and environmental change in the Fen and Fen-edge region of east Cambridgeshire in the nineteenth century', in R. A. Butlin and N. Roberts (eds), *Ecological Relations in Historic Times* (Oxford, 1995), pp.146–68.
23 *Report from the Select Committee on Small Holdings . . ., 9 August 1889* (313), British Parliamentary Papers XII (1889), 275, evidence of C. Bidwell, given on 31 May 1889,
24 J. Rosenthal, *The Fruits of Revolution* (Cambridge, 1992), p. 2.
25 D. Summers, *The Great Level* (Newton Abbot, 1976), p. 47.
26 Summers, *The Great Level*.
27 Darby, *Draining of the Fens* and *Changing Fenland*.
28 S. and B. Webb, *English Local Government*, IV (London, 1922), chapter 1, 'The Court of Sewers'.
29 A. E. B. Owen, 'Land drainage authorities and their records', *Journal of the Society of Archivists*, 2:9 (April 1964), 417–23.
30 Darby, *Changing Fenland*; A. E. Owen, 'Records of Commissions of Sewers', *History*, 52 (1967), 35–8.
31 Summers, *The Great Level*, pp. 90–1.
32 Cambridgeshire CRO, R.59/31/9/8, Minutes of the Adventurers' Proceedings for April 1663; R.59/31/9/12, Minutes of the Commissioners of Sewers for November 1687.

33 Darby, *Changing Fenland*, p. 170.
34 Summers, *The Great Level*, p. 123.
35 J. Beckett, *The Urgent Hour: The Drainage of the Burnt Fen District in the South Level of the Fens 1760–1981*, Local History Publications Board (Ely, 1983).
36 Beckett, *Burnt Fen*, p. 8.
37 Darby, *Changing Fenland*, pp. 170–73, 194–97.
38 C. Taylor, 'The drainage of Burwell fen, Cambridgeshire, 1840–1950', in T. Rowley (ed.), *The Evolution of Marshland Landscapes*, University of Oxford Department of Extra-Mural Studies (Oxford, 1981), pp. 158–77.

Contrasting identities: north-west England and the Basque Country, 1840–1936

Introduction

John Marshall has been a pioneering proponent of regional history, at both a practical and a theoretical level.[1] He has been consistently critical of the tendency to concentrate on a kind of local history which treats particular places for their own sake, with little or no attention to where the place studied might be situated in a wider scheme of things, although he has also – and perhaps more controversially – had reservations about work which uses localities solely as the testing-grounds for theories, subordinating the understanding of the local society to the need to pursue an extraneously-imposed agenda which is driven by currently-fashionable abstract thought.[2] From the beginning of his career, however, John Marshall's work has dealt in larger entities than purely local – even urban – history. His first book was on Barrow, but in the context of the surrounding Furness district within which it developed, and he has since written extensively on counties, combinations of counties, and ways of conceptualising and imagining regions.[3] Regions are, after all, the essential building-blocks for a properly-informed national-level history, which if it is to extend beyond the bankrupt agenda of high politics in isolation, must show awareness of contrasting ways of life, economic systems and indeed political attitudes in different parts of the country, given that no nation is homogeneous and that to understand complex phenomena it is necessary to deconstruct before reconstructing. But such a national history, like the ambitious history of Europe based on trans-national regions which Sidney Pollard has offered us, is itself a comparative enterprise, reminding us that much of the best history is comparative history, whether the comparison is between localities, sub-national regions, nation-states or still larger entities on the world stage.[4] To work well, comparison needs to bring into the equation places which have enough in common to highlight the differences which need explaining, so the best such studies are exercises both in comparing and contrasting, and the careful study of a second place will stimulate new questions about the first one, based usually on counterfactuals: why, when this happens in place B, can I find no evidence of it in place A? The pursuit of such questions enhances the understanding of both the comparators, posing questions which might otherwise have been unthinkable.

It seems fitting, then, that this *Festschrift* should contain a chapter which compares regions across national boundaries, in different parts of Europe, and that it should explore problems of regional identity, looking in the process at divisions within regions (with more scope for comparing and contrasting) as well as at what might unite them. Comparison between north-west England and the Basque Country of northern Spain focuses on regions which industrialised in broadly similar ways, and faced parallel problems of urbanisation, the assimilation of migrants and adaptation to cultural change. The period chosen enables the processes at work to be studied at their highest intensity (although north-west England was already a well-developed industrial economy at the dawn of the railway age, while parts of the Basque Country were expanding rapidly during the later Franco years in the 1960s and early 1970s).[5] Terminating in the 1930s respects the importance of the great watersheds of the Spanish Civil War, which broke out in 1936 and had a particularly traumatic impact in the Basque Country,[6] and the Second World War. The two regions also contained within them differing patterns of change in different geographical areas, with apparent similarities between aspects of the economic development of Guipúzcoa province and south-east Lancashire, Vizcaya province and the western mining and heavy industry districts of north-west England, and Alava province and the more rural districts of the Lake Counties of Cumberland and Westmorland. This enables certain common themes to be sustained, but it also draws attention to the problems which arise in trying to establish agreed sub-national identities for comparative purposes, and in comparing regions in which social changes of ostensibly similar kinds take place to widely differing timetables and with contrasting intensity. Despite these problems, the clearest set of issues to emerge from this discussion concerns identity, and we conclude by asking why the Basque Country developed such a strong cultural and political identity, for all the cross-currents within it, while north-west England, which can be made to look so convincing on the map, exists as an heuristic device or administrative convenience rather than as an entity with which people identify and from which they draw cultural sustenance (see figures 4:1 and 4:2)

Nations and regions

If we look at the current political circumstances of England and Spain the substantial differences between the countries stand out. While in the latter case nationalist or regionalist sentiments (the English word 'regionalist' would have different connotations in Spanish) are intensely felt, in England itself the unifying force of the idea of the nation-state remains undamaged, although the overarching political identity of the United Kingdom, the real although less-imagined nation-state, is as problematic as it has ever been. The situation of Spain becomes all the more arresting when we consider that this is not a nation without its own history or recently constituted, as in the case of so many European countries, but one whose existence spans many centuries. The consensus holds that already at the end of the fifteenth century, with the Catholic Monarchs, a kind of nation-state was being consolidated which was extending its influence throughout the territory. Even so, at the present time the very foundations of the Spanish state are being reconsidered and reconstructed: Spain is being understood as a nation composed of other nations, and not only by the nationalists in Catalonia, the Basque Country and elsewhere. From the advent of democracy in 1977, Spain acquired a new way of organising the state, with the creation of autonomous communities based on perceived or imagined historical identities, with their own governments and parliaments which pulled important powers together.[7] This is in sharp contrast to England (as opposed to the United Kingdom), where local government has been reorganised in various ways and at various times since the 1830s, and county government was democratised in 1889 and recast with new boundaries in 1974, but regional government, with any degree of political autonomy, has never been a serious possibility. Hogwood remarks that positive attitudes to regional government have emerged from time to time, most recently in the 1960s and 1970s (when regional health and water authorities were established); but these faded rapidly in the 1980s although they are pushing out tentative new shoots in the aftermath of the devolution referendums in 1997.[8] As England moved away from regional government, in fact, Spain embraced it with enthusiasm. But the new decentralised system in Spain has not brought an end to discussion about the preferred model of state organisation; on the contrary, there is a lively debate on what the final version of the internal organisation of the Spanish state should be, the more so in face of Spain's steady and cumulative integration into Europe.

Within this pattern of development the Basque Country is, together with Catalonia, the area which maintains most strongly its own sense of identity and where nationalist ideas have gathered the greatest momentum. This is not to say that the Basque Country presents a monochrome image, on the contrary, we should emphasise its diversity and heterogeneity. Within its boundaries we find diverse sentiments and experiences, which produce a richly variegated country in cultural terms. The enduring depth of political divisions is illustrated by the results of the most recent elections, in which the nationalist groupings obtained 45.5 per cent of the vote, while the parties which accepted the Spanish state reached 51 per cent in combination.

Both of the regions under discussion consist of three counties or provinces (the Spanish equivalent) for the purposes of this chapter, and within each region there were contrasting patterns of economic and social change during a period of (in some areas) rapid industrialisation and urban growth, and (nearly everywhere) deepening penetration by the market economy, external trade, migration and the power of the state. In each case, however, the chosen definition of the region is contestable. For current purposes, north-west England consists of the old (pre-1974) counties of Lancashire, Cumberland and Westmorland, with clear geographical boundaries: the River Mersey to the south, the Pennine chain of hills to the east, the Solway Firth to the north and the Irish Sea to the west. But it is not so simple. Rivers can unite as well as divide, and Liverpool's influence crossed the Mersey for several purposes, while the Mersey and its tributaries created a distinctive economy based on Cheshire salt and south-west Lancashire coal, together with (for example) Anglesey copper, which generated distinctive patterns of industrial growth on both banks of the river.[9] Manchester's influence, both as regional capital of the cotton industry and as consumer of agricultural products, also stretched into Cheshire, where 'cotton towns' such as Stockport and Hyde were part of a Manchester economy and Manchester merchants and bankers commuted in from Alderley Edge or Altrincham, while much of Cheshire was geared up to satisfying Manchester's capacious appetite for food.[10]

It is not surprising that many versions of the 'north-west' (including official ones) combine Lancashire and Cheshire, leaving Cumberland and Westmorland to form part of a separate entity called 'the north'. This makes the 'north-west' for this period seem much more agriculturally prosperous and aristocratic, and less scenically dramatic and tourism-orientated, than the more northern version offered in this chapter, which is, however, more interesting for current purposes in that it contains a wider variety of contrasting experiences under a common umbrella of shared characteristics.[11] There is, indeed, a possible greater north-west which, as envisaged (for example) by a regional investment agency in the mid-1990s, extends 'from the Cheshire plain to the Scottish border', although it is held to be suffering from an 'identity crisis' because of the diversity of its economy, which is larger than that of four whole EU countries.[12] As defined here, of course, north-west England also looked across the Pennines; they were not an insuperable barrier, and branches of the cotton and woollen industries were to be found on either side, while there were a lot of cultural similarities between Pennine folk in Lancashire and Yorkshire, just as there were between mining families in north-eastern England and west Cumberland.[13] Moreover, one of the key unifying characteristics of the region lay in its openness to external influences: it was part of an Atlantic and Irish Sea economy, on which its expansion and prosper-

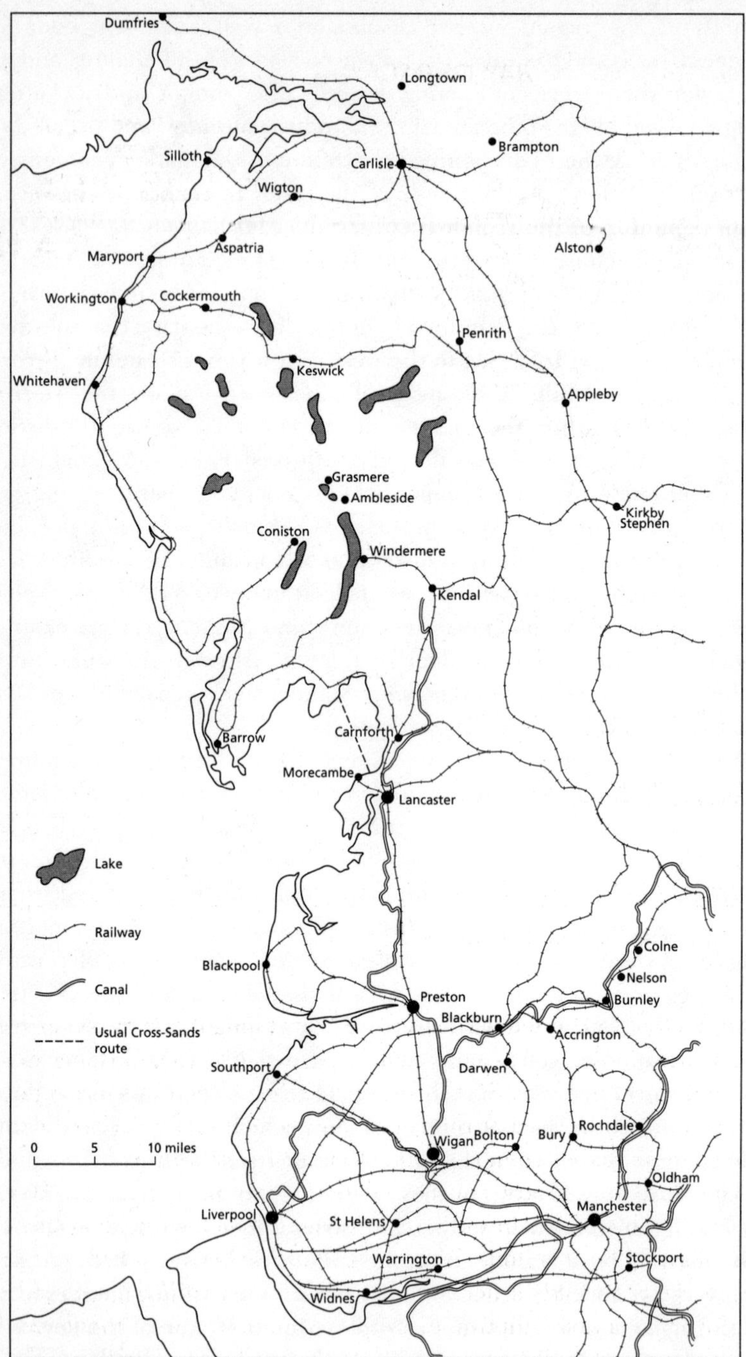

Figure 4.1 **North-west England**

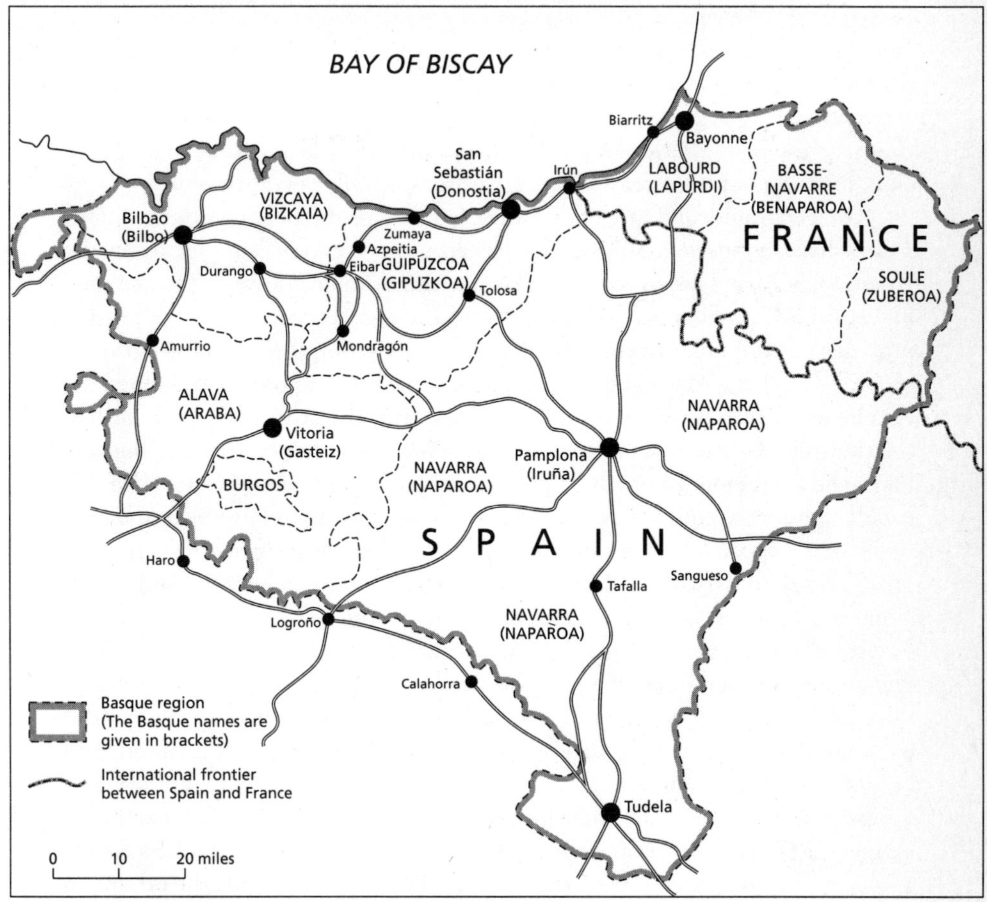

Figure 4.2 **The Basque Provinces**

ity for much of the period was based; and this brought a common experience of Irish migration as well as a common dependence on long-distance maritime trade and world markets. So this was no self-contained, insular region, and nor was it clearly-defined at the edges; but its core can be clearly identified, although more readily so in economic than in cultural terms.[14]

The Basque Country consists of three provinces, Vizcaya, Alava and Guipúzcoa, which contain only 7,261 square kilometres, making this one of the smallest Spanish regions. Its geography is diverse and varied. The region's relief marks out clearly a northern zone in contact with the sea, embracing much of Vizcaya and Guipúzcoa, and a southern area which includes Alava. The northern part is distinguished by its abrupt slopes, surmounted by small mountains which give a particularly undulating aspect to the landscape.

Between the hills open out narrow river valleys in which the population is concentrated. From the coast the land rises steadily, stretching upwards to reach summits of between 200 and 600 metres. Nearer to Alava province are higher mountains, creating a kind of natural barrier between northern and southern zones.[15] Noticeable differences of climate and relief follow this spatial division, marking out two areas which are geographically very different.

The geographical features and the direction of the best communications routes have imposed highly varied patterns of economic contact upon the Basque Country. The northern sector has turned more towards the sea, and has natural links as much with France to the east as with the neighbouring province of Santander to the west. On the other hand, the lack of geographic obstacles between Alava and the high plains of Castile to the south helped the development of a busy communication between the two, while to maintain relationships between Alava and the other Basque provinces natural barriers had to be overcome. Recently impressive efforts have been made to solve this problem and very high levels of infrastructural investment have been made to improve the speed of communications between the Basque provinces. In spite of all this there is still no direct railway service between Vizcaya and Alava, while the road network between the latter province and Guipúzcoa is not exactly a model of convenience. All in all, geographical conditions have favoured the Basque Country's characteristic heterogeneity and the development of different subcultures. By the same token the economic specialisms of each area have been very diverse. Until the beginning of the nineteenth century the main economic foci of the two coastal provinces of Vizcaya and Guipúzcoa, and especially their largest towns Bilbao and San Sebastián, lay in commerce and the iron and steel industry. For its part, Alava based its economy in agriculture, channelling much of its output towards the other two provinces.

In the face of these distinguishing features there were also important aspects which tended to create unifying sentiments between the inhabitants of these provinces. An important role was played by the shared historical experience of the three provinces arising from the existence of a regime exclusive to themselves, the *Fuero*. The Basque provinces were unique in Spain in that from the beginning of the seventeenth century until 1876 they enjoyed a system which accorded them important advantages, including that of not contributing to the state treasury.[16] Shared cultural elements contributed equally to the birth of a sense of collective identity, most prominent among them the possession of a distinctive language, *euskera*. This is a language with distant and unknown origins, the only one in Western Europe with pre-Indo-European origins; and it has characteristics which are alien to the surrounding languages. The survival of *euskera* over a long period has been a fundamental influence on the creation of a feeling of identity which makes it possible to speak of a Basque people.[17] The use of *euskera* in nearby areas such as the adjacent province of Navarra and south-western France is a factor of prime importance for the claim of Basque nationalists that these areas should be considered as Basque and as potentially part of a future Basque state.

This is one of the vexed questions which warn us about the complexity of the Basque Country's problems. There is no agreement about the extent of the Basque Country or Euskadi, to give the Basque name of the proposed state, and while for some protagonists it should embrace the whole area where *euskera* is spoken (including Navarra and the French Basque Country), for others its boundaries are limited to the three provinces on which our attention is centred. Even the linguistic argument lends itself to controversy, because only a little over 25 per cent of the population of these three provinces speak *euskera* fluently, a percentage which diminishes if we include the other territories as well. Moreover, the contrasts between individual provinces are sharply marked and, although in Guipúzcoa about 46 per cent of the population speaks *euskera*, in Alava the figure falls to 8.6 per cent.[18] This draws attention to the distinctive cultural identities of the three provinces, which were strongly marked in the nineteenth century and which remained important in the forging of a new Basque identity by the nationalists and their allies at the turn of the century and onwards. We shall return to this theme.

The two regions thus share problems of definition and internal political and cultural divisions. North-west England has lacked the unifying impetus of a distinctive language, and it has not experienced the political project to define and promote a shared cultural identity which has been increasingly apparent in the Basque Country; but the Basque Country itself has been less unified than nationalist rhetoric has sought to suggest. Before pursuing these themes in greater depth, we need to discuss the economic experiences of the two regions, in which there is considerable common ground as well as divergence in the intensity and timing of economic growth and social change. This is not done in any crude spirit of economic determinism, but because of an expectation that economic development, by affecting ways of life, migration patterns and capital flows, will also have an impact on perceptions of collective identity. We begin with the pioneering (on the world stage) industrial economy of north-west England, in order to set up a comparison with the later-developing and differently-organised Basque Country.

Economy and society: north-west England

North-west England contained within its boundaries contrasting models of early industrialisation. The emergence of the cotton industry in south-east Lancashire and adjoining areas of Cheshire and Derbyshire from the late eighteenth century brought unprecedented demographic growth and population concentration, in association with a novel combination of factories, fossil fuels and the urban location of industry. This grew out of a classic proto-industrial environment of small farms, poor soils, low-key pastoral agriculture and domestic manufacture, and offered opportunities (with their associated social costs) for the employment of whole families.[19] South-west Lancashire, on the other hand, developed on the bases of coal mining and heavy metal-processing and chemical industries, in a flat and potentially-fertile landscape dominated by extensive landed estates. Outposts of a similar economy developed in the mid-nineteenth century in mineral-rich coastal districts further north, with large employers and a predominantly masculine working environment creating an industrial culture that contrasted with the area dominated by the cotton industry.[20] Rival regional capitals developed in the form of Manchester for the emergent 'cotton district', famous as the 'shock city' of the first Industrial Revolution, and the great port of Liverpool, which linked the region to the world economy which increasingly supplied both its raw materials and its markets.[21] Further north lay an enduringly agricultural economy which failed to build on early possibilities of industrial development, although the Lake District tourist trade gave distinctive additional resources to local economies on a seasonal basis.[22]

Within the region as defined here, then, there were distinctive and contrasting economic experiences, which did not correspond with county or other administrative boundaries; as Langton has suggested, the early industrial period created new *de facto* economic regions, based on the migration, raw material and credit flows which defined and followed the new internal transport systems of canals and turnpike roads.[23] These processes began in earnest in the later eighteenth century, although they had deeper roots. The south-east of the region, with Manchester at its hub, had long been in the vanguard of the Industrial Revolution by 1840, when in this part of England it was already the bright morning rather than the dawn of the railway age, with a network beginning to emerge after the successful pioneering of the Bolton and Leigh (1828) and more famously the Liverpool and Manchester (1830) lines. Here was already in existence an urban network based on the cotton industry and related activities, especially in engineering, with an unparalleled concentration of steam-powered factories, and a distinctive dependence more generally on complex machinery which relied on fossil fuels and was developing an increasing appetite for water. The social problems associated with new ways of working, new urban agglomerations of poverty-stricken housing, and new political conflicts were already attracting the fascinated and horrified attention of social commentators from beyond the region and beyond the seas, who saw here the pock-marked but vigorous face of the future.[24]

To the west, beginning in the frontier territory around Wigan and Leigh, was an area where coalmining and heavy industry, including copper, chemicals and glass, were already established in 1840, giving rise to a different social structure, trade cycle and pattern of family structure and living standards from that which prevailed around Manchester, with (for example) less paid labour for women and children, less scope for saving in good times and for political and self-help/mutual aid organisation, and a higher level of insecurity in risky employment.[25] Liverpool, with a distinctive urban economy of its own dominated by overseas trade and the casual and fluctuating work-patterns of dockers, seamen and building workers, presided over this hinterland and shared many of these problems while experiencing a particularly wide gap between a wealthy commercial bourgeoisie and an impoverished and insecure working class.[26] Further north lay an extensive area where neither model of industrial development had taken root, except in occasional patches where circumstances or traditions were favourable, most obviously in west Cumberland where landed capital and the Irish coal trade had fertilised a small but busy industrial belt based on mining.[27] Over most of north Lancashire and Cumbria, however, upland pastoral farming had not provided fertile soil for industry and, although second occupations were common and subsistence elements in farming economies were on the wane, this was a part of the north-west where economic growth and social transformation was much less in evidence, although the rural social system was kept in equilibrium by the out-migration (especially to south Lancashire) of what would otherwise have become a surplus rural population.[28]

These three main sub-divisions could be refined further, but they offer an interesting basis for argument about why, within a given region, similar pressures and opportunities might produce such contrasting outcomes, for by 1840, by and large, the die had been cast. Economic and social changes over the ensuing century, important as they were, followed lines of development which had been firmly laid down by 1840, and the fault-lines and fractures within regional identity were confirmed by the persistence of basic modes of social organisation which had been established by the contrasting nature of early industrialisation, or the lack of it, in the different parts of the region.

By the 1840s the industrial areas of north-west England had marched much further down the path to modernity than had those of the Basque Country, as we shall see, although there were still substantial settlements of hand-loom weavers and other artisans, especially in districts with a rural manufacturing tradition, at and beyond mid-century.[29] The years from 1838 to 1848, in particular, were a difficult transitional period, with a sequence of trade depressions which seemed to threaten the whole equilibrium of the new industrial society in south-east Lancashire, where industrial conflict and a cocktail of angry opposition to new social legislation, or the lack of it, became politicised in Chartism, which was as strong here as anywhere in Britain. But it was comparatively weak outside the cotton-manufacturing areas, although recent work has made a positive reassessment of its popular support in the great commercial metropolis of Liverpool as well as in Manchester itself.[30] Chartism reached its apogee in the seemingly apocalyptic trade depression of 1842, however, and declined rapidly and unevenly as the economy stabilised with the advent of the railway age, and popular support for radical reform was repressed, deterred or bought off by judicious concessions at local and national level.[31] There was, it should be noted, no regional dimension to Chartist demands. A good indicator of the ensuing political stability (though equipoise, the equilibrium of countervailing tensions, might be a better word) is the relative ease with which the mass unemployment and desperate poverty of the 'Cotton Famine' of the early 1860s were negotiated, although blame for this situation was displaced from employers to the American Civil War, and there were sporadic riots and fears of uprising which were carefully played down by those in authority. It does not do to underestimate the persisting scope for social conflict that simmered just below the surface, ready to erupt whenever employers neglected their perceived paternal obligations to workforces.[32] The strong affinity between Chartism and cotton-dominated economies (although most Chartist activists came from artisan and small shopkeeping sectors rather than from the ranks of factory workers) extended to outposts of the industry in the far north in Carlisle and district, and its significance for our purposes lies in the demonstration that north-west England's well-established economic divisions could also be mapped in terms of popular politics.[33] This argument could be extended to broader patterns of popular associational culture, with friendly societies, trade unions, mutual improvement societies, early (and later) co-operatives, and Mechanics' Institutes also much thicker on the ground in the cotton district than elsewhere.[34]

Economic and social change between the mid-nineteenth century and the First World War reinforced the established economic sub-regions within north-west England. The Lancashire cotton district continued to articulate its urban system, as growing towns interlaced grimy fingers along the valley bottoms and cohered indistinguishably (to outsiders) on the plain. Specialisations emerged as urban ways of life became almost universal: the northern towns of the cotton belt became strongholds of the weaving industry, which came to offer the best-paid employment for women in Britain, while to the south around Manchester spinning predominated, with a hierarchical, male-dominated workforce and limited scope for women outside the hard, dirty and generally ill-paid work of the preparation processes. So, within cotton Lancashire, different areas had contrasting family economies and gender relations, although everywhere most adult men worked outside cotton itself, especially in engineering, mining, building and transport. Within this general framework individual towns concentrated on distinctive grades of yarn or cloth for particular markets, and the structure of the firm varied from

Bolton's family-run enterprises to Oldham's abrasively-run mid-Victorian limited companies.[35] By the late nineteenth century local manufacturing identities were well-known and celebrated as part of burgeoning local patriotisms which also embraced town halls, co-operative societies and football clubs. Urban neighbourhoods had been cohering within the towns even as they grew in overall size and complexity, and by the late nineteenth century most populations were being recruited by natural increase rather than migration, reinforcing family and neighbourhood ties. Some towns were already stagnating in population terms. The third generation of workers had been socialised into the routines of the factory and urban neighbourhood as if they were inevitable, to the frustration of an articulate minority of socialists and environmentalists who were unable to understand the widespread acceptance of a way of life they found impoverishing in the fullest sense.[36]

Such social critics were hardly in evidence elsewhere in the region, least of all in the mining and heavy industrial district which abutted 'Cotton Lancashire' to the west and outcropped along the coast further north. Here urban growth could be even more abrasively spectacular than in the cotton towns themselves, as St Helens, Widnes and Barrow carved out ugly industrial identities in mid-Victorian times from small beginnings. In these mining, metalworking and chemical manufacturing towns wage-labour for women was in short supply, especially as women were banished from underground working in the coal mines by 1850. They were incorporated into the economy of the mines as unpaid washerwomen and purveyors of hot water to their menfolk. These areas were masculine republics in thrall to the worship of the breadwinner's brawn and endurance, with a tradition of violent sports on which rugby came to be grafted as the popular team-game of the later nineteenth century, in contrast with the soccer which predominated (never exclusively) in the cotton towns. All kinds of associational and mutual assistance societies developed later and on a smaller scale than in the cotton towns, and this was connected with higher levels of insecurity and labour mobility, with a more prominent Irish presence and more sectarian strife than prevailed further east.[37]

This was even more in evidence in Liverpool, which acquired an unenviable reputation for ethnic and sectarian conflict alongside a generally daunting level of recorded crime, violence and prostitution. Here, too, local neighbourhoods cohered and generated distinctive identities, but limited and unreliable resources and entitlements prevented the dockland and inner-city districts from attaining the level of quiescent stability which became the norm in all but the most disadvantaged districts of the cotton towns, although police authorities claimed to have curbed the worst of Liverpool's excesses by the 1870s. But throughout the period the urban pathology of Liverpool stood out in public health statistics, from death- and infant-mortality rates to appalling levels of overcrowding in fetid slums which outdid the worst even of Engels' Manchester. It was in Liverpool, especially, and industrial south-west Lancashire that the Industrial Revolution had its most clearly adverse and enduring impact on working-class living standards, while the wealthy merchants increasingly fled into Cheshire or along the coastline. There was a better-off stratum of artisans and clerks in late Victorian housing built to improved minimum municipal standards, but Liverpool and its industrial satellites lacked the evidence of emergent consumer choice in leisure, furnishings and food which was becoming visible at mainstream working-class level during the great price fall in the late Victorian cotton towns.[38]

Urban growth in south Lancashire was on a scale which far outweighed developments in the Basque Country. Between 1851 and 1911 Manchester expanded from just over 300,000 to just over 700,000 inhabitants (exact figures vary according to the boundary chosen, as suburbs proliferated), and Liverpool doubled its population from 375,000 to nearly 750,000. In 1851 four other towns (including Salford, adjoining Manchester) had more than 50,000 inhabitants, and a further six claimed more than 20,000. Sixty years later the urbanising juggernaut had accumulated six towns with more than 100,000 denizens (Salford had over 230,000 and Bolton 180,000), while eight others topped 50,000 (including the seaside resorts of Southport and Blackpool) and a further nine occupied the 30–50,000 range.[39] The northern part of the region could display nothing so dramatic, although it contained the mid-Victorian boom-town of Barrow-in-Furness, whose fortunes were founded on iron-mining and steelmaking. But other industrial towns in north Lancashire and Cumbria were faltering after promising progress in the late eighteenth and early nineteenth centuries, and new boosts to the mining and heavy industry-based economies of west Cumberland in the railway age were short-lived, while inland the tourist trade had a limited economic impact. Here the scale of urban growth and industrial development ran more closely parallel to developments in the Basque Country at this time; and over much of the northern area the economy continued to be based on upland pastoral farming, riding out the agricultural depression which made such an impact further south, depending more and more heavily on family labour as migrants headed for urban opportunities to the south and east, drawn more firmly into the market by railways and easier urban access, but still experiencing what was in many ways a recognisably traditional way of life. Upland Cumbria was, perhaps, the Alava of north-west England.[40]

The First World War proved to be a watershed in north-west England, whose by now well-established staple industries were disrupted and distorted by wartime conditions. The Lancashire cotton industry made soaring profits in the short run, but with shrinking workforces and increasing isolation from important markets. The cotton workforce shrank from 620,000 to 500,000 between June 1914 and June 1917, and the flow of male cotton workers into the armed forces (where many were killed in action) brought growing numbers of women into jobs which had been male preserves, especially on the spinning side of the industry. Constraints on raw material supplies tightened towards the end of the war, as shipping space on transatlantic runs was needed for food and munitions, although supplies of Indian cotton remained abundant. At the same time British cotton goods exports to India, Lancashire's key market for its dominant low-quality lines, went into sharp decline due to local and Japanese competition and a fall in demand, while net import tariffs on British goods were introduced for the first time. But prices generally were cushioned by demand from the war effort and lack of competition within Europe, encouraging a complacency which proved ill-judged when the war ended. Meanwhile a succession of crises and problems seemed to have been weathered.[41]

In north-west England more generally the energies of industries were channelled into the war effort, as engineering works went over to munitions and Barrow's shipyards prospered, although here as elsewhere the demand for extra labour brought squalid overcrowding. Liverpool's port facilities were overwhelmed by pressure of demand, and after the dislocations of the war's early months there was full employment everywhere. Women found new niches in the labour market, working hard and playing hard as munitions workers and taking over highly-visible work in public transport. Wages struggled to outpace rising prices, but as the war proceeded rent controls and rationing reduced the stresses on working-class budgets.[42] The wartime prosperity of Blackpool, a resort which depended on the buoyancy of working-class demand, was symptomatic. Here as elsewhere, however, there were wartime labour conflicts against the erosion of real wages while profits soared; and struggles against dilution and in defence of established working practices punctuated wartime production.[43] Despite this willingness to stand up for workplace rights even at some cost to the war effort, what stands out across the north-west, and especially in the cotton towns of Lancashire, was a strong national patriotic sentiment which drew men to the colours as volunteers in large numbers, and which was expressed through locally-raised regiments which drew their identities from particular towns and industries: especially the so-called 'Pals' battalions, some of which were almost wiped out in the great set-piece battles of the Western Front and at Gallipoli. What was not specifically expressed here was a *regional* identity: patriotic support for the war effort was generated at neighbourhood, workplace and town level, for a national cause, through regiments which (incidentally) had county labels, sometimes laid claim to countywide virtues, used the traditional county figurehead of the Earl of Derby as a recruiting talisman in Lancashire, but hardly appealed to any broader regional sentiment.[44]

The immediate post-war years were difficult and transitional, and in their aftermath north-west England lost all claim to economic primacy as the staple industries which had generated its industrial revolution and sustained its comparative prosperity between the mid-nineteenth century and the First World War fell into decline after a fleeting and illusory post-war boom. The cotton industry itself began its long slide to oblivion in the early 1920s, after extensive speculative revaluation without new investment during 1919–20, which was exposed as over-capitalisation based on over-confidence when the boom broke. The loss of Indian markets was particularly damaging during the 1920s, hitting towns which specialised in lower-grade yarns and cloths (such as Oldham and Blackburn) harder than those with more up-market output inventories.[45] Meanwhile the coal industry fell on hard times across the region, with the outposts of mining and heavy industry on the west Cumberland coast faring worst, although there was severe poverty in the pit villages around Wigan which George Orwell made notorious.[46] The older-established chemical industries of south- west Lancashire faltered in the face of foreign competition, although amalgamations brought resources as well as rationalisations.[47] There were positive developments along the Manchester Ship Canal, which opened in 1894 but came into its own after the war, pulling the industrial centre of gravity southwards to its oil refineries and to the pioneer industrial estate at Trafford Park, on Manchester's edge. Liverpool, meanwhile, was damaged by the diversion of some of its port traffic along this alternative route, which by-passed its dock dues; but it suffered even more from depressed trade flows, the decline of staple hinterland industries and the transfer of ocean liner traffic to south coast ports. Attempts to establish new industries met with limited success, and Liverpool had its own problems of structural unemployment as casual labour problems were reduced.[48]

The slump at the end of the 1920s made matters worse and, although only west Cumberland was recognised as a depressed area, with registered unemployment running at over 60 per cent in places in the depths of the depression in 1931, the weaving towns around Blackburn fared little better and unemployment rates of 30 per cent or more were widespread.[49] There were bright spots in the western half of Lancashire as well as along the Manchester Ship Canal, wherever sunrise industries and tourism were prominent in local economies, and towns with broadly-based or adaptable industrial structures like Rochdale or Lancaster (which also had low wages and a quiescent labour force) bucked the trend.[50] Falling prices and family sizes enabled those in work to prosper modestly across the region, and cotton Lancashire's pre-war culture of high-pressure hard work and consumption of sport, holidays and household consumer goods was perpetuated under these conditions, while even the unemployed could seek warmth as well as entertainment in cheap cinema seats. The cinema brought global Hollywood culture to all but the smallest places, although it also provided less-popular British films, and successful comedies which celebrated Lancashire identities based on an idealisation of the unpretentious, good-hearted, neighbourly, hard-working 'gradely folk' of the cotton towns.[51] By the 1930s the radio, too, was penetrating rural Cumbria, where popular mores still danced to the domesticated tunes of an older set of traditions.[52] Most economies within the region were reviving again by the mid-1930s, especially where rearmament contracts were issued; but the secular decline in the cotton industry's output persisted. An interesting effect of patterns of inter-war change was that sub-regional boundaries within the north-west were shifting. The Manchester Ship Canal corridor, following the Langton model, and a triangle of prosperity linking Blackpool, Preston and Lancaster in north-west Lancashire, and extending to Southport and the northern maritime residential suburbs of Liverpool, constituted new areas of development and population growth which formed differently-shaped pieces in the regional jigsaw. A few residential suburbs apart, population growth was modest, especially when compared with the explosive Victorian pattern, but it contrasted with a general trend towards population stagnation or decline in the specialised industrial towns of nineteenth-century vintage, as migration outflows swelled in pursuit of opportunities elsewhere which were no longer evident there.[53]

The immediate post-war years saw labour unrest in parts of north-west England, particularly Liverpool, where the authorities were especially perturbed by a police strike in 1919 which led to looting and brought military intervention, mass sackings and emergency recruitment to restore order. Shortly before this there were race riots against Liverpool's black labour force as post-war labour markets tightened, and sectarian divisions between Protestant and Catholic retained more power than elsewhere in the region.[54] Generally, however, media appeals to English patriotism against the alien godlessness of communism, which was carefully if misleadingly identified with socialism and the Labour Party, were effective here as elsewhere, and the failure of the General Strike in 1926 set the seal on the decline of post-war militancy. Only when employers sought to cut at the heart of the established working practices of generations, as in the attempts to require weavers to operate additional looms at lower rates in north-east Lancashire in the early 1930s, did bitter labour disputes revive; and the unemployed were unable to keep the active support of their more fortunate neighbours, despite marches and occasional riots. The work ethic had been thoroughly internalised.[55]

What is remarkable is the passivity of the working class throughout north-west England in the face of widespread industrial decline, visibly incompetent management and high levels of unemployment, especially when the conditions under which relief was offered were tightened in the early 1930s, when there were even attempts to force female weavers, proud of their skills and independence, into domestic service.[56] Out-migration, moreover, though not insignificant, was a trickle rather than a flood. Working-class families remained attached to towns and neighbourhoods, despite often deteriorating working and living conditions and loss of prospects and job security. Families, savings and survival strategies were rooted in localities and neighbourhoods, and there were significant minorities of houseowners who would have found it hard to realise their assets.[57] Established political and religious cultures attached people to the old political parties, even as the established elites abdicated their old leadership roles, sold up and departed for more salubrious climes. When Labour made headway in the 1920s, beginning to mobilise communities as well as workforces, its hopes were blighted by the lack of alternative economic policy, at local and national levels, and by the political disaster of 1931 which ushered in the National Government.[58] Even in the utterly depressed areas of west Cumberland, local government was evenly balanced between Labour and Independents or Conservatives. Even in Workington, a heavy industry centre which might have been read off as a Labour stronghold, an electoral pact between Labour and its rivals kept the party out of office throughout the 1930s.[59] As before, however, the identities that gave meaning to lives were those of neighbourhood and town at one level, and nation and empire in more abstract and distant but nevertheless powerful terms at another level. There is little evidence of people thinking in terms of regions, or of a north-western identity, despite the widely-shared experience of poverty and insecurity across a broad and identifiable area. Such a sense of identity was no more in evidence in industrial decline than during the prosperous years which had laid down enduring assumptions about what life was for: a 'commonsense' which accepted grim industrial environments and long working hours in repetitive jobs in exchange for a measure of security, access to cheap consumer goods and occasional sanctioned opportunities for escape and carefully-defined acceptable excess. As these trade-offs were almost imperceptibly whittled away during the depression years, there was scant response and little vitality within the culture to orchestrate one.

The north-west England of this chapter thus experienced a long cycle of growth, industrial prosperity and decline during the century after 1840, building on earlier developments. Manifestations of change and continuity took different forms in different parts of the region, and the internal economic boundaries of the region, as notional shapes on the ground or indeed spatially-expressed flows of economic and social relationships, might be argued to have changed over time, especially during the inter-war years. An overarching sense of regional identity, as expressed (for example) in literature, politics or popular culture, was never in evidence, although parts of the region (especially 'cotton Lancashire' and the Lake District) might have generalised characteristics ascribed to them in ways which might command some popular assent.[60] But loyalties were attached to the local and the national/imperial rather than to the regional. We shall return to these issues. Meanwhile, the changing economic and social panorama of the Basque Country needs to be presented.

The Basque Country: economy and society

The Basque Country had enduring economic sub-divisions of its own, with corresponding social implications. Developments here showed similarities with and differences from those that took place in north-west England. An initial feature that stands out is that the Basque provinces also experienced an important industrialisation process, rising to become a key centre of Spanish industrial development. This development came significantly later than in England, but above all its extent and social consequences were decidedly smaller. We are dealing with two zones marked out within economies whose trajectory was strikingly divergent, and in face of the powerful industrial advance in England, Spain throughout the nineteenth century and well into the twentieth continued to base its economy in an unsophisticated agricultural sector. We have to wait until the 1960s before Spain experienced a real industrial awakening when this sector became the basis of development. Until then industrialisation had a limited role in the national economy, although both the Basque Country and Catalonia were the scenes of industrial developments whose levels were important in Spanish terms.[61]

The origins of industrialisation in the Basque Country can be located between the years 1841–72, that is to say, in the intermission between two wars which affected this region in a distinctive manner.[62] The year 1841 marks the point of departure for the economic transformation of the Basque provinces. In this year, and in the context of the end of the First Carlist War, the government decided to move the internal customs barriers between the Basque provinces and the rest of Spain to the frontier and the seaports. The survival of internal customs barriers into the beginning of the nineteenth century came by courtesy of the *Fuero*, which encompassed this peculiar situation, so characteristic of the *ancien régime*. The relocation of the customs created an appropriate environment for the development of textile manufacturing by protecting the Basque industrialists from foreign competition by means of tariff obstacles, at the same time giving them unrestricted access to the Spanish market in which they were most likely to sell their products. From this point began the installation of the first modern factories, both in Vizcaya and Guipúzcoa, at the same time as the traditional ironworking industries entered their final crisis. But until the 1870s the scale of development was limited.[63]

It was from 1876 onwards that the Basque Country's real industrial awakening occurred, in a process which took on varying characteristics and took root to an unequal extent. Vizcaya province, and more especially Bilbao with its extension along the Nervión estuary, was the area of most intensive industrial development. At the same time Guipúzcoa, the other coastal province, also industrialised, although with marked differences from Vizcaya.. Guipúzcoa's industrial development was noticeably more modest, and was not geographically concentrated in that it extended broadly over the province through the spread of medium-sized and small businesses. Equally, manufacturing was not dominated by a single sector; rather it was highly diversified in different branches of production. Industrial growth did not presuppose the elimination of farming activity, which declined but survived in the interior of Vizcaya wherever it had not been affected by large-scale industrialisation, as well as in Guipúzcoa. These were small farms which had to adjust themselves to the broken terrain and which could not support more than a single family. Economic development required these farms to adjust to new circumstances, moving into the market economy and responding to the opportunity to meet a demand for higher-quality produce (such as meat, milk, fruit and vegetables).

For its part, Alava remained on the margins of industrial development and suffered sustained stagnation. It remained a pre-eminently agrarian province as attempts to modernise its economy failed, and recession continued through the nineteenth century. The differences between the coastal provinces and Alava were deepening, as the latter became an economically dependent area which supplied migrant labour and foodstuffs to the other two provinces.[64]

From this initial overview we can extract some parallels between the Basque Country and north-west England, always bearing in mind the unequal scale of their economic processes and the gap between one example and the other. In both areas industrial development became consolidated into clearly-defined economic spaces, some of which were extraordinarily industrialised, while other districts continued to base themselves on agriculture. Within the areas which industrialised, the predominance of heavy industry in both cases made Bilbao and its hinterland resemble south-west Lancashire, while the nature of Guipúzcoa's industries showed some similarity to south-east Lancashire, though on a much smaller and less intensive scale, and without the distinctive impetus and specialisation that Lancashire's cotton industry had provided. The provincial capital, San Sebastián, developed as a seaside resort, although it had its own industries and acted as a vector for new ideas in the same way as Manchester, though through international tourism rather than trade more conventionally envisaged; while the industrial settlements of the valleys had much in common with the smaller and more insular textile towns of Lancashire districts such as Rossendale. The province of Alava showed some similarity with north Lancashire and rural Cumbria in that economic growth lagged behind and the primary sector continued to be the focus of their economies. However, the system of agriculture based on small family farms, which was more in evidence in the two coastal provinces than in Alava, had more in common with the hilly districts of south-east Lancashire and the northern parts of north-west England than with the great estates and sometimes capital-intensive farming which dominated the agricultural scene around Liverpool. So the pattern of farming did not match the pattern of industrial growth in the two regions.[65] But to develop these arguments further we need to investigate the pattern of economic development and social change in the Basque Country in greater depth.

As suggested above, the key change in trend came in 1876. Before this date the Basque provinces were the scene of two conflicts, the so-called Carlist Wars, which occupied the years between 1833–39 and 1872–75 and put a brake of their own on economic development. Although these were struggles of national import, given that the Carlists aimed at installing a new monarch, it was in the Basque Country and the neighbouring province of Navarra that Carlism had its main social base and theatre of operations.[66] Although Carlist motives were not the same in the first conflict as in the second, Carlism was above all a reactionary movement which rejected the consequences of liberal-capitalist society as much for its social implications (an important aspect of the first war) as for the liberal politics with which it was associated (an influential ingredient in the second struggle). Carlism drew on a broad spectrum of support in the Basque Country, which embraced not only rural landowners and peasant groupings, but also pulled in sectors of the urban populace.[67]

The Carlist wars constituted a kind of conflict which reflected very clearly the contrasting rhythms of development of north-west England and the Basque Country, and the differing social problems which each area faced. During the middle years of the nineteenth century the number of urban workers in the Basque Country was very small, and these people had not developed a class consciousness on any viable definition, nor had they even formed organisations of their own. The working people lived segregated lives, divided into strata according to whether they were skilled artisans, factory workers or unskilled, and stable feelings of collective identity did not exist among them.[68] Support for Carlism among the lower orders in the Basque Country reflected the insecurities which capitalist development had brought to these social strata, but the responses that were offered consisted more of defensive postures than of attempts to hold back a process which was already unstoppable. In any case, Carlism became a phenomenon of central importance in the nineteenth-century Basque Country, consolidating an established mentality, a culture, a way of acting communally expressed through a traditionalist ideology; and these and other key elements were to be passed on in good measure to the nationalism of the following century. This offers an interesting contrast with the widespread support for Chartism in the most advanced industrial areas of Lancashire, although the English county developed its own varieties of popular traditionalism, especially in the post-Chartist period, and Chartism itself built on radical traditions within and beyond the region while making its own appeal to a version of English history. Post-Chartist popular traditionalism, however, was identified with national patriotism as expressed through the Conservative Party in its guise as ostentatious proponent of social reform and advocate of a strong navy and forward foreign policy which Lancashire's markets seemed to need, rather than forming a movement harnessing regional identities for political purposes.[69]

Where Chartism itself had been a national movement with regional concentrations of strength, Carlism in the Basque Country drew its strength from an identification with regional political and cultural attachments. The entity which came closest to such a guise in north-west England was the Anti-Corn Law League, with its headquarters in Manchester and its identification with the 'Manchester School' of free-market liberalism and internationalism whose content was in complete contrast with Carlism: it attacked traditions rather than endorsing them, and it lost its tail of popular support very quickly after the repeal of the Corn Laws in 1846.[70] In any case its symbolic affiliation to Manchester fell far short of the full-blooded Basque claim to the defence of an older regional identity. This was associated in the Basque case with an economic protectionism which became anathema to Lancashire workers as well as employers, and which in its English guise had been the central target of the Anti-Corn Law League's wrath. Free Trade remained orthodoxy in north-west England despite the loss of popular support for the original campaigners after mid-century, as the electoral disaster which befell the Conservatives in Lancashire when they took up Protectionism for the 1906 general election was to demonstrate only too clearly.[71]

The year 1876 was important in Spain generally and in the Basque Country in particular, and not only for ushering in the long-drawn-out final resolution of the Carlist question. In the first place it marks the moment in which Spain moved into a new stage of political development, and in which, as in the rest of Europe, new ideologies and forms of mass mobilisation were to surge forth. It also constitutes the starting point for the full-scale industrialisation of the Basque Country, for the beginning of a phase of important economic transformations and the placing of the market economy in a dominant position over older social norms.[72] The detonator which sparked the explosion of industrial growth was the export of Vizcayan iron ore from the 1870s, which enabled the accumulation of capitals from which there arose in this province a vigorous iron and steel industry, subsequently complemented by a metal-working sector. From these bases the rapid industrialisation of Vizcaya was consolidated, in a process whose speed and intensity had no parallel elsewhere in Spain. In a short time the landscape of Bilbao's estuary changed profoundly, as mining and manufacturing activity around Bilbao and on the left bank grew in spectacular style, and with it the population of the area. English influences were prominent here, and English capital played a formative role. The start of the twentieth century saw a second phase in Vizcaya's industrial growth. A greater diversity of production emerged, with shipbuilding enterprises and the growing financial sector standing out, while the web of industry became extended through parts of the province's interior.[73] Guipúzcoa also experienced a considerable industrial boost during this period, characterised by the variety of branches which proliferated, including metalworking, armaments, textile and consumer goods factories and paper mills.

These processes produced spectacular demographic and urban growth wherever there was industrial development, while in those areas with stagnating economies there was hardly any population change. In the first category we find the environs of Bilbao, which saw how towns could issue forth in previously sparsely-populated places. San Salvador del Valle grew from 798 people in 1860 to 5,114 in 1887, while Baracaldo went from 2,688 inhabitants in 1860 to 34,209 in 1930. Bilbao itself grew equally spectacularly, moving from 17,923 inhabitants in 1857 to 112,819 in 1920 (an increase of 529 per cent), while San Sebastián passed from a population of 15,911 to 61,774 between the same dates, combining tourist, administrative and industrial activities. Levels of urbanisation increased in parallel, so that in 1920 more than 50 per cent of the population of Vizcaya and Guipúzcoa lived in towns with more than 5000 inhabitants. On the other hand the population of Alava province, with 98,668 inhabitants in 1920, hardly increased at all during this period.

If we compare these figures with those supplied for north-west England, the differences in population totals attract immediate attention. This is not to suggest that we should play down the substance of the developments in the two coastal provinces of the Basque Country, and especially what took place in Vizcaya. The transformation of this province was very sharply-defined indeed. Consider the case of Baracaldo which was discussed above. In 1857, 91.4 per cent of the active population was included in the primary sector, but thirty years later this accounted for only 12.7 per cent while the secondary sector stood at 79.4 per cent. In the area around Bilbao the old farmsteads were vanishing before the invasion of an urban landscape, and the peaceful rhythms of rural life found themselves pushed aside by industrialisation and its flood of new arrivals from other places. Between 1877 and 1900 about 74,000 migrants arrived in Bilbao's industrial area, making an immediate impact on a population of limited dimensions. The transformation which occurred in Guipúzcoa was more gradual, more restrained, which helped to ensure that social problems were less evident in this province. The rise and development of the tourist industry had an immediate impact on San Sebastián, whose urban expansion from the late 1860s was undertaken on the basis of constructing a high-quality urban environment which would be attractive to a visiting population.[74]

Between 1876 and 1914 the 'social question' emerged as a theme with undeniable impact in Basque society. The stacking up of people in overcrowded, unhygienic and insanitary conditions formed the everyday currency of the working-class districts. The situation of the miners in Vizcaya, a growth sector during the last third of the nineteenth century, was especially hard: they had to find lodgings in dormitory cabins which lacked even the most basic amenities.[75] Mortality rates were very high, with a notable increase during this period, in sharp contrast to the experience of mining settlements in north-west England; but perhaps the most telling aspect of this situation was its socially selective character, as mortality reached widely differing proportions according to the social condition of the districts. Thus the most deprived districts in Bilbao at the start of the twentieth century had a mortality rate of over 45 per thousand, while in those of higher social standing the rate stood at 22 per thousand.[76] In these conditions workers' grievances appeared in full vigour, as strikes and protests took place in the 1890s and at the beginning of the twentieth century, giving rise on occasions to general strikes which affected the mining and industrial basin of Bilbao and its hinterland. This was a movement led by the socialists, who proclaimed their influence over the Vizcayan working class during this period, as the area was converted into one of the bastions of Spanish socialism. The socialists imprinted a forcefully demanding and confrontational tone on employer-worker relations, while the employers collaborated together decisively in denying the workers their most basic rights (those of association, collective bargaining, and so on). In contrast with what happened in north-west England, where workers' organisations in the second or third generation of industrialisation were more developed, employers were less effective at presenting a common front, and relations between trade unions and socialism were more distant, this first generation of Basque industrial workers still had not internalised the conventions of the industrial system, hence the radical nature of many of the protests in which they participated during this period, despite the efforts of Basque nationalists to implant a more moderate trade unionism of their own.[77] The Basque industrial districts had more in common with aspects of labouring culture in Liverpool with its appalling housing, ethnic divisions and propensity for fierce and combustible labour disputes against united employers (though with little sustained socialist content), or in west Cumberland where trade unions made ground late in a decidedly Vizcayan industrial environment, than in the more stable (by this time) setting of the Lancashire cotton district. The First World War was to bring both short-term and long-term changes in both settings.

The war made a great impact on the Basque Country, despite Spain's neutral status. In contrast with what happened in north-west England, industry in general enjoyed a period of strong expansion, with the creation of new businesses and a notable increase in the number of workers. Both societies saw an increase in employers' profits, as well as a rise in prices which was particularly noticeable in basic necessities. The poorer classes lost purchasing power, which brought an extension of social discontent in the Basque Country. The incidence of strikes reached levels unknown until now, and even the hitherto tranquil province of Guipúzcoa found itself convulsed by the wave of conflicts. These were directed by the socialists, who consolidated their favoured position among the workforce, especially when redress of grievances was being sought. Even so, this was a socialism which had become more moderate in its actions, which now no longer sought confrontation with employers, but aimed at negotiation and agreement. In its operations among the workers it put into practice a tradition of trade union action of a reformist character which produced good dividends, although in 1921 it had to confront the communist secession, which had an important following in the Basque Country.[78]

The end of the war brought about a period of industrial crisis. The ample flow of profits obtained by the employers during the conflict was not used to improve either production techniques or productivity levels, so that when peace returned the lack of competitiveness of Basque industries was made all too visible. Even so, this was a fleeting crisis. In contrast with what occurred in north-west England, the 1920s witnessed a period of general economic expansion and industrial revival, although times were sunnier for employers than workpeople. The coming of Primo de Rivera's dictatorship in 1923 put the lid on industrial unrest, and the traditional sectors consolidated themselves, with the steel and metalworking industries, together with shipbuilding and banking, maintaining their strength in Vizcaya. Meanwhile Guipúzcoa continued with its industrial diversity, at the same time as it expanded its sources of income through the continued growth of up-market tourism, despite the closure of San Sebastián's casinos by the Primo de Rivera regime in 1924, which posed revenue problems for local and provincial government. For its part Alava continued along the path of economic atrophy, basing itself on an agricultural sector which had hardly modernised, rather like the Lake District without its tourist trade.[79] The overall picture changed radically with the Second Republic (1931–36), an episode which had an enormous political significance in Spain and which entailed an attempt to bring about a genuine democratisation of society. This experiment coincided with the economic crisis which affected the Western powers and which had repercussions of great intensity in the Basque Country. This crisis was due as much to external factors – the 'crisis of 1929' – as to internal ones. Among the latter are included government policies which gave up the state's role as starter-motor and locomotive of industry, to which was added the adverse competitive effect that arose from increased production costs as a result of wage rises. The overall result was a rise in unemployment, which in Vizcaya at times reached 35 per cent of the workforce; a province-wide figure which was topped only in the most depressed areas of north-west England, the old mining areas and centres for the weaving of low-quality cloth, even in the worst of the lean years of the early 1930s.[80]

During the Second Republic various phenomena, which were already developing during the second decade of the twentieth century, reached their full flowering. They reflected the profound changes which were taking place in all social spheres in the Basque Country. Later than in England and in a more socially selective manner, an incipient consumer society began to emerge as the range of products on offer began to broaden. The industrial transformation of Basque society and the associated economic growth pulled along with them a 'revolution of necessities'(in E. P. Thompson's telling phrase), breaking through the ceiling of what had been considered basic commodities. The decisive and sustained urban development in the Basque provinces since 1880 implied changes without end and the most sharply-defined transformation of daily life and customs. An urban culture became consolidated and with it a culture of escapism, which developed popular preferences for musical and sporting spectacles. Musical genres such as *zarzuela* (a kind of music-hall), *canción española* and others were assured of growing public support, a development which created the new experience of pleasure-seeking crowds gathering in a defined space. Among sporting activities football had a sensational rise. At the beginning of the twentieth century it was almost unknown and more an elite preserve, but in a very short time it attracted a good number of players and spectators, which brought about the construction of closed-off stadia to enable profits to be made by exploiting the game commercially. These developments came a generation or more later than in north-west England, although pelota and bullfighting were already commercially-run spectacles on this model by the 1870s. Thus there was in the Basque Country a trend to the collective enjoyment of leisure, which brought an immediate response in a new social differentiation of recreations. People met together in certain defined spaces or meeting places to pursue leisure activities, or played certain particular sports, according to their economic circumstances. For example, the drinking places which proliferated from the beginning of the century and which were the preferred meeting-places for Basques as centres of sociability, were divided into *tabernas* which gave solace to the popular sectors, and the bars or cafeterias which were frequented by the middle classes, while elite groups preferred to follow the English example of meeting in private clubs. Other patterns of segregation proliferated alongside these.[81]

These developments constitute one similarity among many between the converging experiences of industrialisation in north-west England and the Basque Country, despite wide variations in the scale and timing of events and processes, and sharply contrasting political cultures. In parts of north-west

England industrialisation developed earlier, promoting the rise of specialised urban networks on a scale which the Basque Country was to match only in Bilbao and district. The Lancashire cotton towns already constituted a mature industrial society by the mid-nineteenth century, although the stability of the 1850s remained precarious and vulnerable. Liverpool had already become one of the world's great seaports. Large-scale, transforming industrial development in the Basque Country came later, arriving on the grand scale only in the last quarter of the nineteenth century; there was a time lag of a generation, even when developments around Bilbao are compared with the mushroom towns of the railway age whose natural resources were unlocked in the 1850s and 1860s in north-west England, most obviously Barrow and St Helens. The Lancashire cotton towns were already developing a working-class consumer society when the Basque Country was starting on the muddy road to industrialisation and generating raw poverty and social discontent of a kind which had declined sharply in most of north-west England since the 1840s, although the rough, polluted industrial environments of south-west Lancashire had strong similarities with those of industrial Vizcaya. It was during and after the First World War that Basque industrial living standards began to catch up with those of north-west England, as the industrial climate in the Basque Country became much more benign than in Lancashire and west Cumberland.

The political stability of north-west England for most of this period was built on short-distance migration, social cohesion arising from the consolidation of civic pride and mutual assistance in tightly-knit urban neighbourhoods, and the development of survival strategies which entailed the acceptance of a life revolving around the disciplines of industrial labour. Long-range in-migration was dominated by the Irish and concentrated into the mid-Victorian period, and the Irish presence, while generating conflict in the short run and providing an 'otherness' against which local identities could be measured and tested, proved capable of assimilation into and alongside the dominant popular cultures.[82] Socialism worked in similar ways.

The Basque working class experienced deeper poverty for longer periods, and migration from beyond the provincial boundary proved more indigestible, while socialism also remained a more abrasive ingredient in popular culture than in north-west England, despite moves towards increasing moderation by the war years. The Basque Country was united by Roman Catholic assumptions, although the Basques had a distinctive version of Catholicism, while north-west England experienced a plurality of religious outlooks which permeated party politics but did not generate serious social conflict after the 1870s.[83] On the other hand, Basque politics were much more complex and sub-divided than the two-party structure which continued to dominate in the north-west, although second-party status shifted from the Liberals to (decidedly non-socialist) Labour during the 1920s. But what was distinctive about the Basque Country, despite its internal sub-divisions and complicated political spectrum, was an overriding sense of shared identity among the Basque inhabitants, of which political nationalism as it developed was only one, controversial expression. This question must now be taken further, as we pick up themes which have surfaced repeatedly in earlier discussions and try to explain the contrast between the well-developed sense of collective regional identity which existed and developed in the Basque Country, and the lack of any such shared sentiments in north-west England.

Regions and identities

If economic processes carried the lifestyles and customs of the urban inhabitants of north-west England and the Basque Country towards points of convergence, the political and social panorama offered elements of divergence. While in the English setting patriotic ideals predominated, with their focus on nation and empire, in the Basque Country during the first third of the twentieth century there arose a very powerful nationalist sentiment which rejected head-on any notion that this territory belonged to Spain. Whether or not one sympathises with them, there is no denying that the nationalists ensured that during the Second Republic the question of Basque national identity gathered novel strength and formed itself into a fundamental issue in public life. The nationalists had obtained their first great success in 1918, when they achieved a well-publicised triumph in the parliamentary elections in Vizcaya, winning four of the five seats being contested. After the dictatorship of Primo de Rivera (1923–29), which entailed the suppression of democratic activity, the Second Republic was the opportunity for the nationalists to display the full extent of their power. This showed itself in the parliamentary elections of 1933, when they emerged as the most popular grouping in the Basque Country, with a total of 30 per cent of the vote and 12 of the 17 available seats.[84] The strength of the nationalists expressed itself not only in political action, important though this was. It was rooted fundamentally in their capacity for creating communal ties between the followers of this ideology, forging a kind of community within the wider society. By this means they established a complex communications system, and a whole network of organisations (trade union, cultural and women's groups, and so on) through which they secured the transmission of their ideology and the establishment of a culture of their own which gave an unexpected solidity to the movement.

Basque nationalism drew on old attachments to traditions of autonomy within the Spanish state, to language, and to the idealised cultural identities of the three provinces. At the core of all this, historically, was the *Fuero*. Since the beginning of the seventeenth century the Basque provinces were alone in Spain in enjoying this special system which exempted them from (among other things) contributing to the central Treasury and from military service. This exemption, coupled with linguistic distinctiveness, lay at the core of the development in the eighteenth and nineteenth centuries of an awareness of a distinctive identity among Basques. This consciousness did not go so far as to question belonging to the Spanish state, but it was the foundation for a discourse which highlighted the particular identity of the Basque provinces and demanded on this basis a special status in relations with the monarchy. But the state centralising influence which arose in Spain, as in the rest of Europe during the nineteenth century, required Basque intellectuals to broaden the basis of their claims beyond the *Fuero*.[85] This took two main forms. Firstly, an ample and complex mythology about the past of the Basque Country became the basis for inventing a tradition and an image of the country which justified its peculiar relationship with the Spanish crown. Secondly, there also developed a judicial/political doctrine which opposed to the national state's constitution a kind of 'internal' constitution which existed in each Basque province thanks to the foral regimes. Against the doctrine of constitutional legitimacy as expression of the general will, certain Basque theoreticians of the nineteenth century argued for a superior Basque legitimacy rooted in history and made concrete in the *Fuero*.[86]

In these arguments which came from Basque sources over the nineteenth century there were no explicitly political demands, nor do we find nationalist formulae, nor indeed a unified Basque sense of identity. The basic point of reference for the people continued to be the province and not the Basque Country as a whole, while the rights demanded by these provinces were above all administrative. But the diffusion achieved by these ideas, and the popularity enjoyed by the *Fuero* among the inhabitants, were decisive in creating an atmosphere conducive to the later spread of nationalist ideas, especially after the abolition of the key components of the *Fuero* in 1876. The attachment to the *Fuero* generated a popular belief that Basques had traditional rights and customs which could not legitimately be altered by any external authority. When central government undermined and suppressed the foral system, this aroused a unanimous reaction in the Basque Country in its defence, contributing to the forging of sentiments of identity among the people. The old foral consciousness was validating and giving way to Basque and/or nationalist feelings.

Political nationalism, as it developed, was not a unifying ideology in itself. Two basic identities lived side by side in Basque society from the beginning of the twentieth century. One was Basque nationalist; the other, which defined itself partly in reaction to this, combined attachments to Basque and Spanish elements. This latter posture was less sharply defined, with different strands operating within it, many of which made much of the second set of allegiances, celebrating Spanish roots. The radical nature of early Basque nationalist discourse, with its racist and xenophobic allegiances, together with its political position on the most recalcitrant right, brought about a profound division in the Basque Country. Over and above other fault-lines, such as the social question, the rise of nationalism and the content of its message inflicted serious wounds on the social body and meant that Basque society, which had been drawn together during the nineteenth century by the defence of the *Fuero*, came to appear intensely polarised. With the Second Republic, the nationalist message was moderated ideologically and became more pragmatic, fleeing from the bitter tone which Sabino Arana, the founder and principal ideologue of nationalism, had conferred on it. Even so, it continued to sustain an exclusivist conception that to be Basque was to be nationalist, and sought to reduce the Basque Country to the community of the nationalists, marginalising all who did not accept this system of ideas.[87]

There was a further dimension to this panorama. The 1880s and subsequent years saw the hewing out of other identities on a smaller scale. During this period emerged an abundant literature which, in evoking nostalgically a kind of society which was disappearing before the advance of modernity, gave a more finished form to stereotypes at the level of individual provinces.[88] Portraits of the characteristics of Vizcayans, Guipúzcoans or Alaveses, or on another level Bilbaínos or Donostiarras (people from San Sebastián), were retouched and fixed in these years. These were constructions which met an enthusiastic response, in that provincial attachments had been maintained very much alive throughout the history of the Basque Country, ensuring that these stereotypes gained rapid endorsement. Local and provincial identities were located on a different plane from those of nationalism or of attachment to a Basque identity within the Spanish state. The former did not display the same political dimensions as the latter, operating at a less-articulated level and without carrying the same ideological freight. They could be interleaved with nationalist sentiment, although in a sense they eroded it by implanting loyalties which introduced destabilising cracks into the unified idea of a Basque nation. This was a set of issues which simply was not present in the political discourse of north-west England despite the nostalgia evident in the emerging genres of dialect literature.

Nationalist sentiments grew most obviously between 1880 and 1923, when much of Spain invented itself aesthetically and culturally. The political rise of nationalism was held in suspension during the Primo de Rivera years, although cultural celebrations of Basqueness continued to flourish, and political nationalism surged forth with renewed vigour with the return of democracy. But although it became the leading political force, nationalism did not become hegemonic in the Basque Country during the Second Republic. On the contrary, during this period the tendency to the multiplication of parties, which had been developing as a feature of the region, was accentuated, and alongside nationalism other political options continued to enjoy substantial support. Thus the Left represented by republicans and socialists, the moderate Right which supported the Spanish state, as well as a traditionalist Right which was a more radical legatee of Carlism, continued to be firmly-rooted alternatives whose strengths varied in different areas. During the Second Republic political diversity became consolidated in the Basque Country, with each province responding in its own way to distinctive political tendencies, a pattern of political allegiance which came to coincide with the uneven economic development of the provinces in a manner which was more than coincidental. Specifically, in Vizcaya there was fierce competition between Basque nationalists, the Left and the Madrid-leaning Right. On the other hand in Guipúzcoa the traditionalist Right and the nationalists held the majority, while in Alava the most intransigent sectors of the Right were dominant.[89] The trade union world also reflected these changes and, although socialism continued to have a broad following, it had to confront the strength of the nationalist trade union movement, which made itself into the leading force in Guipúzcoa and obtained widespread support in Vizcaya.[90] None of these complications was observable in north-west England, where a three-party system persisted and communists and splinter groups of the far Right made little headway, while the trade union movement had varying characteristics in different industries but kept its allegiance to the Trades Union Congress despite bitter arguments and accusations of betrayal on particular issues.

Having arrived at this point, we can appreciate the different trajectories which the two areas under comparison followed in their political culture. If it is possible to identify parallels in social and economic aspects, nevertheless, there was one circumstance which differentiated them clearly, and that was the question of regional identity, which was practically non-existent at any conscious level in north-west England but was increasingly intensely felt in various ways in the Basque Country. While in the English region national patriotic ideals prevailed, in the Basque Country feelings of Basque identity became general and political nationalism registered a growing following. The question of the *Fuero* is only part of this story, although it is close to the core of it; and north-west England, on any definition, had nothing remotely parallel to this talismanic (and economically rewarding) legal and administrative peculiarity. Throughout the nineteenth century Spain lacked a strong central state with the capacity to pull together and inculcate national values with which the citizens could identify, given the undemocratic character of the political system. A consequence of this was the feeble development of national identity within Spanish society at large, and this applied especially to the Basques. Moreover, foreign policy and attachment to empire could not arouse patriotic enthusiasm. On the contrary, the loss of the last colonies in 1898 set in train a wave of criticism of the basic conditions under which Spain functioned, while reactions to the military disaster of Annual in 1921 symbolised the failure of north African ventures to revive imperial sentiment.[91] The situation was very different in England, where pride in Empire and in military achievements fostered a powerful and enduring sense of national character and identity which was, perhaps, particularly strong in parts of the north-west, depending as they did on imperial markets and a strong navy. The Irish presence was partly countervailing and partly reinforcing of such attitudes, which not only sustained an unusually strong strand of working-class conservatism but also affected the rhetoric and imagery of other parties, including Labour, and of the trade unions.[92] In this climate there was no room for a political sense of separate regional identity, even though much of the region shared a commitment to an Irish Sea and Atlantic economy which almost made for an integrated economic system, especially as rural areas of the northern part of the region were extensive suppliers of migrants to the industrial towns, a flow off the land which in turn helped to keep rural economies in equilibrium.

There were other obvious distinguishing factors, one of which, and a very important one, was the existence of the distinctive Basque language,[93] which had the capacity to be a much more powerful integrating force than the various dialects of north-west England, celebrated though these were in a proliferating popular literature. Basque society was also held together by the hegemony of Roman Catholicism, expressed in distinctively Basque forms, which contrasted with the plurality of Christian religious adherence in north-west England. At the beginning of the twentieth century, a sense of Basque identity had entered fully into the inhabitants of this territory but (the nationalists excepted) it lay at the margin of their political creed, a feature fully present in society whose basic nature was not a matter for argument. It was a sign of regional identity, a kind of personal and collective definition which was also compatible with feelings of belonging to Spain, and of forming part of the nation in every respect. This sense of Basque identity, which entailed the celebration of ascribed virtues of hard work, honesty, simplicity, courtesy, hospitality and loyalty to family and locality, had no equivalent in north-west England, although literary celebrations of an idealised Cumbrian yeomanry and of a popular culture of unpretentious solidarity and acceptance of hard work and pride in skills in the Lancashire cotton towns went some way towards reinforcing similar territorially-based values.[94]

The rise of political nationalism entailed a breach with this harmonising ideology, introducing a new doctrine based on confrontation between Spain and Euskadi, seen in terms of a dichotomy between 'them' and 'us'.[95] The rapid growth of nationalism had much to do with the sense that an existing culture was menaced by industrial advance, with the destruction of one type of society and a search for new elements which might give a new coherence. The new nationalism, readily employing a variety of channels of sociability, understood how to weave a dense network of social relations, through which it pulled together a culture which issued forth as a kind of secular religion. It created a densely-articulated, backward-looking, conservative cultural system, through which it made firm connections with broad groupings among the population and communicated their problems in its own way in the face of a world which was tending to dissolve cultural differences and to create uniform national states.[96]

Conclusion

The panorama of the Basque Country which we have sketched out should warn us of its extreme complexity and the multiplicity of factors which affected its development. We have shown what, over time, has come to be the great problem of this small territory: its lack of articulation, the absence in certain respects of a basic framework of assumptions held in common by the majority of the population, in spite of the pre-existing and enduring sense of Basqueness which is generally shared and which is capable of transcending the other differences. In the period studied there crystallised contrasting cultures, in some cases ultimately coming into open conflict one with another, creating a situation in which various mutually antagonistic identities might exist within the Basque Country. A special responsibility for this can be imputed to Basque nationalism, which put forward a model for the fatherland in conformity with its party political interests, which carried with it the exclusion and rejection of all those who did not sympathise with its system of ideas.[97] Conflicts have grown from these antecedents with the passage of time, and today the lack of a basic common substratum around which to construct the Basque Country attacks the communal life of the citizenry and impedes the development of a normal civilised society. The development of senses of regional and quasi-national identity can have corrosive and divisive as well as empowering and fulfilling consequences, as is illustrated by events in the Basque Country since the 1930s and especially since the 1970s.[98]

It was, above all, the rise and transformation of these perceptions of regional and national identity, with their connotations of linguistic, cultural and even racial sentiment, which differentiated the Basque experience from that of north-west England in this period. There were significant differences in the economic trajectories of the two regions, especially in the scale and timing of industrialisation and urban growth and the economic experience of the inter-war years; but the outstanding contrasts lie in geographical perceptions of collective identity. Despite the much more complex differentiation between political parties in the rainbow spectrum of Basque politics, as compared with the more monochrome vision of north-west England, the growth of overriding, conscious, articulated senses of Basque identity as political forces has no counterpart in the English case. The working out of Basque nationalism as political ideology created divisions rather than pulling society together, but it did so within a framework of shared values and assumptions without which it could not have developed in the first place. Comparisons with Scotland or Wales might now be fruitful, to see how apparently similar ideologies of nationality below the level of the existing nation-state were articulated in detail and produced differing outcomes. There is already some work on the Basque Country and Ireland and Scotland for later periods; it may be time to extend the agenda further.[99] Meanwhile, this essay in regional comparison between an English experience which can be made to look distinctive but which failed to distil identities or create 'imagined communities' at levels between the local and the national, and a particularly strongly-defined European provincial identity which brought an aspiring but inefficient nation-state into conflict with a nascent nationalism within and beyond its borders, adds additional weight to arguments that might be advanced about English exceptionalism.[100]

It has been interesting and instructive to trace comparisons and contrasts in economic development and social systems between regions with superficial (though never overwhelming) similarities; but the real message to emerge emphasises the vital importance of perceptions of collective identity at levels between the local and the national, and of their political and cultural consequences. Such perceptions do not necessarily flow from common economic experiences, nor are they necessarily impeded by divergent economic trends within a region, as the comparison between north-west England and the Basque Country demonstrates. It is important to be aware of the economic ties that bind areas together, and shared economic activities can provide the basis for economic analyses which may have validity on their own terms; but for regions to be more than shapes on the ground, imposed for the convenience of administrators, planners or historians, they need to have, or to invent, a common and distinctive culture that is capable of forging and sustaining a distinct identity of which the inhabitants are conscious. The case of the Basque Country shows, however, how problematic such a consciousness can be, especially in an environment characterised by rapid and divisive economic change. So this chapter illustrates the working out of a dialogue between the economic and the cultural, and the complexities of the outcomes in areas whose economic trajectory itself might seem superficially similar, and whose internal sub-divisions might seem analogous. The key differences between north-west England and the Basque Country involve the latter's explicit expression (increasingly through a nationalist vocabulary) of regional values and a regional identity; but the contrast cannot be abstracted from the economic and social changes whose effects on the outcomes were fundamental and cannot be ignored. Regional identities are the discursive products of the collective invention and re-creation of traditions, but they are also grounded in the ways in which people made their livings and lived their lives.[101]

Notes

Professor Walton would like to thank the British Council and the University of the Basque Country for his tenure of an Elcano Fellowship at the latter institution between April and June, 1995, when this collaboration was arranged and first discussed. Martin Blinkhorn kindly commented on a draft of the chapter.

1 See especially his *The Tyranny of the Discrete* (Aldershot, 1997), which pulls together the (often heretical) thoughts of a long career.

2 Examples include M. Anderson, *Family Structure in Nineteenth-Century Lancashire* (Cambridge, 1971), and J. Foster, *Class Struggle in the Industrial Revolution* (London, 1974), with its Oldham case study.

3 J. D. Marshall, *Furness and the Industrial Revolution* (Barrow-in-Furness, 1958; reprinted Beckermet [Whitehaven], 1981); *Lancashire* (Newton Abbot, 1974); and (with J. K. Walton), *The Lake Counties: From 1830 to the mid-Twentieth Century* (Manchester, 1981).

4 S. Pollard, *Peaceful Conquest* (Oxford, 1981) and *Marginal Europe: The Contribution of Marginal Lands since the Middle Ages* (Oxford, 1997). See also above, chapter 2.

5 M. García Crespo, R. Velasco Barroetabena and A. Mendizabal Gorostiaga, *La economía vasca durante el franquismo* (Bilbao, 1981).

6 M. González Portilla and J. M. Garmendia, *La posguerra en el País Vasco: política, acumulación, misería* (San Sebastián, 1988).

7 P. Heywood, *The Government and Politics of Spain* (Basingstoke, 1995).

8 B. W. Hogwood and M. Keating (eds), *Regional Government in England* (Oxford, 1982), p. 19.

9 T. C. Barker and J. R. Harris, *A Merseyside Town in the Industrial Revolution* (Liverpool, 1954); S. Marriner, *The Economic and Social Development of Merseyside* (London, 1982).

10 K. Chorley, *Manchester Made Them* (London, 1950); R. Scola, *Feeding the Victorian City* (Manchester, 1992).

11 The official Registrar-General's classification of English regions puts Lancashire and Cheshire together, as does the Longman history of the English regions.

12 *Guardian*, 21 August 1996.

13 But see, for example, D. Elliston Allen, *British Tastes* (London, 1968), pp. 130–1, for sharply-drawn contrasting stereotypes of Lancashire and Yorkshire.

14 The point about openness to external influences applies more to economic relations than to social attitudes, especially in the smaller cotton towns.

15 J. Juaristi, *Memoria(s) del conjunto provincial de Alava, Vizcaya y Guipúzcoa* (Madrid, 1978).

16 J. Arostegui, 'El carlismo y los fueros vasconavarros', in *Historia del Pueblo Vasco* 3 (San Sebastián, 1979); G. Monreal, *Las instituciones públicas del Señorio de Vizcaya* (Bilbao, 1974).

17 A. Tovar, *Mitología e ideología sobre la lengua vasca* (Madrid, 1980); K. Mitxelena, *La lengua vasca* (Durango, 1977).

18 *Euskal urtekari estatistkoa / Anuario estadístico vasco* (Vitoria 1994).

19 J. K. Walton, 'Proto-industrialization and the first Industrial Revolution: the case of Lancashire', in P. Hudson (ed.), *Regions and Industries. A Perspective on the Industrial Revolution* (Cambridge, 1989).

20 See above, note 10; J. Langton, *Geographical Change and Industrial Revolution: Coalmining in South West Lancashire, 1590–1799* (Cambridge, 1979); S. Walker, 'The eighteenth-century landowner as entrepreneur' (unpublished Ph.D. thesis, University of Lancaster, 1988); Marshall, *Furness*.
21 A. Kidd, *Manchester* (Keele, 1993); T. Lane, *Liverpool: Gateway of Empire* (London, 1987); J. Belchem (ed.), *Popular Politics, Riot and Labour* (Liverpool, 1992).
22 Marshall and Walton, *Lake Counties*.
23 J. Langton and M. Freeman, 'The Industrial Revolution and the regional geography of England', *Transactions of the Institute of British Geographers*, new series, 9 (1984), 145–68.
24 J. K. Walton, *Lancashire: A Social History, 1558–1939* (Manchester, 1987), chapters 6, 8–9.
25 See above, notes 10 and 21; Walton, *Lancashire*, chapter 9.
26 Belchem (ed.), *Popular Politics*, provides the best introduction.
27 J. V. Beckett, *Coal and Tobacco* (Cambridge, 1981); C. O'Neill, 'The contest for dominion', *Northern History*, 18 (1982), 133–52.
28 J. D. Marshall, 'Stages of industrialisation in Cumbria', in Hudson (ed.), *Regions and Industries*.
29 J. G. Timmins, *The Last Shift. The Decline of Handloom Weaving in Nineteenth-Century Lancashire* (Manchester, 1993).
30 P. A. Pickering, *Chartism and the Chartists in Manchester and Salford* (London, 1994).
31 N. Kirk, *The Growth of Working-Class Reformism in Mid-Victorian England* (London, 1985), chapter 1.
32 M. E. Rose, '"Rochdale man" and the Stalybridge riot', in A. P. Donajgrodzki (ed.), *Social Control in Nineteenth-Century Britain* (London, 1977); J. King, '"We could eat the police": popular violence in the north Lancashire cotton strike of 1878', *Victorian Studies*, 28 (1985), 439–71.
33 J. C. F. Barnes, 'Popular protest and radical politics: Carlisle 1790–1850' (unpublished Ph.D. thesis, University of Lancaster, 1981).
34 J. K. Walton, 'Co-operation in Lancashire, 1844–1914', *North-West Labour History*, 19 (1994), 115–25.
35 Walton, *Lancashire*, chapter 10. See also below, p. 175.
36 Walton, *Lancashire*, chapter 13; A. Clarke, *The Effects of the Factory System* (reprinted, with an introduction by Paul Salveson, Littleborough, 1985); P. Joyce, *Visions of the People* (Cambridge, 1991).
37 Walton, *Lancashire*, chapter 13; D. Russell, '"Sporadic and curious": the emergence of rugby and soccer zones in Yorkshire and Lancashire, 1860–1914', *International Journal of the History of Sport*, 5 (1988), 185–205.
38 A. T. McCabe, 'The standard of living on Merseyside 1850–74', in S. P. Bell (ed.), *Victorian Lancashire* (Newton Abbot, 1974); J. K. Walton and A. Wilcox (eds), *Low Life and Moral Improvement in mid-Victorian England: Liverpool through the Journalism of Hugh Shimmin* (Leicester, 1991).
39 C. B. Phillips and J. H. Smith, *Lancashire and Cheshire from AD 1540* (Harlow, 1994), p. 136, Table 3.3, and p. 229, Table 4.3.
40 Marshall and Walton, *Lake Counties*.
41 J. Singleton, 'The cotton industry and the British war effort, 1914–18', *EcHR*, 47 (1994), 601–18.
42 M. Dupree, 'Foreign competition and the inter-war period', in M. B. Rose (ed.), *The Lancashire Cotton Industry: A History since 1700* (Preston, 1996), pp. 265–72.
43 J. K. Walton, 'Leisure towns in wartime: the impact of the First World War in Blackpool and San Sebastián', *Journal of Contemporary History*, 31 (1996), 603–18.
44 G. Moorhouse, *Hell's Foundations* (London, 1992).

45 Dupree, 'Foreign competition', in Rose (ed.), *Lancashire Cotton Industry*, pp. 272–95.

46 P. Abercrombie and S. A. Kelly, *Cumberland Regional Planning Scheme* (Liverpool, 1932); G. Orwell, *The Road to Wigan Pier* (London, 1937).

47 A. E. Musson, *Enterprise in Soap and Chemicals* (Manchester, 1965), chapters 18 and 19.

48 D. A. Farnie, *The Manchester Ship Canal and the Rise of the Port of Manchester* (Manchester, 1980); I. Harford, *Manchester and its Ship Canal Movement* (Keele, 1994); Walton, *Lancashire*, chapter 14.

49 R. Pope, 'The unemployment problem in north-east Lancashire, 1920–38' (unpublished M.Litt. thesis, University of Lancaster, 1974).

50 Walton, *Lancashire*, chapter 14.

51 Joyce, *Visions*; Jeffrey Richards, *Stars in their Eyes* (Preston, 1994).

52 G. L. Murfin, *Popular Leisure in the Lake Counties* (Manchester, 1990).

53 Phillips and Smith, *Lancashire and Cheshire*, pp. 304–9.

54 M. Brogden, *On the Mersey Beat: Policing Liverpool between the Wars* (Oxford, 1991); D. Frost, 'West Africans, Black scousers, and the colour problem in inter-war Liverpool', *North-West Labour History*, 20 (1995), 50–7.

55 Dupree, in Rose (ed.), *Lancashire Cotton Industry*, pp. 265–94.

56 D. Martin, 'Women without work: textile weavers in North-East Lancashire 1919–1939', (unpublished M.A. dissertation, University of Lancaster, 1985).

57 Walton, *Lancashire*, chapter 14.

58 M. Savage, *The Dynamics of Working-Class Politics: The Labour Movement in Preston 1890–1940* (Cambridge, 1987).

59 D. McKeown, 'The November confrontation: municipal election campaigns in Whitehaven and Workington' (unpublished M.A. dissertation, University of Lancaster, 1996).

60 Joyce, *Visions*, seems to do this for cotton Lancashire; and see, for example, W. Rollinson, *A History of Man in the Lake District* (London, 1967).

61 G. Tortella, *El desarrollo de la España contemporánea* (Madrid, 1994), provides a good introduction.

62 Useful overviews are M. Montero, *La construcción del País Vasco contemporáneo* (San Sebastián, 1993); M. González Portilla, 'Primera industrialización y desarrollo del capitalismo', in *Gran Atlas Histórico de Euskal Erria* (San Sebastián, 1995).

63 M. Gonzalez Portilla, 'Los origenes de la sociedad capitalista en el País Vasco. Transformaciones económicas y sociales en Vizcaya', *Saioak*, 1.

64 A. Rivera, *La ciudad levitica* (Vitoria, 1992).

65 M. J. Winstanley, 'Industrialisation and the small farm: family and household economy in nineteenth-century Lancashire', *Past and Present*, 152 (August 1996), 157–95.

66 M. Urkijo, *Liberales y carlistas. Revolución y fueros vascos en el preludio de la ultima guerra carlista* (Leoia, 1994); J. Extramiana, *Historia de las guerras carlistas* (San Sebastián, 1980).

67 M. Pérez Ledesma, 'Una lealtad de otros siglos (En torno a las interpretaciones del carlismo)', *Historia Social*, 24 (1996), 113–51.

68 R. Ruzafa, 'Los trabajadores vizcaínos de mediados del XIX' (unpublished doctoral thesis, University of the Basque Country, 1996).

69 Joyce, *Visions*; Kirk, *Working-Class Reformism*; P. F. Clarke, *Lancashire and the New Liberalism* (Cambridge, 1971); Walton, *Lancashire*, chapter 12.

70 N. McCord, *The Anti-Corn Law League* (Cambridge, 1958); V. A. C. Gatrell, 'Incorporation and the pursuit of Liberal hegemony in Manchester', in D. Fraser (ed.), *Municipal Reform and the Industrial City* (Leicester, 1982).

71 Clarke, *Lancashire and the New Liberalism*, pp. 375–6, although he emphasises that there were many cross-currents and alternative issues at work in 1906.

72 M. González Portilla, *La formación de la sociedad capitalista en el País Vasco* (San Sebastián, 1981); L. Castells, *Modernización y dinámica política en la sociedad guipuzcoana de la Restauración, 1876–1915* (Madrid, 1987).
73 M. Montero, *La California del hierro: las minas y la modernización económica y social de Vizcaya* (Bilbao, 1995).
74 M. Arbaiza, 'Estrategias familiares y tension demográfica en Vizcaya (1825–1930)' (unpublished doctoral thesis, University of the Basque Country, 1994); A. García Sanz, 'La evolución demográfica vasca en el siglo XIX (1787–1930). Tendencias familiares y contrastes comarcales de la nupcialidad y la fecundidad', in *II Congreso Mundial Vasco* (Bilbao, 1988).
75 P. Pérez Fuentes, *Vivir y morir en las minas* (Bilbao, 1993).
76 L. V. García Merino, *La formación de una ciudad industrial. El despegue urbano de Bilbao* (Bilbao, 1987).
77 J. P. Fusi, *Política obrera en el País Vasco 1880–1923* (Madrid, 1975); J. M. Eguiguren, *El PSOE en el País Vasco, 1886–1936* (San Sebastián, 1984); L. Castells, *Los trabajadores en el País Vasco, 1876–1923* (Madrid, 1993).
78 L. Castells, 'Una aproximación al conflicto social en Guipúzcoa 1890–1923', *Estudios de Historia Social,* 32–33 (1985); F. Luengo Teixidor, *Crecimiento económico y cambio social, Guipúzcoa 1917–1923* (Leoia, 1990); J. K. Walton and J. Smith, 'The rhetoric of community and the business of pleasure: the San Sebastián waiters' strike of 1920', *International Review of Social History*, 39 (1994), 1–31.
79 González Portilla, *Sociedad capitalista*.
80 J. Diaz Freire, *La república y el porvenir. Culturas políticas en Vizcaya durante la Segunda República* (San Sebastián, 1993); E. Legorburu, 'La sociedad guipuzcoana durante la II República. Los pilares de un conservadurismo' (unpublished doctoral thesis. University of the Basque Country, 1994); Walton, *Lancashire*, chapter 14.
81 L. Castells and A. Rivera, 'Vida cotidiana y nuevos comportamientos sociales (El País Vasco, 1876–1923)', *Ayer*, 19 (1995), 135–65; S. de Pablo, *Trabajo, diversion y vida cotidiana: el País Vasco en los años treinta* (Bilbao, 1995).
82 For these issues with special reference to Liverpool and Manchester, see S. Fielding, *Class and Ethnicity: Irish Catholics in England 1880–1939* (Milton Keynes, 1993).
83 For the exceptional case of Liverpool, see F. Neal, *Sectarian Violence* (Manchester, 1988); P. J. Waller, *Democracy and Sectarianism* (Liverpool, 1981).
84 M. Heiberg, *The Making of the Basque Nation* (Cambridge, 1989).
85 C. Rubio, *Revolución y tradición. El País Vasco ante la revolución liberal y la construcción del Estado espanol, 1808–1868* (Madrid, 1996); J. Aranzadi, *El milenarismo vasco* (Madrid, 1981).
86 J. Juaristi, *El linaje de Aitor. La invención de la tradición vasca* (Madrid, 1987); J. M. Portillo and J. Viejo (eds), *Francisco de Aranguren y Sobrado* (Bilbao, 1994).
87 J. P. Fusi, *El País Vasco: pluralismo y nacionalidad* (Madrid, 1984).
88 J. Juaristi, *El Chimbo expiatorio* (Bilbao, 1994).
89 J. Real, *Partidos, elecciones y bloques de poder en el País Vasco 1876–1923* (Bilbao, 1991).
90 Fusi, *Pluralismo y nacionalidad*.
91 S. Balfour, 'Riot, regeneration and reaction: Spain in the aftermath of the 1898 disaster', *Historical Journal*, 38 (1995), 405–23, is the most recent consideration of the complexities of 1898; S. E. and A. K. Fleming, 'Primo de Rivera and Spain's Moroccan problem', *Journal of Contemporary History*, 12 (1977), 85–99.
92 Clarke, *Lancashire and the New Liberalism*, pp. 344, 367 and *passim*. More work might be done on this.
93 See above, note 17.
94 Heiberg, *Basque Nation*; J. K. Walton, *Doing Comparative Social History: North-West England and the Basque Country from the 1830s to the 1930s*, inaugural lecture, Lancaster University (Lancaster, 1996), pp. 1–10.

95 A. Elorza, *Ideologías del nacionalismo vasco* (San Sebastián, 1987).

96 J. Corcuera Atienza, *Orígenes, ideología y organización del nacionalismo vasco (1876–1904)* (Madrid, 1979); Heiberg, *Basque nation*; Fusi, *Pluralismo y nacionalidad*; and see L. Mees, *Nacionalismo vasco, movimiento obrero y cuestión social, 1903–1923* (Bilbao, 1992) for relations between Basque nationalism, trade unions and socialism.

97 A. Gurrutxaga, *Transformación del nacionalismo vasco. Del PNV a ETA* (San Sebastián, 1996); G. Jauregui, *Entre la tragedia y la esperanza. Vasconia ante el nuevo milenio* (Barcelona, 1996).

98 There is an extensive literature on this. See, for example, in English, J. Sullivan, *ETA and Basque Nationalism: The Fight for Euskadi, 1890–1986* (London, 1988), and C. E. Zirakzadeh, *A Rebellious People: Basque Protest and Politics* (Reno, Nevada, 1991).

99 For example, C. E. Zirakzadeh, 'Economic changes and surges in micro-nationalist voting in Scotland and the Basque region of Spain', *Comparative Studies in Society and History*, 31 (1989), 318–39.

100 B. Anderson, *Imagined Communities: Reflections on the Origin and Spread of Nationalism* (London, 1991).

101 E. J. Hobsbawm and T. Ranger (eds), *The Invention of Tradition* (Cambridge, 1983); N. Kirk, 'History, language, ideas and post-modernism: a materialist view', *Social History*, 19 (1994), 221–40.

5 *John Langton*

The continuity of regional culture: Lancashire Catholicism from the late sixteenth to the early nineteenth century

Introduction

The main purpose of this chapter is to present some maps of the distribution of Catholics in Lancashire between the late sixteenth and early nineteenth centuries.[1] Fernand Braudel has argued with reference to regional identities in France that

> Such particularities go deep into the mass of the . . . population . . . . The vital thing for every community is to avoid being confused with the next tiny *patrie*, to remain *other* . . . . for progress, marching with giant strides through the land, turns out to have changed one *pays* more than its neighbour, or perhaps to have changed it in a particular way, creating a new difference, which becomes a new cleavage. The basic fragmentation has thus been maintained in recognizable form (or very nearly so) since earliest times'.[2]

Have regional cultures been as persistent in England, notwithstanding their neglect in an English historiography[3] which seems more concerned with defining a hegemonic metropolitan stereotype than with any deeply-rooted particularities of the regions?[4] The narrow focus and brevity of this chapter mean that any generalisations and inferences will inevitably be abbreviated, tentative and open to question. However, the maps themselves, unadorned by speculation, do show how much geographical continuity there was in Lancashire Catholicism through times of persecution, missionary effort, civil war, political turmoil, two Jacobite rebellions, and wholesale economic change.

'Dark continent'

Whether or not 'Lancashire [is] alone among our counties to be charged with giving itself the airs of a continent',[5] it was certainly isolated behind the treacherous Irish Sea coast, the Mersey marshes, the Pennines and the Lake District, with a very varied topography. At first these were variations around a very lowly theme. Figure 5.1a[6] shows that at the start of our period much of the county's land surface was marshland ('moss'), sand dunes, moorland, or deeply dissected coalmeasures.[7] The sparse roads of this dark corner of the land were 'gulphes of duste and mire',[8] and a few small and barely accessible harbours linked it only with Ireland; the great arteries of north–south movement and seaward contact with London and Europe lay, like broad rich farmlands, east of the Pennines.[9] For its area, Lancashire had few boroughs[10] or resident aristocrats.[11] In 1515 it was less than half as wealthy as the second poorest county and under one-sixth as wealthy as the richest, with one of the slowest growth rates.[12]

Most of Lancashire was forests, chases and their purlieus in medieval times.[13] As part of the Duchy of Lancaster and a County Palatine, its courts were different from elsewhere. Outside the four town corporations, it was under the specific charge of the Chancellor of the Duchy of Lancaster, a crown appointee.[14] The earls of Derby were almost hereditary Lords

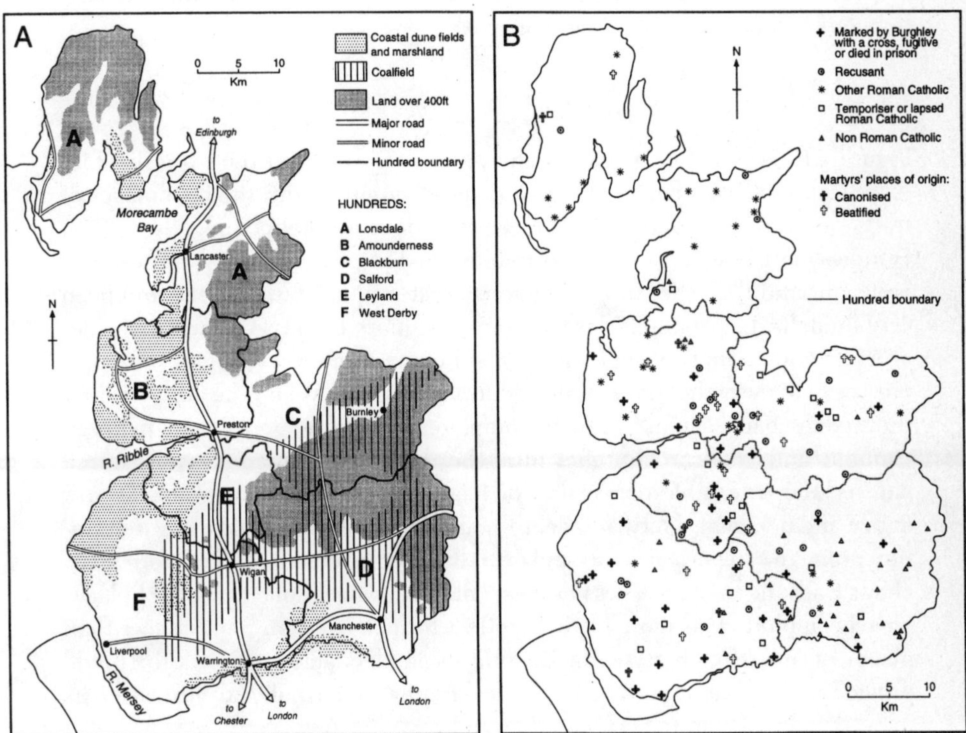

Figure 5.1 **(a) Topography, Hundreds, main towns and roads of early-modern Lancashire (b) Lancashire Catholicism in the late sixteenth and early seventeenth centuries**

Lieutenant: 'all the keys of Lancashire do hang at the Earl of Derby's old girdle'.[15] Ecclesiastically, it was split along the Ribble, literally in corners of the dioceses of Lichfield and York, until the creation of the diocese of Chester in 1541.[16]

Although its economy and population undoubtedly then grew faster,[17] much remained uncultivated in the mid-seventeenth century,[18] when its largest town was only the eighty-second biggest in Britain.[19] Lancashire was still in the 1690s one of the very poorest of English counties.[20] There were in 1701 fewer people in Lancashire than in Norfolk and barely more in than Somerset, counties roughly comparable in area.[21]

A century later land reclamation was well advanced.[22] Lancashire was the third wealthiest county in England and one of the most densely populated.[23] It contained some of England's largest and fastest-growing towns,[24] the major staple industry,[25] one of the most productive coalfields,[26] one of the densest and busiest inland navigation networks,[27] and some of the largest industrial plant[28] and wealthiest people.[29] Most of this efflorescence was on and near the coalfield, between the Mersey and the Ribble. How was the Catholic population distributed across this matrix?

'*Cock-pit* of *Conscience*'[30]

Figure 5.1b is based on Lord Burghley's map of 1590 and the extensive biographical notes which accompanied its publication,[31] with the birthplaces of thirty-one Catholic martyrs.[32] The classifications are not completely certain. Families marked with a cross by Burghley needed 'extra coercion', but were all recusant, and the other map categories must also have overlapped and been very fluid: 'In Lancashire, I have seen myself more than two hundred present at Mass and sermon. People of this kind come to church without difficulty, but they fall away the moment persecution blows up. When the alarm is over, they come back again.'[33] The incompleteness of the separation between Catholic and Anglican churches until the 1580s, the commonness of church papists, the ostensible conversion of heads of household for financial prudence and personal safety, and death-bed reconversions all make any itemisation prone to categorical errors and overall understatement.[34] The information about Catholic martyrs is less evanescent, but spans a long time; birthplaces have been plotted, as more likely to reflect formative cultural influences than places of arrest or martyrdom. Despite its inadequacies, figure 5.1b should provide a reasonable picture of the geography of Catholicism just after its definition as a separate persecuted church.

The sheer density of symbols on the map squares with the county's reputation as 'the very sink of Popery',[35] produced by decades of confused administration and preoccupation with financial matters in the bishopric of

Chester,[36] Catholic missions,[37] and the influence of the earls of Derby and their Justices of the Peace,[38] who kept the Lancashire gentry out of the Northern Rising and other Catholic plots by being 'far too lenient' in their prosecution of the penal statutes.[39] Burghley did not produce a similar map of any other county. It was drawn as alarmist reports reached London that 'The people in moost partes of the countie ... doe slide back from all duetyfull obedyence', as 'The Papists every where are growen so confident that they contempne Magistrats and their authorytie', so that 'the nomber of the recusants is great, and dothe dailie increase' to double that at the start of Elizabeth's reign.[40] Demographically negligible Lancashire sired a disproportionate number of Catholic martyrs,[41] as well as William Allen who 'made a greater contribution to preserving Roman Catholicism in England than any other individual',[42] as its organiser and founder of the seminaries for English missionary priests at Douai and Rome.[43] Sixty Lancastrians – most, doubtless, from its thirty-two Catholic schools – soon went abroad to train as missionaries.[44] Between 1579 and 1673, 200 of them (compared with 130 from much bigger Yorkshire) attended the English College in Rome.[45] Many of its young women took the veil at English convents, such as Gravellines and Rouen. This 'last English outpost of the great Roman Catholic Church' was rather more than the 'pathetic remnant' recognised by its most recent historian.[46]

Taken together, figures 5.1a and 5.1b show that however significant backwardness and remoteness within England were for the survival of Catholicism in Lancashire, this relationship was not duplicated inside the county. It is true that concentrations of ultra-recusants and martyrs' birthplaces existed in the far west and in the north-east of Blackburn Hundred, and there were few Catholics in the Manchester embayment and its flanking hills where, from the mid-sixteenth century, pastoral colonisation and an emergent textiles industry brought rapid economic, demographic and social changes, and much greater business, legal and intellectual contacts with London and the universities.[47] This part of the county was least under the sway of the earls of Derby, and most under that of Puritan ministration from Manchester Collegiate Church and Bolton, 'home of the strongest of the Edwardian Protestant circles'.[48] As Christopher Haigh has observed, 'known Lancashire Protestants were drawn entirely from the south-east of the county',[49] and its three Marian martyrs were born in Salford Hundred.[50]

Even so, only an anachronistic textiles-obsessed Mancuno-centrism can interpret this as a simple equation between remote backwardness and Catholic survival. Catholics were not concentrated in upland areas.[51] Vast majorities of Burghley's crosses, recusants, and martyrs' birthplaces lay within a few miles of the main arterial road from Warrington to Lancaster. They were densest of all at the heart of the county, in its most agriculturally developed parts,[52] around and between the boroughs of Wigan and Preston, its two biggest towns at the time. Parishes there were no larger than in the rest of the county, although neither were they any smaller, and they must have been amongst the choicest of its nationally-celebrated crop of plump livings.[53] Where 'Churches farre do stand / In lay mens hands, and chappels have no land / To cherish learned curates', people 'scarce see priest to give / Them ghostlye counsell';[54] but this made them no more prone to Catholicism than to Puritanism, irreligion or witchcraft.[55]

Neither did Catholicism survive only among and under the protection of 'feudal' magnates with hearts in Counter-Reformation Europe.[56] The role of 'great men' among the gentry in Catholicising and protecting followers[57] is easy to exaggerate: apostates were as dilatory in prosecuting Catholics as most long-term Protestants,[58] perhaps because kinship links criss-crossed religious boundaries, and the Catholic gentry owned so much land in the west that it was impossible to live far from one of their mansions. Many martyrs were from yeoman and lesser stock, and a larger proportion of Lancashire Catholics were plebeian than elsewhere in England.[59] In fact, 'Lancashire . . . had few Catholics of any wealth and none of national standing. Its strong Catholicism was a very localized matter'.[60] Here, perhaps, was the key to its persistence: these people did not strut a national stage, but lived their lives in dense meshes of local relationships where extremes of belief were the norm. Catholic, Puritan or blackly-artful neighbours, who were seen daily, known since childhood, and often kinsfolk, were usually left to their own devices. Mutual acceptance was the only viable quotidian attitude, even if it fell short of amity, and outbursts of sectarian persecution were mostly prompted by the incursion of outsiders, such as soldiers, sailors or excisemen.[61]

Because they were so large, varied greatly in size, and many had non-contiguous parts, Lancashire's parishes are a poor grid of mapping units. Where the sources allow it, figures 5.2–5.3 represent detached or remote parts of parishes separately, so that 65 parishes[62] became 205 areas, common to each map. The data are far from ideal. The total numbers of Catholics represented vary from 310 to 73,500; but assuming that the distributions of recusants shown on figures 5.2a and 5.2b corresponded with those of all Catholics, their conversion to percentages makes them comparable with the data plotted on figures 5.3a and 5.3b. Nonetheless, it should be borne in mind that some variations in the sizes of symbols, and some aspects of their distribution, are due to differences in the areas of the parishes and part-parishes on which the data are plotted.

Despite the fewness of the people mapped on figure 5.2a,[63] they had the same pattern as the Catholics of a generation earlier, strung along the north-south spine of the county, with salients westwards to the north of the Mersey and Ribble and eastwards into the corner of Blackburn Hundred. The forty-one per cent living in parishes containing a town seem to confute the 'remote

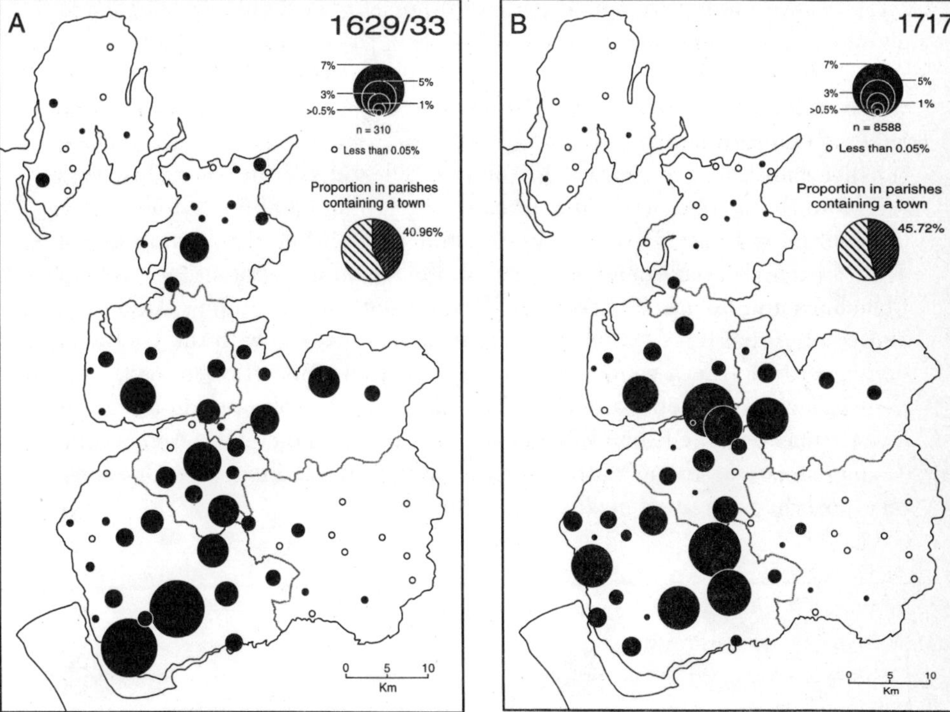

Figure 5.2 **(a) Lancashire Recusants, 1629/33 (b) Lancashire Catholic non-jurors in 1717**

highland' explanation of survival, although many of those parishes were very large and mainly rural, and urban Catholicism is better dealt with at the township level (as on figures 5.4–5.5a). The extremity and nature of their punishment must have made this a tiny sample of Lancashire's Catholics: it is not reasonable to infer little Catholicism from their small proportion of a total population in which a majority had no land to confiscate.[64] The number who chose to suffer these punishments reveals an implacably recalcitrant community, as does much other contemporary evidence. The first English Catholic printing press since the Reformation was set up at Birchley, south of Wigan, by 1620.[65] In 1629 a spy was outraged by Lancashire gentlemen and their priests flaunting themselves at St Winifride's Well in Flintshire,[66] and local shrines and martyrs' relics were increasingly venerated.[67] In 1639 there were 67 secular priests and their dependent laymen in the county, plus 41 Benedictine and 50 Jesuit religious clergy and dependent laymen.[68] Most were of local birth, though trained abroad; three of the Lancashire-born were martyred at Lancaster in the 1640s.[69] Consistent with figure 5.2a, in 1639 there were 'no Catholics, or exceeding few and poor to be found' in dune-strewn North Meols parish along the southern shore of the Ribble estuary. In Salford Hundred 'there are but few Catholics,'[70] whereas Bolton was 'the Geneva of the North'.[71] Two-thirds of the Catholic clergy were in West Derby and Leyland Hundreds.[72]

The battle line of the Civil War was old and sharply drawn. In 1642 'Catholic gentry were most numerous in the lowland and more arable hundreds of West Derby, Leyland and Amounderness, while the Puritan gentry were strongest in the highland and more pastoral hundreds of Salford, Blackburn and Lonsdale'.[73] Military defeat, estate sequestrations, land sales and composition fines,[74] then political turmoil to 1688,[75] with the Catholics under Lord Molyneux gaining control of county administration in 1687,[76] did more to fan than to douse ardour. As Thomas Fuller had observed in 1662, 'this *County* may be called the *Cock-pit* of *Conscience*, wherein . . . *Antient* and *Modern Fanaticks*, though differing much in their wild Fancies and Opinions, meet together in mutual *madness* and *distraction*'.[77]

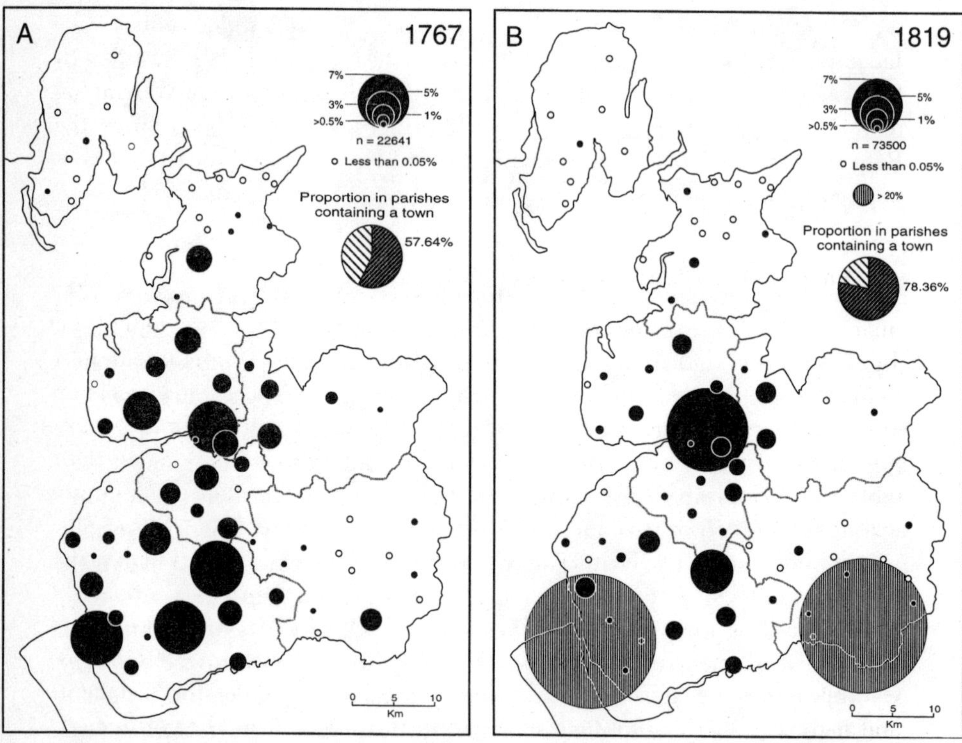

Figure 5.3 **(a) Lancashire Catholics in 1767 (b) Lancashire Catholic chapel congregations in 1819**

The geography of Catholic adherence hardly changed through these desperately fractious upheavals. Jacobitism and anti-Catholicism had just as little effect in the early eighteenth century. These were particularly sharp in Lancashire because of the strong support given by its Catholics to the Jacobite invasion, defeated at Preston in 1715,[78] and the mob violence associated with it.[79] Further persecution, financial penalisation and demographic failure wiped out Catholic gentry families throughout the county. Figure 5.2b[80] shows that by 1717 the northern, south-western and north-eastern extremities of the distribution had been trimmed and thinned, but that these were small modifications to what was basically the same pattern as earlier. By 1767,[81] after resumed Jacobite rebellion in 1745[82] followed by more estate sequestrations, the marginal limbs had withered further, and by 1819[83] they had dropped off altogether (see figures 5.3a and 5:3b).

The main eighteenth-century distributional changes were associated with a rapidly shifting economic geography, including a large increase in urban Catholicism. The predominance of Liverpool and Manchester in 1819, when they contained over 40 per cent of the county's Catholics, came long before massive Irish migration to the county. It was already clearly heralded in 1767, when there were 287 Catholics in Manchester, where Lancashire's only Jacobite regiment had been raised in 1745.[84] Overshadowed though it was by Liverpool and Manchester in 1767 and 1819, the axis from north of Warrington to north of Preston was still as clearly evident as it had been since the Reformation: industrialising as fast as Salford Hundred to the east,[85] it contained four urban townships with more than 1,000 Catholics in 1767.[86]

'Sacred Heart-land' of 'the Pope's Creatures'[87]

Adjacent parts of Amounderness and Blackburn were at least as staunch, but Table 1 shows that West Derby and Leyland Hundreds contained most Lancashire Catholics from the 1590s to 1819.[88] They covered a wide spectrum of topography (see figure 5.1a), contained old towns as well as remote unimproved countryside, and saw the growth of the textiles industry along their eastern margin, as well as coalmining, iron, non-ferrous metals, glass, chemicals and pottery industries on the coalfield between Wigan and Liverpool.

Figures 5.4a–5.4d and 5.5a show the distribution of Catholics across the townships of West Derby and Leyland Hundreds between the 1590s and 1819.[89] Much smaller mapping units cause patterns to differ slightly from those across the equivalent areas of figures 5.2a–5.3b. However, the same absence of Catholics from the coastal strip between Formby Point and Preston is evident, and also the withering away in the extreme south-west. So are the north-south axis along the arterial road, with strong westward salients which appear, at this scale, to be separated by townships containing the principal estates of the earls

Table 5.1 **The proportions of Lancashire Catholics in each Hundred, 1629/33–1819**

Hundred	1629/33	1717	1767	1819
Lonsdale	7.4	1.2	0.9	2.2
Amounderness	23.6	22.7	28.6	17.2
Blackburn	11.9	17.5	11.0	6.1
Salford	2.9	1.8	3.9	21.4
Leyland	17.1	12.0	12.2	8.5
West Derby	37.1	44.7	44.9	45.5
Total numbers	310	8,588	22,641	73,500

Sources: see text.

of Derby. Smaller mapping units are responsible for the much smaller urban share of seventeenth-century Catholicism, too, but they also show it increasing by 1767, then nearly doubling by 1819. The greater volatility of distributions from map to map is at least partly for the same reason, but there does appear to be a consistent tendency to the main changes: the two dense south-west to north-east bands seem to have switched in relative importance, before evening-up in 1715. This might be due to inconsistent imperfections in the sources, but it could equally-well reflect the growth of Catholicism in line with that of total population on the coalfield by 1715 (see figures 5.5b–5.5d).[90]

Parts of the detailed maps can be used to corroborate every customary notion about the reasons for Catholic persistence. Until 1767 it was overwhelmingly rural. The northern transverse strip was in the emptiest part of the area, apart from the near-deserted dune coast (see figure 5.5b). Its parishes were very large, and so were some of its Catholic estates. The north-east end was in uplands. The south-west end was dominated by the famously Catholic Blundells and Molyneuxs, and the latter were grandly aristocratic Europhiles.[91] Large Catholic estates stretched north-east along the salient, across more mossland where flood-prone quagmires gave an excuse not to attend church,[92] and refuge to rioters who stopped the collection of penal taxes.[93] The extreme western end of the southern salient disappeared when Catholic gentry families died out or apostatised. For half the period, Liverpool was an isolated burghal beacon of Puritanism in a markedly Catholic hinterland.[94]

Other parts of the maps confute all customary explanations. Across the whole region, Catholic landowners were among the most avid improvers, spurred to develop their estates by exclusion from civil life, penal fines and taxes, and frequent trusteeships. A strongly Catholic town sat in the centre of the mosslands at Ormskirk (see note 86). Liverpool's meteoric growth offered opportunities to the younger sons and cousinage of local Catholic gentry: the first post-Reformation mass was said there in 1701 and there was a Catholic chapel by 1728, rebuilt by the Blundells in 1746.[95] Given the short distances traversed by most migrants in the region,[96] Liverpool must have sucked in plebeian Catholics displaced from extensive mossland commons by agricultural improvement. They were not a docile flock: by 1788 there were three competing Catholic chapels and doctrinal disputes were as intense as those of Protestants are supposed to be.[97] As it shot into growth, Liverpool switched from an isolated Puritan beacon to an overweening Catholic bastion: Catholicism and capitalist economic development were not antipathetic.

At its other end, the northern salient intersected with the Preston–Warrington axis at Chorley to produce a Catholic epicentre in the triangle between Mawdesley, Brindle and Wigan. This area had everything that is supposed to have been inimical to Catholic survival. There were no grandees: most townships contained two or three manors in different hands. In Leyland Hundred two-thirds of the recusants were tradesmen, craftsmen, yeomen and husbandmen in 1641, nearly twice as many as in West Derby.[98] The hilly coalmeasures and millstone grit, rising to over 500 feet and deeply dissected by the Douglas and Yarrow rivers, industrialised early. Brindle, in the north-east corner, was one of the region's few small parishes; a quintessential upland handloom weaving settlement,[99] it had 170 Catholics in 1715 and 364 in 1767, and only four of its fourteen recusants owned land in 1717, none more than £20's-worth. Nearby Chorley, always a centre of urban Catholicism,[100] had the earliest cotton-spinning mills in Lancashire.[101]

Coalmining developed early and quickly on Catholic estates, notwithstanding – indeed, perhaps because of – the financially straitened circumstances of most recusant gentry.[102] Perhaps in consequence of the strong proclivity of the Catholic gentry to exploit their coal reserves, Catholic recusants were amongst the most important colliery surveyors and undertakers during the explosive growth of mining in the eighteenth century.[103] The iron industry, too, was begun by the then-Catholic Bradshaighs just north of Wigan in the early seventeenth century.[104] Its eighteenth-century expansion was completely in the hands of Catholic recusants. Like Quakers elsewhere, they had geographically extensive ore mining and smelting interests, stretching from their south Lancashire forges and slitting mills, through Cheshire and Liverpool into north Wales, and through Furness into Scotland. One of the most important ironmasters was a lieutenant in the Jacobite rising of 1745 and brother of the Lancashire vicar-general.[105]

At the hub of all this, the ancient borough of Wigan had the usual ornaments of a spa, opulent new houses and wealthy pseudo-gentry (many of them sons of local Catholic landed gentry) by the early eighteenth century. Home of the 'most obstinate and contemptuous Papists' of the sixteenth century,[106] it had by far the biggest urban concentration of Catholics in the seventeenth

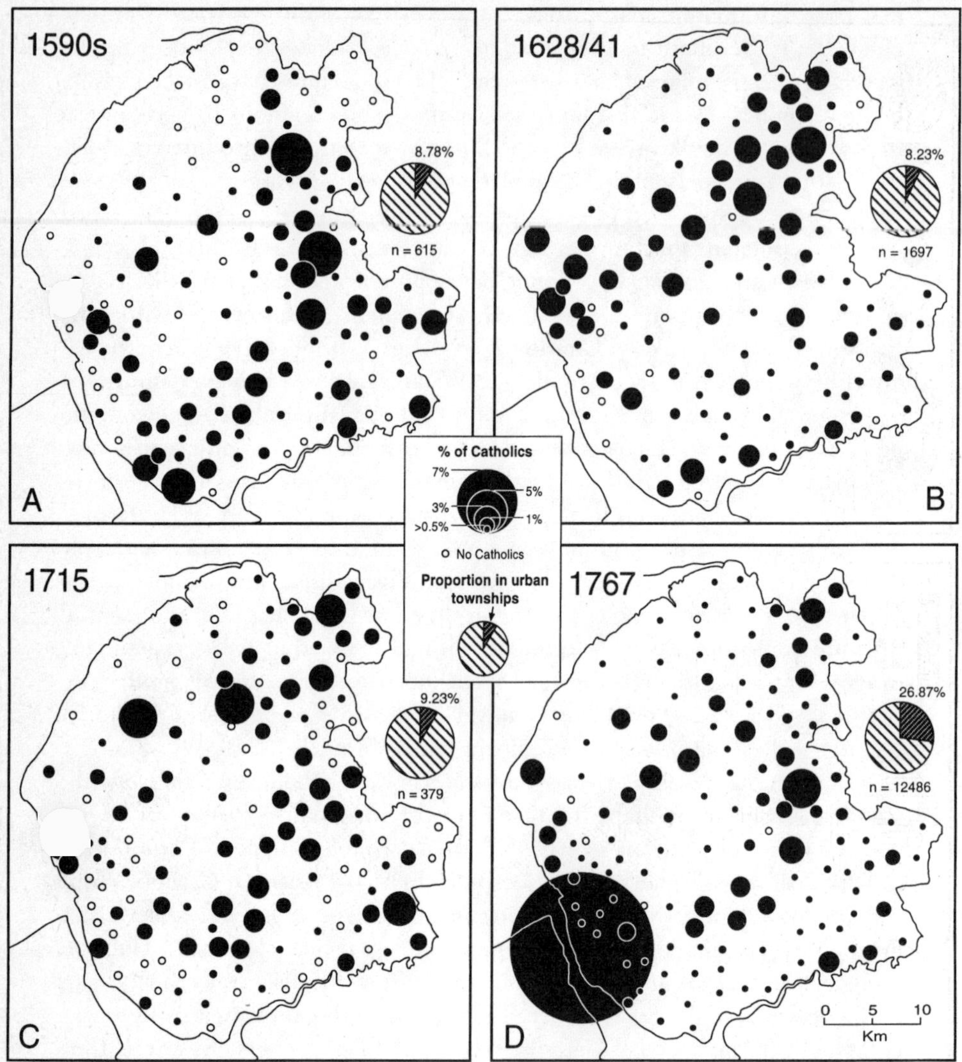

Figure 5.4 **West Derby and Leyland Hundreds (a) Catholic recusants in the 1590s (b) Catholic recusants, 1628/41 (c) Catholic recusants in 1715 (d) Catholics in 1767**

century.[107] They were just as riotous against the collection of penal taxes as those in the mosslands.[108] As a Royalist garrison, Wigan suffered severely from continual sackings in the Civil War, but its non-ferrous metals crafts surged to national prominence soon afterwards, and their guilds dominated the corporation.[109] Meanwhile, the school of its large Jesuit mission had over 100

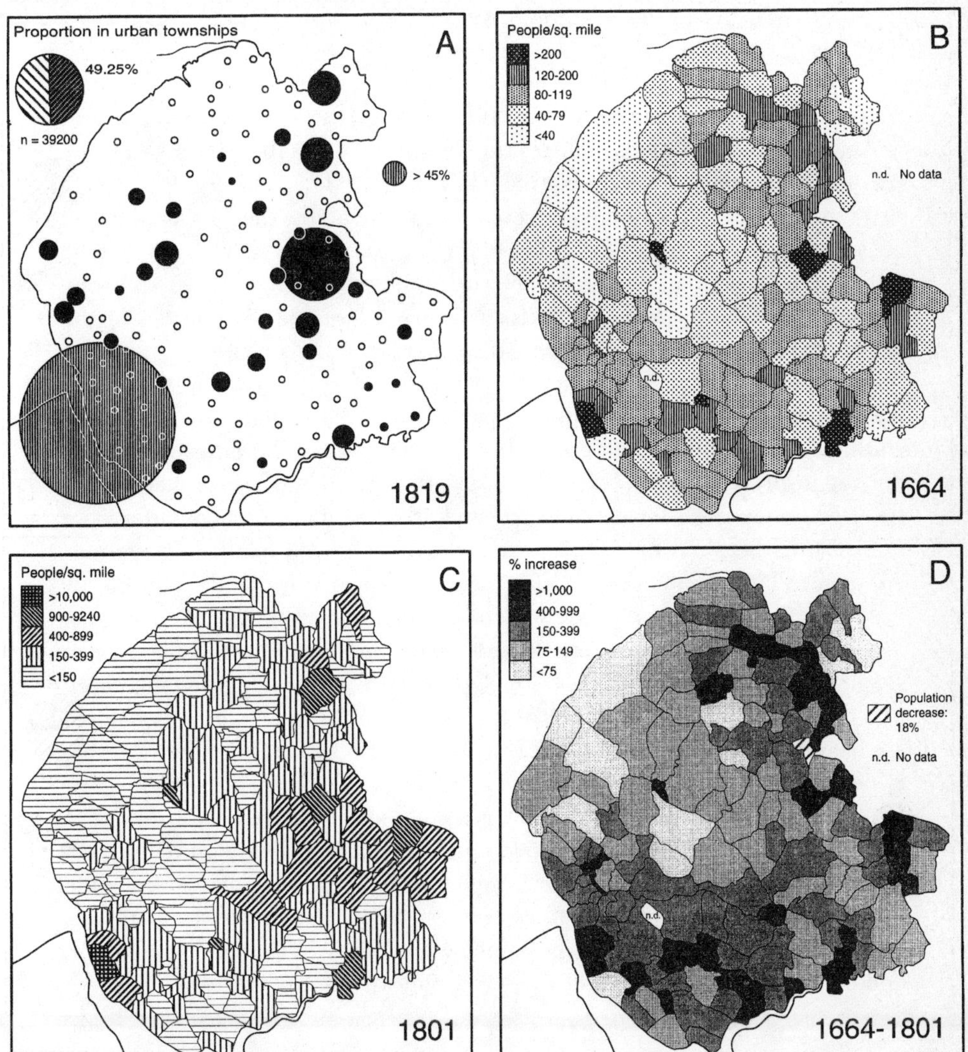

Figure 5.5 **West Derby and Leyland Hundreds (a) Catholic chapel congregations in 1819 (b) Estimated population in 1664 (c) Population in 1801 (d) Estimated population growth, 1664–1801**

scholars and (whatever the law said) 'the mayor or chief magistrate of the town and his suite were accustomed to attend' their chapel, which was 'much better attended than the neighbouring Protestant churches'.[110] Catholics coped with the destruction of their early chapels by mobs; services were held continuously by stipendiary Jesuit priests from the early eighteenth century and, like

Liverpool, Wigan had rival Catholic chapels by the 1780s. Here was something which is supposed not to have existed: a vibrantly old-Catholic borough with a thriving economy. In 1767 Wigan's Catholic population was the biggest outside London and Liverpool (see note 86) and, as it transmogrified into Coketown during the next half-century, more Catholics flocked in from the surrounding farmland and industrial villages.

Because of the phenomenal growth of Liverpool, the percentages plotted on figures 5.4d and 5.5a give a misleading impression of declining Catholic strength in other areas where, in fact, the numbers of Catholics were increasing strongly. Chorley and Wigan, for example, increased their shares of the Catholic population by more than they increased their shares of the total population as they industrialised.[111] Figures 5.6a–5.6d show the townships where higher than average estimated proportions of the total population were Catholic. The mapped data are highly speculative. Population estimates are derived from the Hearth Tax returns and Catholic numbers are estimated from the Recusancy Rolls for the mid-seventeenth century; 1767 populations are interpolated between the 1664 and 1801 figures, and Catholic congregations are divided by the populations only of the townships in which the chapels lay in 1819.[112] The resulting data are so deficient that they would be utterly worthless if they did not show patterns which we would by now expect. Figure 5.6a suggests that the proportions of both Catholics and total population increased in the handloom weaving uplands of the extreme north-east, and in a coalfield arc from Leigh through Wigan to Prescot, as well as in Liverpool, before 1767. Especially if the very high figures for townships with chapels in 1819 are envisaged spread across the adjacent townships which must have contributed to their congregations, figures 5.6b–5.6d suggest what is, given their provenance, a remarkably stable heartland where, notwithstanding the wholesale economic transformation of some, but not other, parts of the two hundreds, Catholics consistently accounted for a very significant minority of the total population, and perhaps a majority of practising Christians in a few of the townships.

Conclusion

Even though the accuracy of these data is as oft-lamented as they are much-used, their map patterns are very robust. All environmental, economic and social-functional explanations of this resilience fail utterly in one part of the region or another: Catholicism continued not because of what else Catholics were, but simply because of where they were. Neither the giant boots of progress nor the jack boots of persecution shifted their geography by much. Liverpool and Manchester became massively predominant through the short-distance migration of displaced and aspirant Lancashire Catholics, long before Irish immigration can have had much effect. Where Catholicism had

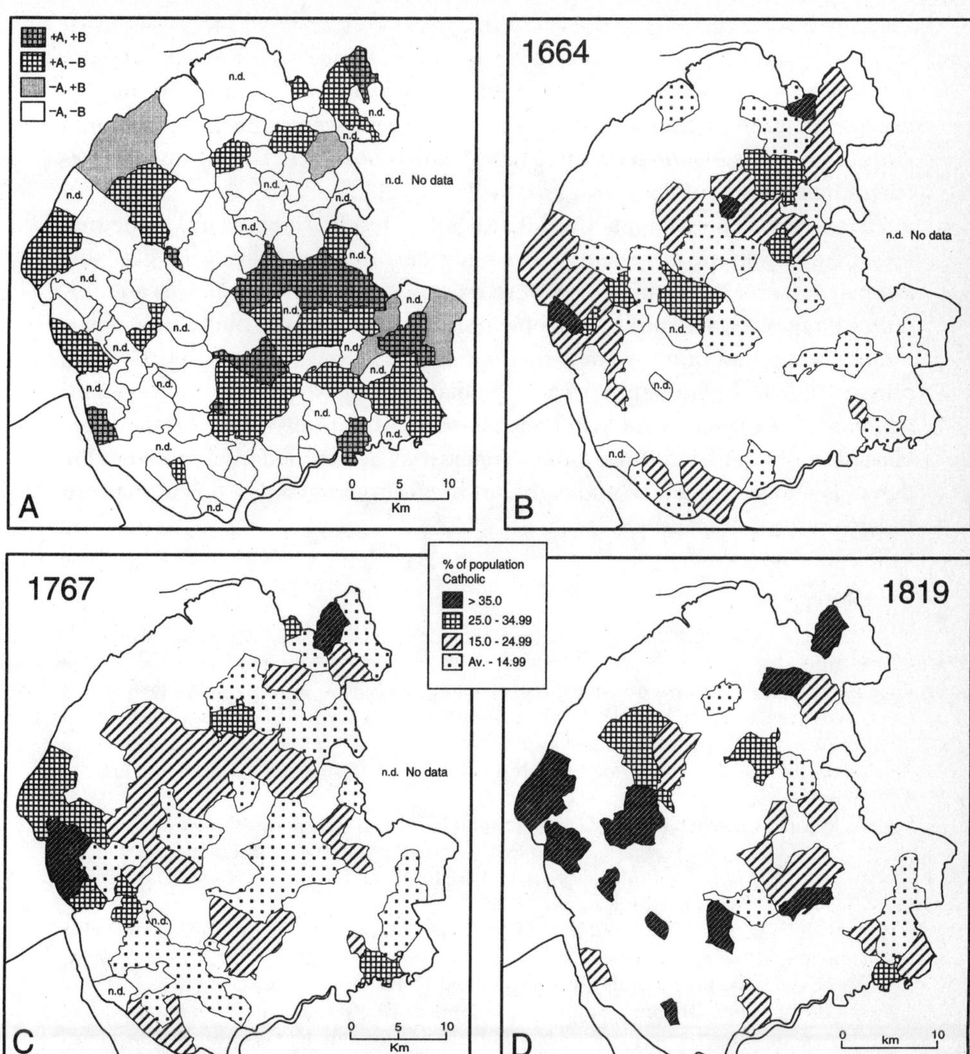

Figure 5.6 **West Derby and Leyland Hundreds (a) Townships where the percentage share of Catholics grew (+a) and declined (−a) and the percentage share of estimated total population grew (+b) and declined (−b), 1664–1767 (b) Estimated proportions of the population who were Catholic in 1664 (c) Estimated proportions of the population who were Catholic in 1767 (d) Estimated proportions of the population who were Catholic in 1819**

been strong at the end of the sixteenth century, it remained so in 1819. As it still does: the hand of St. Edmund Arrowsmith continues to work miracles in the urban sprawl which now covers what was heath and moss when he was born there more than four centuries ago.[113] The answer to the question posed at the start is yes, regional cultures have been as persistent in England as elsewhere in Europe.

However, this was not a 'Catholic region'. Despite their woeful inadequacies, figures 5.6b–5.6d are valuable as reminders that Catholics were probably not in a majority even where they were most numerous. Rather, it was a multicultural region, where other religious minorities were just as obdurately maintaining what they most valued in their non-material lives, excluded from, scorned by, and contemptuous of the bland, supposedly national, cultural hegemony which was notable in Lancashire only for its absence.[114] Implacable obsession with alien cultural values was just as accommodating to economic dynamism in seventeenth- and eighteenth-century England as it is in many of today's multi-cultural societies.

Notes

1 Drawn by Peter Hayward at the School of Geography Cartography Unit, University of Oxford.

2 F. Braudel, *The Identity of France*, vol. 1, *History and Environment* (London, 1988), p. 41.

3 A neglect castigated by D H. Fischer, *Albion's Seed: Four British Folkways in America* (Oxford, 1989), pp. 788–805. See also, M. A. Kishlanski, 'Community and continuity: a review of selected works on English local history', *William and Mary Quarterly*, 37 (1980), 139–46.

4 As in J. G. A. Pocock, *Virtue, Commerce and History* (Cambridge, 1985); J. C. D. Clark, *English Society, 1688–1832. Ideology, Social Structure and Political Practice during the Ancien Régime* (Cambridge, 1985); P. Langford, *A Polite and Commercial People: England 1727–1783* (Oxford, 1989).

5 J. Betjeman, in N. Kerr (ed.), *John Betjeman's Guide to English Parish Churches* (London, 1993), p. 304.

6 Based on T. W. Freeman, H. B. Rodgers and R. H. Kinvig, *Lancashire, Cheshire and the Isle of Man* (London, 1966), p. 8; J. P. Smith, *The Genealogists' Atlas of Lancashire* (Liverpool, 1930), facing p. iv, and H. Moll's map, *The South Part of Great Britain, called England and Wales* (London, 1710).

7 F. Walker, *Historical Geography of Southwest Lancashire before the Industrial Revolution* (Manchester, 1939), pp. 56–7. 'Many places in all parts of West Derby', the wealthiest hundred, were still mainly 'moss and moor' in the mid-sixteenth century.

8 T. Corser (ed.), *Iter Lancastrense: A Poem written A.D. 1638 by the Rev. Richard James, B.D.* Chetham Society VII (Manchester, 1845), p. 2.

9 F. Musgrove, *The North of England: A History from Roman Times to the Present* (Oxford, 1990).

10 Lancaster, Liverpool, Preston and Wigan were chartered and parliamentary boroughs. Clitheroe and Newton-le-Willows were pocket boroughs. Markets were held in over 40 other places. G. H. Tupling, 'Lancashire markets in the sixteenth and seventeenth centuries', *Transactions of the Lancashire and Cheshire Antiquarian Society*, 57 (1945–46), 1–34.

11 In the Civil War, the Stanley Earls of Derby at Lathom, Molyneux Viscounts Maryborough at Sefton, and Parker Barons Morley and Monteagle at Hornby Castle in east Lonsdale. B. G. Blackwood, *The Lancashire Gentry and the Great Rebellion 1640–60* (Manchester, 1978), p. 4.

12 R. S. Schofield, 'The geographical distribution of wealth in England 1334–1649', *EcHR*, 18 (1965), 483–510.

13 W. Farrer and J. Brownbill (eds), *Victoria History of the County of Lancaster*, vol. 2 (London, 1908), map facing p. 438.

14 S. Webb and B. Webb, *English Local Government from the Revolution to the Municipal Corporations Act: The Parish and the County in England* (London, 1906), pp. 310–18; L. K. J. Glassey, *Politics and the Appointment of Justices of the Peace 1675–1720* (Oxford, 1979), pp. 270–96.

15 Walker, *Historical Geography*, p. 64.

16 C. Haigh, *Reformation and Resistance in Tudor Lancashire* (Cambridge, 1975), pp. 6–7.

17 J. K. Walton, *Lancashire: A Social History, 1558–1939* (Manchester, 1987), pp. 20–33 and 60–83.

18 T. Fuller, *The History of the Worthies of England*, 4 parts (London, 1662), part 2, p. 105.

19 Based on English and Welsh Hearth and Scottish Burghal Taxes. Only six others were in the biggest 200.

20 E. J. Buckatzsch, 'The geographical distribution of wealth in England, 1086–1843, *EcHR*, 3 (1950), 180–202.

21 P. Deane and W. A. Cole, *British Economic Growth 1699–1959* (Cambridge, 1964), p. 103.

22 There were still 82,000 acres of moor and common and 26,500 acres of moss and fen in 1815. G. Rogers, 'Customs and common right: waste land enclosure and social change in west Lancashire', *Agricultural History Review*, 41 (1993), 138.

23 Buckatzsch, 'Distribution of wealth'; Deane and Cole, *Economic Growth*.

24 Liverpool and Manchester, each with approaching 100,000 inhabitants, were the second and third biggest British towns in 1801, having been 274th and 82nd largest in the mid-seventeenth century, and ten other Lancashire towns were in the largest 100 in Britain in 1801. J. Langton, 'Urban growth and economic change from the seventeenth century to 1841', forthcoming in P. Clark (ed.), *The Urban History of Britain*, vol. 2 (Cambridge, 1999).

25 The value of cotton textiles production increased from £600,000 in 1770 to £10,500,000 in 1805. Deane and Cole, *Economic Growth*, p. 212.

26 M. W. Flinn and D. Stoker, *The History of the British Coal Industry, Vol. 2, 1700–1830: The Industrial Revolution* (Oxford, 1984), p. 26.

27 J. Langton, 'Liverpool and its hinterland in the late eighteenth century', in B. L. Anderson and P. M. S. Stoney (eds), *Commerce, Industry and Transport: Studies in Economic Change on Merseyside* (Liverpool, 1983), pp. 1–25.

28 Thomas Williams' copper works, mainly at St Helens, were worth £800,000 in 1799, and the British Plate Glass Company made glass worth £90,000 in St Helens in 1801. T. C. Barker and J. R. Harris, *A Merseyside Town in the Industrial Revolution: St. Helens 1750–1900* (London, 1954), pp. 81 and 116.

29 D. Rubinstein, 'Wealth and the wealthy', in J. Langton and R. J. Morris (eds), *Atlas of Industrializing Britain 1780–1914* (London, 1986), p. 157.

30 Fuller, *Worthies*, p. 124.

31 'Lord Burghley's map of Lancashire, 1590', *Catholic Record Society*, 7 (1907), 162–222.

32 Compiled from D. Attwater and J. Cumming, *A New Dictionary of Saints* (Tunbridge Wells, 1993) and J. Gillow, *Bibliographic Dictionary of the English Catholics*, 5 vols [1885] (London, 1972).

33 P. Caraman (ed.), *John Gerard: The Autobiography of an Elizabethan* (London, 1951), pp. 32–3.

34 Haigh, *Reformation and Resistance*; E Duffy, *The Stripping of the Altars: Traditional Religion in England 1400–1580* (New Haven, 1992); A. Walsham, *Church Papists: Catholicism, Conformity and Confessional Polemic in Early Modern England* (Woodbridge, 1993); K. Hylson-Smith, *The Churches in England from Elizabeth I to Elizabeth II*, vol. 1, *1558–1688* (London, 1996), pp. 77–92.

35 R. C. Richardson, *Puritanism in North-West England: A Regional Study of the Diocese of Chester to 1642* (Manchester, 1972), p. 5.

36 Haigh, *Reformation and Resistance*, pp. 1–19.

37 First by priests who refused to become Protestant, then by missionaries from Douai, the first three of whom arrived in England in 1573 and who numbered over 100 by 1580, when they were joined by Jesuits. M. D. R. Leys, *Catholics in England 1559–1829: A Social History* (London, 1961), pp. 27–9.

38 In 1564, 50 of the 78 Justices of the Peace in the Diocese of Chester (18 out of 24 in Lancashire) had a religious outlook unfavourable to the Established Church. W. R. Trimble, *The Catholic Laity in Elizabethan England 1558–1603* (Cambridge, Mass., 1964), pp. 26–8.

39 A. L. Rowse, *The England of Elizabeth: The Structure of Society* (London, 1951), p. 440.

40 'Burghley's map', p. 162, quoting reports to the Privy Council from the Bishop of Chester.

41 31 (14 per cent) of the 216 with known birthplaces. Only Yorkshire, with 55 (25 per cent), produced more. 104 (48 per cent) were born in the six northern counties.

42 Hylson-Smith, *Churches in England*, vol 1, p. 82.

43 C. M. Haile, *An Elizabethan Cardinal: William Allen* (London, 1914).

44 J. A. Hilton, *Catholic Lancashire: From Reformation to Renewal 1559–1991* (Chichester, 1994), p. 9.

45 Rowse, *England of Elizabeth*, p. 452.

46 Hilton, *Catholic Lancashire*, p. 6.

47 Walker, *Historical Geography*, pp. 60–1; Haigh, *Reformation and Resistance*, pp. 159–77.

48 *Ibid*, pp. 13 and 176.

49 *Ibid*, p. 175; see also Richardson, *Puritanism*, pp. 8–9.

50 Fuller, *Worthies*, p. 108.

51 As in northern England as a whole according to J Bossy, *The English Catholic Community 1570–1850* (London, 1975), pp. 84–7. Catholics were distributed even less 'as if they were types of vegetation' (p. 86) than he supposed.

52 'West Derby and Leyland were by far the most important Hundreds' in the Assessment of 1576 and the Levy of 1587, due to their productive arable/mixed farming system. Walker, *Historical Geography*, pp. 53–4.

53 According to Fuller in 1662, the 36 parishes of Lancashire, 12 fewer than in Rutland, one fifth of its size, were the most highly-coveted in England. Haigh mapped 60 parishes for c.1600. Fuller, *Worthies*, p. 105; Haigh, *Reformation and Resistance*, pp. xii–xiii.

54 *Iter Lancastrense*, p. 10.

55 The north-east corner of the county produced Catholic martyrs, witches and early Quaker congregations, as did the Aspull-Blackrod area between Wigan and Bolton. K. Thomas, *Religion and the Decline of Magic; Studies in Popular Beliefs in Sixteenth- and Seventeenth-Century England* (Harmondsworth, 1973), pp. 39 and 627n; N. Morgan, *Lancashire Quakers and the Establishment 1660–1730* (Halifax, 1993), p. 288.

56 Rowse, *England of Elizabeth*, pp. 450–1.

57 Richardson, *Puritanism*, pp. 5–6; G. P. Connolly, 'Catholicism in Manchester and Salford, 1770–1850: The Quest for "Le Chrétien Quelconque"' (unpublished Ph.D. thesis, University of Manchester, 1980), pp. 16–17.

58 A. J. Hawkes, *Sir Roger Bradshaigh of Haigh, Knight and Baronet* (Manchester, 1945).
59 B. G. Blackwood, 'Plebeian Catholics in the 1640s and 1650s', *Recusant History*, 118 (1986), 51.
60 Trimble, *Catholic Laity*, pp. 206–7.
61 C. Haydon, *Anti-Catholicism in Eighteenth-Century England, c.1714–80: A Political and Social Study* (Manchester, 1993), p. 11.
62 They increased continually as new parishes were carved out of large old ones. My base map was derived from Smith, *Genealogical Atlas*, pp. 2–15.
63 Recusant landowners who compounded with the Crown for two-thirds of their estates for refusing to conform to the established religion, from J Brownbill, 'Lancashire recusants about 1630', *Transactions of the Historic Society of Lancashire and Cheshire*, new series 24 (1908), 171–80.
64 As in Rowse, *England of Elizabeth*, p. 452, and Hilton, *Catholic Lancashire*, p. 6.
65 F. O. Blundell, *Old Catholic Lancashire*, vol. 1 (London, 1925), p. 2.
66 'Registers of Holywell', *Catholic Record Society*, Miscellany 3 (1906), 108.
67 B. Camm, *Forgotten Shrines* (London, 1910).
68 G. Anstruther, 'Lancashire clergy in 1639. A recently discovered list among the Towneley papers', *Recusant History*, 4 (1957–58), 38–46.
69 *Ibid*, pp. 40–1.
70 *Ibid*, pp. 44 and 39.
71 Haigh, *Reformation and Resistance*, p. 176.
72 Lonsdale is absent from the list of clergy. The percentage figures for the hundreds included in both sources are: West Derby, 41.4 in 1629–33 and 54.4 in 1639; Leyland, 19.1 and 16.5; Blackburn, 12.2 and 13.3, and Amounderness, 27.3 and 15.8.
73 Blackwood, *Lancashire Gentry*, p. 28.
74 *Ibid*, pp. 112–30.
75 Hawkes, *Sir Roger Bradshaigh*, pp. 21–30; Kenyon MSS, *Historical Manuscripts Commission, 14th Report, Appendix*, part IV (London, 1894).
76 *Ibid*, pp. 187–8; Glassey, *Politics*, p. 274.
77 Fuller, *Worthies*, p. 124.
78 Haydon, *Anti-Catholicism*.
79 P. K. Monod, *Jacobitism and the English People, 1688–1788* (Cambridge, 1989), p. 192.
80 Statistics gathered by the Bishop of Chester, reproduced in 'Lancashire Catholicism', *Transactions of the Historic Society of Lancashire and Cheshire*, 54 (1902), 212–21.
81 'Account of Papists within the Diocese of Chester', reproduced in *ibid.*
82 Monod, *Jacobitism*, p. 195.
83 *The Catholic Chapels, and Chaplains, with the number of their Respective Congregations, in the County of Lancaster, as taken at the end of 1819* (Liverpool, nd.).
84 Monod, *Jacobitism*, p. 332.
85 J. Langton, *Geographical Change and Industrial Revolution: Coalmining in South West Lancashire, 1590–1799* (Cambridge, 1979).
86 Liverpool (1,748), Wigan (1,194), Ormskirk (1,086) and Preston (1,043). London had 1,492. York's 642 was the next largest urban total outside Lancashire. Connolly, *Catholicism*, following p. 9.
87 Hilton, *Catholic Lancashire*, flyleaf; Haydon, *Anti-Catholicism*, p. 62.
88 Irritatingly, but perhaps inevitably, hundred boundaries cut right through the most Catholic area of Lancashire, which stretched from north of Preston in Amounderness, southwards through Walton-le-Dale township in the western promontory of Blackburn, through Leyland, into the north-east corner of West Derby Hundred.
89 The sources of data are somewhat different from those of the county maps because civil returns, unlike ecclesiastical ones, always specified townships. They are as follows: Figure 5.4a, H. Bowler, 'Recusant Roll No. 1 Mich. 1592–1593', *Catholic Record Society*,

18 (1907), 156–212; 'Recusant Roll No. 2 Mich. 35–36 Eliz. (1592–4)', *ibid.*, Miscellanea, 53 (1965), 52–87; 'Recusant Rolls No. 3 Mich. 36–37 Eliz. (1594–5)' and 'No. 4 Mich. 37–38 Eliz. (1595–6)', *ibid.*, 61 (1970), 36–42 and 160–77. Figure 5.4b, 'Subsidy Roll, Leyland Hundred, Co. Lanc. 1628', *Record Society of Lancashire and Cheshire*, 12 (1885), 164–88 and 'Recusant Roll for West Derby Hundred, 1641', *ibid.*, 50 (1898), 231–46. Figure 5.4c, E. A. Estcourt and J. O. Payne, *The English Catholic Non-Jurors of 1715* (London, 1885). Figure 5.4d, E. S. Worrall, 'Returns of Papists 1767, Diocese of Chester', *Catholic Record Society*, Occasional Publications, 1 (1980). Figure 5.5a, as Figure 5.3b.

90 Based on the Hearth Tax of 1664 and the Census of 1801. The former are very unreliable estimates.

91 Blundell, *Old Catholic Lancashire*, vol. 1, pp. 67–73.

92 Walker, *Historical Geography*, p. 73.

93 Kenyon MSS (1894), pp. 134 and 185.

94 Richardson, *Puritanism*, pp. 7–8.

95 Blundell, *Old Catholic Lancashire*, vol 1, pp. 49–64.

96 J. Langton, 'People from the pits: the origins of colliers in eighteenth-century south-west Lancashire', forthcoming in D. R. Siddle (ed.), *Migration, Mobility and Modernization in Europe* (Liverpool, 1998).

97 M. Burke, *Catholic History of Liverpool* (Liverpool, 1910), pp. 7–29. In a dispute of 1783, the Vicar Apostolic complained that the demands of one Liverpool Catholic congregation to choose its own clergy 'strike at the very root of ecclesiastical authority and subordination . . . [and are] . . . a most preposterous attempt to exalt the sheep above the pastor . . . a sacrilegious effort to disturb the order established by our Blessed Redeemer and disturb the system of Infinite Wisdom', quoted in Hilton, *Catholic Lancashire*, p. 66.

98 Blackwood, 'Plebeian Catholics', p. 51.

99 G. Timmins, *The Last Shift: The Decline of Handloom Weaving in Nineteenth-Century Lancashire* (Manchester, 1993), p. 46.

100 Chorley township contained 4.23 per cent of the Catholics in Leyland and West Derby in 1629/41, compared with 2.93 per cent of the total population (estimated from the Hearth Tax) in 1664; 3.98 per cent of the Catholics in 1819 compared with 2.13 per cent of the total population in 1821.

101 Farrer and Brownbill, *Victoria County History*, vol. 6, pp. 148 and 130.

102 Langton, *Geographical Change*, pp. 74–6, 123–5 and 217–23.

103 Such as John Halliwell of Tunley, John Chadwick of Burgh and Charles Dagnall of Eccleston, *ibid.*

104 Hawkes, *Sir Roger Bradshaigh*, p. 9.

105 B. G. Awty, 'Charcoal ironmasters of Lancashire and Cheshire', *Transactions of the Historic Society of Lancashire and Cheshire*, 109 (1957), 102–5.

106 Farrer and Brownbill, *Victoria County History*, vol 4, p. 125.

107 Hilton, *Catholic Lancashire*, p. 13. The absence of Wigan from the Recusant Rolls for 1641 is one of the obvious inaccuracies of these sources. In the 1590s, Wigan housed 5.53 per cent of the Catholics in Leyland and West Derby Hundreds, compared with the aggregate of 3.25 per cent in all the five other towns; it contained 7.96 per cent of the Catholics in the two hundreds in 1819 and 5.15 per cent of their total population in 1821.

108 Kenyon MSS (1894), pp. 128 and 132.

109 Langton, *Geographical Change*, pp. 52–3; J. Hatcher and T. C. Barker, *A History of British Pewter* (London, 1973), pp. 125–8 and 261; J. Langton, 'Industry and towns 1500–1730', in R. A. Dodgshon and R. A. Butlin (eds), *An Historical Geography of England and Wales* (London, 1978), pp. 188–9.

110 Farrer and Brownbill, *Victoria County History*, vol 4, p. 127.
111 See notes 100 and 107.
112 The total populations of some small townships containing chapels were less than their Catholic congregations, giving figures in excess of 100 per cent.
113 Edmund Arrowsmith (1585–1628) was a Jesuit priest, executed in 1628. His hand is preserved as a relic at St Oswald's church in Ashton-in-Makerfield.
114 Langford, *Polite and Commercial People*, pp. 673–4.

6 Norman McCord

The regional identity of north-east England in the nineteenth and early twentieth centuries

Introduction

In recent decades much attention has been devoted to consideration of the nature of local history and regional history, their relationship to each other and their interaction with wider perspectives. John Marshall has for many years been one of the leading contributors to these debates, and has done much to clarify the issues involved. It is now clear that the relative significance of local, regional, national and international topics within history is far from simple or uniform, but instead is something capable of infinite variation in both time and place. Within this broad field, this chapter has the limited aim of offering a single example by discussing how far north-east England can reasonably be seen as a discrete region in the nineteenth and earlier twentieth centuries. The area involved is taken as covering the historic counties of Durham and Northumberland, and including Newcastle upon Tyne, Berwick upon Tweed, with the northern fringe of Yorkshire along the lower Tees, centred on Middlesbrough (see figure 6.1)

For much of history, it would be difficult to maintain that the region as defined here provided any striking degree of recognisable coherence. Archaeologists have preferred terms like the 'Forth-Humber cultural province' for the centuries of the pre-Roman Iron Age. Early tribal boundaries in the North seem to have followed very different lines, and our concept of the north-east appears to have little relevance to either Roman Britain or Anglo-Saxon Northumbria. During the medieval centuries, there were differences between Durham and Northumberland and little to indicate any particular regional uniformity. However, it can be argued that in certain respects there was a greater coherence within the north-east region during the nineteenth and early twentieth centuries than in earlier and later periods.

At a time when industrial and commercial developments were of crucial importance, there was a basic topographical unity to this region. Wide gaps intervened between the industrialising centres on the rivers Tyne, Wear and

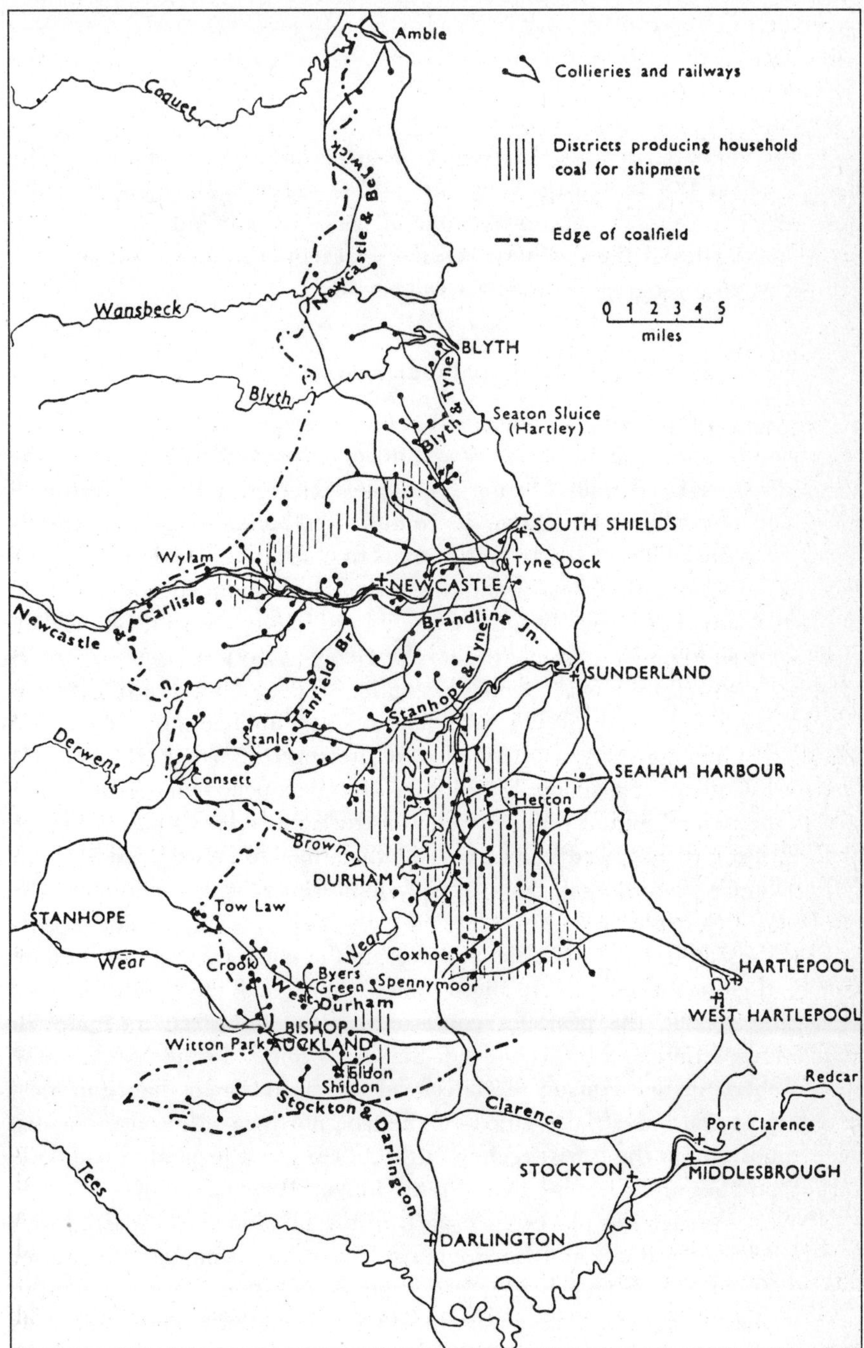

Figure 6.1 **The north-east of England in 1850**

Tees and the nearest similar districts. The Cheviot Hills to the north, and a wide stretch of essentially farming country, separated the north-east from Scottish centres of development. To the south, the Cleveland Hills and the agricultural North Riding intervened between the region and the main Yorkshire industrial centres. To the west, substantial stretches of poor quality land, such as the Bewcastle Fells, always bearing a small population, lay between the north-east centres of economic development and Cumbria. The leadmining dales of the northern Pennines present a minor exception here, but the general geographical point is valid enough.

The national and international dimensions

Even in this period, it is obvious that any concept of a completely separate region is untenable, for it is easy to think of a variety of factors linking the region to the rest of Britain. The north-east played its role in the constitutional machinery of the United Kingdom. Its counties and boroughs elected MPs; its peers sat in the House of Lords. Northerners frequently held high office in the national government. Earl Grey and the Earl of Durham took leading parts in the enactment of the Great Reform Act, and Lord Eldon was Lord Chancellor, with one brief interval, from 1801 to 1827. Sir George Grey was Home Secretary 1846–52, 1855–58, 1861–66, Colonial Secretary 1854–55; Sir Edward Grey was Foreign Secretary 1905–16. The 3rd Duke of Northumberland and the 6th Marquis of Londonderry were viceroys of Ireland; the 4th Earl Grey was Governor-General of Canada; Sir Charles Trevelyan occupied a senior position in the government of India as well as introducing reforms into the home civil service. Others played leading parts in the armed forces; the 3rd Marquis of Londonderry and the 5th Duke of Cleveland were prominent soldiers, the 6th Duke of Northumberland was an admiral as well as briefly serving as First Lord of the Admiralty. As new elements within the north-east attained prominence, their achievements received much more than a merely regional recognition, as in the peerages conferred on the industrial magnate Sir William Armstrong and the coalowner Sir James Joicey. In the years around 1900, Robert Spence Watson of Gateshead was a prominent figure in local government and industrial relations within the north-east, but also encouraged opposition to the tsarist regime in Russia (as other local men had done earlier) and became a leading figure in the Liberal Party nationally.[1]

Northern magnates played their parts in the London social season, with Northumberland House and Londonderry House, for examples, serving for many years as two of the centres of the capital's high life. It was common to find northern magnates taking part in other national pursuits, perhaps as Fellows of the Royal Society or of the Society of Antiquaries or as trustees of the British Museum. The 8th Duke of Northumberland was President of the

Royal Archaeological Institute in 1883–92. Thomas Hodgkin, partner in an important Newcastle bank, was also one of the most eminent historians in mid-Victorian Britain, with a scholarly reputation which was much more than merely regional.

The extent to which the interests of individuals had a specifically regional bias was a considerable variable. Many northern magnates had additional interests in other regions.[2] If the estates of the Earl of Durham were essentially within the north-east, Dukes of Northumberland in addition to their extensive northern properties were significant landowners in Surrey and Middlesex. Lord Londonderry owned land in Durham, Montgomeryshire, Merioneth, Donegal and County Down. In 1883 the Duke of Cleveland owned property in Durham, Shropshire, Sussex, Somerset, Northamptonshire, Wiltshire, Kent, Cornwall, Staffordshire, Devon and Gloucestershire.

There were some northern landowners whose principal properties and interests lay elsewhere. The relative significance of different properties in a family's income varied enormously. Viscount Barrington, Lord Hastings and the Earl of Carlisle derived a greater income from their Northumberland estates than from more extensive properties elsewhere. In all of these cases the landowner preferred to live outside the north-east. Sir Walter James, Bt, later Lord Northbourne, depended heavily on income from a relatively small but highly profitable acreage in the Gateshead area, but his preferred base was Betteshanger Park, near Sandwich in Kent. Lord Hastings received much more from his Northumberland than from his Norfolk estates, but preferred to live at Melton Constable.

Even where landowners were generally absent from the north-east, they might exercise a considerable influence on local affairs. The Northumberland property of the Duke of Portland was much smaller than his Nottinghamshire estates, but its position meant that the Duke and his agents could control important development in north Newcastle and the expanding Northumberland mining centre of Ashington. Even if Sir Walter and Lady James were not resident on Tyneside, they carefully cultivated a long-standing family connection there, including the creation of public parks and generosity to other local philanthropic causes. In 1874 this assiduity, coupled with their important property within the constituency, provided the family heir with an easily-won parliamentary seat at Gateshead, despite his political inexperience.[3] The owners of land within the north-east played a major part in the region's history in this period, but the scale and the quality of their participation in the region's affairs was varied.

There were other kinds of links between the north-east and other parts of the country. A key feature in the national economy was the east coast trade, with its vital supply of coal from north-east ports for a variety of communities all the way down the coast to culminate in the crucial London coal connection. Domestic hearths and industrial furnaces in the capital depended on fuel from the north-east, while the revenue from coal sales there was an essential component in the regional economy of the north-east. Before the end of the eighteenth century, all the important coalowners in the north-east found it necessary to maintain permanent agents in London.[4] In the buying, transporting, distribution and selling of coal, there grew up intricate financial connections between north-east producers and the extensive markets in Britain and elsewhere which they served.

Commercial connections were not confined to the coal trade. By the early nineteenth century, the east coast carrying trade generally had achieved a high level of organisation. Regular freight services sailed to and from the north-east ports, with a sophisticated network of collection and delivery points established throughout the region to feed into the regular sailings. In 1827, destinations of these regular services included Leith, London, Hull, Dundee, Gainsborough, Glasgow, Liverpool, Ipswich, Whitby and Rotterdam, and this is not a complete list. In addition to cargo carriage, the coasting trade provided a relatively cheap passenger service which was widely used. The region's ports developed an extensive range of overseas contacts, with a continuing concentration in trading with the states along the eastern periphery of continental Europe. The dependence of the regional economy on distant markets at home and abroad was itself enough to inhibit any myopic restrictions in outlook within the more powerful elements in north-eastern society.

Even before the development of the railway system, the region played a part in a complex national network of road freight services.[5] In 1827, Pickersgill's warehouses in Newcastle organised daily post wagons to and from London, Manchester, Sheffield, Barnsley, Wakefield, Birmingham, Huddersfield, Halifax, Leeds, Bradford, Coventry, Leicester, Nottingham and other centres, providing transport 'to all parts of England and Scotland'. Other major carriers concentrated on regular services to various points in Scotland and Cumbria. Another range of services contributed the stage coach lines which provided quicker passenger carriage between the north-east and other parts of England, Scotland and Wales. The coming of the railways, and the development and expansion of steamship services, saw an increasing elaboration of the transport links between the north-east and other regions in Britain and abroad.

The diversity of the region

On the other hand, smaller units than the north-east region could offer their own coherence and more local significance. The organised life of individual counties made important contributions to political, social and administrative concerns. There was no regional forum which quite matched the regular county Quarter Sessions as occasions which focused a variety of forms of interest. It is unlikely that any other meetings within the region provided such recurring occasions for contacts and discussions between dominant elements, as well as a variety of shared social occasions. County Councils, after their inauguration in 1889, never matched Quarter Sessions in these respects.

Until well into the twentieth century, individual local authorities, especially counties and county boroughs, enjoyed a substantial degree of financial independence. The bulk of the money spent in local official spending was raised from local sources, mainly the rates, and expended under the control of local authorities elected by local ratepayers. Many ambitious men might find their aspirations adequately covered by prominence within a single local council rather than by more elevated positions. Interventions in local affairs from Whitehall were often resented, and there were many instances of such bodies as Poor Law Unions effectively going their own way despite strenuous efforts by central authority to make them toe the line of national policy. There was no serious attempt to establish significant units of official administration on a regional basis.

As organised sporting activities became more sophisticated during the Victorian period, loyalties to individual teams, often with a very local ambience, became matters of primary importance to many of the region's inhabitants. It was not uncommon for an active individual to concentrate his energies on the administration of such an event as an annual local flower show, a local sporting league, a masonic lodge or a friendly society branch. Religious activity was rarely organised on a regional basis but could be expressed in membership of a nationally organised sect, a diocese, a Methodist circuit, or a variety of other forms of administrative district. For many individuals the affairs of individual churches or chapels might be in practice the effective limit of their active participation. It is worth remembering though that the essential nature of religious faith would often discourage excessive interest in local secular affairs. There were agencies which served to incorporate localised activities within a wider regional context. As the provincial press developed in the later nineteenth century, newspapers such as the *Newcastle Chronicle* provided accounts of an immense variety of activities within the region to an extent which might inspire embarrassment among their less thorough and careful successors of the late twentieth century.

For most of the region's inhabitants, life could still be overwhelmingly concentrated on immediate local and family concerns. Although levels of literacy were greatly improved, and the region's achievements here were above average in extent, illiteracy remained widespread, and for many years the relatively high cost of books and journals limited their availability. While the remarkable achievements and wider interests of such largely self-taught working men as Thomas Burt and John Burnett have properly attracted much attention, it is as well to balance this admiration with a realisation that they were far from typical members of their social groupings. Progress in education was nevertheless striking, although its significance for regional developments could vary. Many students of the University of Durham and the Newcastle School of Medicine after their creation in the 1830s went on to become clergymen and doctors serving within the region, although not all of them stayed there. As the state's role in education increased, the nature of the elementary curriculum became more standardised in national rather than merely local or regional terms. Many men and women rarely moved far from home, even in the earlier years of the twentieth century, and the majority of the people of the region could have very limited horizons, which rarely included any particular concern for the entire north-east region.

The local, the regional and the national

The period considered here saw the emergence of a complex set of conditions, in which some important instances of distinctively regional developments occurred. At the same time, smaller scale loyalties could remain significant, and there was a growing body of national institutions which incorporated north-eastern elements within a greater whole. By the end of the nineteenth century, many trade unions and professional organisations had come into existence, with a central existence and a network of branches on a national scale. To take a single example, Newcastle received its branch of the United Kingdom Commercial Travellers Association six years after that body's foundation in 1883. By 1914, the local branch's annual handbook listed, among a variety of similar 'perks', special premium rates offered to its members by the Norwich Union insurance company. In trade unions, friendly societies, sporting activities and many other areas, the nineteenth century saw an accelerating development of national, as well as regional or local, organisations.

In the period considered here, it would therefore be difficult to maintain that regional history could reasonably be studied without reference to both smaller and larger units. It would not be easy to find a better illustration of the connections between political, social and economic history, or between local, regional and national history, than the example offered by the experiences of the ports of north-east England during the nineteenth century. The expansion of the industrial economies of Tyneside, Wearside and Teesside depended heavily upon the development of effective transport facilities, especially seaborne freight carriage, including the coal trade. In turn, the emergence of the distinctively urban society of the region's main towns was a product of industrial and commercial growth and its ancillary attributes. For a number of reasons, the progressive improvement of the north-east harbours could not have taken place without resort to a national political process, especially in the securing of the necessary parliamentary legislation.

A crucial element on Tyneside was the breaking of Newcastle's stranglehold on the whole Tyne harbour, which in earlier years was marked by a determination to exploit chartered rights to subsidise the town from harbour revenues and to impede the development of any rival ports. Such tactics worked for many years, though at the cost of retarding any significant modernisation of the Tyne harbour. The eventual checking of these policies was a process helped by such political developments as the granting of municipal institutions and their own MPs to other Tyneside towns in the Whig national reforms of the 1830s. Gateshead, South Shields and Tynemouth all became parliamentary boroughs in 1832. Gateshead became a municipality in 1835, Tynemouth and South Shields followed suit in 1849 and 1850 respectively. Anyone standing as a parliamentary candidate or leading municipal figure in these towns must have as part of his appeal a willingness to champion the interests of the other Tyneside communities as against the over-mighty self-interest of the principal regional centre. These political changes were a vital part of the background to the Tyne Improvement Act of 1850, an essential prerequisite for the harbour developments which facilitated the development of Tyneside as one of the world's major industrial districts. The Act extinguished Newcastle's monopoly of authority and revenue within the whole Tyne harbour, and transferred control to a new Tyne Improvement Commission, made up of members appointed by all of the major towns on the lower Tyne, the Admiralty and representatives of the trade of the harbour. During the remainder of the nineteenth century, the Tyne Improvement Commission, dominated by men who possessed a keen personal interest in the district's economic health, contrived to improve the harbour in time to facilitate the expansion of Tyneside industry and commerce, with all the social changes which this involved. Legislation was needed for many of the other harbour improvement projects in the northern ports during the nineteenth century. Without these initiatives, involving the national legislature, the development of the industrial north-east would have been much more difficult, if not impossible.

The development of a regional identity

If both larger and smaller loyalties remained effective, in some important respects the north-east did develop a strong regional identity during the nineteenth and early twentieth centuries. One crucial element in this lay in the economic sphere. Here a number of characteristics tended this way. The key role of the Great Northern Coalfield was one of these. Mining came to employ a remarkably high proportion of local labour in the course of the nineteenth and early twentieth centuries. In 1911, there were well over 54,000 miners in Northumberland, representing nearly 20 per cent of all employment. In Durham there were then more than 152,000 miners, or not far short of 30 per cent of all local employment. These figures are for direct employment only, taking no account of those employed in such related elements as the coal-carrying railways and collier fleet, or the many additional thousands whose employment was concerned with the sale and distribution of coal at home and overseas.

It was not just a matter of scale. The coalfield's patterns of trade, both within Britain and in overseas markets, differed from those of other coalfields. They included the dominance of the key London market at home and a unique distribution of export shipments, which saw much of the coalfield's expanding output sent to western European destinations in a wide arc stretching from Scandinavia and the Baltic to the Mediterranean.[6] Underground working practices in northern collieries differed from those of other coalfields, and both miners and coalowners on the coalfield developed their own institutions. In the North of England Mining Institute, founded in 1852, north-eastern coalowners and their principal technical advisers came together to pursue their joint interests. Although for many years after the establishment of permanent mining unions Durham and Northumberland had separate organisations, they closely resembled each other in their principal characteristics and were often out of step with other mining unions. There were other regional peculiarities in the mining sphere, as for example the very large proportion of northern mining families who lived in houses provided by their employers. Like the high density terraces of the region's towns, north-east colliery houses developed into a distinctly regional form of vernacular building which flourished until the First World War. Mining was one major element within an industrial pattern which discouraged high levels of female employment, in contrast to the experience of the principal textile regions. Engineering and shipbulding were other important industries within the region which strengthened this male domination of the regional work force.

The influence of the coalfield was a pervasive one within the regional economy. The winning and distribution of coal required inputs which contributed to the development of related industries, including the manufacture of iron and steel and a varied engineering sector. The important Newcastle engineering firm of Robert Stephenson came into existence to provide locomotives for coal-carrying railways. For many years the Consett Iron Company depended on the manufacture of rails, again with coal-carrying lines among its principal early customers. The building of collier ships was an important branch of local shipbuilding both before and after the introduction of iron screw steamships into the trade in the mid-nineteenth century. When the market for rails showed signs of drying up, with the substantial completion of railway networks, at home and abroad, Consett Iron Works came to depend on the mass manufacture of ships' plates as a main source of business for many years.

The ready availability of supplies of cheap coal encouraged the development within the region of other industries. Chemical manufacture, glass-making and paper-making were among these. By 1860, Tyneside chemical plants used about 300,000 tons of coal annually. Special sands for use in local glass-works might be brought back to the north-east as ballast in local colliers. The expanding paper industry was not only a customer for coal, but also contributed an essential input for the parallel expansion of administrative activity and commercial correspondence which the coal trade generated. A publicity tribute to a leading Newcastle printer noted that, 'the Mines Regulating Act of 1887 has still further increased Mr. Reid's connection with the leading colliery owners of the district, and an extensive business is done in the printing of special rules, abstracts, books and forms.'[7] The coalfield contributed significantly to expansion over a wide range of activities. Law, banking, stockbroking and insurance all found growing business in the affairs of colliery companies. The increasingly numerous miners and their families provided more work in the retail, building and recreational sectors. Coal mining was an important element in the development of various institutions which gave the local economy a distinctively regional aspect. Perhaps the best example here was the evolution of the North Eastern Railway, as one of the largest, most efficient and most profitable of the pre-1914 railway companies.

The North Eastern Railway came into existence as a regional amalgamation of various smaller enterprises, all of which had been created to serve distinctive local economic interests. In many cases, the economical carriage of coal had been the primary factor in the creation of the local railways which came together in the North Eastern Railway. For example, the North Eastern Railway absorbed the Stockton and Darlington Railway in 1863, the Blyth and Tyne Railway in 1874, and the Londonderry Railway in 1900. The regional network continued to be dominated by men closely associated with a variety of aspects of the region's economic life, and throughout its policies were directed to serving those interests. In 1898 its directors included Sir Joseph Pease, from a notable Darlington family of entrepreneurs, Sir David Dale of the Consett Iron Company, Sir Isaac Lothian Bell, another prominent iron-master, the coalowner Sir James Joicey, and Sir William Gray, a leading West Hartlepool shipbuilder. Members of the landowning Grey and Ridley dynasties, also North Eastern Railway directors, reflected the extent to which the northern aristocracy was concerned with many other economic activities as well as agriculture. By the end of the nineteenth century, the North Eastern Railway was firmly established as a kingpin of the regional economy, with a regionally based direction and a total of 40,000 shareholders.

The nature of the North Eastern Railway, and its strong regional commitment, provided one of the most powerful expressions of the essential interdependence which pervaded the developing regional economy. The kind of overlapping direction seen there had many parallels throughout the north-east, with coalowners, for example, frequently appearing as directors of coal-using industries. Such links reflected the ways in which many of the key industries within the region were highly inter-dependent. Perhaps the best example here is provided by coal, iron and steel and engineering. Increasing demand for coal brought colliery developments which required more iron or steel and developments in engineering, including not only mining machinery but also the building of more colliers in local shipyards. Increasing demand for iron and steel, or for engineering products, similarly triggered off additional growth in the other members of this triple alliance. The twentieth century was to discover, the hard way, that such a spiral of inter-dependence could be as effective in decline as in expansion.

The development of service elements, such as banking, insurance and stockbroking, took on significant regional features. Local banks were much involved in the financial affairs of local companies, and their directors often included men with a variety of business interests within the region. For example, the support of the Newcastle-based banking partnership of Hodgkin, Barnett, Pease, Spence and Co. was crucial in the reconstruction of the Hawthorn engineering company on Tyneside in the early 1870s. In 1866, that bank's support made all the difference in enabling Wigham Richardson's shipyard to survive in business during a short but sharp recession in shipbuilding. The catastrophic failure of the Northumberland and Durham District Bank in 1857 was in great measure due to the bank's adventurous financing of local industrial enterprises, including collieries and iron works. Some of the north-eastern banks built up networks of branches serving much of the region. In the later nineteenth century, Hodgkin, Barnett, Pease, Spence and Co., in addition to their Newcastle headquarters (with local suburban satellites at Byker and Westgate), had branches at North and South Shields, Morpeth, Alnwick, Rothbury, Shotley Bridge, Consett, Jarrow, Blyth, Wallsend, Bellingham and Amble, with sub-branches at Stanley, Annfield Plain and Ashington.

The Newcastle branch of the Bank of England was established in 1828, amidst widespread local suspicion of the national bank's intervention in local affairs. Prompted by the existing local banks, the Newcastle Chamber of Commerce protested vigorously but vainly against this intervention from the centre. After the creation of the branch, there followed, during the tenure of the first managing Agent, a period of conflict with the existing local banks.[8] In those years, the branch sought in a rather heavy-handed fashion to establish its own primacy among the local banks, in ways which aroused considerable resentment among the private banks already active in the area. Thereafter, successive Agents adopted a more conciliatory approach which brought more success. After its somewhat shaky beginning, the Bank of England branch in Newcastle established itself as a kind of regional banking centre, providing a crucial back-up for other north-eastern banks in such troubled times as the banking crises of 1847 and 1857. In those two years, major local joint stock banks collapsed disastrously, threatening ruin to the many local enterprises which had relied upon their services and backing. Especially in the 1857 crisis, building on experience gained ten years earlier, the national Bank of England reacted briskly and effectively to the collapse of the important Northumberland and Durham District Bank. The rapid provision of emergency credits to the failed bank's customers throughout the north-eastern region enabled a largely successful damage limitation exercise to be implemented, which saved a number of important north-east enterprises.

Another aspect of the Bank of England's operations within the region was the way in which, over a prolonged period, most of the important local banking houses were, one by one, persuaded to abandon their independent note issue. They agreed to act instead as agents for the issue of Bank of England notes, in return for financial sweeteners offered by the national bank. The correspondence of the Newcastle branch shows a growing range of connections with a great variety of local companies, as well as with other northern banks, and also the development of something like a regional network of financial intelligence. This branch of the Bank of England provided a significant connection controlled from outside the region but essentially involved in regional financial activity. Most of the region's banking activity was still in the hands of local banking enterprises within the north-east. Although from an early date these local banks developed standing connections with other banks in London and elsewhere, until the years around 1900 their autonomy and regional significance remained essentially intact.

Northern suspicion of the potentially aggressive role of the Bank of England did not die away entirely. A regional Bankers' Clearing Association based in Newcastle was established in 1872, after a series of earlier attempts to create efficient clearing facilities. By 1882, most banks north of York had affiliated to it. A few major banks, including some on Tyneside, remained outside the association, however, mainly because in this clearing house's operations a key part was allotted to the Bank of England.[9]

The coming reduction of the region's economic independence was foreshadowed in the years around 1900, when a number of the leading local banks succumbed to the embraces of wider groupings. Of the Newcastle banks, in 1897 the long-established banking firm of Woods and Company was taken over by Barclays Bank, while Lloyds Bank absorbed Hodgkin, Barnett, Pease, Spence and Company in 1893 and the venerable (founded 1790) Lambton Bank in 1908.

By the early Victorian years professional stockbroking was an established activity in Newcastle. The Newcastle Stock Exchange was founded in April 1845, and it is possible to identify about twenty enterprises in this field within the town by the end of that year. Much of the exchange's business consisted in the buying and selling of shares in companies based in the north-east.[10]

As the shipping using the northern ports expanded, the necessary ancillary services were largely supplied by enterprises based within the region. Marine insurance was a flourishing and expanding local business. The Northern Maritime Insurance Co., Newcastle, paid a 12½ per cent annual dividend in 1878–81, 10 per cent in 1881–88. Another group of Newcastle-based associated marine insurance companies insured 501 steamships in 1888–89.[11] Similarly, a variety of local enterprises provided northern shipping with the necessary supplies of food and drink. A substantial proportion of the shipping using the north-east ports was owned and managed within the region. Northern shipbuilders established their own distinctive patterns of repetitive orders and long-term co-operation with shipowners at home and abroad. In 1884 the region's engineers and shipbuilders followed the earlier example of coal-mining in founding their own regional forum, The North East Coast Institution of Engineers and Shipbuilders. During the discussions on the creation of this body, F. C. Marshall, one of the most prominent and effective of the Tyneside engineers, with important marine engineering interests, argued strenuously and successfully against an amalgamation with the existing North of England Mining Institute. On the other hand, he also succeeded in his advocacy of a deliberately regional organisation, which would comprehend all of the shipbuilding interests within the north-east rather than just the Tyneside element.[12]

Much of the north-east's economy in the nineteenth century was controlled by a relatively small group, who were themselves linked together by a variety of social as well as business connections. Apart from such obvious examples as family ties, including frequent marriages within the dominant group, there existed a wide range of social, political, cultural and recreational activities which brought together many of the north-east's leading entrepreneurial interests. Many of them shared educational experiences, whether in schooling in such institutions as Newcastle's Royal Grammar School or in apprenticeships within local enterprises. At the end of the century, there were several key figures in local industrial firms who had been apprentices at Armstrong's Elswick Works. The principal gentlemen's clubs in centres like Newcastle and Durham, and Newcastle's learned societies such as the Literary and Philosophical Society, the Society of Antiquaries or the Natural History Society, brought together important elements from both county landed society and industrial, commercial and professional groups. The regional economy was largely controlled by these groups, and as yet it remained possible for this dominance to be distinctively regional, with most important concerns essentially independent of control from outside the north-east.

The weakening of identity

The successes of the north-east economy during the nineteenth century provided the region with a coherent and largely autonomous structure of employment and income. However, where a company flourished particularly this might lead to a dilution of the distinctively regional flavour of the regional economy. A good example here is provided by the intensive rivalry in armaments production and related activities during the mid-Victorian period between the Armstrong company on Tyneside and the firm founded by Sir Joseph Whitworth at Openshaw. In 1897 the long-standing competition ended when Armstrong's bought up the Whitworth company. This meant that the new giant enterprise of Armstrong Whitworth was no longer so exclusively tied to Tyneside, but must be concerned with affairs elsewhere too. A number of Tyneside shipyards became involved in shipbuilding enterprises in other countries. A more general feature of the regional economy was a widely-shared dependence on export markets, especially in continental Europe, which meant that attention to more than regional matters was essential. By the end of the nineteenth century, for example, there was an increasingly intricate network of company representatives in other parts of Britain and abroad. Large firms required extensive sales organisations. In 1890 Sowerby's Ellison Glass Works at Gateshead employed travellers in Germany, Holland, Belgium, Russia, Canada and the USA as well as its home sales staff.[13]

Other forms of success could lead to individual experiences with a more than local or regional significance. John Philipson (1849–1923) provides a good example here.[14] Initially working as a coke-burner for a Tyneside colliery, he obtained positions of greater responsibility and reward before setting up his own photographic and printing business in Newcastle in 1900. He had become a teetotaller at the age of 13, and was for many years an active Methodist and a keen member of the Independent Order of Rechabites, a friendly society based on temperance principles with a quasi-masonic organisation. Philipson joined the Order in 1879, and by 1887 was Secretary of its Durham and Northumberland District. Experience in various capacities within the Order's national organisation was followed by his elevation to the top post of High Chief Ruler in 1909. This coincided with the Order's 75th anniversary, marked by a gathering of 1,000 guests in the Free Trade Hall, Manchester, over which he presided. In 1910–11, Philipson made official visits to Rechabite Tents (as local branches were known) in Australia and New Zealand, where the Order had many adherents. Stays in Ceylon, India and South Africa as a kind of

Rechabite ambassador followed. No doubt this was an unusual career, but it illustrates the varied ways in which success within the region could lead to wider distinction over a much larger field.

One of the most striking developments in Victorian Britain was the expansion of the retail sector, and this could both embody and transcend local and regional affiliations.[15] The expanding Newcastle establishment owned by the Bainbridge family has a strong claim to be considered the first of all department stores. It developed a network of local agents seeking new business for the store, covering much of the north-east, but also acquired a textile factory in Leeds to meet its clothing needs.[16] As industrial and commercial developments brought about an accelerating increase in population, and technical changes improved carriage by land and sea, the remarkable achievement of feeding these swollen numbers involved the evolution of an increasingly intricate network of supplies. The food shops in the north-east by the end of the nineteenth century had long outstripped merely regional resources and, as with other retail sectors, now depended upon importing goods from a wide spectrum of suppliers at home and abroad. But, despite the remarkable complexity of this development, most of the retail enterprises in the north-east of 1900 were still owned and controlled within the region.

Conclusion

The nineteenth and earlier twentieth centuries saw the evolution of distinctively north-eastern regional traits, especially in the economic sphere. The development was never absolute, and understanding of the region's experiences in those years must recognise the continued existence and importance of elements in its make-up which reflected both wider national and even international connections, as well as many smaller, more local, influences. By the end of the nineteenth century, the spread of nationally organised institutions in many spheres was already threatening the extent of the regional autonomy which had developed, especially in the economic sphere, during the Victorian period.

Notes

1 P. Corder, *The Life of Robert Spence Watson* (1914); D. Saunders, 'Tyneside and the making of the Russian revolution', *Northern History*, 31 (1996), 259–84.
2 J. Bateman, *The Great Landowners of Great Britain and Ireland* (London, 1883).
3 Anon, *The Durham Thirteen* (Darlington, 1874), pp. 122–7.
4 M. Flinn, *The History of the British Coal Industry. Volume 2, 1800–1830* (Oxford, 1984), p. 227.
5 W. Parson and W. White, *History, Directory, and Gazetteer of the Counties of Durham and Northumberland* (Leeds, 1827), pp. 133–41.

6 N. R. Elliott, 'A geographical analysis of the Tyne coal trade', *Tijdschrift voor Econ. an Soc. Geografie* (April 1968), 85–93.
7 Anon, *Tyneside industries* (London, 1889), p. 95.
8 I am grateful to the Bank of England for allowing me, some years ago, to consult in its main archives the early correspondence of the Newcastle branch
9 M. Phillips, *History of Banks, Bankers and Banking in Northumberland, Durham and North Yorkshire, illustrating the Commercial Development of the North of England from 1755 to 1894* (London, 1894).
10 J. R. Killick and W. A. Thomas, 'The Stock Exchanges of the North of England, 1836–1850', *Northern History*, 5 (1970), 121, 123.
11 Anon, *Tyneside Industries*, pp. 156, 153.
12 J. F. Clarke, *A Century of Service to Engineering and Shipbuilding. A Centenary History of the North East Coast Institution of Engineers and Shipbuilders 1884–1984* (Newcastle, 1984).
13 Anon, *Tyneside Industries*, p. 184.
14 O. Checkland, *Sobriety and Thrift. John Philipson and Family* (Newcastle upon Tyne, 1989).
15 See chapter 8.
16 A. and J. Airey, *The Bainbridges of Newcastle. A Family History 1679–1976* ([Newcastle], 1979); Anon., *Report of the Proceedings of the Business Jubilee of Alderman G. B. Bainbridge, J.P.* ([Newcastle], 1917).

7 *Winifred Stokes*

Regional finance and the definition of a financial region

Introduction

The argument of this chapter is that in the second quarter of the nineteenth century the development of joint stock companies, initially to finance railways but subsequently to finance a diversity of enterprises, engendered a sense of regional identity in an area of north-east England whose geographical boundaries were fluid, but which could be delimited roughly by Durham City to the north, Northallerton or even York to the south, Wolsingham in Weardale to the west, and Hartlepool, Teesside and possibly Whitby to the east.[1]

In the first decades of the century this was what might be considered an economically and socially static area of moderately prosperous small farming, some mining and quarrying for local use and linen and woollen manufacture in the small market towns of Teesside and north Yorkshire. The north Pennine valleys to the west were dominated by large-scale leadmining companies; on the eastern seaboard Whitby was the only port of any size with its whaling and fishing fleets and shipbuilding for the coal trade. Stockton's aspirations to seaport status were frustrated by the town's up-river location and the navigational difficulties of the Tees. Viewed from this distance in time the only characteristics the region would seem to have had were negative ones. Yet there is evidence that even before the advent of railways there was some notion of a possibly more dynamic identity.

Historical geographers and transport historians alike have made a good case for the importance of the role of canals and railways in altering the economic geography of an area and thereby potentially changing both its spatial dimensions and its regional identity.[2] While in no way denying their theses, this chapter looks rather at the means whereby such capital intensive ventures were brought into being and the role of joint stock enterprise in changing contemporary perceptions of the extent and character of this particular region. A commentator in the *Newcastle Chronicle* reviewing the census returns of 1851, noted that in the preceding twenty years the population of the county of

Durham had increased more than that of any other county in the kingdom and that much of that increase was in the southern half of the county.[3] This dramatic demographic expansion completely changed the area's social character, for most of these incomers were manual workers, either in the coal industry or on the railways. The minor gentry, small farmers and rural artisans, the owners of small scale textile manufactures and providers of services in the little market towns, found themselves numerically swamped and their region regarded by the middle of the century as an industrial area to be compared with Tyneside. The agency of that change was a range of joint stock companies to which many of them, as individuals, were subscribers.[4]

The Stockton and Darlington railway

Any study of early joint stock companies in south Durham has to start from the Stockton and Darlington railway. What is not widely realised, despite the coverage given to the early stages of that company's gestation by Maurice Kirby, is that the line that was finally constructed was only a pale reflection of the one envisaged by the original promoters, which was intended to stretch from Weardale to north Yorkshire. This wider vision is demonstrated in the phrase used in promoting the company 'to serve the country in general' and in the nature of the commodities to be carried, 'coals, lead and lime', as well as by the location of the individuals whose support was solicited.[5] Yet by the time the bill for the incorporation of the Stockton and Darlington railway came before Parliament, the focus had narrowed to the area that could be served by a railway between the Auckland coalfield and the textile manufacturing towns of Stockton and Darlington. This narrowing of focus was interpreted in 'the country at large' as a concentration on the interests of the major subscribers, particularly those in Darlington, to the neglect of others, and marks the beginning of the love-hate relationship that grew up between the Stockton and Darlington supporters and the 'rest'. In contrast to the wider vision of the initial promoters, the 1821 version of the Stockton and Darlington prospectus made a point of stressing the limited nature of the venture. 'Local circumstances entitle this undertaking to the support of the Public. The line passes through a populous district in which an extensive trade already exists (thus maintaining trade and capital in their wonted channels without detriment to old establishments)'.[6] (See figure 7.1)

This appeal to the 'Public' was not just empty words. At the beginning of the second decade of the nineteenth century 'public utility' remained the only recognised justification for bringing before Parliament the bill for incorporation which gave a joint stock company legal identity and allowed public investment and transferability of shares. Incorporation also, as in the case of the turnpike trusts and canal companies on which this and subsequent joint stock

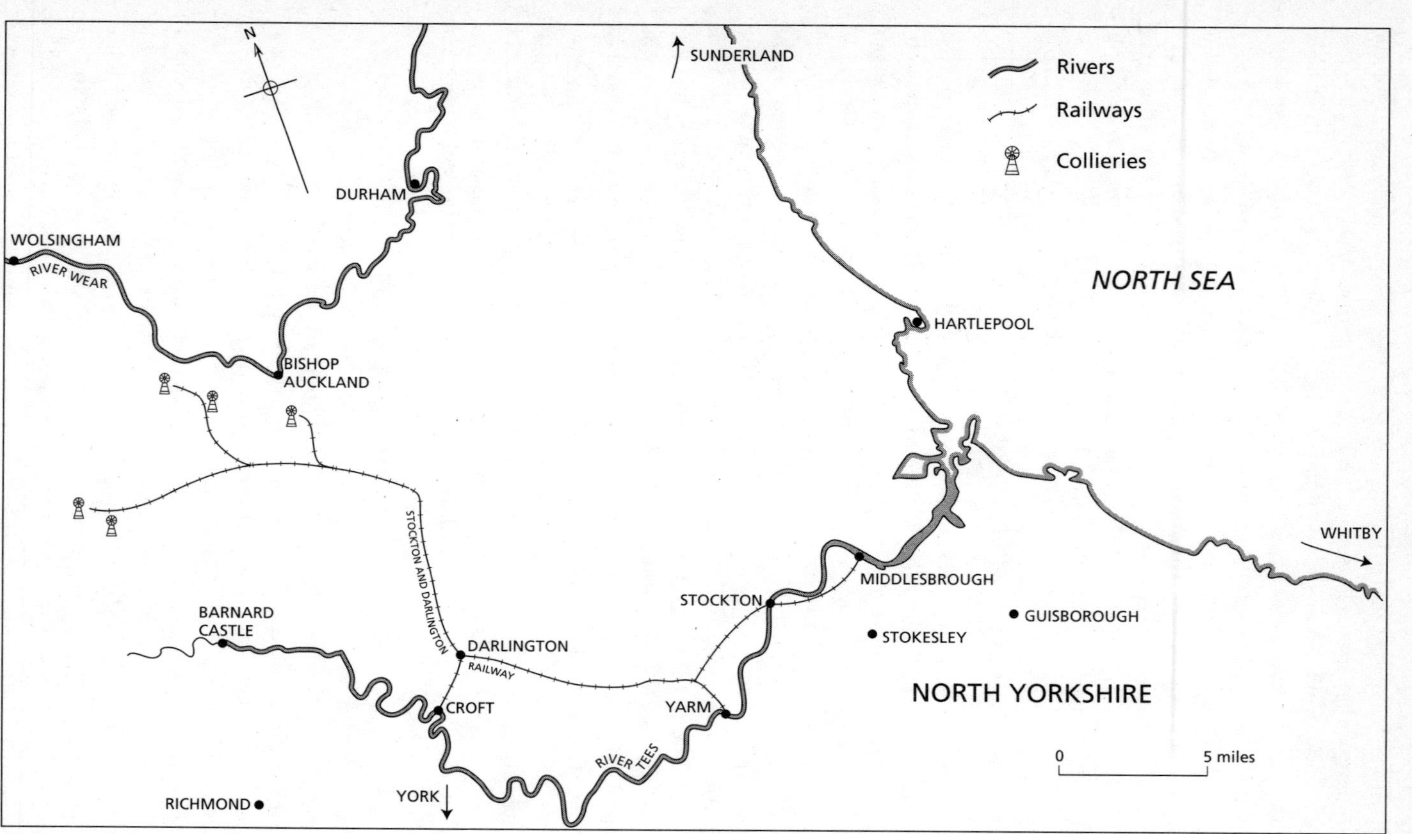

Figure 7.1 **South Durham in 1831**

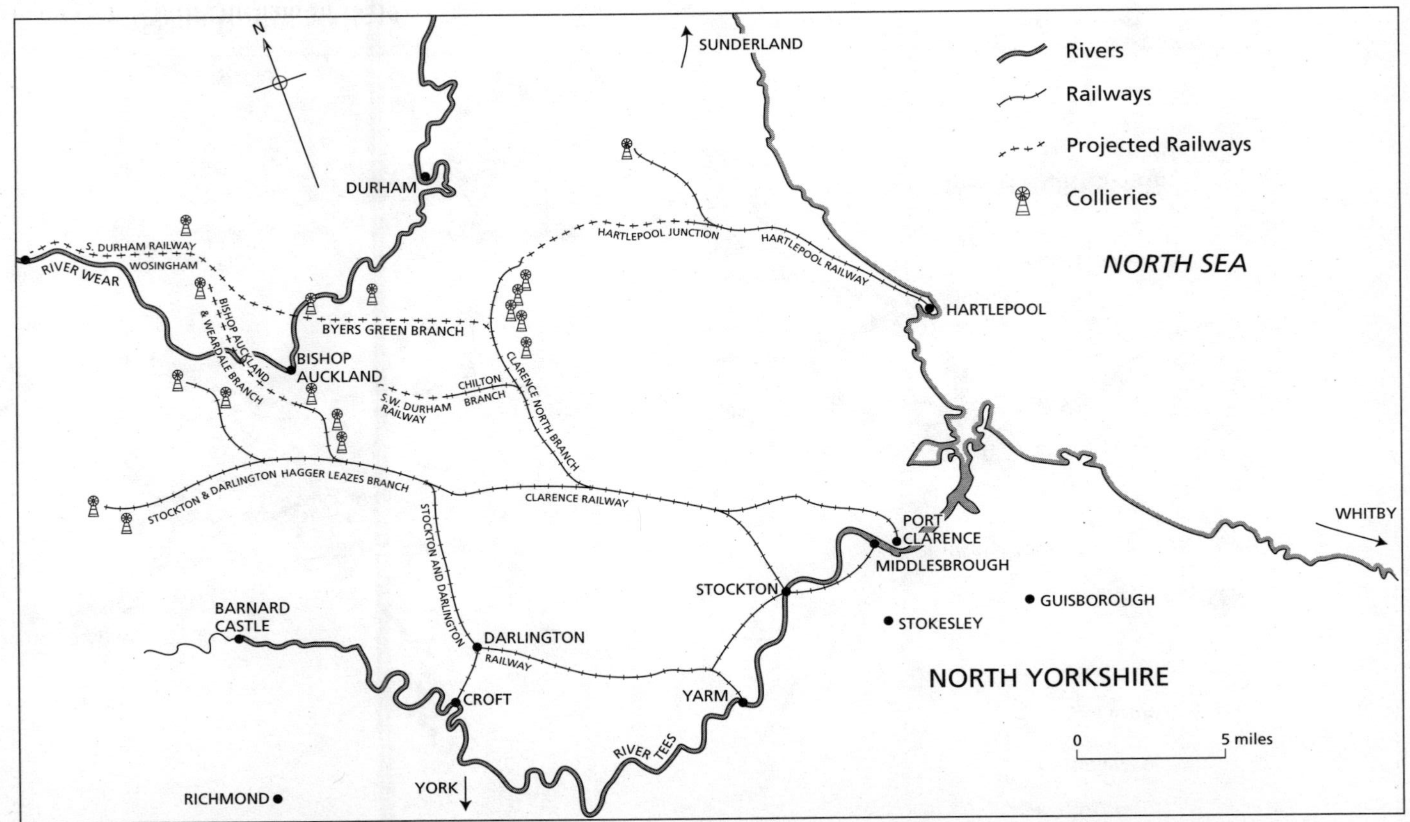

Figure 7.2 **South Durham in 1836**

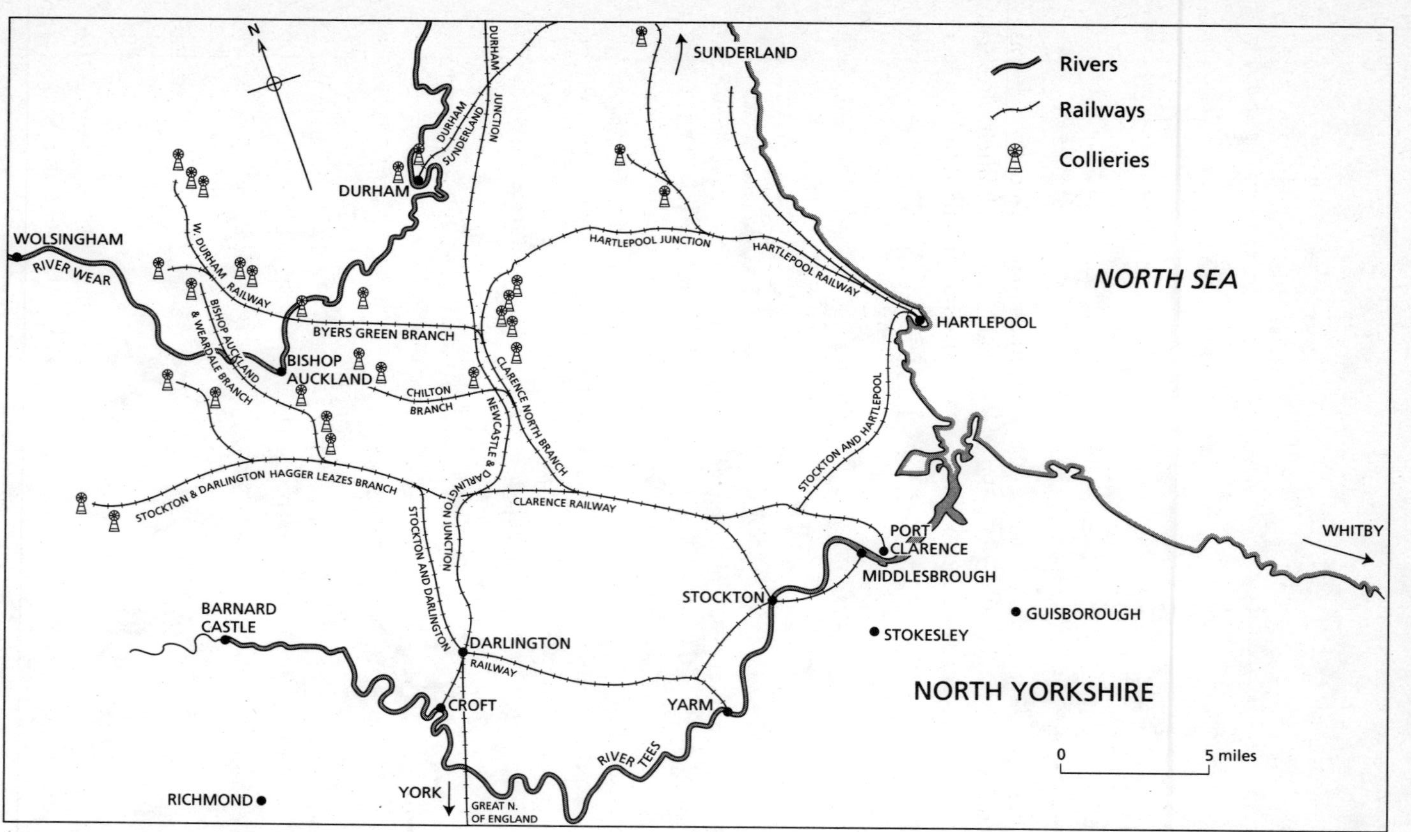

Figure 7.3 **South Durham in 1844**

financed railways were modelled, allowed the company to purchase the land over which the railway was to pass, rather than paying a 'wayleave' rental to the local landowners. For the Stockton and Darlington company with its motto of *Periculum privatum utilitas publica* – roughly translatable as 'Private risk for public benefit' – the public envisaged in the more spatially limited final version of the scheme consisted mainly of the woollen and linen manufacturers and domestic consumers of the two towns which gave the line its name and the land and coal owners along its route with goods to be transported. These, the practical beneficiaries, were the people from whom investment was forthcoming with the added incentive of an 'ample return' of 5 per cent.

But even while the Stockton and Darlington railway was under construction there was a change in the wider public's attitude to investment which was reflected in a growing disregard for the century-old law which limited partnership numbers in unincorporated companies to six and prevented the transfer of shares without prior dissolution of partnership, except when bequeathed. The unprecedented flight of capital into highly speculative ventures overseas in the early 1820s demonstrated that there were those with both the inclination and the resources to flout these regulations on a grand scale, and to force the repeal of the old limitations which occurred, coincidentally, in the same year, 1825, that saw the opening of the Stockton and Darlington railway.[7]

This deregulation had little immediate effect on railway development in the north-east because of the need for land purchasing powers. Only when confronted by intransigent opposition from business rivals did promoters in the region resort to 'non parliamentary' lines. However, the deregulation of 1825 did provide the opportunity to extend to other enterprises, where land purchase was not required, the Deed of Settlement mode of operation already used by insurance companies and also for its use as an interim stage to full incorporation.[8]

The subsequent history of the Stockton and Darlington Railway Company has been so well explored by Maurice Kirby as to require no further coverage here except in so far as it relates to issues raised in this chapter. This was the company that inaugurated the redefinition of the region but despite its pioneering quality it did not enjoy the status among local contemporaries that it has since acquired among historians. The growing exclusivity of its management, the narrow shareholding base which concentrated the eventual profits in so few hands – most of those belonging to the Pease family and their fellow Quakers – and the stroke of good fortune that gave the company and the few collieries it then served an entry into the exclusive London market, were enough to arouse the envy if not the downright animosity of those outside the privileged circle.[9] However for the eight years following its opening the Stockton and Darlington provided the only rail link between the Auckland coalfield and the Tees and the value of coal royalties over a wide area of south

Durham was measured according to their proximity to that link. Even after the appearance of rival lines the coalowners' interests remained paramount and they did not allow anti-Stockton and Darlington prejudice to get in the way of those interests. They were just as likely to support a Stockton and Darlington branch line as any other if it was going to serve their collieries.

The precise means whereby the Stockton and Darlington managers broke into the coastwise London coal trade are not entirely clarified even by Kirby, although it seems likely that a combination of moves by local investors, and the ever present metropolitan pressure for cheaper fuel, provided the incentive to take the chance offered by a temporary gap in the 'vend' regulation imposed by the Tyneside-dominated, north-eastern, coalowning establishment.[10] The apparently totally unremunerative tariff offered for coastwise shipped coal by the line's pared-down group of promoters, who had deliberately chosen not to enter the London trade for fear of both an 'establishment' backlash and the loss of support from conservative local businessmen, was undoubtedly a prime incentive in the London approach.

The Stockton and Darlington management thus found itself plunged almost from the outset into what a later writer described as 'a powerful and complex system of machinery over which it is by no means easy for either Parliament or the public to exercise any effectual control' – the London coal trade.[11]

The popular identification of Tyneside with that trade, although no longer entirely valid even in 1825, reflected a century of supply regulated by Tyneside coalowning grandees and Newcastle merchants. At the time when the Stockton and Darlington managers entered the trade, Tyneside's pre-eminence was already being challenged by two Wearside land and coalowners who were also substantial political figures, Lambton and Londonderry, neither of whom wished to see a further extension of sources of supply and a concomitant drop in prices.

Whilst gratified by the traffic generated, the Stockton and Darlington management was not really prepared for the local reaction which was to press for the building of branch lines to enable other coalowners to share the benefits. It was the Stockton and Darlington's initial financial inability, widely construed as unwillingness, to extend branches further into the coalfield, combined with its decision in 1827 to move its coal wharves away from Stockton to a new development at Middlesbrough, that helped revive south Durham and north Yorkshire support for the long-standing scheme of the Stockton-led splinter group of the original promoters which had retained the initial more ambitious concept of a 'country' stretching from Weardale to north Yorkshire.

The Clarence Railway Company

This scheme, which ultimately became the Clarence Railway Company, should not be seen merely as a focus of anti-Stockton and Darlington sentiment. In fact on more than one occasion during its development its promoters unsuccessfully sought to co-operate with the established line in order to realise their vision of a west–east transport system with the south Durham coalfield as its central link rather than its western limit. But Stockton shippers had their eyes on the coastwise trade from the beginning and resented the detour to serve Darlington manufacturers which in their view added unnecessarily to transport costs. The Stockton and Darlington decision in 1827 to move coal shipment away from Stockton was a further blow.

The list of original local shareholders in the Clarence company shows clearly the strength of support from Stockton tradespeople particularly those with shipping connections. But the interest of coalowners not served, or likely to be served, by the Stockton and Darlington, and of local notables with money to invest, is also apparent. Among these were some who had supported the first proposals and then withdrawn, and some whose connection with the trade was only indirect. There was Robert Appleby, deputy lieutenant of County Durham, who held land north of the Tees crucial to later development; William Ward Jackson of Normanby and Sir William Foulis of Ingleby, both from the south side of the Tees and neither of them coalowners, although Ward Jackson had ironstone on his estate which improved transport might make worth developing. There was also W. T. Salvin of Croxdale, a member of an old Durham Catholic landowning family which already operated a paper mill and a tile works and was looking to develop its coal royalties; and Christopher Mason of Chilton, a former banker and would-be coal exporter whose coal-bearing land, like that of the Salvins, lay in an area south of Durham city unlikely to be served by any branch of the Stockton and Darlington; and, less obviously, Henry Vansittart of Kirkleatham in north Yorkshire, grandson of a governor of Bengal, a former high sheriff of the county and a man with national political connections as well as investment capital. Vansittart is an interesting example of a locally based individual who does not seem to have had any direct business interest in the regional companies in which he invested, but who became involved from a general belief in the viability of joint stock enterprise and its importance to the local economy. He and Appleby were the most important of the initial subscribers but in terms of shareholding they were closely rivalled by one of the Stockton tradespeople, Thomas Allison Tennant, a sail cloth and rope manufacturer whose elder brother Christopher was the leading local promoter of the line.[12]

By the time the act of incorporation for the Clarence railway got through Parliament in 1828, Christopher Tennant had become a well known figure locally. It was he, as a former sailor, who named the line in homage to the Duke of Clarence, at this date the Lord High Admiral and subsequently King William IV. It was Tennant who was involved from the outset in the various proposals to open up the coal reserves of South Durham by improved transport facilities and who during the 1820s emerged as leader of the group which continued to support the longer line from Weardale to the Tees. Despite his local fame, biographical details are hard to come by. There is no indication of whether the sail cloth and rope making business run by his younger brother was a family concern and, whatever his maritime past, by the mid-1820s Christopher's main source of income was a coal-using lime-burning plant close to the upper part of the Stockton and Darlington railway.[13] The lime came from Weardale and was in increasing demand as an agricultural fertilizer, hence his – and others' – support for the longer line serving a greater diversity of interests. Early joint stock railway companies provided a means for bringing together such interests through improved transport. Clearly at this stage in this part of county Durham most of those who subscribed, whether to the Stockton and Darlington or to the Clarence, were looking not simply for dividends but also to benefit their own enterprises, or as landowners to explore the potential value of what they possessed.

Christopher Tennant is interesting not only as a possibly typical element in an evolving regional business network but also as an early example of a new type of entrepreneur. He became an almost professional 'projector' who was consulted on most of the subsequent joint stock projects in the region. Although there were those who treated such 'projectors' as objects of derision, Tennant's undoubted commitment to the wider interests of the region in which he operated seems to have preserved his standing with local company promoters.[14]

He is also interesting as part of a generation to whom the speed of joint stock financed economic change in the region offered a chance to enter the world of business that might otherwise have been denied them.[15] To Tennant and a number of those mentioned by name in this chapter, this was an opportunity for involvement in promotional and entrepreneurial activity; for others advancement was based on the demand for technological expertise. The much-trumpeted Stephensons were archetypal figures from a whole generation of engineers, surveyors, builders, inventors and manufacturers who emerged in the region during the quarter century that followed the opening of the Stockton and Darlington and the relaxation of the regulations governing company formation.

Shipping and the London trade

With the wisdom of hindsight and knowledge of the extent to which after 1850 the Teesside iron industry, using south Durham produced coke and Cleveland ironstone would come to dominate the regional economy and modify regional identity yet again, the historian can afford to be critical of the south Durham coalowners' and railway promoters' earlier obsession with the London market. Yet given the long-established social and economic pre-eminence of the Tyneside coal trade and the more recent rise to prominence of owners in north Durham, it is understandable that coalowners in a relatively backward area like the southern half of the county should seek to enter this hitherto exclusive club once the opportunity presented itself. Moreover, it is arguable that the mechanisms developed to finance and implement the first phase of changing regional identity through improved transport systems, were necessary preconditions of its further development.

The importance of local landowning and coalowning involvement in the initial lists of Clarence subscribers should not be allowed to obscure another of the company's fundamental differences from the Stockton and Darlington. Not only had it a much wider shareholding base but at a general estimate something like a third of its capital came from shipping. What any study of the expansion of the coal industry based primarily on railway development tends to underestimate is the importance of shipping in that 'complex system of machinery' that operated the London trade. Thus it was not only the number of shareholders but the nature of their business involvement and the sources of their capital that differentiated the two companies. The economic development of the region was based not only on coal and railways but also on shipping and the Clarence had been aptly named for it was fundamentally a shippers' company .

Within the London trade it was the normal, though not universal, practice for the shipper – whether an individual master, a partnership or, in the period under consideration, a joint stock shipping company – to buy the coal from the owners at the quayside and it was they, the shippers, who sold it to the London distributors. The more cheaply the coal could be brought to the shipping point, the greater their profit margins in what was from every point of view a capitally-intensive and risk-ridden business. How much of the existing coal shipping in 1828 was London based and financed is impossible to assess. A London office address or vessel registration often masked family as well as business connections with the north-east. There were London links in the Tyneside trade that went back over a century. London shippers or coal factors had shares in Tyneside collieries, and Tyneside coalowners and shippers sent their sons to work for London coal factors to learn the business.[16] The legal restriction of partnership numbers to six before the deregulation of 1825 applied also to shipping. The arrival of Teesside coal on the London market, coinciding as it did with the relaxation of regulations on partnership numbers, favoured the creation of joint stock shipping companies. However, although these companies figure in newspaper advertisements from the early

1830s onwards, it is difficult to know where to look for details of share ownership if indeed such details still exist, or to what extent they were concerned with coal-carrying, since technically joint stock shipping companies which *bought* the coal they carried remained illegal until 1836.[17]

The potential development of coal-shipping links between the Thames and the Tees may have been what brought in Henry Blanshard, a London shipowner, as a major shareholder in the Clarence railway. His other main business interest was in marine insurance which like other areas of insurance was already moving into the joint stock mode of operation even before 1825. Blanshard had family connections in north Yorkshire[18] and was friendly with Sir William Chaytor, a well-known local landowner and businessman and one of those early supporters of the Stockton and Darlington who had withdrawn over the company's failure to provide branch lines and its increasing domination by the Pease family. Chaytor's enormous surviving correspondence provides a vivid if idiosyncratic view of business and politics in the region during the 1830s. He dabbled, not always very profitably, in railways, banking, lead mining, harbour development and coal mining as well as county and Durham City politics. It was probably only the fact that his own coal measures were closer to the Stockton and Darlington than the Clarence that kept him from investing in the latter despite his continuing friendship with Blanshard. His were the sorts of cross-business linkages that built up the network of intelligence and investment that, it is the contention of this chapter, were among the elements that helped remould the regional identity.[19]

Confronting the establishment

Blanshard, both as a shipper and because of family connections, may have been interested in the early proposals for a transport link between Weardale and the Tees. Certainly at one point he and Tennant considered buying into a colliery not far from the latter's lime kilns.[20] From 1827 onwards when he outbid the Peases for the royalty of Coxhoe to the south-east of Durham City, however, Henry Blanshard identified himself totally with the Clarence and became not only one of its major shareholders but also ultimately the chairman of the board of management. Indeed once the railway became operational he seems to have abandoned most of his other business interests and he was still actively engaged on the railway's affairs until within weeks of his death some twenty years later.[21]

Blanshard's purchase of the Coxhoe royalty made him a Durham county freeholder and when he proudly claimed in 1830 that, as such, he had 'fought hard to put down the power of these great coal lords',[22] he was referring to another potent element in contemporary regional consciousness – opposition to the north-eastern coalowning establishment which had been based on

Tyneside, and was by then also dominating Wearside. There were in existence two committees of coalowners, one for those shipping from the Tyne, the other for those shipping from the Wear, who tried, not always successfully, to maintain the price of coal on the London market at what they considered a remunerative level, by limiting the output of collieries shipping from these two rivers.[23] Shipments from the Tees were still not covered by this regulation when the miners' strikes of 1831–32 in the Tyne and Wearside coalfields offered Teesside coalowners and shippers a virtually open market and in doing so consolidated the financial stability of the Stockton and Darlington Railway and the limited number of collieries it served. At national and local level, the years between 1830 and 1832 were ones in which the principles of political economy and parliamentary reform were hotly debated. But so far as the coal trade was concerned they were years in which the pressure of the north-eastern coalowning establishment helped achieve a legislative simplification of the London end of the trade whilst fighting off any threat to its own monopolistic activities whether inside or outside Parliament. Once the miners' strikes were over the two existing coalowners' committees invited the Tees owners to form their own committee and collaborate in the maintenance of the regulation. As the Tees owners at this date were those using the Stockton and Darlington, this was tantamount to inviting the Pease family to join the coalowning establishment. One of its number had already entered the political establishment with the election of Joseph Pease as an MP for the newly created south Durham division of the county. Despite the Peases' Liberal anti-monopolistic general political alignment, as coalowners and railway operators they were prepared to use all the means available to check the encroachments of any rival enterprise. So in 1828 they reputedly spent over £1,700 lobbying Parliament to block the Clarence bill[24] and in 1836 made common cause with the Tory Lord Londonderry to prevent the passage of measures to extend the Clarence network.

Within the geographical region the ultimate effect of the economic and political changes of the early 1830s was to strengthen the control of a coalowning establishment, still dominated by Tyneside and Wearside interests despite the Teesside entrée, and potentially to enhance the role of the Clarence and other south Durham 'independent' joint stock companies in opposing it.

Communication networks: banks

Of these 'independent' joint stock companies, one of the most important in the long term was probably the Darlington District Bank. In 1826 provincial joint stock enterprise had been given a further boost by the relaxation of the Bank of England's monopoly of joint stock banking. It is a measure of the growing confidence of the regional economy that, despite the banking preeminence of Newcastle upon Tyne, the first joint stock bank in the north-east was the Darlington District set up in 1831. For the next decade joint stock banks became an essential adjunct to company promotion in all sectors of the economy and existing partnership banks often eventually converted to joint stock operation to draw in extra capital.[25]

The Darlington District Bank joint stock bank seems to have been founded partly to supply banking provision south of the Tees but also probably to establish an alternative non-Quaker bank in Darlington should the existing Skinners' partnership bank fail, as it had almost done in 1825. The initial shareholders in the joint stock bank were thirty 'gentlemen, merchants and tradesmen' of whom, despite the title, only six were from Darlington; another six were south Durham landowners and of the remainder at least ten were from the north Yorkshire rather than the Durham side of the Tees. This geographical spread was reflected in the location of the branches which, apart from one in Stockton and one in Barnard Castle, were all in the market towns of north Yorkshire.[26]

The bank at its inception had no direct connection with the Clarence railway Company who banked with Skinners'. The Skinners, father and son, are listed by Kirby in 1822 as major shareholders in the Stockton and Darlington and also as Quakers but they were actually Methodists.[27] This fact, and the input of Quaker bankers from outside the region into the Stockton and Darlington, may account for their transfer of allegiance to the Clarence. Another reason may have been that the source of their capital lay in shipping – Whitby whaling. There is no space in this chapter for an exploration of Whitby's claims for inclusion within the region but it is worth noting that the town was not only a mineral-shipping and shipbuilding centre but also a source of banking capital.

Although there has been some attempt to examine the discount networks and correspondence systems of provincial partnership banks,[28] there seems to have been no similar work done on their joint stock counterparts. There have been suggestions that the advent of joint stock banking lessened provincial dependence on the London money market but this was not the case in the north-east whose coal trade-based economy by its very nature relied on the credit facilities offered by London houses. As the metropolitan-induced financial crisis of the late 1840s demonstrated, this could have disastrous and unforeseeable effects on the fragile credit structures that underpinned many joint stock concerns, but this was not apparent in the rising markets of the previous decade.

The extension of banking provision resulting from the relaxation of the law in 1826, followed by the repeal in 1833 of the old, long-evaded usury law limiting interest rates on loans to 5 per cent, had an incalculable effect on the volume of commercial transactions taking place, particularly in a region already undergoing a process of industrial development, and these commercial transactions by their very nature created networks of communication the ramifications of which, like most aspects of early joint stock, have yet to be explored.

Communication networks: solicitors

Banking was one such network; another, arguably equally important, was provided by firms of solicitors. The existing professional contacts between firms of local solicitors were further extended by the increased business generated by railway and mining enterprise since every joint stock company had to have a solicitor. Within the context of south Durham railway development and entry into the London coal trade, existing links between local firms of solicitors and their London counterparts also assumed added importance as metropolitan solicitors became involved in easing the passage of bills of incorporation through Parliament or assessing the merits of rival claims in lawsuits.[29] Frequently professional and family connections overlapped as in the case of another major shareholder in the Clarence, Folliot Stokes. Stokes was, like Blanshard, London-born, a partner in a stockbroking business set up by his father in the City, but his sister was married to G. L. Hollingsworth whose family had interests in Darlington, Weardale and Sedgefield. Hollingsworth and Stokes' brother were partners in the London firm of solicitors Stokes Hollingsworth and Tyerman which handled the affairs of several joint stock companies both in London and in the region. But that was not the full extent of the linkage. In the period before 1815 another of Stokes' brothers, Hollingsworth and, for a time, a man already mentioned as a major Durham shareholder in the railway company, Christopher Mason, had also been partners in a Darlington based bank which fell victim to the post-Napoleonic wars recession.[30]

It is not merely the family and business connections that are important here but the nature of the businesses involved. Solicitors and bankers acted as financial advisers to their clients and were the chief outlets for the initial share issue of joint stock companies. Stockbroking and share dealing, before the surge in railway speculation, were essentially metropolitan functions; in the provinces in the early days of joint stock and even until the 1840s, after the initial issue, shares changed hands, if at all, along with other commodities through local auctioneers.[31]

The London connection and regional initiative

Blanshard and Stokes were far from being the only London based shareholders in the Clarence. Indeed the evidence points to a deliberate attempt by

Tennant and Blanshard to bring in individuals linked to shipping or to the London end of the coal trade. There were also some with family or business connections in the north-east. Involvement with the trade, or family loyalty, meant that the major early London investors remained loyal throughout the vicissitudes that beset the company. The extent of their stake was also a factor. Smaller and later investors seem to have been understandably more volatile as alternative investment opportunities became available and returns were slow to materialise.[32]

It might be argued that, however close the family and business connections, the location of substantial shareholding outside the geographical area to be served by the Clarence railway invalidates the notion of that company's centrality to a contemporary consciousness of regional identity based on investment in public works to benefit the local economy. But for this argument to be tenable it would be necessary to show both that the London investors were the main beneficiaries of the enterprise and that they formulated the policy of the company. The first is clearly not the case. In terms of dividends all the major investors, local as well as London, lost more than they gained, although as participants in one or other branch of the coal trade or as local suppliers of material for railway construction they may have recouped themselves in other ways. The question of policy making is more difficult and becomes crucial after 1833 when, as explained below, the control of company finance was moved to London. However, despite the increasingly improved communication between the metropolis and the south Durham coalfield, the managers in London remained at the mercy of those on the spot and it is clear from the minutes of the London committee that within two years the initiative had returned to the north-east, and the lines of communication provided by Stokes and Blanshard were repeatedly used to convey only such information as those in the north-east deemed it prudent to reveal.[33]

The transfer of management to London was the direct result of a financial crisis that confronted the company in 1833 just as the main line was almost completed and parliamentarily sanctioned branch lines under construction. There was provision for an incorporated company in this situation to apply to the Exchequer for a loan the granting of which was contingent upon the availability of funds and the proven probity and viability of the enterprise. The Stockton and Darlington company at a similar stage of its construction had also applied for such a loan although without success. It seems likely that the Clarence acquired its loan precisely because of its City connections. The negotiation was done by John Labouchere, a partner in Williams Deacon, the company's London bank and a shareholder, but the security was provided by Christopher Mason whose coal royalties were on the branch nearest completion.

Labouchere insisted that one of the conditions imposed by the Exchequer loan commissioners was the transfer of financial control to a committee of leading London shareholders with himself in the chair.[34] The understandable opposition to the move from north-eastern shareholders was only overcome by the prospect that, in the event of non-completion, the Quakers would consolidate their hold over the region, a fear which had assumed more substance with the election of Joseph Pease to Parliament and which had been further reinforced by the revival of the 'vend' regulation and its extension to south Durham collieries shipping from the Tees.[35]

The evidence of the company minutes suggests that Labouchere saw his role as protecting the interests of the bank and that he had little grasp of, or interest in, the detail of what was happening in the region. Blanshard and Stokes remained the chief managerial links with those actually involved in the construction and the running of the line, and in Blanshard's case, given his own coal royalty at Coxhoe, with any other potential transport developments in the area to the south and east of Durham City .

The Hartlepool harbour scheme

The earlier business connections between Blanshard and Tennant and the personal friendship between him and Sir William Chaytor may well account for Blanshard's subsequent ambivalence about what had been happening further north while the Clarence was under construction. Again, as with the wider vision of the 'country' to be served by the first improved transport link, the key figure seems to have been Tennant. For in 1831, just as the construction of the Clarence was getting under way, he gave his backing to, and took employment with, another joint stock company developing the harbour at Hartlepool. Hartlepool, situated on a bay to the north of the mouth of the Tees, had declined from a position of some importance at an earlier period to virtually a fishing village and a not particularly fashionable watering place. The Hetton mining company, which in 1822 had achieved the technological breakthrough of extracting coal from below the limestone layer north-east of Durham City, had considered building a short railway to ship its coal out of Hartlepool but lacked the capital to improve the silted-up harbour. By 1831 joint stock finance offered a possible solution. In that year a partnership developing the coal measures at Thornley somewhat to the south of the Hetton colliery, unwilling to have its shipping arrangements at the mercy of either the Pease-dominated development at Middlesbrough to the south or Lord Londonderry's newly opened Seaham harbour to the north, sought advice from Christopher Tennant about reviving the harbour and railway scheme on a joint stock basis. Thornley was about twelve miles from Hartlepool and only a matter of five or six miles from Blanshard's Coxhoe royalty and a projected branch of the Clarence.[36]

Hartlepool's harbour fell within the jurisdiction of Stockton so for

Stockton shippers there was not necessarily a clash of interest in this new development but this was not the case for Stockton tradespeople. The only Stockton manufacturer among the initial investors in the Hartlepool enterprise was Tennant's brother. There was some overlap of shareholding between the Clarence and the Hartlepool companies among local land owners but the Durham City connections of the Hetton and Thornley coal companies provided the largest single group of investors, drawn primarily from members of the legal profession that flourished in the county and diocesan centre and reinforced by their family and business contacts. Among the largest investors were the holders of the Thornley royalty and Sir William Chaytor who had strong family as well as business connections with the Durham City legal profession. One of his sons had sat as MP for the city and his partnership bank based in Sunderland, but with a large input of Whitby capital, had a branch in Durham which aspired to handle the dock and railway company's account. Although the list of initial Hartlepool Dock and Railway Company subscribers included at least two London bankers, one of them John Hinton Tritton of Barclay Tritton, a relative of Sir William's, there was markedly less London capital involved than in the Clarence railway. Despite financial problems similar to those experienced by the Clarence, by the autumn of 1834 the harbour was beginning to ship its first coal.[37]

The consolidation of the network

Thus by the beginning of 1835 there was already, in south Durham and north Yorkshire, the basis of an economic region whose services, financed by joint stock investment, included railways, harbour installations, shipping and banking. But as yet the network was not self-financing and apart from the more limited Stockton and Darlington, the companies involved were labouring under a burden of accumulated indebtedness. The promoters of the Hartlepool Dock and Railway Company correctly felt that without a longer rail link to serve more collieries the new dock would not be a commercial proposition. There was no capital to build such a link and any attempt to gain parliamentary authorisation for it was likely to run into opposition not only from the Tyneside and Wearside coalowning establishment but also from the Peases, and even from alienated Stockton investors in the Clarence.

The Clarence itself was in a different but comparable situation, with branch lines constructed to serve as yet not fully productive collieries and insufficient income from existing traffic to provide the capital required to build a further branch on which the authorisation was rapidly running out. The needs of the limestone producers of lower Weardale were still unserved. But for both the Hartlepool company and the Clarence, as for the region in general, the needs of the coastwise coal trade remained paramount.[38]

Limited in vision, in retrospect, these south Durham entrepreneurs may have been and starved of capital by over zealous London bankers doubtful of provincial business acumen, but in fact all the evidence for 1835–36 points to vigorous regional initiative as the overlapping groups endeavoured to relieve their common frustration by further joint stock enterprise.

In October and November 1835 advertisements appeared in the *Durham County Advertiser* for two new railway companies, the South Durham Railway and the South West Durham Railway.[39] Ostensibly these were independent promotions but in fact they were part of a determined effort to use joint stock to consolidate the region's economy by developing the potential of the Clarence's branch lines. They also demonstrate the ways in which local interest groups could manipulate Clarence policy to serve their ends. Although the advertisements did not appear until the last months of the year, the first of these promotions was set on foot as early as May when the Clarence management committee received a proposal from a group of businessmen headed by John Charles Ord, a York based solicitor, which was seeking to develop a colliery at Roddymoor on the western edge of the south Durham coalfield and was preparing to set up a company to build a line to link up with either the Chilton or the Byers Green branch of the Clarence. The Chilton branch was almost completed, the Byers Green branch not yet started, but the colliery developers seemed to be prepared to offer collateral security on the latter as giving a more direct route. There was also, although they did not admit this to the Clarence committee until several months later, the possibility of an alternative shipping point via a further link to the Hartlepool railway and docks. By October the group supporting this proposal had been expanded to include Weardale limestone and lead producers and the line envisaged began to echo those earlier ideas of a Weardale–Tees link, but with an additional shipping point at Hartlepool. This was the scheme advertised as the South Durham railway.[40] It had Tennant's support, but once it became clear that the railway promoters were going to use the Byers Green link he also proposed a much less ambitious extension of the Chilton branch into the coal-bearing area to the east of Bishop Auckland.[41] This was the South-West Durham railway (see figure 7.2.)

The two railway schemes were advertised contemporaneously with the Great North of England Railway project which, unlike the existing east–west coal trade-oriented railways of the north-east, was envisaged as linking urban centres from south to north, initially between York and Newcastle and ultimately between London and Edinburgh. At first the Clarence management was open-minded about this proposal but when it became clear that the involvement of Joseph Pease would ensure that any linkages would not be via branches of the Clarence, it put considerable energy and money it could ill afford into opposing it. Tennant went on record as publicly accusing Pease of wanting 'to get possession of the county'.[42]

The Clarence management committee minutes note that at a meeting on 5 December 1835 a group of Durham coalowners declared themselves prepared to take half the shares in Tennant's proposed South-West Durham line if the Clarence shareholders would take the rest, and if the proposal could be perceived as emanating from the Clarence. There is no evidence that, at this stage, there was any agreement to that effect, but as explained below the coalowners were themselves looking towards joint stock as a solution to their developmental problems and would then demand a *quid pro quo*. It also seems likely that there was collusion from within the ranks of the Clarence management team, for Blanshard had been in the north-east during November 1835.

Further research on the individuals involved in episodes such as this can uncover unexpected information that highlights the complexity of the regional and even inter-regional connections. For example, John Charles Ord, the solicitor to the South Durham railway, was not only a colliery developer; he also had interests on the London coal exchange and seems to have been responsible for bringing a number of York City shareholders into the subsequent joint stock coal company.[43] Similarly at a later stage another leading protagonist in local joint stock enterprise, Ralph Ward Jackson, tapped substantial sources of Lancashire capital through his wife's relatives.[44]

The Durham County Coal Company

At what stage, and by whom, the scheme to launch a joint stock coal company was conceived, it is difficult to say. It was clearly intended to tie into the two railway projects. Again, one of those involved was a solicitor, Thomas Wheldon, the Barnard Castle based solicitor to the South-West Durham Railway Company, who was also the agent for John Bowes whose mineral royalties in the Evenwood area of south-west Durham were being developed by a partnership led by Charles Barrett, the manager of the Darlington District bank.[45] Bowes was Pease's parliamentary colleague for the South Durham division but this did not prevent the Stockton and Darlington management from overcharging and obstructing coals from his royalties when he transferred to the rival line. Bowes later distanced himself from the joint stock coal company promoters but he was happy to accept Barrett's proposals to pull in more capital to develop his collieries and he certainly gave parliamentary support to the railway bills.[46]

Barrett's development proposals, like Ord's approach to the Clarence board, were made in May 1835. This could have been coincidental, but it is clear that by the end of that year there was some element of collaboration between the various groups although it is not echoed in the Clarence's London management committee minutes. Wheldon, Blanshard, Tennant and Barrett were in close communication with each other in November and December

1835. Wheldon wrote to Barrett at the Coal Exchange, 'I count on your attending the meeting on Saturday. The result of your interview will materially influence all proceedings in the North . . . All must depend on the acts of the London gentlemen. . . . We must be extremely cautious in all our proceedings'.[47]

What Barrett was seeking was financial support, in the short run for the extension of the Evenwood venture, but in the long term for a joint stock coal company which in addition could help finance Ord's Roddymoor project and other under-capitalised coalowning partnerships along the routes of the proposed rail links. It was to be, as the prospectus when it was issued declared, a challenge to the coalowning establishment, 'by a combination of Energy and the Employment of Capital on an extended scale'.[48] However, the coal company promotion seems to have remained a well-kept secret during the first months of 1836 when the South-West Durham railway scheme was before Parliament. The Stockton and Darlington management, having denounced this proposal as a 'sinister attempt to injure their line by depriving it of traffic', offered it 'determined and unyielding opposition' and Joseph Pease made common cause with Lord Londonderry to attack it as a 'Clarence job' and to elicit as much damaging information as he could about the Clarence's precarious financial situation. As a result the bill was lost.[49]

The South Durham railway proposal was less easy to dismiss. In the form in which it reached Parliament, not only did it draw its support from individuals representing a wider range of local economic interests, but some of those individuals were important members of south Durham society whose political connections were not to be trifled with.[50] It was also accompanied by well-orchestrated anti-monopolist demonstrations, parliamentary petitions and letters to the Press attacking the operation of the coal trade regulation in the north-east as against the interests of independent producers and the inhabitants of the metropolis and contrary to the principles of political economy. The railway bill got through the Commons despite Pease using funds from the northern coal owners' committees to subsidise the opposition, but it was defeated in the Lords by members of the landholding coalowning aristocracy led once again by Lord Londonderry.[51]

It is uncertain whether either Londonderry or anyone else involved in the opposition to the South Durham railway bill was aware at the time of any connection between the railway and the coal company but the fact that Londonderry's agents in the north-east stepped in to prevent the sale of an independent colliery to a group of the coal company's promoters suggests that he knew that something was afoot.[52] It was a further telling example of the power of the coalowning aristocracy.

Advertisements for the coal company appeared in both the local and the national press at the end of May and the beginning of June 1836. Although

Charles Barrett resigned his post as manager of the Darlington District bank in order to devote his time to the new venture, his carefully chosen managers in its north Yorkshire branches played a key role in the establishment of the company through the sale of shares to their clients, thereby consolidating still further the existing cross-county boundary links established by the Clarence and to a lesser extent the Stockton and Darlington.[53]

Barrett himself is another of those figures whose varied interests typify the way in which the regional network operated, and whose business acumen had emerged through the openings provided by joint stock. The fourth son of a long-dead Stockton master mariner, trained as a clerk in Skinners' bank, by the late 1820s he was already investing in mining ventures and acquiring shares in ships. His relations by marriage came to include the coal 'fitter' or agent to the Clarence railway and one of the leading Stockton shipbuilders.[54] Furthermore he was, like the Skinners, a Wesleyan Methodist whose religious affiliation brought him into contact with other Methodist businessmen and potential investors in the north-east.[55]

The anti-monopolist agitation that accompanied the debates on the two railway bills was not only designed to put the case of the London consumer against the operation of the north-east's price-fixing cartel, it was also intended to remove the last legal impediment to free trade in coal – the Act of 1788 which forbade partnerships of more than five persons within the trade. This was achieved when the resulting committee of enquiry recommended the repeal of the Act 'to leave the coal trade free . . . to the competition of capital and free enterprise'.[56] This legalised joint stock coalmining and coalshipping companies, but did nothing to stop the operation of the coalowners' committees in the north-east trade.

Those frustrated by the defeat of the railway bills represented a majority of actual or potential investors in a multiplicity of industrial concerns in the region. Nor was it merely a question of the disappointed expectations of producers of goods; both the Hartlepool company and the Clarence were now facing possible takeover and sale by the Exchequer loan commissioners for failure to pay the interest on their borrowing. The position of the Clarence was rendered the more acute by the sudden death of Christopher Mason, the guarantor of their loan, and the dawning realisation by those who had had business dealings with him that his estate as it stood, with his collieries not yet in full production, was close to bankruptcy.[57] The processes of probate concealed this from the outside world, including the Stockton and Darlington management, for the next eighteen months, but even without that knowledge the damaging allegations about the Clarence's finances made in the course of the debates on the South-West Durham railway bill had undermined public confidence in the ability of the company to build the Byers Green branch before the expiry of its parliamentary authorisation in 1837.[58]

At local level such loss of confidence was largely, but not entirely, offset by fear of a Stockton and Darlington takeover. The promoters of the South Durham railway almost immediately announced their determination to proceed as an unincorporated company using wayleaves to run a line out of Weardale and into the coalfield but, in the absence of the Byers Green link to the Clarence system, might well, albeit reluctantly, have accepted instead a possible alternative link southwards to the Stockton and Darlington.[59]

So the financing of the Byers Green branch became crucial to the survival of the network. Ord, in collusion with Stokes, tried unsuccessfully to persuade the other promoters of the South Durham line to take financial responsibility for the branch; but they were also keeping their options open in case there was a more advantageous offer from the Stockton and Darlington. In a hectic round of negotiations during July and early August 1836, Stokes and the promoters of the coal company reached an understanding that, in effect, the coal company would share the responsibility for the construction of the Byers Green branch by setting up a subsidiary company for which half of the capital would be raised by the coal company and half through the Clarence. The Clarence management committee minutes suggest that even some of the company's major investors were kept in ignorance of these manoeuvrings so that this outcome was presented as the eleventh hour salvation of a stricken company rather than the adoption of a locally initiated move towards consolidation in the face of the continuing threat from the Stockton and Darlington compounded by the growing risk of Stockton and Darlington collaboration with George Hudson.[60]

Thus in the short term at least the agreement with the coal company to build the Byers Green branch enabled Stokes and Blanshard as Clarence representatives at the relevant meetings to avert the danger of south Durham coalowners transferring their support to a Stockton and Darlington-linked counter proposal.[61]

The detail of these tortuous negotiations is relevant to the proposition put forward in this chapter because it shows not only provincial initiative in manipulating metropolitan opinion but also the networks of communication by which such initiative was sustained. However, the consolidation that might have resulted from the shared disappointment of the Hartlepool company and the Clarence at the loss of the South Durham railway bill, and their apparent reprieve by the coal company's financing of the Byers Green branch, was prevented by the London board's fear that the revival of the scheme to provide a junction between the Hartlepool railway and the Byers Green branch, instigated to save the Hartlepool company would ultimately siphon off revenue from the parent company.[62] In financial terms this was probably correct but the south Durham coalowners were more interested in getting their coal on to the London market at a profit than in providing revenue for the London shareholders in the Clarence, and the 'Hartlepool Junction' railway bill had a relatively easy passage through Parliament precisely because Pease and Londonderry considered it would take revenue from the Clarence.

A financial region?

It was during this hectic summer of 1836 that the Chancellor of the Exchequer endorsed joint stock as the motor of economic development, declaring it to be 'one of the great discoveries of modern times'.[63] Within the region the extended use of joint stock became a crucial element in a struggle to control that development which tacitly recognised the existence and identity of the region over which the struggle was taking place. By the end of the year independent coalowners like Chaytor and Salvin of Croxdale were wondering whether it might not be to their advantage to sell developmental rights to the coal company. As the former commented, 'I hear they are taking almost the whole County of Durham'.[64]

This was manifestly an exaggeration. The coal trade establishment still controlled access to the London market and, after holding out for the better part of two years, the new company found itself forced to accept the vend limitation. But as a condition of that acceptance it secured representation on the Tees owners' committee to offset the existing domination by the Stockton and Darlington interest upon which the coal trade establishment relied for support.[65]

It is indicative of the speed at which industrial and commercial development was taking place nationally that hardly two years after the launch of the Durham County Coal Company, individuals within it seem to have decided to seek outlets and investment outside the London market. It would be over simplistic to attribute this simply to the company's need to tap new sources of capital although that undoubtedly played a part, or to irritation with those control mechanisms within the London trade that still worked for the benefit of the major producers. A proportion of south Durham coal had always continued to be consumed by local industry and the scale of that consumption had increased steadily in response to the demands of the railways themselves as well as those of other industrial developments. Barrett had attracted investment not only from fellow Methodist iron founders on Wearside but also from Tyneside industrialists, among them one Thomas Cummings Gibson who, in addition to owning ships, operated a range of coal-consuming enterprises, brick and tile works, paint, lamp black and coal tar manufactories and lime-burning works.[66] As both a shipper and a processor he had contacts with East Anglian maltsters and brewers, and processors in Liverpool and Edinburgh. So in 1838 a group headed by Gibson and the Sunderland iron founders hived off a working colliery from the parent company to set up what was ostensibly an independent new company drawing much of its capital from industrialists outside the immediate region who used coal or coke for processing purposes.[67]

As in the case of the London shareholders in the Clarence or the Durham County Coal Company, the extent of extra-regional capital invested in the Northern Mining Company must raise the question of how far this invalidates the notion of a regional financial identity. In this case there can be even less doubt that the enterprise was firmly in the hands of the promoters and their associates. Shareholders in places as far apart as Norfolk, Edinburgh, Liverpool and even Exeter could have little control over the disposal of their capital in the south Durham coalfield. Similarly, although Gibson and two of the other leading promoters of the new company came from outside the more strictly defined region and brought in two collieries from the Lanchester area of north Durham, the main thrust of the new operation was to develop the good coking coal along the branches of the Clarence railway.[68]

The retention of regional initiative was also related to the structure of the coal companies themselves, for neither of them sought parliamentary incorporation. They operated like joint stock banks or insurance companies, under a Deed of Settlement. In the first instance Charles Barrett had gone to London to get extra share capital for the specific collieries that he and his associates had undertaken to develop on the Strathmore royalties around Evenwood and that J. C. Ord and his partners were developing at Roddymoor. The only way in which this could be financed was as a joint stock company but the electoral registers show the names of individual shareholders as attached to particular collieries. In fact the management teams of the two concerns seem to have oscillated uneasily between behaving like a corporate entity and acting as agents, linking groups of shareholders to particular royalties or to existing collieries whose owners were seeking development capital. In either case they retained control within the region.[69]

These developments, however, did not alter the regional perception of railways as an adjunct to shipping since the coal and coke for processing unless used in the region was still largely seaborne and, despite the development of north–south passenger and freight carrying link lines, the fortunes of the railway companies of south Durham remained tied to shipping and the coastal trade.

There may have been a further factor in the decision to launch the second coal company. In 1837 the Stockton and Darlington sponsored railway project, from which Stokes and Blanshard had turned local support in the troubled summer of the previous year, received parliamentary sanction. It now became a race to provide an extension to the skeletally completed Byers Green branch which could tap the coal measures in the Roddymoor area before the rival line reached them. There is clear evidence that the newly revived truncated version of the South Durham railway (now confusingly named the West Durham railway) and the second coal company were part of the same scheme.[70]

The Clarence railway management committee minutes which might have thrown further light on the connections between the various enterprises are missing between July 1837 and August 1838. Nor does Tomlinson, the historian of the North Eastern railway, seem to have had access to them since his account at this point is based on a later newspaper report.[71]

The surviving minutes recommence at a point where there was a serious risk of dissension both within the management and between the Clarence and the coal companies. Dividend starved shareholders in the Clarence main line were becoming concerned that collieries, whether privately or company owned, along the northern branch of the line, as well as those along the Byers Green branch and its projected extension, the West Durham railway, would, as feared, ship from Hartlepool. Among the owners on that northern branch was Blanshard himself who, unbeknown to the rest of the Clarence management, was in the process of selling the developmental rights in his royalty to the Durham County Coal Company with every intention of shipping through Hartlepool. After several difficult meetings it was eventually agreed to require a formal undertaking from the coal companies to send at least a quota of their coals down the main line of the Clarence, as the price of continued co-operation.[72]

Of all these companies the only one run from London was the Clarence and what also emerges from the renewed minutes is a clear impression that during the previous year operational control of developments in the south Durham coalfield had passed definitively to the region. Some of this power shift may be attributable to the Clarence's appointment of a new company solicitor in the north-east, Ralph Ward Jackson, who first appears in the minutes entrusted with the delicate task of drafting and implementing the quota agreements. He had been appointed during the period not covered by the minutes so the circumstances of the appointment are unknown, but it is possible that his name was put forward by Tennant. He was one of the sons of that William Ward Jackson already mentioned among the first Clarence shareholders and he had recently returned from a legal practice in Preston to go into partnership with one of the Skinner family in Stockton. In the midst of the Clarence management committee's discussions about enforcing quotas he revealed the existence of a scheme to provide a link between the main line of the Clarence near Billingham and the docks at Hartlepool which would offer coalowners a choice of shipping points whilst still keeping traffic on a Clarence controlled route all the way. To avoid expensive parliamentary confrontations the link was to be initially a wayleave line and the company a Deed of Settlement company.[73]

On the face of it this seems a perfectly innocuous means of resolving a potentially damaging situation but there is documentation that shows this proposal (subsequently called the Stockton and Hartlepool railway) to have been part of yet another locally conceived 'package' which included, in addition to the railway, plans for a joint stock bank and an alternative dock facility on the west side of Hartlepool Bay.[74]

The dock scheme was temporarily shelved when the existing Hartlepool company offered preferential terms for coal shipped along the proposed new line, but the bank, the Stockton and Durham, was launched at the same time as the railway company and was manifestly an adjunct of that enterprise. The promoters of the bank were local businessmen but the timing of its launch just as yet another financial crisis hit the Clarence, and the facts that the new bank discounted with Williams Deacon and rapidly became the Clarence's northern banker, and that Labouchere and other London shareholders of the Clarence soon acquired a large stake in the new railway company, suggests once again a regional initiative subsequently taken up by the Clarence management team.[75]

Within the next few years Ward Jackson became an increasingly important manipulative and managerial force in the region although he did not emerge fully into the limelight until after the period covered by this study. However, it is clear from the letter, signed by nineteen other south Durham and north Yorkshire shareholders, that he sent to the Clarence directors in November 1839, that virtually from the outset he was working for the formal return of the management to the region. That there was a need for 'some efficient plan of conducting the affairs of the company on the spot' had been recognised by the London committee but only to the extent of sending Stokes as resident manager.[76]

Crisis and survival

During 1840 the network that had emerged so painfully from the 1836 setbacks was nearing completion. It was only a matter of months before coal and coke would start coming down the West Durham railway along the Byers Green branch and either down the main line of the Clarence to the Tees or by the link line to Hartlepool, which makes it the more suspicious that it should have been at the autumn 1840 general meeting of shareholders in the Durham County Coal Company that doubts were first raised about that company's viability.

As in all enterprises supported by public investment, the maintenance of public confidence was all important. There are no extant minutes but it is clear from the press reports that what occurred at the next meeting of the coal company in February 1841 had been carefully planned and that the managers were aware of what was going to happen and had prepared their own strategy, which was to absent themselves from the meeting and resign if the proceedings turned nasty. So Stokes, who had been put on the board to look after the interests of the Clarence, was forced to take the chair and to explain the company's inability to declare a dividend. The meeting, led by one of the York shareholders, demanded a committee of enquiry into the operation of the company and the commissioning of an independent coal viewer to review the company's prospects.[77]

It is significant that between this and the subsequent meeting on 27 April one of the men whom Stokes brought in was Ward Jackson who became the new company solicitor. The report on the operation of the coal company was condemnatory of the way in which it had been set up and of its links with the Northern Mining Company but the evaluation of its prospects by Matthias Dunn, a reputable local coal viewer, was relatively optimistic. That the enquiry was led and pursued by two York shareholders who were also actively involved in Hudson's company, justifies suspicion of ulterior motives, but that there had been elements of deception particularly in the setting up of the two companies was hardly in doubt.[78] However, the coal company was connected with too many other concerns in the region for it to be allowed to go under, so in the short term the network held, partly because of a local news blackout. The nearest newspaper to report the shareholders meeting was in York.

Manifestly the news ban could not be maintained indefinitely. The London based but nationally read *Mining Journal* got hold of the story and those London shareholders brought in by Barrett in the early days of the Durham County Coal Company backed out, but those whose links were through the Clarence retained their holding, while the north Yorkshire investors recruited by the branch managers of the Darlington District Bank picked up the abandoned shares and within two years had taken over the direction, thus in effect keeping the regional network together.[79]

In the light of subsequent developments, the instigator of this move could have been Ward Jackson whose own family came from north Yorkshire, but in the absence of company minutes there is no direct evidence of this. He was certainly becoming increasingly active in regional affairs in his multiple roles as solicitor to both the coal company and the Clarence railway and the behind-the-scenes promoter of the Stockton and Hartlepool railway and the Stockton and Durham bank. In the autumn of 1841 he made another attempt to bring the management of the Clarence back to the north-east, which was foiled only by the need to retain London support in the face of another threatened Exchequer loan commission takeover.[80]

If it is possible that Ward Jackson engineered the north Yorkshire takeover of the Durham County Coal Company then it is pretty well certain that it was Thomas Cummings Gibson who brought in the Norfolk shareholders to take over the Northern Mining Company and thus ensure supplies of coke for their brewing and malting enterprises.[81]

Even if connections within the City enabled the Clarence to stave off foreclosure by the loan commissioners the inevitable gaps in production attendant on the restructuring of the coal companies left the railway vulnerable to takeover by Hudson's company which by 1842 had already acquired the 'junction' line linking Hartlepool with the Byers Green branch of the Clarence and seemed poised to acquire control of the whole network. How this might have affected the nature of the region's identity is an unanswerable question since in the event the takeover was averted by another adroit move on the part of Ward Jackson.

The Clarence management, on the advice of Labouchere, bought time by converting the existing company bonds into shares. Ward Jackson's group running the Stockton and Hartlepool railway revived the original scheme for a new dock on the west side of Hartlepool Bay and launched a new joint stock company to finance it. The company, chaired initially by Vansittart, included a number of investors from the existing concerns as well as new businessmen fearful of the spread of Hudson's empire and of links between Hudson and the Peases. One of its working directors was Charles Barrett who had survived the upheavals in the coal companies and now became Ward Jackson's right-hand man. Ward Jackson's next step was to persuade the management of the Clarence to lease that line to the Stockton and Hartlepool for a period of years. By this 'tail wagging the dog' manoeuvre he hoped to ensure that the rail and colliery networks were sufficiently integrated to withstand piecemeal takeover and that, should the existing Hartlepool shipping facilities fall into hostile hands, there would be alternative provision.[82] (see figure 7.3.).

From the surviving documentation it seems likely that these measures were the product of economic necessity as perceived by those whose own solvency was at stake rather than part of a coherent plan, but in retrospect they can be seen as providing the framework upon which the continuing identity of the region came to rest.

Limitations of space preclude the examination of the impact of the legislative changes and the 'boom and bust' processes of the national economy of the later 1840s on a region still suffering from the effects of the prolonged miners' strike of 1844. Suffice to say that the close ties formed with the London markets through the banking system and the coal trade proved a source of weakness when those markets were in disarray. The credit squeeze imposed by the London banks in the wake of the collapse of the metropolitan-induced speculative boom of the middle years of the decade left none of the companies in the region – including the Stockton and Darlington – untouched.[83]

Some of the elements in the post-1850 restructuring of the regional economy are clearly rooted in the networks established in the previous two decades. So, although a subsidiary partnership of the Pease family acquired the collieries in the Roddymoor area, most of those developed by the coal companies remained part of a Clarence, Stockton and Hartlepool system, a solution which was achieved largely through the machinations of Ralph Ward Jackson, Charles Barrett, Thomas Cummings Gibson and their associates.[84]

But there was a significant change, although even that had been foreshadowed by the increased use of coal for processing. As with the Stockton and Darlington's entry into the London market twenty-five years earlier, there seems to be no convincing explanation of why the Cleveland ironstone, considered of such inferior quality as to be not worth large scale development at an earlier period, should suddenly acquire economic importance in the years following 1850. The myth of its accidental discovery does not stand up to close scrutiny for it was already being used before then. It is much more likely that there was a conscious decision by the Stockton and Darlington connection to develop it to retrieve the fallen fortunes of the Middlesbrough proprietors after the disasters of the late eighteen-forties and their loss of shipping to Hartlepool. Certainly the decision by the already established local ironmasters, Bolckow and Vaughan, to open new mines at Eston at the end of 1850 was seen as a turning point in Middlesbrough's fortunes and one which brought prosperity to those collieries (Roddymoor among them) along the branches of the Stockton and Darlington railway whose coal was more suited to coking than to the London market. Within three years Ward Jackson had taken the same path, leasing land at Port Clarence, the original Teesside shipping point of the railway now largely superseded by Hartlepool, to the Bell brothers, the innovative Tyneside ironmasters. He also leased them the ironstone deposits on his family's estates at Normanby. So large areas of north Yorkshire which had supplied investment capital to the early railways and coal companies now became adjuncts of the Teesside industrial complex.[85]

Thus these enterprises, despite continuing for another decade the rivalry begun in 1828, also consolidated the regional identity that had been formed through opportunities opened up by ramshackle risk-taking and sometimes downright fraudulent unregulated joint stock operations bringing railway, shipping, mining and banking interests together in a regional community of mutual self-interest.

Principal manuscript sources

Public Record Office, Kew (PRO): The largest single source used is the documentation of the Clarence Railway which is in the PRO under Rail 117. There are 28 volumes of surviving documentation. Of these nos 1 and 2 are minutes of shareholders meetings, 3 to 7 are minutes of management committee meetings, and most of the rest comprise letter and account books of various kinds including one dealing with the long-running dispute about the overcharging by the Stockton and Darlington on coal that switched from one line to the other. Also used are PRO 668/7 and 668/20, the 'Journal ' and letter book of the Stockton and Hartlepool Railway.

Durham County Record Office (DCRO): HH 1/3 and 4, Hanby Holmes papers; Str. B1/3 and 4, Strathmore papers; PR, Parish Registers; ER, Electoral Rolls; NRC14, West Hartlepool

North Yorkshire County Record Office: NYCRO Chaytor papers

Notes

1 The background to much of the material used in this study may be found in the following: Maberley Phillips, *History of Banks, Bankers and Banking in Northumberland, Durham and North Yorkshire, Illustrating the Commercial Development of the North of England from 1755 to 1894* (London 1894); W. W. Tomlinson, *The North Eastern Railway: Its Rise and Development* (first published 1915, reprinted Newton Abbot, 1967); and M. W. Kirby, *The Origins of Railway Enterprise: The Stockton and Darlington Railway 1821–1863* (Cambridge, 1993).

2 J. Langton and M. Freeman, 'The Industrial Revolution and the regional geography of England', *Transactions of the Institute of British Geographers*, 9 (1984), 145–67 and 507–12.

3 *Newcastle Chronicle*, 7 Oct. 1853.

4 The material used in this chapter is drawn from a wider, as yet unpublished, study which seeks to explore the place of early joint stock companies in the transition from family firms to corporate capitalism in mid-nineteenth century Britain.

5 Quoted in Tomlinson, *North Eastern Railway*, p. 40.

6 *Ibid.*, p. 68

7 See F. Griffith Dawson, *The First Latin American Debt Crisis* (New Haven and London, 1990).

8 A Deed of Settlement was a legal document assented to and signed by all the shareholders, in which the objectives of the company and the rights and duties of the shareholders and directors were spelt out. How far such undertakings were enforceable at law seems to have remained a matter of debate until the Company Act of 1844.

9 Tomlinson, *North Eastern Railway*, p. 69; also see NYCRO, Chaytor papers, Blanshard to Chaytor, 13 Feb 1830, 'problems with the Quakers'; Allison to Chaytor, 20 Jan 1832, warning him not to be seen to be publicly associated with the Hartlepool Dock and Railway Co. 'or the Quakers will cut up rough'. DCRO, HH 1/3/3, Thomas Wheldon writing about the Stockton and Darlington, Dec 1835, refers to 'thraldom in the Auckland Valley'.

10 P. M. Sweezey, *Monopoly and Competition in the English Coal Trade 1800–1850* (Cambridge, Mass., 1938) remains the most comprehensive study of the attempts during this period to maintain an 'economic' price for coal produced for the London market by limitation of production, but see also J. A. Jaffe 'Competition and the size of firms in the north east coal trade', *Northern History*, 25 (1989), which argues against the coalowners' committees' effectiveness. The minutes of the North East Coal Owners' Committees on which Sweezey's work is based still survive at the

Northumberland CRO (NCRO). Regulation was intermittent during the 1820s but continuous from 1834 until after the miners' strike of 1844. To control the market there had to be co-operation between the coalowners, shipowners and the coal factors on the London Exchange, and this provides the context for the anti-monopolistic propaganda of 1836 touched on later in the study.

11 *Mining Journal* (hereinafter *MJ*), 17 Oct. 1838, editorial.

12 Rail 117/1, Clarence railway, Minutes of shareholders meetings, list of those present, 8 July 1828.

13 W. Parson and W. White, *History, Directory and Gazetteer of the Counties of Durham and Northumberland* (hereinafter Parson and White) vol. 1 (1827), p. 319, lists Thomas Allison Tennant as a rope maker and sail cloth manufacturer; vol. 2 (1828), p. 209, lists Christopher Tennant as lime-burner at East Thickley.

14 Guildhall Library, London, 'Coal-trade scrapbook 1800–1840', has a newspaper cutting referring to Christopher Tennant in 1836 as 'that notorious projector and tramping quack', but all the local company promoters seem to have valued his experience and there are no derogatory references to him in any of the local sources consulted.

15 For a more extensive treatment of this point see W. Stokes, 'The Joint-Stock Generation', *Durham Co. Local Hist. Soc. Bulletin*, 55 (1996),. 5–23.

16 Sweezey, *Monopoly and Competition* pp. 50 *et seq*.; R. Smith, *Sea Coal for London; The History of the Coal Factors in the London Market* (London, 1961) pp.106–7 and 164–5; Tomlinson, *North Eastern Railway*, pp. 175–8; Corporation of London RO, 429 a, Applications of those intending to deal on the coal exchange 1827–33, *passim*.

17 Smith, *Sea Coal*, p. 244.

18 In Pigot's *London Directory* for 1826–27 he appears as 'Merchant and insurance broker' of 1, Old Broad St. In subsequent editions up to 1835 he is listed as 'Merchant and ship owner'. After that date he is listed only at his private address in Great Ormond St. There is a specific reference in Rail 117/5, 14 Sept. 1838, to his going north on family business.

19 NYCRO, Chaytor papers. Despite his derogatory nickname, 'Tater Willie', a reference to his unkempt appearance, Sir William was a force to be reckoned with in County Durham – see Tomlinson, *North Eastern Railway*, p. 62. The fact that he kept both incoming letters and drafts or actual copies of his own replies makes him an invaluable source for this ill-documented period.

20 DCRO, Str B1/4/2–6, shows Tennant and Blanshard investigating Deanery colliery, 1827. Despite Kirby, *Origins*, p. 81, I have found nothing to connect Henry Blanshard with the Stockton and Darlington, but a Richard Blanshard was certainly a shareholder.

21 On Coxhoe, see Kirby, *Origins*, pp. 36, 71–2, and Tomlinson, *North Eastern Railway*, p. 170. The manoeuvrings of the two groups in the early 1820s add substance to the notion of a pre-existing awareness of a regional identity which was given a different emphasis by the new investment network. Blanshard's long-term identification with the Clarence is attested not only by the amount of capital he put into it but also by his long service as chairman of the company from 1841 until it was finally taken over in 1853. He chaired the last meeting on 31 Dec. 1853, Rail 117/7, and died on 28 March 1854. Rail 117/1, 2 Feb. 1832, shows him as holding forty-five of the original £100 shares; Rail 117/3 shows that on 24 Jan. 1835 he lent the company £800 for a month to meet immediate expenses, on 16 May he lent a further £1200, on 23 Sept. he took fifty-two shares of a new issue and at the end of 1837 he took company bonds for £10,000.

22 NYCRO, Chaytor papers, Blanshard to Chaytor, 6 Sept.1830.

23 Sweezey, *Monopoly and Competition*; NCRO, Minute Books of the Committees of the two rivers, 1827–32.

24 Kirby, *Origins*, p. 83.

25 Phillips, *History of Banks*, pp. 102 *et seq.*

26 *Ibid.*, pp. 236–8; NYCRO, Chaytor papers, 9 Feb. 1832.
27 G. Milburn, 'Piety, profit and paternalism. Methodists in business in the North East of England c.1760–1920', *Proceedings of the Wesley Historical Society*, 44 (1983–84), 40; Records of Methodism in Sunderland held at the Sunderland Society of Antiquaries, include a list of circuit deputies on which the Skinners' names appear.
28 Ian Black, 'Geography, political economy and the circulation of finance in early industrial England', *Journal of Historical Geography*, 15 (1989), 366–85.
29 DCRO, HH 1/3 and 4. The relevant volumes are the correspondence books of Thomas Wheldon, a partner in the Barnard Castle firm of solicitors that handled a considerable amount of colliery and railway related business throughout the period covered by this study.
30 London Guildhall RO, PR, St Mary Moses; Greater London RO, PR, St George Bloomsbury; see Pigot's *London Directory*, *London Post Office Directories*, and *Mining Journal* for companies for which Stokes, Hollingsworth and Tyerman were solicitors.
31 J. G. Killick and W. A. Thomas, 'The Stock Exchanges of the North of England 1836–1850', *Northern History*, 5 (1970), 115–16. See also press advertisements of shares for sale, e.g. *Durham Co. Advertiser*, 18 Apr. 1834, sale by a local auctioneer of eighteen shares in the Darlington District Bank in three lots of six; or *ibid.*, 30 Oct. 1835, Great North of England railway shares for sale though sharebrokers in London as well as by the company solicitors in Darlington.
32 Rail 117/8, Share registers.
33 See below for the episodes in 1835–36 and 1838 when this was clearly the case and Rail 117/3–7, Management committee minutes, *passim*.
34 Rail 117/3, Meetings of 15, 12, and 29 Nov. and 13 Dec. 1834.
35 NCRO, Coal owners' committees minute books, 1833–4. At the first United committee meeting the Tees representatives were all coalowners associated with Pease, although there were others who used the Stockton and Darlington. The secretary of the Tees committee was Thomas Storey, the Stockton and Darlington's resident engineer.
36 NYCRO, Chaytor papers, *passim*. Chaytor corresponded regularly on Thornley colliery and Hartlepool Dock and Railway Co. affairs with John Burrell, the prominent Durham City lawyer who was, like himself, a leading shareholder in both companies.
37 Hartlepool Local Studies library, printed list of subscribers to the Hartlepool Dock and Railway Co.
38 NYCRO, Chaytor papers, letters of 28 Oct. 1835, 12 Dec. 1835 and 15 Jan. 1835. Rail 117/3, spring and summer 1835, *passim*.
39 *Durham Co. Advertiser*, 30 Oct. 1835, South Durham Railway promotion; 13 Nov. 1835, S. W. Durham Railway.
40 Rail 117/3, letter considered at meeting of 30 May 1835. NYCRO, Chaytor papers, letter from Joseph Wooller of Wolsingham, 6 Feb. 1836, 'If they [the South Durham railway promoters] get the act they will bring limestone down to the coals, using the small coals that are now lost.' He suggested that there could be links to Yarm and Croft and into Cleveland to supply the farmers of North Yorkshire with 'the famous Frosterley lime, a manure superior to all others.'
41 Rail 117/3, Tennant's proposals were discussed at the meetings of 3 and 10 Oct. 1835
42 Kirby, *Origins*, p. 125.
43 PRO, B450, 12–14 Aug. 1843, Bankruptcy of J. C. Ord coal factor of Waterloo Pl. Pall Mall.
44 DCRO, NRC 14, collection of letters to and from Ralph Ward Jackson and printed material relating to the Hartlepool West Dock Co.
45 DCRO, Str. B1/3/87 and 94.
46 R. Church, assisted by A. Hall and J. Kanefsky, *The History of the British Coal Industry*, vol. 3 (Oxford, 1986) was apparently unaware either of the context of the foundation of

the company or of the extent of John Bowes' earlier involvement – DCRO, HH 1/3/4 and 1/4/30.

47 DCRO, HH 1/3/3, 18 Nov. 1835, Wheldon has had a meeting with Blanshard, 2 Dec. 1835, note to Barrett while he was in London.

48 *Durham Co. Advertiser*, 23 May 1836; *Gateshead Observer*, 23 May 1836; *Newcastle Courant*, 11 June 1836.

49 Kirby (*Origins*) gives a summary of these debates based on Tomlinson, *North Eastern Railway*, pp. 11–13; see also *Hansard's Parliamentary Debates*, 3rd ser., 33, House of Lords (3 May 1836), 511–14; and 35, House of Lords (11 and 15 July 1836), 60, 225–7.

50 Notably the Woollers of Wolsingham, William Russell of Brancepeth Castle, G. H. Wilkinson of Harperley Park, R. E. D. Shafto of Whitworth Hall, and Col. Mills of Willington. HH 2/16/11, a printed petition of 'the landed proprietors of South Durham against the combined interference of great coal owners of Northumberland and North Durham' in the passage of the railway bills.

51 *MJ*, 2 Jan. and 4 June 1836, letters; Smith, *Sea Coal*, p. 241; Newcastle upon Tyne Central Library Local Studies Collection, Matthias Dunn's Diary, ed. Michael Sill, 16 March 1836, records the decision of the Coalowners' Committee to oppose the South Durham Railway 'with every exertion' and notes that 'Pease took a conspicuous part'; NCRO, Coalowners' Committee minutes, 5 Sept. 1836, record payments to those who had opposed the bill.

52 Dunn's Diary, 17 May 1836 and 18 June 1836. Having recorded in mid-May that 'arrangements for the purchase seem to be progressing very steadily', Dunn reported a month later 'that all are surprised that Mr Gregson says he has a better offer' and commented 'upon the whole the transaction does not savour too much of honour'.

53 NYCRO, Chaytor papers, 2 Jan. 1829; *MJ*, 12 June 1841, letter signed Crito. Allegedly the banking and legal network disposed of '£40,000 of coal company shares in Helmsley and neighbourhood, at York £10,000, at Masham and in Wensleydale between £10 and £20,000 and £14000 at Bedale and Richmond'. There is no way of checking these figures but the named leading shareholders who attended general meetings bear out this geographical distribution.

54 For Barrett's background, see W. Stokes, 'The Joint-Stock Generation', *Durham Co. Local Hist. Soc. Bulletin*, 55, 5–23.

55 Records of Methodism in Sunderland, vol.1, records Barrett as a circuit deputy in 1838 and 1839 along with other known Methodist businessmen who were shareholders in the coal companies.

56 Smith, *Sea Coal*, p. 244.

57 Durham University, Special Coll. Mason's will shows that he left under £5000; Rail 117/4, the management committee of the Clarence on 24 Aug.1836 recommended seizure of 60 wagons belonging to Mason which probably indicates that Stokes who had been on the spot knew the situation; Bell Coll., 14. p. 55, has a press advertisement for the sale of Mason's colliery in Sept. 1836; Rail 117/5 shows that on 19 Sept. 1839 six members of the directorate including Blanshard and Stokes agreed to cover Mason's bond.

58 Rail 117/4, 27 Aug. 1836, letter from J. Wooller, 'An impression prevails in the North that the Byers Green branch can not be made by the limit of the time allowed by the Act of Parliament'.

59 Kirby, *Origins*, p. 117, dates the line from 1837 but it is clear from what follows that it was under consideration in the summer of 1836; NYCRO, Chaytor papers, Chaytor, 1 Aug. 1836, recorded that he had been approached by Storey the Stockton and Darlington resident engineer about a branch coming through the Witton Castle estate up into Weardale with a further branch to Mown Meadows (about a mile from the intended route of the South West Durham).

60 Rail 117/4. Indications of the various approaches and responses are contained in the management committee minutes of the sparsely attended meetings of 16 and 23 July and 6, 8 and 12 Aug. 1836. Stokes was in Durham between 23 July and 6 Aug. and the arrangements were ratified on 13 Aug.

61 *Ibid*., meeting of 27 Aug.; *Durham Co. Advertiser,* 2 Sept., account of Stokes' speech at the meeting; 21 Sept., Blanshard was deputed to attend the second meeting.

62 Rail 117/4, 29 Dec. 1836, letter from Hartlepool Co. announcing the launch of the 'Junction' railway; Rail 117/1, General meeting, 22 Nov. 1838, alerting shareholders to the threat of competition from the 'Junction' line.

63 *Hansard's Parliamentary Debates*, 3rd ser., 33, House of Commons (12 May 1836), 862.

64 NYCRO, Chaytor papers, 23 May 1836; HH 1/3/3, 23 July 1836.

65 NCRO, Coalowners' committee minutes. The negotiations took place in the summer of 1838 and on 4 Aug. Captain Watts, one of the directors, represented the company on the Tees committee.

66 Records of Methodism in Sunderland, vol.1. For further details on T. C. Gibson, see W. Stokes, 'The Joint-Stock Generation'.

67 *MJ*, 15 May 1841, revelations about the origins of the Northern Mining Co.

68 *Ibid*., between May and Dec. 1836, the letters and editorial comment confirm the importance of Norfolk, Suffolk and Edinburgh shareholding in the Mining Company and also that the company was in the process of establishing a depot in Exeter; *ibid*., 16 Apr. 1842. In a court case in Liverpool, Gibson claimed he had established offices for the company in six places, presumably Edinburgh, Ipswich Great Yarmouth, Liverpool, Exeter and his native Newcastle upon Tyne where he was also a shareholder in a joint stock bank, *Newcastle Journal,* 7 Feb. 1846. DCRO, Str. B1/4/38, records one of the company's collieries being saved from receivership by the arrival of cash from Exeter in Feb. 1842.

69 *MJ*, 6 Nov. 1841, claims that the collieries were sold from the 'winners', i.e. those who developed them, to the companies. This is borne out by the Electoral Registers for the wards of the South Durham constituency in which the partnerships who developed the collieries and the shareholders in the railway companies are listed as voters under the terms of the 1832 Reform Act – see ER 1837–38, Evenwood and Barony; 1838–39 Coxhoe and Whitwell; 1839–40 Framwellgate Moor; 1840–41 Whitworth, Willington etc., although later registers simply say 'the owners of X colliery'.

70 *Durham Chronicle,* 30 Mar. 1838, for launch of the W. Durham; Kirby, pp. 118–19.

71 Tomlinson, *North Eastern Railway*, p. 335.

72 Rail 117/5, Minutes of management committee, Aug.–Dec. 1838.

73 Eric Waggott, *Jackson's Town* (Hartlepool, 1980) provides useful background material on Ward Jackson and some indication of his character but most of the information on him used in this chapter is taken either from the Clarence minutes, DCRO, NRC 14, a collection of material relating to West Hartlepool, or Rail 668/7 and 668/20, an account book and letter book of the Stockton and Hartlepool railway. The first mention of the proposal was in a letter from Ward Jackson dated 28 Aug. 1838 but it was not discussed by the Clarence management until 14 Nov.

74 Rail 668/20, Stockton and Hartlepool Railway Co. Journal.

75 Rail 117/5, meeting of 27 Sept. 1839, when Labouchere refused to discount £1243 of bills the accountant in Stockton was told to pay all revenues into the Stockton and Durham until further notice. The bank then offered the company a loan in return for all their future business. It was with the Stockton and Durham that the Clarence directors sorted out the problems arising from Mason's security. The chairman of the bank's board of directors at the meeting of 15 Nov. 1839 was T. A. Tennant. See Rail 668/20, pp. 5 *et seq*., for Labouchere's subsequent involvement with the company.

76 Rail 117/5, letter from Ward Jackson dated 4 Dec. 1839.

77 *MJ*, 6 Mar. 1841 onwards. The meeting at which no dividend was declared took place on 25 Feb. but the subsequent meeting of 27 April achieved front page status under the headline 'Extraordinary Disclosures'. The demand for the initial enquiry came from Thomas Leadbitter, a York solicitor. He was backed by George Leeman, subsequently a chairman of the North Eastern railway and also a solicitor in York, and George Andrews, an associate of Hudson and the architect of the first York railway station opened that year on the Great North of England railway. The editor of the *MJ*, who was a guarded supporter of joint stock enterprise, was bombarded with correspondence from both supporters and detractors. As with most press coverage and correspondence, there are provable errors of fact. There is some reference in the correspondence to the intransigent hostility of the coal-owning establishment and the Stockton and Darlington but this is not picked up by the editor.

78 The *MJ* report of the meeting of 27 April was taken from the *York Courant* and *York Herald*. The 'independent' investigator was Matthias Dunn and his report, which the editor of the *MJ*, had difficulty in getting hold of and published on 29 May 1841, concentrated on the prospects of the collieries held by the company rather than the misdeeds of its promoters. Rail 117/5 – the only references to the coal company's affairs in the railway minutes are demands that Stokes ensure the prompt payment of outstanding accounts.

79 *MJ*, 17 Feb. 1844, report of the general meeting held 9 Feb. with Andrews in the chair. ER, as early as 1841–42 show shareholders from Helmsley taking over Evenwood and another varied group of Yorkshire shareholders at Whitworth.

80 Rail 117/2, Special General Meetings, 23 Aug. and 12 and 15 Oct. 1842.

81 ER, 1841–12, shows Martin William Seppings of Norwich taking over shares in the W. Durham Railway formerly held by the Northern Mining Company and in 1842–43 a Norfolk group at Framwellgate Moor colliery. Norfolk CRO, BR 1/44, Steward Patteson and Finch letter book, shows the brewers dealing with the Northern Mining Co. and Seppings as the Norfolk representative in the north-east. *Norfolk Chronicle* 14 Sept. 1844, reports a Special General Meeting of the company held in Norwich. Several of the major shareholders were also associated with the East of England Commercial joint stock bank and were either brewers, maltsters or solicitors. W. White's *Directory* (1845); W. Rye, *Norfolk Families* (Norwich, 1913).

82 Rail 117/2, Special General Meetings, 24 Aug.1842; Rail 668/1, letter of 23 May 1843. The bill for the Hartlepool West Harbour and Dock Company got through Parliament the following year and the Dock was opened with great ceremony on 1 June 1847 – see newspaper report, Hartlepool Local Studies Library; see also DCRO, NRC 14, printed reports of company meetings.

83 On the crisis itself, see H. M. Boot, *The Commercial Crisis of 1847*, University of Hull, Occasional Papers on Economic History no. 11 (1984); for local repercussions, see Kirby, *Origins*, p. 139; Tomlinson, *North Eastern Railway*, p. 493.

84 The assets of the Durham County Coal Company were gradually sold off although the company was not finally wound up until 1853. *Durham Co. Advertiser,* 30 Jan. 1846, 'Joseph Pease jnr. has purchased Roddymoor and Job's Hill collieries'; the adjoining colliery at Whitelea was in the hands of Bolckow and Vaughan the Middlesbrough ironmasters by 1853; Rail 117/18, letter from Thomas Sturge to Joseph Pease 10 Oct. 1849, 'In respect of some of the collieries we are told they are taken and worked by a company, the leaders of which are interested in the West dock and Stockton and Hartlepool railway'; also, see DCRO, NRC 14, letters from Ward Jackson to Robinson Watson, one of his associates which show Cummings Gibson's involvement. By 1854, T. Y. Hall, 'Treatise on . . . the Northern Coalfield' (Newcastle upon Tyne, 1854), was listing ten collieries worked by Robson and Jackson, all of them previously belonging to one or other of the coal companies.

85 For a perspective on the development of the Teesside iron industry see T. Nicholson. '"Jacky" and the Jubilee: Middlesbrough's creation myth', in A. J. Pollard (ed.), *Middlesbrough Town and Community 1830–1950* (Stroud, 1996).

8 *Michael Winstanley*

Women and the grocery trade in Britain, 1851–1911: a regional analysis

Introduction

In 1974 Eric Richards argued that the nineteenth century witnessed a 'substantial diminution of the economic role of women' and their confinement to 'non-market household labour'.[1] Since then, the relationship between British industrialisation and the gendering of occupational roles has generated considerable academic debate.[2] The decline in women's participation was initially associated with the period of the 'classic' industrial revolution, but Jane Humphries has suggested that 'historians of women's paid work should revise their periodisation and their priorities', pointing to the fall in women's activity rates after 1851, and 1871 in particular.[3] She attributes this to 'sluggish growth, relative industrial decline and persistently slack labour markets', but a number of other explanations for this phenomenon have been put forward, ranging from technological developments to the emergence and social diffusion of a patriarchal ideology which stressed the importance of 'separate spheres' and a male 'breadwinner's wage'.[4]

The emphasis on the universality of women's declining participation in the national workforce during the nineteenth century has been increasingly questioned since the mid-1980s, however, with doubts being expressed about the reliability of census occupational data and contemporary commentaries on which this interpretation was based. A plethora of local case studies has documented the diversity of women's experiences which persisted within the developing market economy. Maxine Berg and Pat Hudson, for example, have stressed how central female labour was to the high-productivity factory and workshop sectors which provided the engines of growth in the late eighteenth- and early nineteenth-century economy.[5] Others have pointed to women's importance in a wide range of 'sweated' or workshop trades in the late nineteenth century, and in the provision of accommodation.[6] Women's incomes also remained crucial to many working-class families for whom sole reliance on an adequate male breadwinner's wage remained an unrealistic ideal.

Although not formally acknowledged in official sources like the census, women, especially married women, remained a 'hidden workforce' of part-time, casual and seasonal workers in agriculture, home-based manufacturing and the service sector.[7]

There has also been a growing awareness, in the words of Pat Hudson and W. R. Lee, that 'the local and regional structure of production was crucial in influencing gender-specific economic roles' and that consequently 'the process of industrialization needs to be examined as a highly diverse regional phenomenon, involving a variegated pattern of sectoral balance and attendant levels of technological development'.[8] The adoption of a more overt regional perspective by agricultural historians has already resulted in a move away from the discussions of women as a casual labourers in the arable districts of the south and east, towards an increasing recognition of the variety of roles which they undertook as members of family farming units, 'general' servants and bondagers in mixed and pastoral economies in other parts of Britain.[9] Marked geographical variations in employment opportunities for both unmarried and married women in industrial and service sectors are now recognised as an enduring characteristic of the labour market throughout the nineteenth and twentieth centuries with important consequences for marriage patterns, fertility and gender relations.[10]

This study uses census data at national, county and town level to explore women's work in the most important components of the retail sector during the late nineteenth century, grocery and general shopkeeping. It argues that it is not possible to understand the changing nature and extent of women's participation in these trades from aggregate national figures or from isolated, local case studies. Women's importance in these sectors was determined by the distinctive characteristics of regional patterns of industrialisation and urbanisation.

Structural and regional change in the grocery trade

It is tempting to portray the development of the retail sector as a linear, national narrative which involved the progressive, inevitable marginalisation of women. During the early modern period, perishable food production and small-scale retailing were viewed as women's domains, an extension of, and compatible with, their domestic roles and culinary 'arts'.[11] The increasing scale and complexity of production, processing and distribution, involving extended chains of supply, the physical separation of shopkeepers' homes from workplaces, and the emergence of new forms of large-scale retail organisations like the co-op and multiples, undermined these functions. Legitimised by a dominant patriarchal ideology, women's importance and autonomy in the retail sector declined. Their marginalisation in the marketing and processing of food is usually associated with the late eighteenth century. As markets became 'more organised, less casual and less private', the 'women's market' in poultry, fruit and vegetables was gradually taken over by 'wealthier and more aggressive business people' such as jobbers and higglers.[12] Men dominated the meat trades and gradually took over women's role as bakers, while male workers in the new creameries and cheese factories displaced female-dominated farmhouse dairy production in some parts of the country.[13]

Catherine Hall's study of family retail businesses, published in 1982, remains the most lucid and influential explanation of how women's role in the grocery trade was redefined during the early nineteenth century. Extrapolating from a case study of the socially-mobile Cadbury family, Hall argued that women withdrew, or were excluded by a variety of circumstances, from active involvement in the family businesses, and that the grocer's shop consequently became a male domain. Two mutually supporting processes contributed to this. On the one hand she argued that 'the physical environment which combined work and home, was gradually changing in our period. . . . This separation between work and home had important effects on the organisation of work within the family and the marking out of male and female spheres'. Consequently the 'increasing complexity of the commercial world and its increasing formalisation in the period meant that it was becoming more difficult for women to participate even informally'. This was underpinned by the emergence of a 'domestic ideal' of womanhood which 'well-to-do shopkeepers were not slow to attach themselves to'. Popularised from the late eighteenth century by evangelical Christians, this postulated that women's proper role was the 'private' sphere, and redefined the 'public' world of business as a male preserve.[14]

Hall's analysis of gender relations in the early nineteenth-century grocery trade, however, privileged one aspect of the sector which, as she herself recognised, was not necessarily the most typical nor even the most numerically dynamic during the period. By concentrating exclusively on 'well-to-do shopkeepers' or high-street traders, what one might call 'family capitalists', she deliberately excluded from her remit the 'small shopkeepers running general stores who serviced the working-class population' which were 'rapidly on the increase in the early nineteenth century'.[15] Although the absence of national data on the number, size, ownership, and turnover of shops makes it is impossible precisely to quantify the changing importance of different types of shops, the work of Hoh-cheung and Lorna Mui, Janet Blackman, Roger Scola and David Alexander all strongly suggest that these small general shops were an integral component of the expanding urban market economy from as early as the late eighteenth century. They continued to increase in numbers well into the following century at a faster rate than high-street grocers, and gradually extended the range of goods which they sold.[16] Christopher Hosgood's analysis of trade directories for Leicester between 1880 and 1906 suggests that only about 10 per cent of shopkeepers, mainly drapers, chemists, town centre grocers and wine merchants, conformed to the behaviour patterns described by Hall. The majority of retailers continued to live over and behind their shops.[17]

For these small-enterprise families, as Geoffrey Crossick and Heinz-Gerhard Haupt in their recent study of the European *petite bourgeoisie* stress, 'The separation of business and home which became central to bourgeois culture was rarely feasible. . . . That is why the role of the family was more important for the *petite bourgeoisie* than for any other social group'.[18] Oral and autobiographical evidence from manufacturing towns consistently suggests that the late nineteenth and early twentieth century witnessed the 'heyday of the little corner shop' in which women played as essential role as an unwaged, residential, family labour force.[19] The continued viability of small shops was blamed by organisations representing high-street food retailers, especially grocers, for undermining the profitability of their trade, and prompted demands for legislation to restrict shopkeepers' ability to exploit relatives' labour.[20] Inter-war economic surveys estimated that 'family type' shops still comprised as many as two-thirds of all retail outlets and that there were only sixty people for every shop in Britain.[21] Retail analysts, planners and male trade unionists now joined the condemnation of '"the family shop", employing no assistants from outside the shopkeeper's family', and in particular 'parlour shops' which expropriated part of the private domestic sphere for public business use, as one of the major shortcomings of the 'existing machinery for distribution' and as an obstacle to the introduction of better working conditions and pay for waged assistants.[22] Only in the second half of the twentieth century, however, did the number of small shops in many sectors of the economy decline dramatically.

Business histories of retailing, however, rarely focus on family enterprises; they are more likely to dwell on the food multiples and the co-operative movement which developed rapidly from the 1870s. Unlike the small general shop or the high-street grocer, who might have developed a few local branches, national multiples like Liptons, Home and Colonial, and Maypole sold a limited range of groceries and provisions, mainly imported or processed produce, and compensated for low margins by the achieving a large volume turnover.[23] The co-op's success was based on a strategy of distributing surpluses to members in the form of a quarterly dividend in proportion to their purchases at the stores which had been popularised by the Rochdale Pioneers after 1844. In addition to high-street premises, larger successful co-operative societies frequently developed branch networks of smaller stores selling groceries and provisions in working-class neighbourhoods. Although many had secure foundations by the 1860s, it was only from the 1880s that membership levels and turnover rose dramatically.[24]

Although the 'retailing revolution' of the late nineteenth century is often associated with the expansion of occupations for young, single female shop assistants, this trend was particularly evident in the clothes trades with their feminine associations and the glamorous environment of metropolitan department stores.[25] Large-scale grocery concerns would seem to have been overwhelmingly staffed by men. Historians of the co-operative movement have largely ignored its role as an employer, and indeed most of its retail functions, in preference for a study of its ideology and culture, and in-house co-operative histories provide only fragmentary, incidental references to the composition of the labour force, but photographs of white-aproned shop assistants proudly standing outside co-op premises, which litter the pages of individual societies' jubilee histories around the turn of the century, strongly suggest that the co-op's retail, if not its productive, workforce was overwhelmingly male.[26] Business histories of successful food multiples refer to their workforces only in passing, but it is clear nevertheless that retail, as opposed to manufacturing or clerical, employees were usually what John Sainsbury and numerous practical guides to the grocery trade referred to as 'bright young fellows'.[27] Multiples only tended to employ saleswomen in what were viewed as unskilled or semi-skilled trades selling branded, packaged products like tobacco.[28] Census data for 1911, although far from comprehensive, confirms this impression, with the industrial classification returning 11,538 males employed by food multiples as opposed to just 729 females.[29] More women were recruited during the First World War, but only a few were kept on in the fairly universal reversion to male labour in the immediate post-war period. Not surprisingly, therefore, the expansion of women's employment in the grocery trade is usually associated with the mid-twentieth, rather than the late-nineteenth century.[30]

Each of these business forms was characterised by distinctive regional concentrations. Twentieth-century studies suggest that small shops were particularly prevalent in the industrial north and Midlands. In 1929 a survey estimated that there were just 50 people per shop in Lancashire, but that in Buckinghamshire and Surrey the figure was 70, in Essex 72 and in Middlesex over 80. A Home Office investigation the following year stated that over three-quarters of all shops in Leeds, Birmingham and Sheffield were of the family type, 'i.e. employing no assistants except members of the family'.[31] James Jefferys' analysis of customers' registrations for sugar rations in 1919 and 1949 suggest that these differences in scale were not restricted to independent shops but also affected branches of grocery multiples and co-ops. Registrations per shop were high in Scotland but within England, 'In all three cases the number of registered customers per shop is highest in the London and Home Counties area and in all three cases the number of registrations per shop increases as one moves down the map from the Northern region to London'.[32] Subsequent Censuses of Distribution provided convincing proof that regional variations in shop density, size and turnover persisted well into the post-war period with the south-east and Scotland having the most people per shop and the highest sales per retail establishment in Britain, while the north-west (Lancashire and Cheshire) and the East and West Ridings of Yorkshire had the lowest.[33] Small shops, therefore, were closely associated with what J. B. Priestley characterised as the 'industrial England of coal, iron, steel, cotton, wool, railways' which covered 'the larger part of the Midlands and the North'.[34]

Only a few multiples had achieved national coverage by the outbreak of the First World War. Most would appear to have concentrated their investments in London, the south-east and parts of the north, especially large cities or ports such as Liverpool and Newcastle, and in industrial Scotland.[35] Lipton moved his headquarters from Glasgow to London in 1891 and the capital 'rapidly became the new centre of gravity' for the firm, with a massive programme of expansion in the region; by 1898 seventy-two of the firm's 400 shops were in the capital. The bulk of the one hundred shops run by Pearks by 1910 were also south of the Trent. Although the multiples' penetration of co-op strongholds remains to be explored in detail, it is highly probable that most chains followed the Home and Colonial Stores' decision to leave areas of the north well alone, and adopted instead a 'deliberate policy of endeavouring to obtain branches in the developing suburbs of London and also in the South'.[36] Rural areas and, for less obvious reasons, the industrial districts of the Midlands, would also seem to have remained relatively unaffected by them.

The retail co-operative movement, as Martin Purvis has meticulously shown, also displayed 'bold regional contrasts in its strength'. Unlike the privately-owned multiples, the movement developed in the industrial districts of Lancashire and Yorkshire. Societies were established in the south and Midlands before the First World War, but the textile and mining districts of Lancashire, the West Riding and Scotland, with their distinctive social structures, shared experiences and cultural values, and relatively high and regular family incomes, still accounted for three-quarters of the movement's total sales before 1914. The co-ops' importance only declined in these areas when the social conditions which gave birth to the movement in the first place passed away in the second half of the twentieth century.

There is sufficient, if patchy, evidence, therefore, to sustain the view that grocery and provisions retailing during the nineteenth century became characterised by a variety of ownership patterns, modes of trading, sizes of operation, and employment patterns. It would seem reasonable to surmise that the level and nature of women's involvement in both grocery and general shopkeeping would have been influenced by shops' distinctive regional geographies.

The census and retail employment

The only national figures on employment in the retail sector during the nineteenth century were those published in the occupational tables of the decennial censuses from 1841. The reliability, comprehensiveness and consistency of occupational data in these Victorian censuses have come under increasing scrutiny in recent years. That of 1841 has been shown to have seriously under-numerated occupations of both males and females. Occupational categories changed significantly between censuses, making meaningful measurement of developments in a single trade or industry over time particularly problematic. Edward Higgs has also demonstrated in convincingly depressing detail how the nineteenth-century census seriously under-represented women's involvement in the market economy by ignoring their roles as part-time, seasonal or casual workers, members of family businesses, and 'general servants'.[37] The removal of the categories of 'shopkeeper's wife' and 'butcher's wife' from published tables after 1871 was symptomatic of the gendered ideology which influenced the compilation of the census during the mid-Victorian decades.

These problems have deterred many historians from using the census, but some of the difficulties we associate with the Victorian census arise because it accurately, if sometimes belatedly, reflected many of the significant changes in economic activity during the period. New or revised categories, for example, were introduced to take account of the changing nature of retail business. 'Tea', and later 'Coffee' and 'Chocolate Dealer' were added to the 'Grocer' category. The category of 'Multiple Shop, Multiple Store, Proprietors, Workers' was separated from 'General and Undefined Workers and Dealers' in 1911 in response to the emergence of the department store.[38] The increasing separation of production, processing and distribution was acknowledged by attempts to devise occupational classifications which distinguished 'makers' from 'dealers'. By the end of the century, the development of physically-distinct processes within the food trades was recognised by the removal of 'Chocolate, Cocoa-Makers' from the category of 'Grocers: Tea, Coffee, Chocolate-Dealers'. Separate columns for employees, employers, the self-employed and 'others' were also incorporated into the enumerators' schedules from 1891, although the results were deemed to be 'excessively untrustworthy' and no reference was made to them in the general report of that year, and the problem of distinguishing between merchants, wholesalers and retailers remained.[39] But this data continued to be collected and published and can be used to provide valuable clues about the structure of trades in specific parts of the country.

By the turn of the century the fact that women's work was being significantly under-recorded was also acknowledged as a problem since there was growing concern about the possible consequences of women's employment, particularly married women's work. Details of the marital status of occupied females were incorporated into the published tables after 1891 and increasing efforts were made to record wives and relatives engaged in family businesses. In 1911 enumerators were instructed that 'the occupation of women . . . generally engaged in assisting relatives in trade or business must be fully stated'. This was considered at the time to have had most impact on the food retail sector. Between 1901 and 1911 there was a disproportionate increase in the numbers of married and widowed women returned as butchers, grocers, dealers in bread and confectionery, milksellers, cheesemongers, greengrocers and fruiterers, fishmongers and general shopkeepers which was largely attributed to 'the greatly extended return of wives and other relatives assisting in the business' who 'have now for the first time been included as occupied in the businesses in which they assist'.[40] These changes mean that the census of 1911 provides a more comprehensive and reliable guide to employment patterns than its late Victorian and early Edwardian predecessors.

Nevertheless, we should not understate the difficulties which remain. Few of the categories relevant to the retail sector distinguished between those engaged in production, processing and distribution.[41] Indeed, it was argued at the time that in several trades the distinctions themselves were often false ones. As the general report of 1891 acknowledged, it was often a case of 'the maker and the retail seller being very frequently one and the same person; and further that, when the two are distinct persons, they very generally have one and the same occupational title'. The boundaries between occupational categories did not remain constant over time. Entries in trade directories would tend to support the hypothesis that most petty undifferentiated general shopkeepers retitled themselves as grocers from the late nineteenth century as they expanded their stock or turnover, while others diversified into new specialities as tobacconists, newsagents, confectioners or fish and chip shops.[42] By 1901, the young age profile of 'general shopkeepers' and the large proportion of females returned as employees, suggest that many were unclassified shop assistants rather than small-scale retailers trading in their own right. Identifying assistants in earlier periods, however, is problematical. Higgs has suggested on the basis of his survey of Rochdale in 1851 that 'general servants' employed by retailers might have assisted in shops but there is no way of quantifying this nationally.[43] Although there was a category for 'Shopwomen; Assistants' in the earlier censuses, the printed tables provide no clues as what sorts of shops they were employed in, while 'Shopmen' were returned with mechanics and manufacturers of 'Indefinite Employment' in 1851.[44]

Although critics of the census have identified fewer problems with using census data to analyse regional patterns of employment at any particular time, it is possible that regional linguistic and cultural factors could have resulted in occupational descriptions such as 'grocer' or 'general shopkeeper' being interpreted in different ways in different parts of the country, especially in the mid-Victorian period. Male concepts of what constituted married women's 'proper' role might also have been regionally differentiated, and this could have resulted in women's involvement in the economy in some parts of the country not being fully acknowledged in the enumerators' returns. While the statistics on which the following analysis is constructed may not be totally precise, however, regional distortions in recording would have had to be considerable to undermine the general patterns which they appear to reveal.

Regional employment patterns in grocery and shopkeeping, 1851–1911

Regional studies of retailing based on census data have arrived at very different conclusions. Clive Lee found a low coefficient of variation for employment in the distributive trades throughout the Victorian period which led him to argue that retail provision was largely proportionate to population.[45] Martin Phillips's analysis of a number of food trades, however, has suggested that this was not the case, but his work has otherwise proved inconclusive, even puzzling, with 'major, and fluctuating variations' in provision over time and huge discrepancies in regional densities which 'do not seem to correspond to many of the existing macro-scale, "evolutionary" explanations of retail development'.[46] Although Phillips acknowledged that the changes in occupational classifications which were introduced between 1841 and 1911 pose potential problems for temporal comparisons, he failed to take any account of them in his analysis, and neither he nor Lee considered the age or gender profiles of the workforces which will be our main concern here.

In 1851 males outnumbered females in grocery by nearly four to one in Britain, but females outnumbered males in the less prestigious shopkeeper category by three to two. National gender ratios, however, disguise the existence of significant regional diversity which suggests that women's participation in retailing was related to the varying social structures and labour markets associated with different forms of economic activity (figures 8.1 and 8.2). The most obvious common characteristic of both grocers and shopkeepers is the contrast between women's low participation in the retail workforces in virtually every English county to the east of Hampshire in the south, up past the east Midlands to the Humber, and their relative importance in rural areas to the south west and far north. In agricultural regions associated with pastoral or mixed farming and smaller family-units of production, it would seem that women were much more likely to be involved in business than in those in which large-scale arable production, dependent primarily on male-waged labour and selling on a national market, had become the norm. The extent of

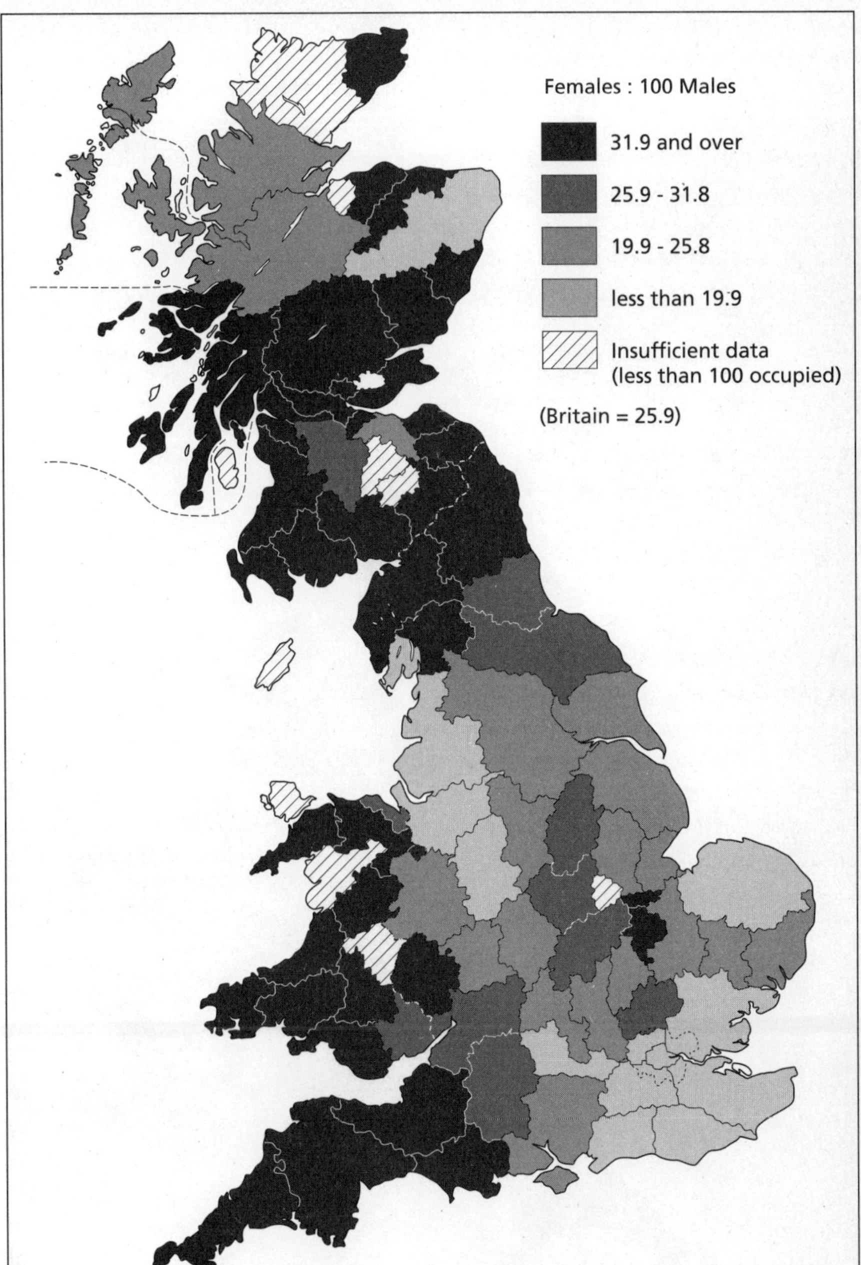

Figure 8.1 **Gender ratios in the grocery trade, 1851: females per 100 males**
Source: Census occupational tables, 1851

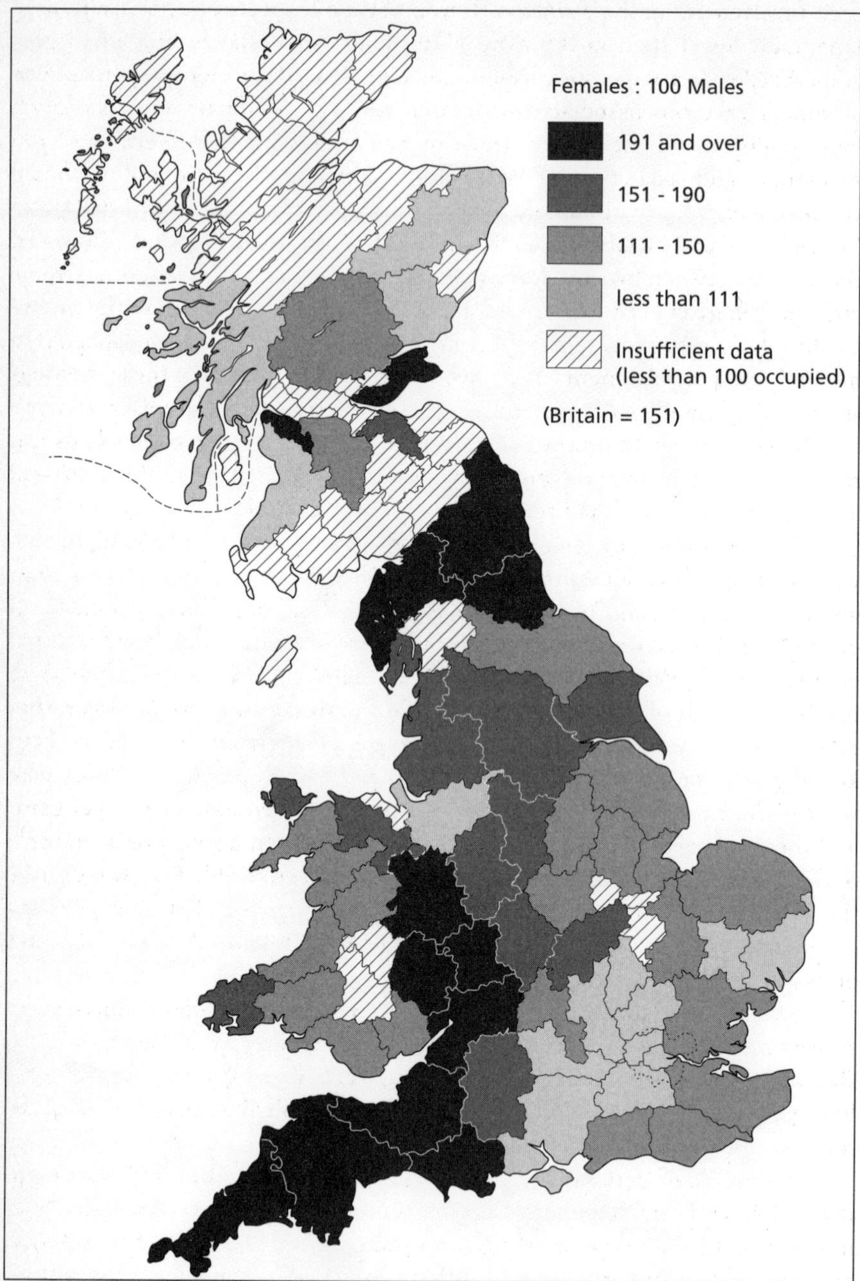

Figure 8.2 **Gender ratios in shopkeeping, 1851: female shopkeepers and shopkeepers' wives per 100 male shopkeepers**
Source: Census occupational tables, 1851

their involvement in the 'Principal Towns' of their respective regions, although marginally lower than in the rural hinterlands, also reflects this broad geographical division, suggesting that urban areas shared the cultural perceptions of gender relations associated with rural society.[47] Women were also much more important in the grocery trade in Scotland, with the exception of the highlands and islands and Edinburgh, and significantly outnumbered shopkeepers, who were largely absent from sparsely populated districts. In London, the industrialising north and most of the west Midlands, however, there were between two and four times as many female shopkeepers as female grocers. Whereas both trades were male-dominated in London, in the manufacturing districts a low female presence in grocery was counterbalanced by a much higher involvement in shopkeeping. Taken together these findings suggest that small-scale, general shopkeeping from fixed premises was primarily associated with urbanisation, but that women played a more significant role in catering for the growing urban working-class demand in the industrial areas outside London than they did in capital. (see tables 8.1–8.3.)

The age profiles of females engaged in grocery and shopkeeping in 1851 were considerably older than those for males. Only 25.8 per cent of male grocers in England and Wales were aged 45 or over as opposed to 53.7 per cent of the female workforce; equivalent figures for Scotland were 28 and 58.8 per cent (table 8.1). Whereas the age profile of male grocers was much the same north and south of the border, the female workforce in Scotland was rather older than that in England and Wales, but the position was reversed in shopkeeping. The proportion of female shopkeepers in England and Wales who were under 25 was 6.8 per cent, but was higher in Scotland at 17.1 per cent; and there was also a much lower proportion of women aged 45 or over north of the border, 42.9 per cent as opposed to 51.4 per cent (table 8.2). But despite these differences, overall the national figures suggest that most women entered retailing relatively late in life, probably trading on their own account or assisting in family businesses.

Over the next sixty years, census figures were undoubtedly influenced by revised instructions regarding the recording of women's work. Changes in the size, age and regional composition of workforces in grocery and shopkeeping, however, broadly reflect what is known about the radical transformation of the retail sector which occurred during the period.

The profile of 'general shopkeepers' in 1911 was very different from that of 1851. Male and female general shopkeepers in Scotland rose dramatically in numbers until the 1880s, but the figures then declined between 1891 and 1901, and only male numbers revived a little in 1911. Older women aged 45 or over shared in the early expansion, but from the 1890s their numbers dropped dramatically, suggesting that small-scale general retailing in this sector was in rapid decline by that period. On the other hand under 25s increased their

Table 8.1 **Structure of the grocery workforce in Britain, 1851 and 1911**

England and Wales

	Age structure				Gender ratio	
	Males (%)		Females (%)		Females per 100 males	
	1851	1911	1851	1911	1851	1911
10–14	2.83	2.68	0.77	1.24	6.3	14.9
15–19	15.64	20.01	4.48	10.13	6.6	16.4
20–24	14.59	15.43	6.42	10.31	10.2	21.6
25–34	23.41	23.41	15.06	18.16	14.8	25.1
35–44	17.74	17.57	19.62	20.59	25.5	37.9
45–54	12.73	11.25	20.86	18.36	37.8	52.7
55–64	7.96	6.52	18.08	13.06	52.4	64.7
65 & over	5.10	3.13	14.71	8.17	66.5	84.5
N=	58228	165981	13430	53638	23.1	32.3

Scotland

	Age structure				Gender ratio	
	Males (%)		Females (%)		Females per 100 males	
	1851	1911	1851	1911	1851	1911
10–14	4.24	3.01	0.45	1.94	4.4	16.9
15–19	16.05	25.93	2.71	21.27	7.1	21.6
20–24	11.96	16.48	3.65	18.28	12.8	29.2
25–44	39.75	37.10	34.44	28.66	36.2	20.3
45–64	21.87	14.40	44.31	21.22	84.7	38.7
65 & over	6.13	3.07	14.44	8.63	98.5	73.9
N=	9621	24548	4024	6451	41.8	26.3

Source: Census occupational tables, 1851 and 1911

share of the female workforce from just 17.1 per cent in 1851 to 51.9 per cent by 1911. Since no such fall occurred among the numbers of older male shopkeepers, however, by 1911 Scottish 'shopkeeping' came to be characterised by self-employed males and young female employees (though not necessarily working only in the food trades). A similar, though less complete, transformation is evident in the figures for England and Wales. During the 1870s and 1880s the numbers returned in the census as general shopkeepers began to decline. The report for England and Wales in 1891 conjecturally attributed this to falling populations in rural districts and the absorption of the trade of small shops by larger businesses in market towns.[48] This would appear to have been

Table 8.2. **Structure of the 'shopkeeping' workforce in Britain, 1851 and 1911**

	England and Wales					
	Age structure				Gender ratio	
	Males (%)		Females (%)		Females per 100 males	
	1851[a]	1911[c]	1851[b]	1911[c]	1851	1911
10–14	1.25	1.71	0.33	2.20	41.0	157.7
15–19	4.74	12.21	2.01	17.70	65.4	177.4
20–24	6.81	10.09	4.43	14.23	100.2	172.6
25–34	20.87	20.80	18.28	17.86	135.0	105.0
35–44	22.67	20.36	23.61	16.35	160.5	98.3
45–54	19.86	16.21	21.59	14.60	167.6	110.2
55–64	13.75	11.95	16.71	10.77	187.3	110.3
65 & over	10.05	6.68	13.05	6.28	200.2	115.0
N=	12900	38697	19886	47345	154.2	122.3

	Scotland					
	Age structure				Gender ratio	
	Males (%)		Females (%)		Females per 100 males	
	1851[a]	1911[c]	1851[b]	1911[c]	1851	1911
10–14	2.09	1.25	0.54	2.81	28.6	333.3
15–19	11.06	12.64	6.45	27.64	64.9	325.0
20–24	13.75	10.91	10.14	21.45	82.1	292.1
25–44	42.30	39.32	39.96	30.56	105.1	115.5
45–64	22.65	29.11	32.03	13.07	157.4	66.7
65 & over	8.15	6.76	10.88	4.46	148.6	98.1
N=	1338	3830	1489	5691	111.3	148.6

Notes

[a]excluding 'shopmen': these were not distinguished from unclassified mechanics and manufacturers in the 1851 tables

[b]female shopkeepers and wives (figures exclude 'shopwomen', 2248 in England and Wales, and 174 in Scotland)

[c]'General and Unclassified Shopkeepers and Dealers'

Source: Census occupational tables, 1851 and 1911

the case since, as in Scotland, the decline was largely accounted for by a substantial drop of 43.7 per cent in the number of females aged 25 or over between 1871 and 1891, while the number of women under 25 dropped by only 7.7 per cent and then nearly doubled in number between 1891 and 1901. Even after

Table 8.3. **Regional changes in female participation in grocery and shopkeeping, 1851–1911**

	Females per 100 Males			
	Grocers		Shopkeepers	
	1851	1911	1851[a]	1911[b]
England and Wales	23	32	154	122
Scotland	42	26	111	149
London	9	27	110	74
Middlesex	15	14	99	74
Surrey	15	12	99	82
Suffolk	25	22	106	118
Devon	62	31	308	159
Staffordshire	19	54	173	232
Warwickshire	22	48	184	216
Leicestershire	27	51	134	137
Nottinghamshire	26	41	140	105
Lancashire	18	38	188	172
West Riding of Yorkshire	21	39	178	139
Northumberland	39	32	448	213
County Durham	28	31	338	200
Glamorgan and Monmouth	31	29	122	166
Flint and Denbighshire	33	34	152	128
Rest of Wales	37	63	145	129
Lanarkshire	31	23	142	169
Edinburghshire	25	15	164	235

Notes

[a]1851: shopkeepers (male and female) and shopkeepers' wives

[b]1911: unclassified general shopkeepers and dealers

Source: Census for England and Wales, Scotland, 1851 and 1911

the issuing of the new instructions in 1911 about the recording of married women's work, over a third of the female workforce was under 25, over a half was unmarried and four-fifths of them were employees. Unlike in Scotland, however, the ratio of females to males in shopkeeping had deteriorated over the period (table 8.2).

The grocery workforce also increased dramatically up to 1891 during which time it also became younger. In England and Wales, men under 25 accounted for 34.1 per cent of the male workforce in 1871 and 42.1 per cent twenty years later, but the figure slipped back to just 40 per cent in 1901 and 38.1 per cent in 1911 reflecting the slower pace of expansion from the 1890s. The proportion of the female labour force who were under 25 years old rose to 15.6 per cent by 1871 and 21.7 per cent by 1891, due in part to the inclusion of young chocolate and cocoa workers and tea packers in the figures, but then stagnated. North of the border these trends were rather more defined. By 1891 men under 25 accounted for 49 per cent of the male workforce, but the figure declined marginally thereafter as the pace of expansion slackened, and with it recruitment into the trade. The female workforce also became much younger from the 1870s. As the number of older women stagnated and then declined, women under 25 increased their share of the female labour force from just over 10 per cent in 1871 to 23.7 per cent in 1891 and 41.5 per cent by 1911. In Scotland, however, women's overall participation plummeted from 41.8 females per 100 males in 1851 to just 26.3 in 1911, the most substantial fall occurring between 1871 and 1891 (table 8.1). This trend was evident throughout eastern and southern Scotland but was particularly pronounced in the densely populated, urbanised counties of central Scotland, especially Lanarkshire and Edinburgh, where gender ratios in the trade fell from what were already relatively low figures by Scottish standards of 31 and 25 females per 100 males in 1851, to just 23 and 15 by 1911 (table 8.3). This was in marked contrast to England and Wales where women comprised an increasing share of the workforce, the number of females per 100 males rising from 23.1 in 1851 to 34.1 by 1891, dropping to 28.3 in 1901 but then reviving to 32.3 in 1911. Furthermore, the 25–44 age group accounted for an increasing proportion of this expanding female workforce in England and Wales, rising from a low of 30.4 per cent in 1871 to 38.8 per cent by 1911 (table 8.1). Some of this may have been due to the tendency to reclassify small general shopkeepers as grocers during this period, but it nevertheless implies that such businesses continued to be viable despite the growth of large scale retailing. To understand where they may have persisted we need to disaggregate the most reliable and detailed national figures we have – those for 1911.

Figures 8.3 and 8.4 and table 8.3 reveal that women remained significantly under-represented in both grocery and shopkeeping throughout south-east England, especially in the Home Counties. Only in London, where the emergence of exceptionally large numbers of unmarried employees belatedly raised the female–male ratio in grocery from 15.4 per 100 males in 1901 to 26.5 ten years later, was there any evidence of substantial female incursion into what still remained an overwhelmingly male workforce. Elsewhere in the region women were virtually absent from grocery, and in several counties, including

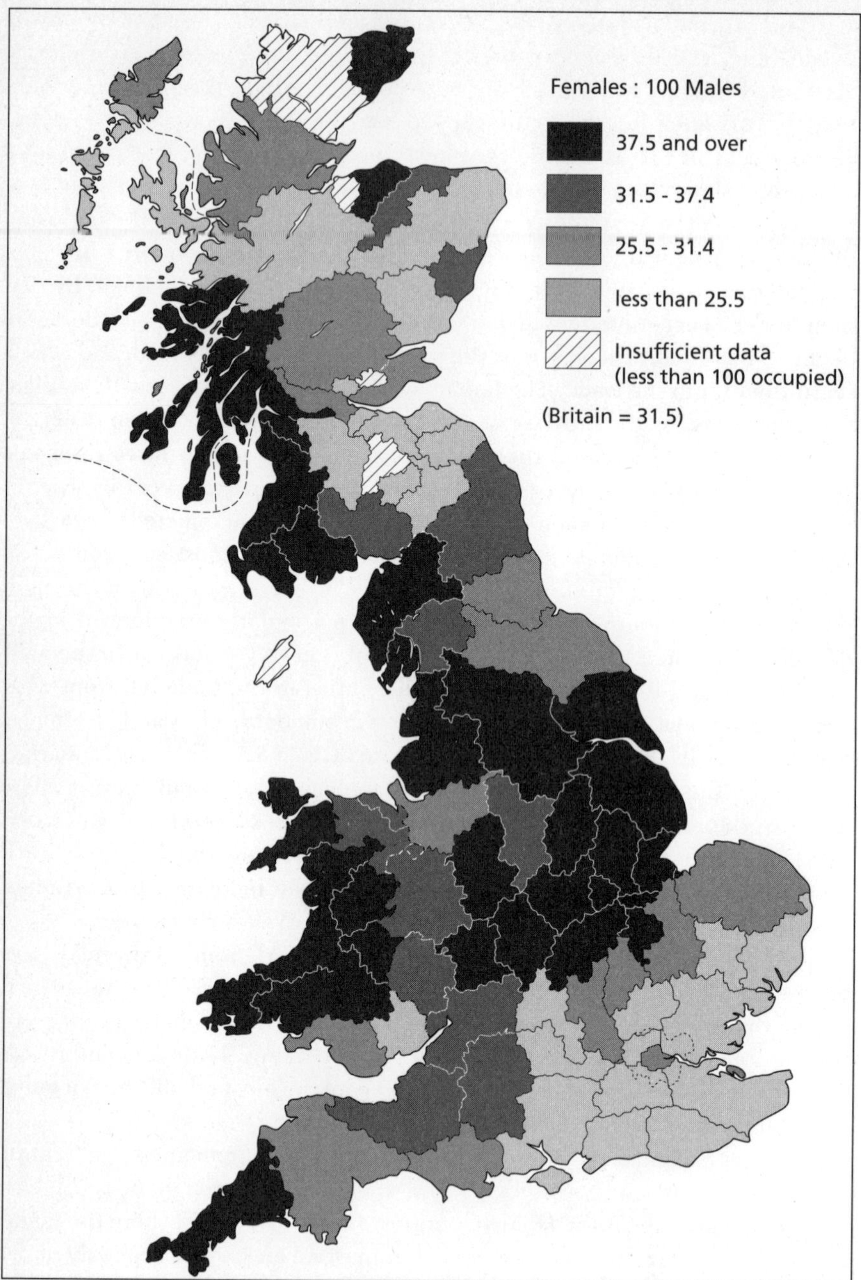

Figure 8.3 **Gender ratios in the grocery trade, 1911: females per 100 males**
Source: Census occupational tables, 1911

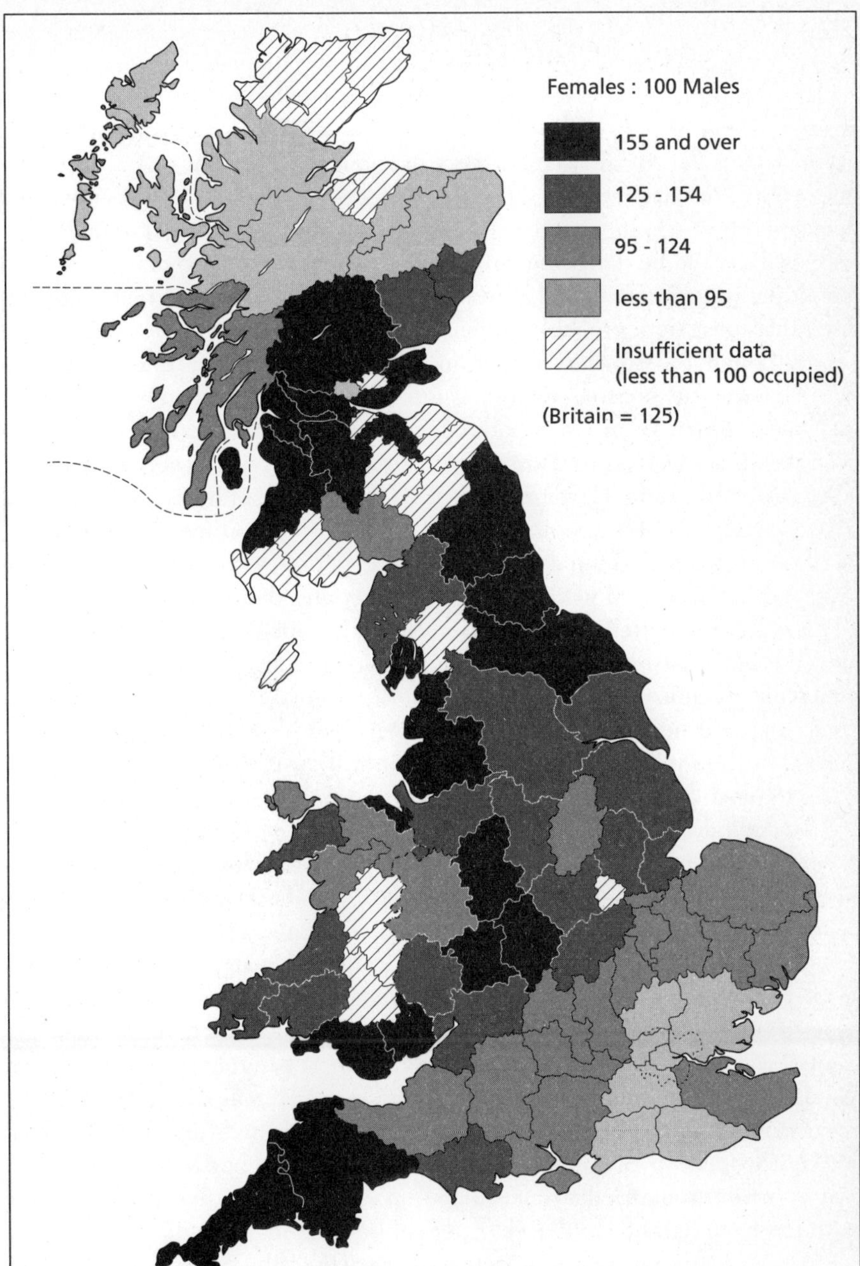

Figure 8.4 **Gender ratios in general shopkeeping, 1911: females per 100 males**

Source: Census occupational tables, 1911

Surrey, Kent and Middlesex, their importance actually declined over the period, contrary to the national trend (figure 8.3; table 8.3). Despite above average increases in the number of married women after 1901 in the counties around London, they still accounted for only around 6 per cent of grocers (table 8.4) and a trivial 10–11 per cent of shopkeepers (table 8.5) in 1911. The majority of female grocers and shopkeepers in London were unmarried women, few of whom worked on their own account or as part of family businesses. It would be dangerous to assume that these 'shopkeepers' were even employed in general or food retailing by this date; the census report considered that most were probably drapers of some description.

Although the south-west continued to display higher rates of female participation, the contrast with the south-east was less marked by 1911 than it had been in 1851. Women's importance in both shopkeeping and grocery actually declined in Devon, Dorset and Somerset over the period while in Gloucestershire and Herefordshire they made only marginal inroads into grocery and were far less involved in shopkeeping. Cornwall's experience, however, remained unique throughout the period with exceptionally high numbers of unmarried women in both grocery and shopkeeping.

Yet another pattern emerged in north and south Wales, central Scotland and the north-east of England, areas whose growing prosperity in the late nineteenth century had been primarily based on the expansion of mining, quarrying and heavy industry. Here women had been relatively over-represented in the mid-century grocery trade, but by 1911 this was no longer the case. In most counties in these regions the gender ratio deteriorated over the period and now reflected the national figure (figure 8.3). Women's over-representation among general shopkeepers in the north-east was also far less evident by 1911, but their share of the workforce in Scotland and South Wales had increased (figure 8.4; table 8.3). Apart from the grocery trade in Glamorgan and Monmouth, where their involvement in the workforces was close to the national figure, these regions had relatively few married women in their retail workforces (tables 7:4 and 7:5). They accounted for around 6 per cent of grocers in the north-east and only around 1 per cent in Scotland. That gender ratios had not deteriorated further since 1851 was due entirely to the increasing number of unmarried women who accounted for nearly a half of all shopkeepers in Scotland and over a third in the north-east and South Wales, while unmarried women made up nearly one in five of the grocery workforce on Tyneside and over 15 per cent of that in Scotland.

The situation in the manufacturing districts of the Midlands and northern England, however, was very different. In 1851 women had been relatively under-represented in the grocery trade in the west Midlands, Lancashire and the West Riding; by 1911 they were significantly over-represented. Their importance in the east Midlands also increased but from a rather higher base

Table 8.4. **Regional variations in female participation in the grocery trade, 1911 (%)**

	Female Workforce		Total Workforce		
	married	widowed	married	widowed	unmarried
England and Wales	42.2	18.8	9.6	4.6	10.3
Scotland	6.1	18.1	1.3	3.8	15.8
Lanarkshire	5.4	*	1.0	*	
Glasgow	5.7	*	0.9	*	
Edinburghshire	3.9	*	0.5	*	
Edinburgh	4.3	*	0.5	*	
London	30.8	7.4	6.4	1.6	12.9
Middlesex	54.1	10.4	6.4	1.2	4.2
Surrey	50.8	13.2	5.6	1.5	4.0
Suffolk	44.9	14.3	8.2	2.6	7.4
Devon	41.5	18.4	9.9	4.4	9.6
Northumberland	21.6	18.3	5.2	4.4	14.4
County Durham	27.9	18.5	6.6	4.4	12.6
Tyneside boroughs[a]	24.0	15.9	7.4	4.9	18.6
Teesside boroughs[b]	35.2	20.8	8.1	4.8	11.2
Glamorgan and Monmouth	41.6	19.1	9.4	4.3	8.9
Flint and Denbighshire	34.5	25.1	8.7	6.4	10.2
Rest of Wales	31.4	24.7	12.1	9.5	16.9
Lancashire	42.2	18.8	11.6	5.1	10.7
Merseyside[c]	31.2	16.0	4.7	2.4	8.0
Textile boroughs[d]	45.2	20.1	14.2	6.3	10.8
West Riding of Yorkshire	41.5	22.1	11.6	6.2	10.2
Textile boroughs[e]	44.3	19.0	12.2	5.2	10.1
Staffordshire	42.2	23.6	14.8	8.3	12.0
Stoke on Trent	48.9	22.2	19.1	8.7	11.4
Warwickshire	45.2	20.0	14.6	6.5	11.3
Birmingham	46.8	19.9	16.5	7.0	11.8
Leicestershire	47.3	20.6	15.9	6.9	10.8
Leicester	56.8	19.3	18.8	6.4	7.9
Nottinghamshire	49.2	19.7	14.3	5.7	9.1
Nottingham	53.8	17.2	17.1	5.5	9.2

Notes
*Figures for widows' employment in Scottish counties and towns were published only for 'principal occupations'
[a]Gateshead, Newcastle, South Shields, Sunderland, Tynemouth
[b]Darlington, Middlesbrough, Stockton, West Hartlepool
[c]Liverpool, Bootle
[d]Blackburn. Bolton, Burnley, Bury, Oldham, Preston, Rochdale
[e]Bradford, Dewsbury, Halifax, Huddersfield
Source: Occupational tables, Censuses for England and Wales, and Scotland, 1911

Table 8.5. **Regional variations in female participation in shopkeeping,[a] 1911** (%)

	Female workforce		Total workforce		
	married	widowed	married	widowed	unmarried
England and Wales	29.3	16.2	16.1	8.9	30.0
Scotland	7.5	10.7	4.5	6.4	48.9
Lanarkshire	12.0	*	7.6	*	
Glasgow[b]	15.4	*	9.1	*	
Edinburghshire	6.8	*	4.8	*	
Edinburgh[b]	8.0	*	5.7	*	
London	27.3	12.7	11.6	5.4	25.5
Middlesex	25.3	12.6	10.8	5.4	26.4
Surrey	24.6	11.2	11.1	5.0	29.0
Suffolk	31.9	17.7	17.3	9.6	27.3
Devon	30.2	16.8	18.6	10.3	32.5
Northumberland	22.9	19.7	15.6	13.4	39.0
County Durham	26.1	21.2	17.4	14.2	35.1
Glamorgan and Monmouth	24.5	18.0	15.3	11.2	35.9
Flint and Denbighshire	19.7	20.4	11.0	11.4	33.7
Rest of Wales	23.9	16.5	13.5	9.3	33.6
Lancashire	29.4	17.2	18.5	10.8	33.8
West Riding of Yorkshire	26.7	15.3	15.5	8.8	33.8
Staffordshire	36.8	21.6	25.7	15.1	29.0
Warwickshire	36.9	21.0	25.2	14.4	28.7
Leicestershire	41.9	15.1	24.3	8.8	24.6
Nottinghamshire	35.8	13.5	18.3	6.9	26.0

Notes
*Figures for widows' employment in Scottish counties and towns were published only for 'principal occupations'
[a]general and unclassified shopkeepers and dealers
For female/male ratios, see Table 8.3 and Figure 8.4
[b]It is not possible to compare towns in England and Wales because the Condensed Occupational Tables for County Boroughs merged general shopkeepers and pawnbrokers; Scottish tables presented them separately.
Source: Occupational tables, Censuses for England and Wales, and Scotland, 1911

(figures 8.3 and 8.4; table 8.3). The reason for this lay not in the increased incidence of single women but in the importance of wives and widows who accounted for over 20 per cent of grocers throughout the Midlands (table 8.4). Female workforces in the region had considerably older age profiles than in the rest of the country. Under 25s accounted for only 18.3 per cent of female grocers in Birmingham, 13.4 per cent in Stoke, 10.6 per cent in Coventry, 10.4 per cent in Walsall, and 9.9 per cent in Leicester, as opposed to 45.5 per cent in Newcastle upon Tyne and 48.9 per cent in London. Against the trend in most of England, general shopkeeping also became more female-dominated in Staffordshire and Warwickshire but, unlike in Scotland or the north-east where single women made up the majority of the female workforce, married women were much more important, comprising around 25 per cent of all shopkeepers in Staffordshire, Warwickshire and Leicester, while widows also were important in Staffordshire and Warwickshire (table 8.5).

Although gender ratios in the grocery trade were somewhat lower in Lancashire and the West Riding, the county figures disguise the fact that the cotton textile towns and, to a lesser extent, the woollen and worsted districts of the West Riding, exhibited similar characteristics to the industrial Midlands. Married and widowed women comprised 20.5 per cent of the workforce in the seven cotton textile boroughs in Lancashire for which detailed statistics were published, 18.4 per cent in Salford and Manchester and 17.4 per cent in the West Riding woollen and worsted towns (table 8.4). Comparable figures for the Lancashire seaside resorts (Southport and Blackpool) and for Merseyside were just 13.8 and 7.1 per cent. In Liverpool 38.1 per cent of the female workforce were under 25 years old; in the textile towns of Preston, Blackburn, Oldham and Burnley the figure was under 10 per cent.[49] Not surprisingly, these older women were less likely to be engaged as employees, and more likely to be in family businesses or working on their own account. Whereas 65.4 per cent of female grocers in London and 53.4 per cent of those in Scotland were described as 'working for employers' only 31.8 per cent were so returned in Lancashire.[50]

Explanations and observations

What do these findings contribute to our understanding of the impact of British industrialisation on retailing and gender relations? Although they do not necessarily invalidate Hall's interpretation of the declining involvement of females in high-street grocery shops, they shed doubts on the extent to which the retail form which she studied was representative of family businesses during the nineteenth century. The virtual disappearance of older female general shopkeepers between 1851 and 1911 was counterbalanced by the increasing role which women in the 25–44 age group played in grocery. There were, however, marked regional variations in patterns of women's involvement which were far from constant over time. In 1851 female involvement in businesses was much lower in the south east than in the rural west and north of the country. Small family shops in which married and widowed women worked were insignificant in south-east England in 1911, and they had also declined wherever large-scale grocery chains emerged, especially in urban Scotland, but they became important elements of the retail structure in the industrial Midlands, and even the co-op strongholds of the Lancashire textile districts.

There is no obvious monocausal explanation of these regional variations in retail provision and employment. Rather they would appear to have been related to a variety of economic and cultural factors, including the organisation of the family economy, the labour market, the structure of demand, patterns of property ownership, and the timing and nature of urban residential development.

First, the early Victorian figures suggest that the extent of women's role in retailing was determined in part by the nature of agriculture in a particular region. In the south-east, as far west as Wiltshire and as far north as Lincolnshire, women had already been marginalised before 1851; they played a much more significant role in the predominantly rural counties in the west and north of Britain, apart from the Scottish highlands and islands. With the exception of the north-east coast above the Humber, the region where they were least important bears a remarkable resemblance to James Caird's mid-century line between corn-growing and grazing counties. It is also virtually identical to that identified by the Muis as having more advanced retail facilities as early as the mid-eighteenth century, a feature which they also associate with the nucleated settlement patterns typical of arable farming areas.[51] Gender relations in societies characterised by large-scale capitalist arable farmers employing male labour and selling in a national market were apparently conceived very differently from those in more pastoral regions to the north and west where smaller family-units of production predominated.

The development of a service-dominated, urban economy in London and the Home Counties in the late nineteenth century did little to enhance women's importance in the south-east. Middle-class demand, fuelled primarily by wealth derived from the expansion of international commerce and the professions, created an urban society in which women were restricted to the domestic environment, as unoccupied family members or domestic servants, and in which most business activity was dominated by males. The market in London's sprawling middle-class suburbs offered little scope for women's involvement in small-scale retailing. Rather, it created a labour-intensive retail system in which tradesmen solicited orders and delivered to customers' doors. Young, single women employed as indoor domestic servants were divorced from the market economy, and they lacked the incentive, experience and confidence which were necessary for conducting business on their own account later in life. Not surprisingly, women's increasing role in the distributive trades in this region during the twentieth century took the form of employment as waged-shop assistants, retail rather than domestic servants, and this stands in marked contrast to the more independent nature of married women's and widows' involvement in the industrial north and Midlands during the preceding century.

Regions which became increasingly dependent on mining and heavy industry in the late nineteenth century were characterised by declining or static female representation in grocery, the emergence of young female shop assistants, and married women's relatively insignificant roles in both workforces. The slack labour markets here offered few other employment opportunities for young single women and widows, with the consequence that they pushed married women out of retailing. The masculine ideology and concept of a male breadwinner's wage generated by the dominant local industries further militated against the involvement of wives in public business activities. Even so, married and widowed women's participation in the workforce was higher in south Wales than the north-east, especially Tyneside, and was exceptionally low in Scotland. The contrasting patterns of property ownership and residential development in these regions could have been responsible for this. Scottish urbanisation was characterised by the subdivision of large central properties and frenetic bouts of construction of densely-packed four-storey tenement flats, neither of which offered their inhabitants opportunity for engaging in retail business.[52] Small-scale, residential businesses were simply not catered for by the large-scale developers and landlords of this new urban landscape. The provision of purpose-built retail premises at street level and the 'great density of the local market in these tenement block districts' were particularly conducive to the rapid expansion of Scottish multiples, which were able to lease the purpose-built premises as lock-up shops.[53] Similar conditions were evident in other overcrowded inner-city districts characterised by the subdivision of large properties and among Tyneside's small terraced flats. Elsewhere in the north-east single-storey cottages provided by colliery owners also offered little scope for independence but where property ownership was less concentrated, as in the mining valleys of south Wales and to a lesser extent Teesside, there were fewer obstacles to small-scale enterprise and married women and widows were marginally more important.[54] The exceptionally low level of married women's and widows' participation in Scotland, however, suggest that other, as yet unidentified, cultural factors were also important.

Unlike the overstocked urban labour markets of London, Liverpool or the heavy industrial and mining areas, the manufacturing districts of the north and Midlands offered more opportunities for juveniles and young adults to obtain relatively well-paid work in factories and workshops. This may have meant that large-scale food retailing businesses, with their long hours and close personal supervision, would have found it more difficult to recruit cheap labour and consequently to compete with small-scale businesses dependent on unpaid, older family labour. Textiles, pottery, boot and shoe manufacturing, hardware and smallware production provided plentiful, regular jobs outside the home for young women and, since some continued to work into early marriage, raised rates of married women's employment well above the national average and challenged the concept of a male 'breadwinner's wage'. Areas like the Potteries and the textile towns were characterised by family structures and strategies in which women – wives, mothers and daughters – played key roles in shaping families' responses to changing economic circumstances.[55] Small-scale retailing which catered for the daily needs of the communities in which they lived was one way in which such women could contribute to family income.

Furthermore, the nature of working-class demand and patterns of residential development in these industrial areas were also conducive to the establishment of small, family-run shops.[56] Working-class purchasers effectively demanded convenience: easy access to retail outlets; long opening hours and a range of packaged, part-processed, cooked and raw food products.[57] The linear bye-law terraces of manufacturing towns and sprawling overgrown industrial villages encouraged the diffusion of neighbourhood shops offering a range of goods and services, rather than concentrating them in the high street. With fewer large landlords than Scotland or the north-east, there were also fewer restrictions on adapting front rooms abutting the public thoroughfare for retail business.[58] From the last quarter of the century developers of working-class estates frequently erected purpose-built residential shops at the junctions of adjoining streets. There is some local evidence to suggest that co-ops and local multiples were beginning to colonise corner shops in working-class estates from the late 1880s but this was far from universally the case.[59] The viability of many family-run neighbourhood shops in these industrial districts was only seriously undermined later in the twentieth century when diminishing employment opportunities in industry, large scale retail development, urban renewal and housing programmes destroyed the social infrastructure of which they were a part.

Conclusion

The relationships between nineteenth-century industrialisation, urbanisation, retail development and employment, therefore, were complex, influenced by factors as diverse as the nature and timing of residential development, patterns of property ownership and the structure of the labour market. We can only begin to appreciate and understand the diverse patterns of women's participation in the labour force in Britain and their possible significance for gender relations, however, if we adopt a long-term comparative perspective which acknowledges that the national picture is composed of a variety of regional identities and experiences. Where women lived was as important as when they lived in shaping their experiences of work.

Notes

1 E. Richards, 'Women in the British economy since about 1700: an interpretation', *History*, 59 (1974), 337–57.

2 For syntheses of the huge historiography which has emerged since Richards see J. Thomas, 'Women and capitalism: oppression or emancipation? A review article', *Comparative Studies in Society and History*, 30 (1988), 534–49; E. Roberts, *Women's Work, 1840–1940* (London, 1988 and Cambridge, 1995); J. Rendall, *Women in an Industrialising Society: England, 1750–1880* (Oxford, 1990); P. Hudson and R. Lee (eds), *Women's Work and the Family Economy in Historical Perspective* (Manchester, 1990), chap. 1; J. Lown, *Women and Industrialisation: Gender and Work in Nineteenth-Century England* (Oxford, 1990); S. Rose, *Limited Livelihoods: Gender and Class in Nineteenth-Century England* (London, 1992); D. Bythell, 'Women in the workforce', in P. O' Brien and R. Quinault (eds), *The Industrial Revolution and British Society* (Cambridge, 1993), pp. 31–53; P. Sharpe, 'Continuity and change: women's history and economic history in Britain', *EcHR*, 48 (1995), 353–69; J. Humphries, 'Women and paid work', in J. Purvis (ed.), *Women's History: Britain, 1850–1945* (London, 1995), pp. 85–106.

3 Humphries, 'Women and paid work', p. 98. This chapter draws heavily on her collaborative work with S. Horrell on re-working pre-census data, 'Women's labour force participation and the transition to the male-breadwinner family, 1790–1865', *EcHR*, 48 (1995) 89–117, and on C. Hakim, 'A century of change in occupational segregation, 1891–1991', *Journal of Historical Sociology*, 7 (1994), 435–54.

4 W. Seccombe, 'Patriarchy stabilised: the construction of the male breadwinner norm in nineteenth-century Britain', *Social History*, 11 (1986), 53–76; S. Rose, 'Gender at work: sex, class and industrial capitalism', *History Workshop Journal*, 21 (1986), 113–32; E. Jordan, 'The exclusion of women from industry in nineteenth-century Britain', *Comparative Studies in Society and History*, 31 (1989), 309–26.

5 M. Berg and P. Hudson, 'Rehabilitating the Industrial Revolution', *EcHR*, 45 (1992), 24–50; M. Berg, 'What difference did women's work make to the Industrial Revolution?', *History Workshop Journal*, 35 (1993), 22–43; Hudson and Lee (eds), *Women's Work*, *passim*.

6 J. A. Schmiechen, *Sweated Industries and Sweated Labour: The London Clothing Trades, 1860–1914* (Beckenham, 1984); J. Morris, *Women Workers and the Sweated Trades: The Origins of Minimum Wage Legislation* (Aldershot, 1986); L. Davidoff, 'The separation of home and work? Landladies and lodgers in nineteenth- and twentieth-century England', in S. Burman (ed.), *Fit Work for Women* (London, 1979), pp. 64–97.

7 E. Roberts, 'Working wives and their families', in T. Barker and M. Drake (eds), *Population and Society in Britain* (London, 1982); S. Alexander, 'Women's work in early nineteenth-century London', in A. Oakley and J. Mitchell (eds), *The Rights and Wrongs of Women* (Harmondsworth, 1976), pp. 59–111; S. Pennington and B. Westover, *A Hidden Workforce: Homeworkers in England, 1850–1985* (London, 1989); E. Ross, 'Survival networks: women's neighbourhood sharing in London before World War One', *History Workshop Journal*, 15, (1983), 4–27.

8 Hudson and Lee (eds), *Women's Work*, pp. 9, 33; See also Sharpe, 'Continuity and change'.

9 K. D. M. Snell, 'Agricultural seasonal employment, the standard of living and women's work in the South and East, 1690–1860', in K. D. M. Snell, *Annals of the Labouring Poor: Social Change and Agrarian England, 1660–1900* (Cambridge, 1985), pp. 15–66; S. McMurry, 'Women's work in agriculture: divergent trends in England and America, 1800 to 1930', *Comparative Studies in Society and History*, 34 (1992), 248–72; M. Winstanley, 'Industrialisation and the small farm: family and household economy in nineteenth-century Lancashire', *Past and Present*, 152 (August 1996), 157–92; M. Bouquet, *Family, Servants and Visitors: The Farm Household in Nineteenth and Twentieth Century Devon* (Norwich, 1985); T. M. Devine, 'Women workers, 1850–1914', in T. M Devine (ed.), *Farm Servants and Labour in Lowland Scotland* (Edinburgh, 1984), pp. 98–123.

10 D. Gittins, *Fair Sex: Family Size and Structure, 1900–39* (London, 1982); M. Glucksman, *Women Assemble: Women Workers and the New Industries in Inter-War Britain* (London, 1990); E. Jordan, 'Female unemployment in England and Wales, 1851–1911: an examination of the census figures for 15–19 year olds', *Social History*, 13 (1988), 175–90; M. W. Dupree, *Family Structure in the Staffordshire Potteries, 1840–1880* (Oxford, 1995); E. Roberts, *A Women's Place: An Oral History of Working-Class Women, 1890–1940* (Oxford, 1984 and 1995).

11 A. Clark, *Working Life of Women in the Seventeenth Century* (1919, reprinted, London, 1982), pp. 200–27; I. Pinchbeck, *Women Workers and the Industrial Revolution, 1750–1850* (London, 1930), pp. 293–300.

12 W. Thwaites, 'Women in the market place: Oxfordshire, c. 1690–1800', *Midland History*, 9 (1984), 23–42; see also E. P. Thompson, *Customs in Common* (Harmondsworth, 1991), pp. 315–16.

13 J. Burnett, 'The baking industry in the nineteenth century', *Business History*, 5 (1963), 98–108; D. Valenze, 'The art of women and the business of men: women's work and the dairy industry, 1780–1840', *Past and Present*, 130 (February 1991), 142–69.

14 C. Hall, 'The butcher, the baker, the candlestick maker: the shop and the family in the Industrial Revolution', in E. Whitelegg *et al.* (eds), *The Changing Experience of Women* (Oxford, 1982), pp. 2–16. For further details of the elucidation of this explanatory model see C. Hall, 'The early formation of Victorian domestic ideology', in Burman, *Fit Work for Women*, pp. 15–32 and L. Davidoff and C. Hall, *Family Fortunes: Men and Women of the English Middle Class, 1780–1850* (London, 1987).

15 Hall, 'Butcher', p. 3.

16 H.-C. and L. Mui, *Shops and Shopkeeping in Eighteenth-Century England* (London, 1989); J. Blackman, 'The corner shop: the development of the grocery and general provisions trade', in D. J. Oddy and D. Miller (eds), *The Making of the Modern English Diet* (London, 1976), pp. 148–60; J. Blackman, 'The development of the retail grocery trade in the nineteenth century', *Business History*, 9 (1967), 110–17; R. Scola, 'Food markets and shops in Manchester, 1770–1870', *Journal of Historical Geography*, 1 (1975), 153–68; D. Alexander, *Retailing in England during the Industrial Revolution* (London, 1970), pp. 89–109; C. P. Hosgood, '"The Pigmies of Commerce" and the working-class community: small shopkeepers in England, 1870–1914', *Journal of Social History*, 22 (1989), 439–60; Z. Lawson, 'Shops, shopkeepers and the working-class community: Preston, 1860–1890', *Transactions of the Historic Society of Lancashire and Cheshire*, 141 (1991), 309–28.

17 C. P. Hosgood, 'Shopkeepers and society: domestic and principal shopkeepers in Leicester, 1860–1914' (unpublished Ph.D. thesis, University of Manitoba, 1987), p. 13.

18 G. Crossick and H-G. Haupt, *The Petite Bourgeoisie in Europe, 1780–1914* (London, 1995), pp. 97, 111.

19 A. Foley, *A Bolton Childhood*. Workers' Educational Association, Bolton Branch (Bolton, 1973), p. 19; R. Roberts, *The Classic Slum: Salford Life in the First Quarter of the Century* (Manchester, 1971; Harmondsworth, 1973); M. Tebbutt, *Women's Talk: A Social History of Gossip, 1880–1960* (Aldershot, 1995).
20 M. Winstanley, *The Shopkeeper's World, 1830–1914* (Manchester, 1983), pp. 97–8.
21 L. E. Neal, *Retailing and the Public* (London, 1932), p. 6.
22 H. Smith, *Retail Distribution: A Critical Analysis* (Cambridge, 1937), pp. 90, 98; D. Braithwaite and S. P. Dobbs, *The Distribution of Consumable Goods* (London, 1936), p. 242; Neal, *Retailing*, p. 8. Only H. Levy, *The Shops of Britain: A Study of Retail Distribution* (London, 1948), sympathised with and supported the small shopkeeper – 'and perhaps his wife', p. 11.
23 J. B. Jefferys, *Retail Trading in Britain, 1850–1950* (Cambridge, 1954); P. Mathias, *Retailing Revolution* (London, 1972).
24 M. Purvis, 'The development of co-operative retailing in England and Wales, 1851–1901: a geographical study', *Journal of Historical Geography*, 16 (1990), 314–31; M. Purvis, 'Co-operative retailing in Britain', in J. Benson and G. Shaw (eds), *The Evolution of Retail Systems, c. 1800–1914* (Leicester, 1992), pp. 107–34; G. D. H. Cole, *A Century of Co-operation* (Manchester, [1944]), pp. 390–2; Jefferys, *Retail Trading*, pp. 164–7.
25 L. Holcombe, *Victorian Ladies at Work* (Newton Abbot, 1973), pp. 105–7; H. Bradley, *Men's Work, Women's Work: A Sociological History of the Sexual Division of Labour in Employment* (Oxford, 1980), pp. 176–81; B. Lancaster, *The Department Store: A Social History* (Leicester, 1995), pp. 137–42.
26 Although the majority of women members of early shop assistants' unions were co-operative employees, this cannot be taken as symptomatic of their importance within the movement's workforce as a whole. Sir W. Richardson, *A History of Many Trades: The History of USDAW* (Manchester, [c.1979]), pp. 318–19.
27 B. Williams, *The Best Butter in the World: A History of Sainsbury's* (London, 1994), pp. 65–6; Mathias, *Retailing Revolution*, pp. 65, 144.
28 Jefferys, *Retail Trading*, pp. 260, 275. Exceptionally the Victoria Wine Company exclusively employed women as manageresses from an early date; A. Briggs, *Wine for Sale: Victoria Wine and the Liquor Trade, 1860–1984* (London, 1985), pp. 80, 113.
29 Census Report for England and Wales, 1911, p. cxxi.
30 Mathias, *Retailing Revolution*, pp. 143–4.
31 'What the consumer wants', *Planning* (PEP), 7 (18 July 1933), 9. I am grateful to Douglas Farnie for this reference. Neal, *Retailing*, p. 6.
32 Jefferys, *Retail Trading*, p. 168.
33 Census of Distribution, 1961, reproduced in Department of Economic Affairs, *The North West, a Regional Study* (1965), p. 171.
34 J. B. Priestley, *English Journey* (London, 1934), pp. 398–9.
35 Jefferys, *Retail Trading*, pp. 164–8.
36 Mathias, *Retailing Revolution*, pp. 101, 139–40, 151.
37 E. Higgs, 'Women, occupations, and work in nineteenth-century censuses', *History Workshop Journal*, 23 (1987), 59–80; B. Hill, 'Women's work and the census: a problem for historians of women', *History Workshop Journal*, 35 (1993), 78–94; E. Higgs, *Making Sense of the Census: The Manuscript Returns for England and Wales, 1801–1901* (London, 1989) is an excellent introduction to this source; I would be grateful for any reference to comparable work on the Scottish census.
38 The term is confusing but meant to reflect the varied, or 'multiple' nature of department store trading. Most of those in this category were considered to have been drapers' assistants. Those employed by the chains of multiples were returned under the specialist trades.

39 Census Report for England and Wales, 1891, p. 34. The 1911 census published data on employment status for London, Lancashire and Yorkshire (three Ridings combined).

40 Census Report for England and Wales, 1911, pp. xxxvi and cxii. The number of female grocers in England and Wales rose by 26.5 per cent over the decade as opposed to an increase of just 9.8 per cent for males. Although the absolute rise in the number of married/widowed women exceeded that for the unmarried the percentage increase was somewhat lower at 24.4 per cent as opposed to 29.7 per cent.

41 C. H. Lee, *British Regional Employment Statistics, 1841–1971* (Cambridge, 1979), chap. 1 provides a balanced discussion of these problems.

42 Winstanley, *Shopkeeper's World*, pp. 41–3.

43 E. Higgs, 'Domestic servants and households in Victorian England', *Social History*, 8 (1983), 208.

44 The same problem applies to shopkeepers and their wives in general, although for the purposes of this analysis I have assumed that they were all 'general shopkeepers', rather than engaged in specialist trading. In the analysis of 1851 which follows shopmen and shopwomen have both been excluded from the calculations of sex ratios and age profiles.

45 C. H. Lee, 'The service sector, regional specialization, and economic growth in the Victorian economy', *Journal of Historical Geography*, 10 (1984), 147.

46 M. Phillips, 'The evolution of markets and shops in Britain', in Benson and Shaw, *Retail Systems*, pp. 64–73. esp. pp. 71, 73.

47 This observation is based on calculations derived from occupational data on 'Principal Towns' in the 1851 census

48 Census Report for England and Wales, 1891, p. 57.

49 Calculated from the 1911 Census for England and Wales, Occupational Table 13, Occupations (Condensed List) of Males and Females in Administrative Counties, Rural Districts and Boroughs over 50,000 population. It is not possible to calculate comparable figures for general shopkeepers since the figures were merged with department or 'multiple' store workers and pawnbrokers.

50 1911 Census for England and Wales, Occupational Tables 9 and 10; 1911 Census for Scotland, Occupational Table xxvi. Figures were published only for Lancashire, Yorkshire and London.

51 J. Caird, *English Agriculture in 1850–51* (1851, reprinted, London, 1968), frontispiece; H.-C. and L. Mui, *Shops and Shopkeeping*, pp. 38–9.

52 For national surveys of regional variations in house design and ownership see M. Daunton, *House and Home in the Victorian City: Working-Class Housing, 1850–1914* (London, 1983), pp. 38–59 and S. D. Chapman (ed.), *The History of Working-class Housing. A Symposium* (Newton Abbot, 1971). On Scotland, see particularly M. Horsey, *Tenements and Towers: Glasgow Working-Class Housing, 1890–1990*, Royal Commission on the Ancient and Historical Monuments of Scotland (Edinburgh, 1990), pp. 1–7; R. Rodger, 'Crisis and confrontation in Scottish housing, 1880–1914', in R. Rodger (ed.), *Scottish Housing in the Twentieth Century* (Leicester, 1989), pp. 34–5; D. Niven, *The Development of Housing in Scotland* (London, 1979), pp. 21–6.

53 Mathias, *Retailing Revolution*, p. 65.

54 K. Pearce, 'Newcastle's Tyneside Flats, 1835–1900', in B. Lancaster (ed.), *Working-Class Housing on Tyneside, 1850–1939* (Whitley Bay, 1994), pp. 39–85; the contrast with south Wales is drawn by M. J. Daunton, 'Miners' houses: South Wales and the Great Northern Coalfield, 1880–1914', *International Review of Social History*, 25 (1980), 143–75.

55 Dupree, *Family Structure*, *passim*, esp pp. 267–8; R. Whipp, 'Women and the social organisation of work in the Staffordshire pottery industry, 1900–1930', *Midland History*, 13 (1988), pp. 103–18; J. K. Walton, *Lancashire: A Social History, 1558–1939* (Manchester, 1987), pp. 287–90; Roberts, *Woman's Place*, pp. 135–48.

56 Case studies of housing in the manufacturing districts include M. J. Daunton, 'Cities of homes and cities of tenements: British and American comparisons, 1870–1914', *Journal of Urban History*, 14 (1988), 283–319 (Birmingham and Glasgow); R. Rodger, 'The built environment', in D. Nash, D. Reeder, P. Jones and R. Rodger (eds), *Leicester in the Twentieth Century* (Leicester, 1993); S. M. Gaskell, 'A landscape of small houses', in A. Sutcliffe (ed.), *Multi-Storey Living* (London, 1974) pp. 88–121; G. Timmins, 'Healthy and decent dwellings – the evolution of the two-up and two-down house in nineteenth-century Lancashire', in A. Crosby (ed.), *Lancashire Local Studies in honour of Diana Winterbotham* (Preston, 1993), pp. 101–22; N. Morgan, *Deadly Dwellings: Housing and Health in a Lancashire Cotton Town, Preston from 1840 to 1914* (Preston, 1993); L. Caffyn, *Workers' Housing in West Yorkshire, 1750–1920* (London, 1986).

57 Roberts, *Woman's Place*, pp. 158–61.

58 Z. Lawson, 'In defence of the shopkeeper', *Lancashire Local Historian*, 9 (1994), 28–36.

59 A. White and M. Winstanley, *Victorian Terraced Houses in Lancaster*, University of Lancaster, Centre for North-West Regional Studies (Lancaster, 1996), pp. 43–8.

9 *David Neave*

The identity of the East Riding of Yorkshire

Introduction

'After a thousand years of history the county of Yorkshire was abolished on All Fools Day 1974.'[1] Thus David Hey ends his survey of *Yorkshire from AD 1000*. Yorkshire may have been officially 'abolished' but it will not go away; the geographical county may be no longer marked on maps but Yorkshire people retain a strong 'belief in themselves as a breed set apart from the rest'.[2] Organisations such as the Yorkshire Agricultural Society with its annual Great Yorkshire Show, the Yorkshire Tourist Board, the Yorkshire Cancer Campaign, Yorkshire Television and Yorkshire Electricity, do much to support this belief. There is also the *Yorkshire Post* and the various journals with Yorkshire in their title, products such as Yorkshire Tea and of course Yorkshire pudding – the list is endless. Probably for no other county is this sense of a separate identity promoted so extensively.

But is Yorkshire, or any historic county, a self-contained cultural or economic region? John Marshall has long questioned the validity of the county as an area of study for the regional historian. He has written, 'So accustomed are we to the identification of 'county' with 'region' that the two words have become synonymous . . . richly documented it [the county] may be, but is it of any use at all in defining social boundaries, before or after the rise of a mature industrialism?'[3] The county, as a social entity, has been defended by Charles Phythian-Adams for geographical and cultural reasons, and because each county 'had its own customary identity, its own administrative reality, its own particular spatial distribution and hierarchy of settlement, and its own territory to be defended specifically by its own inhabitants for much of its past'.[4] Phythian-Adams has grouped the English counties, or sometimes parts of counties, into 'cultural provinces', that is areas with 'a set of distinguishable cultural traits, not the least of which will be a shared susceptibility to the same outside influences'.[5] One of his cultural provinces is the county of Yorkshire.

In this chapter the idea of the county as a cultural region will be examined from the viewpoint of the East Riding, an area that does not appear to be at one culturally with the rest of Yorkshire. The inhabitants of Holderness and Craven will proudly boast of their Yorkshireness but the places where they live have far less in common with each other than with Lincolnshire and Lancashire respectively. What do the prosperous arable farmers of the Yorkshire Wolds have in common with the pastoral farmers of the Yorkshire Dales or the timber importers of Hull with the textile manufacturers of Halifax or cutlers of Sheffield? How can a villager living near Withernsea relate to someone living near Sedbergh? Yorkshire is too large and diverse to be a cultural or economic entity.

Perversely it is the very size of Yorkshire that appears to be the one feature that has long united the disparate people of Yorkshire. They are united in the pride of belonging historically to the largest English county, a county covering about an eighth of the whole country. In 1684 the Dean of Ripon, in his sermon on the occasion of the seventh annual feast of the Yorkshire Society in London, claimed 'No *County* in all his Majesties Dominions was ever yet corrival with *Yorkshire* for *Greatness* or *Goodness*.'[6] Two centuries later when this annual feast was revived by the Society of Yorkshiremen in London in 1891, the principal speaker, Sir A. K. Rollitt, Hull solicitor and MP, suggested that 'it was because of its size that Yorkshiremen were proud of their county'.[7] This pride in the scale of a place of birth or residence is much the same pride that unites the people of Texas or indeed the people of the whole of the United States.

The making of Yorkshire

What is the historical reality of Yorkshire? It is generally accepted that the county of Yorkshire was created during the late tenth or early eleventh century.[8] When first 'described' in the Domesday Book in 1086 the boundaries of Yorkshire to the west and north-west were not yet fixed. An area later covered by Lancashire and much of Cumberland was included with the Yorkshire Domesday entries and it was not until well into the twelfth century that the modern boundaries of the geographical county of Yorkshire, with some minor later changes, were firmly established. Already by 1086 Yorkshire was divided up for administrative purposes into the three ridings and York. The divisions may have been devised by the Anglo-Scandinavian rulers, for riding comes from a Scandinavian word 'thrithing' meaning a third part, but it is possible that they just attached this title to already existing territories.

Pre-conquest territorial boundaries within the area covered by Yorkshire are a matter for speculation but some elements of continuity from the Roman period are evident. At the time of the Roman occupation, the 'Yorkshire' area was divided between two British 'tribes' – in the east were the Parisi and to the north and west the Brigantes.[9] These tribal divisions were not swept away by the Romans and they had their legacy in the early Anglian period. By the sixth century eastern and parts of northern Yorkshire were ruled by the Anglian kings of Deira but west Yorkshire was largely divided between the surviving British kingdoms of Elmet and Craven. In the early seventh century Anglo-Saxon rule expanded westwards and by the end of the century, after Deira had been absorbed by its northern neighbour Bernicia, the whole of the Yorkshire area was taken into the newly established kingdom of Northumbria. It is only in the later ninth century, ten years after the capture of York by the Vikings in 867, when their leader Healfdene 'shared out the land of the Northumbrians', that Yorkshire as a distinct entity began to emerge and the territory's eastern, northern and southern boundaries were established. The eastern and southern boundaries of the Danish kingdom of York were those of Northumbria, and the northern boundary was almost certainly the river Tees, the old northern boundary of seventh-century Deira.[10] We do not know to what extent territorial sub-divisions persisted under the kingdom of Northumbria or kingdom of York, but there is no clear evidence to suggest that the area of the future Yorkshire was an identifiable administrative unit. That it had an entity by the eleventh century cannot be disputed but already by then the existence of the three ridings underlined that Yorkshire's geographical identity was of greater importance than its administrative unity.

Although in the middle ages the Crown and Parliament governed the localities through county-wide structures, particularly for the administration of justice and tax collecting, it was not, in the opinion of Peter Borsay, until the early modern period that the English county 'emerged as a vitally important administrative and political unit, one which provided a focus around which the ruling elite could organize themselves in the localities and develop a sense of social cohesion'.[11] This new found 'county self-consciousness' was centred on the county town, and largely confined to the local gentry who met there periodically to dispense justice, organise the militia, and discuss national and local matters.[12]

Yorkshire, with York as its capital, can be seen as developing a 'county consciousness' in the sixteenth and seventeenth century, at least for the gentry. As well as being the county capital, York was the centre of a large diocese and archdiocese, and as the home of the Council of the North until 1641, it was the administrative capital of the north. For Yorkshire gentry it was the assizes, parliamentary elections and lieutenancy meetings that brought them together at York. It was only on these occasions that the county functioned as a single unit.

The elections to return two Members of Parliament for Yorkshire which took place in the Castle Yard at York were amongst the greatest of events that involved the whole county, but they were few and far between in the Georgian period. There was no contested election between a by-election in 1742 and the great Yorkshire election of 1807. Of the latter event the *York Herald* reported:

> Nothing since the days of the revolution has ever presented to the world such a scene as has been for fifteen days and nights passing within this great county. Repose or rest have been unknown in it, except it was seen in a messenger, totally worn out, asleep upon his post-horse, or on his carriage. Every day the roads, in every direction, to and from every remote corner of the county have been covered with vehicles loaded with voters; and barouches, curricles, gigs, flying waggons, military cars with eight horses to them, crowded sometimes with forty voters, have been scouring the country, leaving not the smallest chance for the *quiet* traveller to urge his humble journey, or find a chair at an inn to sit down.[13]

The twice-yearly assizes for Yorkshire were also held at York Castle and presided over by the High Sheriff, the only significant county official remaining by the end of the seventeenth century. The assizes and the August race meetings on the Knavesmire were the occasion for the great gatherings of the county gentry and their families. Sydney Smith described the three weeks of York assizes as a time 'where there is always a great deal of dancing, and provincial joy'.[14] Then the county's far-flung ruling elite met at the races, the assembly rooms, the theatre and promenading along the New Walk. It provided the opportunity for romance and the brokering of marriages and thus the unity of the county was further advanced.

York's position as the social centre of the north was in decline by the end of the Georgian period. The gentry went elsewhere for their entertainments and the new middle-class 'elite' looked more to the expanding towns of Leeds, Sheffield and Hull. The city's limited county-wide administrative role was eroded by the Reform Act of 1832, which dismembered the county constituency and created parliamentary divisions for each riding, and by the creation of the diocese of Ripon in 1836. York Castle remained the seat of the High Sheriff of the county, but after 1878 there was no longer a civil prison there. The prisoners from the city and the ridings were largely accommodated in new or enlarged West Riding gaols. During the Victorian period the whole focus of Yorkshire moved from York to the West Riding. The final break-up of the county came in 1889 when the three ridings became administrative counties in their own right.

The identity of the East Riding

The emergence of the ridings as counties can be charted from the Restoration when the single Lord Lieutenant for the county was replaced by one for each of the ridings. At the same time each riding began to develop its own sense of 'county-consciousness' focused on the meetings of gentry at Quarter Sessions. In each riding a 'county town' developed, Wakefield in the West Riding, Northallerton in the North Riding and Beverley in the East Riding. York and Hull were administratively outside any of the ridings. Beverley, because it was the largest town in the East Riding, and remained so until the early twentieth century, was in more ways the capital of a riding than either Wakefield or Northallerton, which in their respective ridings had rivals in size if not in role. The Quarter Sessions for the East Riding, having met periodically in other towns, was firmly based at Beverley by the late seventeenth century.[15] To this was added, in 1708, the registry of deeds for the East Riding and Hull with the much sought after post of Registrar and by the mid-eighteenth century the town had also become the base for all the militia and lieutenancy meetings for the riding. The gatherings of the gentry for official business led naturally to the increase in social and cultural provision. There was horse-racing on the Westwood, cock fighting and outings with the local hunt; there were purpose-built assembly rooms and theatre, a library, regular concerts and in the 1780s the New Walk, a promenade to the north of the town, was laid out.[16] The East Riding gentry not only met at Beverley but also at Driffield where the monthly meetings of the Driffield Hunt played an important part in developing 'county-consciousness'. This was acknowledged by Sir Christopher Sykes of Sledmere when writing to Thomas Grimston, president of the Driffield Hunt, in 1792:

> When the pleasures of the chase can be made the means of calling the gentlemen of the country together, they become really useful and beneficial to society. They give opportunities of wearing off shyness, dispelling temporary differences, forming new friendships and cementing old, and draw the gentlemen of the country into one closer bond of society.[17]

A growing sense of an East Riding identity is apparent from the mid-1760s when places mentioned in Acts of Parliament and Proclamations are described as being specifically in the East Riding of the County of York rather than just the County of York as hitherto.[18] Also by 1768 an East Riding of Yorkshire Agricultural Society had been established.[19] The East Riding's independence was further emphasised with the building of a new Sessions House and House of Correction at Beverley in 1805–10, the creation of the East Riding constituency in 1832, the East Riding police force in 1856 and finally the East Riding County Council in 1889. It was with the blessing of the East Riding Education Authority that Horace Browne's *The Story of the East Riding of Yorkshire* was published in 1912. A copy of this book was placed, if not in every school desk, then in every classroom, and a sense of belonging to an historic riding was instilled in every child.[20] By the early twentieth century the residents of the East Riding must have felt separated from the rest of Yorkshire. They had an

Figure 9.1 **The East Riding of Yorkshire**

independent administration and were isolated from the new heart of Yorkshire, the industrial West Riding. Many of the new organisations serving 'Yorkshire' founded in the Victorian period, for example the Yorkshire Archaeological Society and the Yorkshire County Cricket Club, were West Riding based.[21]

To what extent does the East Riding have a cultural unity? Is it more of a cultural region than Yorkshire as a whole? One of Charles Phythian-Adams requirements for a cultural province is 'an unambiguously definable area' and this can be claimed for the East Riding.[22] Its boundary, almost 200 miles in length, is only land-based for seven miles between Stamford Bridge and York in the north-west, and eight miles between Binnington Carr and North Cliff, Filey in the north-east. The boundaries on the north, west and south are the rivers Derwent, Ouse and Humber respectively, and the North Sea forms the eastern boundary. (Figure 9.2).

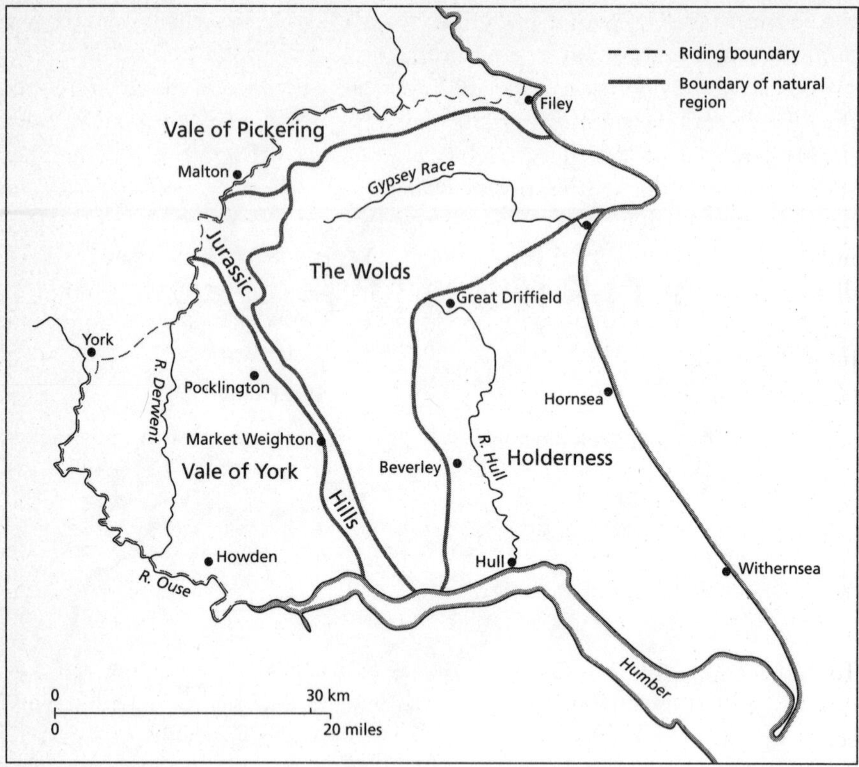

Figure 9.2 **East Riding: natural regions**

The separation of the East Riding, both physically and culturally from the rest of Yorkshire is a well established theme. J. E. Morris noted it in the introduction to his excellent *Little Guide* to the riding first published in 1906:

> The [East] Riding belongs, in the spirit of its landscape, far more to the South than to the North. Differences there are, felt rather than perceived, between this Riding, on the one hand, and Oxfordshire, or Hampshire, or Sussex, on the other. Yet in general spirit – in their leading features – all these districts are closely akin. Between the E. Riding, on the contrary, and Westmorland, or Northumberland – even between the E. Riding, . . . and the rest of Yorkshire – the gulf is apparent and profound. [23]

For J. B. Priestley, on his journey through England in the early 1930s, this south-east corner of Yorkshire 'which is not on the way to anywhere but Hull' had 'a curiously pleasant remoteness of its own'. Of Hull he remarked, 'It is not really in Yorkshire, but by itself, somewhere in the remote east where England is nearly turning into Holland or Denmark' and he commented that the residents were 'pleasant but queer. They are queer because they are not quite Yorkshire and yet not quite anything else.'[24]

Because of its position to the south-east of the line from the River Tees to the River Exe, a line which divides the highland zone of older, harder rocks from the lowland zone of secondary and tertiary rocks, many would classify the East Riding as part of the south rather than the north. [25] The East Riding has four main natural divisions, the plain of Holderness, the Wolds with the Jurassic hills to the west, the Vale of York and the Vale of Pickering. Only the first two divisions, Holderness and the Wolds, are completely within the East Riding.[26]

The physical make-up of the riding has determined that its dominant industry is agriculture. In his *General View of the Agriculture of the East Riding of Yorkshire,* published in 1812, Henry Strickland, noted:

> Fortunately for this district, it is as nearly as possible exempt from manufactories, and consequently from the vices, the corruption of manners, and poverty that are attendant upon them: it may indeed be looked upon as almost purely agricultural; perhaps there is not another in the kingdom of equal extent more completely of that description. . . . The surface of this Riding is little calculated for manufactures of any kind, having neither coal, nor wood for charcoal within itself, nor any rapid streams for working machinery. . . .[27]

To a great extent this description holds true today for the East Riding 'remains one of the most completely rural areas in England'.[28] It is an area with a landscape largely created in the Georgian period. In the early eighteenth century up to fifty per cent of the riding was still being farmed under the open-field system. This was largely transformed in the century 1725–1825 when seventy per cent of the Wolds, forty per cent of Holderness and the Hull valley and some twenty-five per cent of the Vale of York were enclosed by Act of Parliament. New rectangular fields were laid out, hedgerows planted, new straight roads constructed and, in many places, farmhouses were built outside the villages for the first time.[29] The initiative for enclosure and the uniformity of the result owed much to the great landowners who dominated landholding in the East Riding. Sixty per cent of the 700,000 acres of farmland in the riding were in the hands of only ninety-three owners in 1873, each holding over 1000 acres.[30]

The agricultural workforce of the East Riding in the nineteenth century was relatively well paid and a high proportion lived-in as farm servants hired by the year. Young men left home at around thirteen and for the next twelve years or so moved from farm to farm rarely staying more than a year in one place.[31] Statistics compiled by Dunbabin from the census returns show that in 1851 only two counties, Cumberland and Westmorland, had a higher proportion of farm servants living-in to agricultural labourers than the East Riding.[32] The continuance of hirings and living-in in an arable area into the twentieth century is one of most distinctive features of the East Riding.

The East Riding is characterised by a paucity of surviving traditional culture. Pre-1750 houses are rare in town or country and, with the exception of the ubiquitous tumbled-gable, few display any decorative features internally or externally. The late-medieval Wealden houses of Kent, the timber-framed houses of East Anglia and the west Midlands, the seventeenth-century houses of the Dales and Westmorland adorned outside with decorative datestones and crammed inside with ornate woodwork, or nearer at hand the thatched cruck-framed longhouses of the North Riding with their witchposts, seemingly have no parallels in the East Riding. This relative absence of vernacular architecture can be partly explained by the wholesale rebuilding that took place after enclosure but it also owes much to the want of good building materials, the lack of substantial yeoman farmers working their own land, and the purely agricultural nature of the economy.[33] It is in the textile areas of East Anglia and the iron-working areas of the Weald that the earliest and most substantial traditional buildings are found. Evidence from surveys, glebe terriers, probate inventories and hearth tax returns indicates that a typical East Riding farmhouse and cottage was small, two- or three-roomed, of mud, chalkstone or crude timber, covered with thatch and rarely with more than one hearth.[34]

It is rare to find much decoration in an older East Riding farmhouse; beams have the simplest of stops and there is no evidence of regional furniture styles or indeed little identifiable pre-1800 East Riding furniture. In the churchyards of the riding it is hard to find a pre-1750 gravestone and virtually none before the mid-nineteenth century have any form of decoration; yet in other counties, for example parts of Oxfordshire and south Lincolnshire, highly decorative gravestones of the seventeenth and eighteenth centuries abound. Such paucity and plainness of what might be called pre-industrial folk art or regional craftsmanship cannot be explained by poverty. East Riding farmers were not noticeably less wealthy than their southern counterparts. It must therefore be cultural.

One important factor could be the strength of Nonconformity in the riding from the late-eighteenth century. The Society of Friends had a substantial following in the East Riding from the mid-seventeenth century but the sect had largely died out by the mid-eighteenth century when Methodism first appears. The latter gained an immediate following in the riding and expanded to such an extent that on Sunday 31 March 1851 only Cornwall of all English counties had higher attendances at Methodist places of worship. The East Riding was the fourth most dissenting county in England. In the Driffield district total attendances were: Anglican 3,646 (31 per cent), Methodist 7,057 (60.5 per cent) and other Dissent 987 (8.5 per cent). The strength of Primitive Methodism was particularly marked.[35]

The dissenting tradition of the rural community must be a factor explaining the virtual absence of surviving folk-song, custom and superstition. The

'Old Culture' apparently disappeared much more effectively in the East Riding than in many other purely rural communities. This lack of folk culture presented problems to Mrs Gutch, at the very beginning of the twentieth century, when she set about compiling her work on the folk lore of the East Riding. In her preface she remarks:

> I have formed the opinion that the folk of the East Riding are more reticent of tongue and pen than are those of other parts of Yorkshire, for I cannot believe that they are freer from superstition than their neighbours. . . . Ethnic influences may account for their reserve. . . . The special blend of diverse blood which circulates hereabout tends, perhaps, to check self-revelation: the result may sharpen the interest of the anthropologist, but it foils that of the lover of folk-lore.[36]

A folk culture survives best in a settled community, and the highly mobile young agricultural workers are unlikely to be the best vehicles for carrying on tradition.[37] Caunce in his perceptive work on the hired farm servants remarks that the East Riding's relative prosperity made it until the 1920s 'one of the most self-confident rural areas of England and its cultural pattern was more evolutionary than preservationist'.[38]

It is tempting to trace the cultural unity of the East Riding back to fourth or fifth century BC when the area was settled by the people of the 'Arras' Culture. This Iron Age culture is named after the square barrows (burial mounds) excavated at Arras, near Market Weighton, some of which contain 'chariot' or cart-burials. The geographical distribution of this type of square barrows is almost totally restricted to East Yorkshire and the people of the Arras Culture are identified with the Parisi who are known to have occupied the area in the Roman period. The cultural identity of East Yorkshire at this time was not just confined to burial practices, for example in the third and fourth centuries AD the household pottery of the area was markedly different from that of its surroundings.[39] Herman Ramm defines the area of the Parisi as comprising the East Riding, minus the area to the west of the Derwent but 'with the addition of the limestone hills opening on to the north side of the Vale of Pickering'.[40] This is much the same area that Higham attaches to the sixth-century Anglo-Saxon kingdom of Deira, the boundaries of which he defines as the North Sea to the east, the Humber to the south, the North York Moors to the north and 'the frequently-drowned landscape of the Vale of York' on the west.[41]

Such an area may indeed be a more acceptable cultural region than that provided by the boundaries of the administrative county of the East Riding. Those parts of the Vale of York and the Vale of Pickering that lie within the East Riding naturally equate with the rest of these natural regions that lie in the West and North Ridings. The River Derwent to the north was less of a

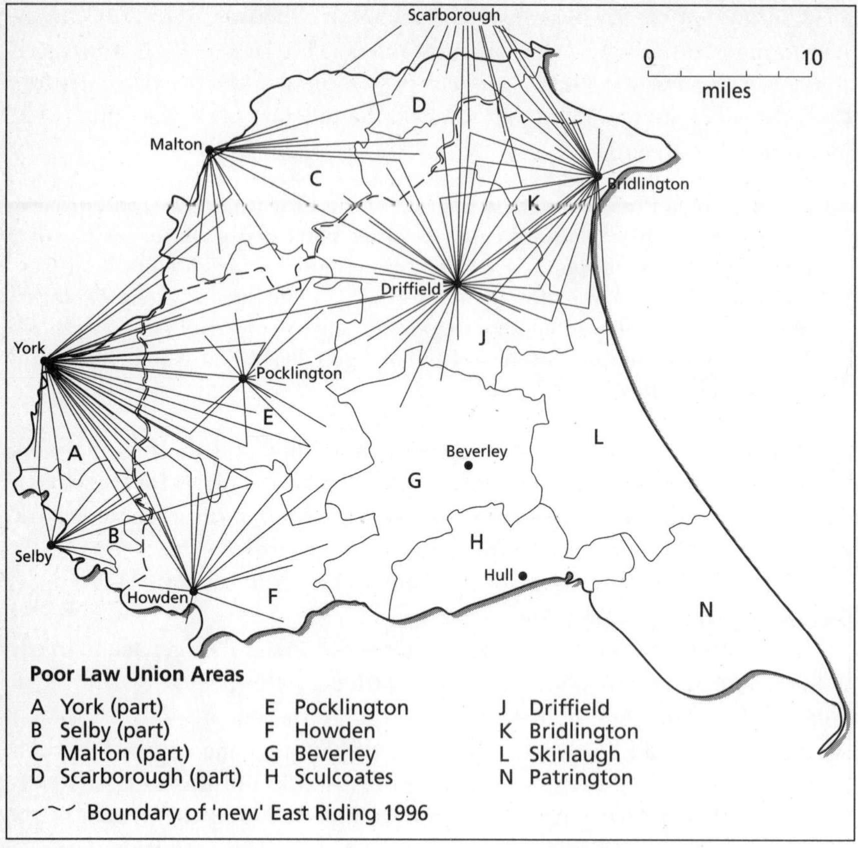

Figure 9.3 **East Riding: carrier services to northern and western market towns 1846–49 and Poor Law Union areas**

barrier than the oft-flooded valleys of the Rivers Ouse and lower Derwent to the west in the Vale of York, and there could be some justification in extending the cultural boundary of the East Riding northwards up to the edge of the North Yorkshire Moors to include the whole of the Vale of Pickering. Conversely that area of the Vale of York between the Rivers Ouse and Derwent has more akin with the adjoining areas of the West and North Ridings. Its separateness from the rest of the East Riding was recognised in the early middle ages by those determining boundaries of ecclesiatical jurisdiction for until the early twentieth century it lay in the Deanery of Bulmer and Archdeaconry of Cleveland. The rest of the East Riding was in the Archdeaconry of the East Riding which stretched northwards to include Scarborough and parishes adjoining.[42]

One oft-used method for defining economic, and to some extent, cultural

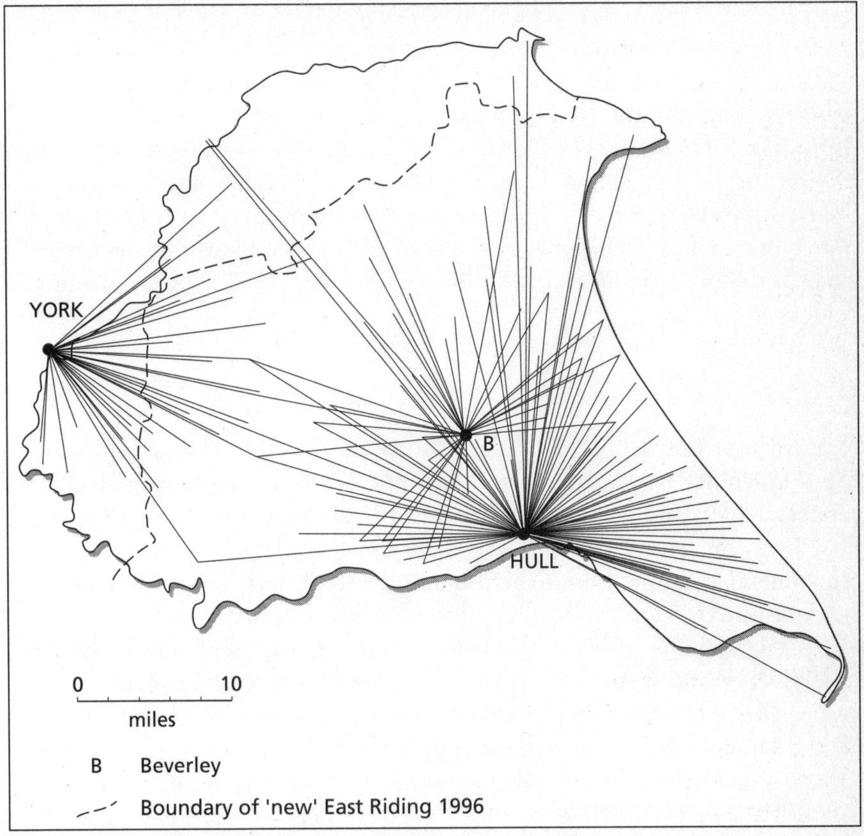

Figure 9.4 **East Riding: carrier services to chief towns 1846–49**

sub-regions for the nineteenth century is the mapping of carrier services to provide marketing areas.[43] In figures 9.3 and 9.4 the extent of carrier services for the principal market towns of the East Riding and the surrounding areas is shown.[44] What is immediately obvious, as one would expect, is that the administrative region does not equate with the economic region; the riding is not a self-sufficient marketing area. In the west the farming community looks to York and Selby and in the north to Malton and Scarborough. The identification of certain East Riding communities with market centres in the North and West Ridings was clearly understood by the Poor Law Commissioners who following the Poor Law Amendment Act of 1834 established Poor Law Unions that took this into account. Blocks of East Riding settlements became part of Poor Law Unions based in York, Selby, Malton and Scarborough. To the local residents this must have made sense and there is no record of any opposition. The Union areas were also Registration Districts. This idea was not followed in 1894 and the new Urban and Rural District Council areas were firmly located within the historic boundaries of the ridings.[45]

Figure 9.4 shows the greater significance of Hull than York or Beverley as a trading centre for the East Riding community. It had long held this position. Around 1642 Henry Best of Elmswell, near Driffield, who chiefly marketed at Malton and Beverley, noted in his farming book: 'This side of the Country, viz. the East ridinge of Yorkeshiere, repayre (for the most part) to Hull when they stande in neede of such things as the industrious merchant-venturer fetcheth from forreigne Countryes towards the reliefe of his owne Countries defeckts'.[46]

Humberside connections

Hull was not only the chief trading centre for the East Riding but also for north Lincolnshire. It was at Hull that Lincolnshire gentry sought specialist services and goods. When Colonel Edward Rossiter rebuilt Somerby Hall, near Brigg, in 1660, he used Hull craftsmen, including a plumber whom he recommended to the Massingberd family at South Ormsby, further south in Lincolnshire. In 1674 the Hull bricklayer, William Catlyn, pleaded his inability to take on the office of sheriff because of his 'great undertakings in Lincolnshire' and at the end of the century Sir William Massingberd obtained bricks, tiles and timber from Hull when building Gunby Hall near Spilsby.[47] By the nineteenth century Hull had become the 'Mecca' for much of north Lincolnshire. When the Revd Benjamin Armstrong was presented to the living of Crowle, Isle of Axholme, in 1842 he gave orders to tradesmen of Hull to furnish the old-fashioned 'but comfortable' vicarage.[48] At that date market packets were going twice-weekly to Hull from Crowle, as well as Barton, Goxhill, Grimsby, Skitter, Stallingborough and Winterton and carriers were going to Hull market on Tuesdays and Fridays from thirty-three north Lincolnshire villages.[49] In 1892 carriers from forty north Lincolnshire towns and villages were attending Hull market by boat and cart.[50]

From the mid-eighteenth century Hull newspapers circulated in north Lincolnshire. In March 1759 the publisher of the *Hull Courant* complained of the 'country people' who collect the paper for their neighbours who 'break open the same, particularly in our Lincolnshire Circuit, who reads and dirty it, and afterwards keeping it the best part of a week by them, before the delivery of the same, to the great prejudice of the printer hereof'.[51] In the nineteenth century Hull newspapers frequently incorporated the word Lincolnshire in their titles beginning with the shortlived *Humber Mercury and Hull, Yorkshire and Lincolnshire General Advertiser* of 1805–6 and the *Hull and Lincoln Chronicle* founded May 1807. In the late 1880s the Hull, East Yorkshire and North Lincolnshire Conservative Newspaper Co. was publishing the [Hull] *Daily Mail* which included north Lincolnshire news and the weekly *Hull and Lincolnshire Times*.[52] The Hull printer, Noble, produced a *Hull, Yorkshire and Lincolnshire Almanac* regularly in the years 1834–48 and directories published by Kelly in 1896 and 1900 covered Lincolnshire and Hull.

A surprising number of societies and associations also existed on a cross-Humber basis. The *Hull Advertiser* mentions the following: Hull, East Yorkshire and North Lincolnshire Unitarian Association (1833); Hull, East Riding and North Lincolnshire United Law, Merchants and Bankers' Clerks Society (1838); Hull, Yorkshire and Lincolnshire Floral and Horticultural Society (1843); and the Beverley, East Riding and North Lincolnshire Congregational Association (1843).[53] At the end of the century there existed the following: the Hull and East Riding, and North Lincolnshire Discharged Prisoners' Aid Society, the Hull, East Riding and North Lincolnshire Orthopedic (*sic*) Hospital, the Hull, East Riding of Yorkshire and Lincolnshire Female Penitentiary, the Hull, East Yorkshire and North Lincolnshire Institution for the Deaf and Dumb and the Hull, East Yorkshire, and North Lincolnshire Perpetual Benefit Building Society.[54]

Such facts add another dimension to the defining of the East Riding as part of a wider region. Has the riding more in common with north Lincolnshire than the rest of Yorkshire and did the County of Humberside have an historical basis? It cannot be denied that many of the East Riding's distinctive characteristics are paralleled in north Lincolnshire, including living-in, Methodism, arable farming and high wages. The two areas are part of the same geological region, have almost identical natural regions and therefore agricultural practice. The settlement history of the East Riding has closer affinities with north Lincolnshire than with the other areas of Yorkshire and there are similarities in dialects. Mid-nineteenth century census returns show much migration across the Humber. In 1851 over 8 per cent of the population of Hull was Lincolnshire born, and on the south side of the Humber 13 per cent of the population of Barton-on-Humber and 10 per cent of the population of Barrow-on-Humber were Yorkshire born.[55]

The catalogue of trans-Humber links could be extended greatly to stress north Lincolnshire's historical reliance on Hull, but as Humberside County Council discovered, the Humber is as much a barrier in the late twentieth century as when it formed the barrier between the Parisi and the Coritani in the first century, and Northumbria and Mercia in the seventh century. When, in March 1990, the Local Government Boundary Commission for England proposed no radical change to Humberside it received twenty-six petitions with more than 81,500 signatures opposed to Humberside and only two petitions bearing 101 signatures supporting Humberside. Opponents condemned the county of Humberside as 'unhistorical', 'an unnatural creation bestriding the natural boundary of the Humber and joining together two separate communities of Yorkshire and Lincolnshire people'.[56]

The people of North Humberside wanted to return to Yorkshire, and also achieve the 'return of the ridings'. On the creation of Humberside in 1974 two segments of the historic East Riding, one to the west between the Ouse and Derwent and the other the northern quarter of the county, were detached and placed in the new North Yorkshire County Council. These areas were almost identical to those portions of the East Riding that were included in the Selby, York, Malton and Scarborough Poor Law Unions in the nineteenth century. Re-organisation in 1996 has left these areas in North Yorkshire and an enlarged City of York and therefore the area covered by the newly created East Riding of Yorkshire Council, which is a unitary authority but not a county or a district, is somewhat smaller than the historic East Riding. To this area has been added that section of the former West Riding, including Goole, that was placed in Humberside in 1974. If this last area is discounted then figures 9.3 and 9.4 suggest that the remaining area of the 'new' East Riding has some historical justification as an economic region, being largely a self-sufficient marketing area in the mid-nineteenth century.

Conclusion

Should this new area now be taken as an area for historical study? Experience of the limited life-span of administrative areas indicates that this would not be wise. The historic English counties, administrative units for a thousand years or more, did develop an identifiable social entity through the interaction of their principal inhabitants in the administration of justice and military organisation, but they cannot be seen as economic regions, nor with rare exceptions, for example Cornwall, are they defineable cultural regions. It has to be accepted that the boundaries of economic, cultural and administrative regions are unlikely to coincide. The historic county will long remain the main unit of study for local historians, partly for sentiment but chiefly as John Marshall has stated it 'is a fine repository of convenient statistics'.[57] This has been the basis of much of the present writer's work on the East Riding over the past twenty years. However, as has been shown, the East Riding has a distinctive cultural, economic and physical identity which though not strictly confined by the riding's physical boundaries justifies it being studied as a separate entity to the rest of Yorkshire.

Notes

1 D. Hey, *Yorkshire from AD 1000* (London, 1986), p. 314. On 1 April 1974 the greater part of the East Riding was included in the new administrative county of Humberside, part

of the North Riding taken into the new administrative county of Cleveland, Sedbergh passed to the new Cumbria, Upper Teesdale to County Durham, Bowland and West Craven to Lancashire and Saddleworth to Greater Manchester.

2 *Ibid.*, p. 5.

3 J. D. Marshall, 'Discussion article: regions, regionalism and regional scholarship' *JORALS*, 10:1 (Summer 1990), 67–8.

4 C. Phythian-Adams (ed.), *Societies, Cultures and Kinship, 1580–1850: Cultural Provinces and English Local History* (Leicester, 1993), p. 19.

5 *Ibid.*, pp. 9–10.

6 *Yorkshire County Magazine*, 1 (1891), 296.

7 M. Bradford, *The Fight for Yorkshire* (Cherry Burton, 1988), p. 35

8 Hey, *Yorkshire*, p. 1.

9 N. J. Higham, *The Kingdom of Northumbria* AD *350–1100* (Stroud, 1993), p. 25.

10 R. Hall, *Viking Age York* (London, 1994), p. 16; Higham, *Northumbria*, pp. 83, 141.

11 P. Borsay, *The English Urban Renaissance* (Oxford, 1989), p. 189.

12 A. Everitt, *Change in the Provinces: The Seventeenth Century* (Leicester, 1972), p. 25.

13 *York Herald*, 6 June 1807 quoted in E. A. Smith 'The Yorkshire Elections of 1806 and 1807', *Northern History*, 2 (1967), 81.

14 A. Bell, *Sydney Smith* (Oxford, 1980), p. 97.

15 G. C. F. Forster, *The East Riding Justices of the Peace in the Seventeenth Century*, East Yorkshire Local History Society (1973), p. 30.

16 D. Neave, 'Beverley, 1700–1835', in K. J. Allison (ed.), *Victoria County History, Yorkshire East Riding* vol. 6 (Oxford, 1989), pp. 112–13.

17 D. C. Itzkowitz, *Peculiar Privilege: A Social History of English Foxhunting 1753–1885* (Hassocks, 1977), p. 19.

18 K. A. MacMahon (ed.), *Acts of Parliament and Proclamations relating to the East Riding of Yorkshire and Kingston upon Hull 1529–1800* (Hull, 1961).

19 *York Courant*, 17 Jan 1769.

20 H. B. Browne, *The Story of the East Riding of Yorkshire* (London, 1912).

21 The Yorkshire Archaeological Society had its origins in Huddersfield in 1863. In 1875 out of a total membership of 388 only nine were from the East Riding and seven from Hull. There were only five East Yorkshire residents amongst the 101 Yorkshire subscribers to the Society's Jubilee fund in 1913. *Yorkshire Archaeological Journal*, 3 (1875), 420–5; 23 (1915), 46–8.

22 Phythian-Adams, *Societies*, p. 9.

23 J. E. Morris, *The East Riding of Yorkshire* (2nd ed, London, 1919), p. 6.

24 J. B. Priestley, *English Journey* (London, 1934), pp. 352–4.

25 H. M. Jewell, *The North-South Divide: The Origins of Northern Consciousness in England* (Manchester, 1994), p. 8.

26 Holderness is the most distinctive of the sub-regions of the East Riding. B. English 'Holderness in the Early Middle Ages', *JORALS*, 13:2 (1993), 44–50.

27 H.E. Strickland, *A General View of the Agriculture of the East Riding of Yorkshire* (York, 1812), p. 284.

28 S. Caunce, *Amongst Farm Horses: The Horselads of East Yorkshire* (Stroud, 1991), p. 1.

29 J. Crowther, 'The incidence and chronology of parliamentary enclosure', in S. Neave and S. Ellis (eds), *An Historical Atlas of East Yorkshire* (Hull, 1996), pp. 50–1.

30 J. T. Ward, *East Yorkshire Landed Estates in the Nineteenth Century*, East Yorkshire Local History Society (1967), p. 72.

31 *See* Caunce, *Amongst Farm Horses;* G. Moses, '"Rustic and Rude": hiring fairs and their critics in East Yorkshire c. 1850–75', *Rural History*, 7 (1996), 151–75; D. Neave, *Mutual Aid in the Victorian Countryside: Friendly Societies in the Rural East Riding 1830–1914* (Hull, 1991), pp. 11–13.

32 J. P. Dunbabin, 'The incidence and organization of agricultural trades unionism in the 1870s', *Agricultural History Review*, 16 (1968), 123–4.

33 N. Pevsner and D. Neave, *The Buildings of England. Yorkshire: York and the East Riding* (London, 1995), pp. 23–9.

34 *Ibid.*; J. D. Purdy, *Yorkshire Hearth Tax Returns*, University of Hull Centre for Regional and Local History (Hull, 1991).

35 D. Neave and S. Neave, *East Riding Chapels and Meeting Houses*, East Yorkshire Local History Society (1990), p. 4; R. W. Ambler, 'Attendance at religious worship, 1851', in Neave and Ellis (eds), *Historical Atlas*, p. 44; A. Everitt, *The Pattern of Rural Dissent: The Nineteenth Century* (Leicester, 1972), p. 69.

36 Mrs Gutch (ed.), *County Folk Lore: East Riding of Yorkshire*, Folk Lore Society (London, 1912), p. xi.

37 The East Riding fishing village of Flamborough with generations of close-knit fishing families has a much better preserved folk culture than local agricultural settlements. R. Fisher (ed.), *Flamborough: Village and Headland* (Hull, 1894), pp. 59–66, 142–8.

38 Caunce, *Amongst Farm Horses*, p. 3

39 P. Halkon (ed.), *New Light on The Parisi*, East Riding Archaeological Society and the University of Hull, School of Adult and Continuing Education (Hull, 1989), pp. iii, 38.

40 H. Ramm, *The Parisi* (London, 1978), p. 25.

41 Higham, *Northumbria*, p. 81.

42 D. M. Smith, *A Guide to the Archive Collections in the Borthwick Institute of Historical Research*, Borthwick Institute of Historical Research, University of York (York, 1973), pp. 86–7.

43 Phythian-Adams in emphasising the significance of the impact of local market centres has cautioned against seeing the populations of their clearly demarcated hinterlands as comprising recognisable social entities. C. Phythian-Adams, *Re-thinking English Local History* (Leicester, 1987), p. 23.

44 F. White and Co., *General Directory of Kingston upon Hull and the City of York, etc.* (Leeds, 1846), pp. 262–8, 319–21, 424, 439–40, 455, 459, 468; *Slater's Royal National Commercial Directory and Topography of Yorkshire and Lincolnshire* (Manchester, 1849), pp. 22, 319–20, 358, 411–12, 566.

45 M. Rogers, 'Administrative Units' in Neave and Ellis (eds), *Historical Atlas*, pp. 66–70.

46 D. Woodward (ed.), *The Farming and Memorandum Books of Henry Best of Elmswell, 1642* (London, 1984), p. 131.

47 D. Neave 'Artisan mannerism in north Lincolnshire and east Yorkshire: the work of William Catlyn (1628–1709) of Hull', in C. Sturman (ed.), *Lincolnshire People and Places*, Society for Lincolnshire History and Archaeology (Lincoln, 1996), pp. 18–25.

48 D. Neave (ed.), *Armstrong's Crowle Journal 1842–44* (Crowle, 1986), p. 8.

49 *Slater's Directory of Yorkshire and Lincolnshire*, 1849, pp. 222–3. See Fig. 21.5 in R. W. Ambler 'The small towns of south Humberside', in S. Ellis and D. R. Crowther (eds), *Humber Perspectives: A Region through the Ages* (Hull, 1990), p. 301.

50 T. Bulmer, *History and Directory of East Yorkshire* (Preston, 1892), pp. 846–8.

51 *Hull Courant*, 20 March 1759.

52 K. J. Allison (ed.), *Victoria County History, East Riding*, vol. 1 (London, 1969), pp. 428–32.

53 D. Parry (ed.), *The Meadley Index to The Hull Advertiser, 1, 1826–45* (Hull, 1987).

54 Bulmer, *East Yorkshire*, pp. 911–12.

55 Census Enumerators' Returns, 1851, *ex inf.* Rex Russell.

56 Letter from the Local Government Boundary Commission for England to the Chief Executives of Humberside and Lincolnshire County Councils, 27 November 1990, p. 16.

57 Marshall, 'Regions, regionalism and regional scholarship', p. 68.

Regional dynamics: north Wales, 1750–1914

Introduction

Understanding the regional nature of north Wales properly begins with the questions left unanswered by the classic analysis of industrialisation in the area, A. H. Dodd's *The Industrial Revolution in North Wales*, published in 1933 and frequently back in print in the period since then.[1] That work is inevitably the base which all subsequent expeditions take, but some of the crucial issues were left unasked, as much as unanswered, by Dodd.

Professor Dodd was a north Wales man; he was born in Wrexham and spent his academic career mainly within the University College of North Wales at Bangor. For some of the time he was an Extra-Mural Tutor. Consequently he seems to have taken his territory for granted; it was his own *bro* and its coherence seems not to have been an issue for him. The extent of the integration of the area is questionable, however, and it might aid analysis to see the emergence of different regional economies and identities within the territory in the course of the 'long industrial revolution' of 1750–1914.[2] It took this longer period for the regional dynamics of north Wales to work themselves out; a mid-century ending of the period of industrialisation will not allow us to see the processes fully at work. The other unasked questions concern the background to and outcomes of industrialisation in the area. Dodd gave uneven consideration to these aspects and a new approach to them must address them more consistently and directly. This leads on to the third of the concerns; whether the impact of industry was sufficient to create a social revolution – the 'more than industrial revolution' that Professor Perkin drew our attention to almost three decades ago.[3]

The question of what constitutes a region is central and necessary for any book celebrating the work of John Marshall who has done so much to promote reflection on regions and their nature. The approach taken here is to conceive of any given region as being in dynamic relations with other regions; static conceptions and boundaries always come to grief, run into problems of definition and miss much of the benefit to be derived from a regional approach to history. A useful point of departure is the observations which D. W. Meunig has made on American history as they can be applied more widely: 'It is a view of America as an ever changing *place*, and an ever changing *congeries of places*, an ever-changing *structure of places*, and an ever changing *system of places*.'[4] Meunig rejects any static conception of regions – or the sectional approach of F. J. Turner. Rather, for him regions are complex, ambiguous and changing – abstractions which exist in the mind but which are also imbued with emotion and capable of influencing action. When they change they change not so much as units but by means of changes in their constituent parts.[5] The most succinct encapsulation of his view is almost a slogan: '... places are created by history.'[6]

Others have taken a similar stance. Harold Carter has stressed the historical shifts in the urban hierarchy in Wales, an approach which speaks loudly to regional analysis, by emphasising the shifting location of central places over the centuries.[7] Indeed, A. H. Dodd himself wrote a penetrating account of relations along the Anglo-Welsh border focusing on Wrexham; in this streams of influence flow back and forth leaving traces for the historian in place and personal names in particular.[8] More recently Bernard Deacon has rejected the static nature of core – periphery analysis for an approach which recognises that the world system is made up of a series of cores and peripheries. Cornwall is peripheral to London, but still part of the global core. Within Cornwall there was the mining core of Cambourne-Redruth, while north Cornwall and the Lizard Peninsula were peripheries of it. These problems are compounded by changes in relationships which occur during historical development.[9] This approach to regions has the advantage of making the notorious problems of definition into one of the virtues. Shifting boundaries can be incorporated into the argument: indeed they become pivotal to the analysis. What has to become central is movement, both in the sense of migration of people and the flows associated with economic activity. Regions are, by definition, part of a larger entity and are open to influences from outside.[10]

Such an approach is at the opposite end of the spectrum from the idea of 'natural regions' as elaborated by some geographers and geologists in the past, though even their geographical/geological determinism had to be modified by the realisation that only in the modern period did the distribution of mineral resources play any significant role in shaping the location of the population.[11] It is not necessary to be a geographical determinist – or an economic one for that matter – to recognise that regional coherence might be defined also by the relationships between a variety of geographical, economic, social and cultural factors. This is an approach which John Marshall himself has taken when he strives to find a working definition of regions:

> The base, then, is social, whether expressed in the form of class analyses or not; the economic is closely related to it in historical analysis and measurement. With the social and the economic together goes the political; with the social goes the demographic; and, where the decisions are put into effect, goes the administrative. It should be the regional historian's ambition to show the processes of change within society. The long term movements within a regional society are those which display its true identity.[12]

Regions are therefore best regarded as complex but shifting social formations in which movements of peoples and goods – and the consequent reordering of spatial relations – are regarded as central aspects. With this is mind it is possible to approach the problems of the industrialisation of north Wales. There is one further preliminary to be dealt with first. That concerns the trajectory of industry in a particular area. Dodd had a fairly simple, though not fully elaborated, view of this. His north Wales was underdeveloped and backward in 1750 and then saw rapid industrial development, though this was succeeded by what would now be called pastoralisation or 'backwash' over large parts of the area.[13] He left the outcome unresolved; the lack of an effective conclusion in the book meant that it was unclear whether north Wales had undergone an industrial revolution or not. The title certainly appeared to proclaim that it had, though it could be read as expressing a concern with the effects of the industrial revolution (which largely happened elsewhere) on north Wales. The text contained much scattered discussion of the reasons for industrial decline and showed how widespread this was though there was no overall evaluation.[14] This was a quite typical analysis in Welsh historical writing of the period; it stressed the sharpness of the break at the industrial revolution, though it implicitly qualified this by showing the de-industrialisation which rapidly followed in its wake in many cases. More recent historical thinking sees a great flexibility of approach and stresses the variety of perspectives on 'modernisation' which are possible.[15] Recent research has questioned both the 'backwardness' of the early modern period and also stressed that what were once seen as pre-modern attitudes, behaviours and values persisted well into the nineteenth century and beyond.[16] Both approaches stress that change might have been more complex and less dramatic than was once imagined. Regional analysis is a vital way of gaining a purchase on this issue and that we need to conceive of a regional pattern of variation in the outcomes.

Dodd bequeathed us north Wales as a unit of analysis and John Marshall has argued for the utility of this six-counties approach seeing it as a region comparable to the Cumbria which he has done so much to illuminate.[17] Yet Dodd's rather cavalier approach to geography contrasts with the care with which John Marshall considered it as a prelude to his own entry in the regional history classic stakes.[18] While the north Wales which Dodd delineated has some utility, it is in one sense too small to be useful as a unit of regional analy-

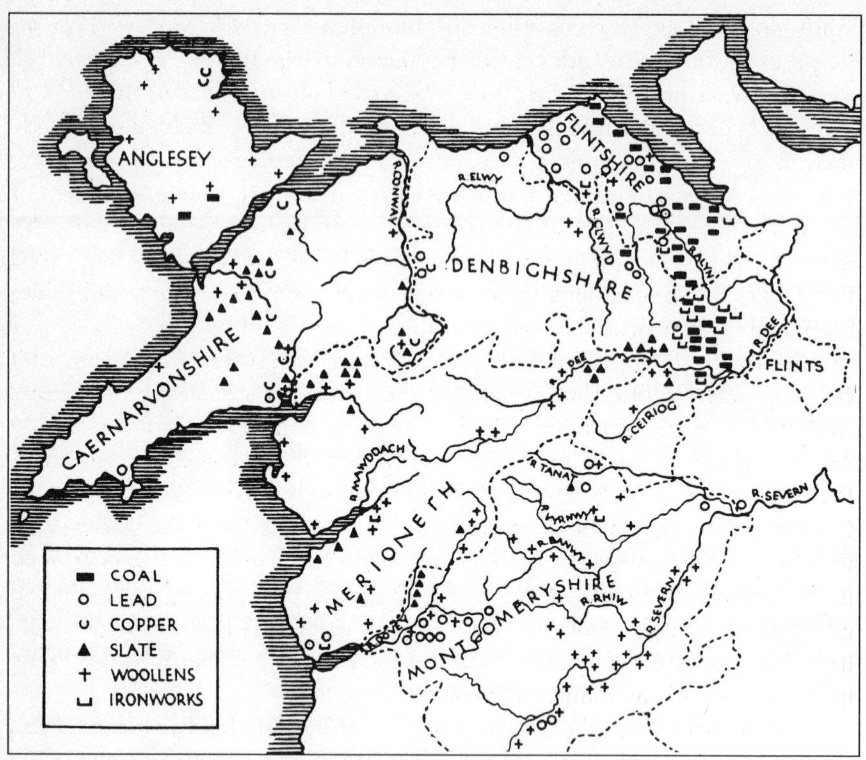

Figure 10.1 **North Wales: industrial, 1760–1850**
Source: A. H. Dodd, *The Industrial Revolution in North Wales* (University of Wales Press, Cardiff, 1971)

sis but in another it is too large. That area will be used here as a vantage point from which to view the process by which regions were formed within it. John Marshall's view, that Dodd's north Wales had 'geographical coherence and validity, even homogeneity in its way of life, industries and traditions', needs to be qualified.[19] (see figure 10.1.)

Pre-industrial north Wales

Pre-industrial Wales had many internal divisions – one recent attempt to come to terms with its diversity makes it seem as plural as a recent analysis of America which deliberately stresses the varied peoples who collided on the continent.[20] Yet much of it shared an upland economy which was pastoral and based on the export of cattle and woollen cloth with limited grain production.[21] In this sense the whole of Wales could be taken as the unit of analysis or, if we anticipate the industrialisation to come, only the area of the south

Wales coalfield and the coastal strip it dominated need be excluded for our purposes. In the eighteenth century no Glamorgan gentry family intermarried with one from north Wales as there was little contact between them.[22] Pre-industrial coastal south Wales, and to some extent the coalfield, moved to the rhythm of Bristol's impulses to a much greater degree than did the rest of Wales, which is another reason for excluding it from consideration here.[23] If we are to consider a unit as large as Dodd's north Wales, there is no real rationale for excluding Radnorshire, Breconshire, Cardiganshire and north Pembrokeshire. Dodd's line through the middle of Wales bisects mid-Wales, for which there is little real justification.

Pre-industrial north and mid-Wales was also part of a larger unit. Geographically it fitted into upland Britain and had something in common with the societies which scratched a living from difficult terrain along the Atlantic fringes of the British Isles. Administratively it was located within the Port of Chester which stretched from Barmouth to the River Duddon in Cumbria. The city of Chester was a powerful influence over the whole of this terrain, while Shrewsbury dominated its cloth trade long after the ending of its legal monopoly in 1624.[24] With this wider territory various areas of mid- and north Wales stand out from the rest by reason of the particular economic activities and orientation to the sea (which is a marker of unusual economic activity) on the eve of the industrial revolution.

Cardiganshire was the area of western Wales most closely connected with the sea by the seventeenth century and had a quite extensive trade which shaped much of its internal life [25] By the early eighteenth century extensive lead workings in the southern part of the county increased the orientation to the sea and Aberystwyth's preliminary smelting of lead was on a sufficient scale to fool Defoe into thinking that coal was mined there. His description of the town was as a veritable mini-Coketown. The county would continue to be characterised by substantial industrial activity in textiles and metals which would leave no mark in terms of urbanisation.[26]

To the north was Merioneth, with its cloth trade becoming focused on Dolgellau and the port of Barmouth from the mid-eighteenth century. The cloth trade was widely diffused in the whole area but only in Merioneth and Montgomeryshire was it well organised and market-oriented. The diffuse industry was given some coherence by the dominance of the Shrewsbury Drapers. It suffered in comparison with the west of England because of the lesser agricultural productivity of north Wales. Gloucestershire was productive enough agriculturally to employ 40 per cent of its adult male population in clothing. North Wales had to import grain in bad years. This meant there was no real industrial proletariat totally dependent on wages in Wales; woollen manufacture remained a supplement of agriculture.[27] The abundant small streams of north Wales served to scatter the industry and it never achieved the degree of concentration which characterised the West Country. Dolgellau was the focus of the short staple 'strong cloth' and wool was imported from Denbighshire and yarn from Caernarfonshire and Anglesey to feed its weaving sheds and fulling mills. It made it 'no despicable little Town for these Parts' by 1775, according to one of the growing band of tourists. The establishment of a depot for export at Barmouth in 1772 was the first step in the breakdown of Shrewsbury's monopoly which was completed by the end of the century. It became self-contained and broke the hold of external capitalists, though Liverpool merchants may have established the depot in the first place.[28]

Montgomeryshire also had a distinctive economic base. Most of its crafts and trades were adjuncts to agriculture, but woollen manufacture had achieved a non-local market. There were large flocks of sheep in the upland parts of the county where wool manufacture was concentrated and there were enough fulling mills and weaving workshops to impress travellers. Of a sample of 560 wills proved between 1690 and 1750, 43 mentioned looms and 193 stocks of wool and yarn. Between 1681 and 1801, the 17 cloth-making parishes grew by 99 per cent compared with a mere 38 per cent for the 14 lowland parishes in the county. Until the late eighteenth century it was a domestic industry; from the late seventeenth century it had shifted from coarse broad cloths to finer, more finished flannel and taken over some of the finishing processes from the Shrewsbury Drapers. Shrewsbury remained the major market and this was the one area of north and mid-Wales with noticeable industrial development which looked inland rather than to the sea.[29]

Caernarfonshire also had quite extensive trade by sea in a range of commodities though imports seem to have been predominant and its slate export trade was intermittent. Extensive smuggling supplemented the legal activities. Salt, pots and coal came in from Liverpool and Flintshire while Beaumaris served as the entrepôt for the whole area, and Caernarfon had the busiest trade. Bangor was the chief centre of slate export.[30]

The most extensive site of industry, and of orientation to the sea, was in Flintshire. Its export trade relied on the estuary of the River Dee and the access to the western coasts of Britain which it provided. The coal industry had expanded quite steadily from the middle ages but was stimulated by the development of lead smelting from 1692, and iron, copper, and brass supplemented this from the early eighteenth century. As early as 1673 it had been observed by Richard Blome that Flintshire had 'plenty of pitt coal, and adjacent mountains [contain a] store of lead ore'. Extensive lead discoveries on the Halkyn Mountain in 1728 added to the industrial impetus, and Quaker entrepreneurs played a crucial role in their exploitation. Lead was exported to London, through the contacts of Chester merchants. Buckley's pottery works added to industrial activity from the mid-eighteenth century.

Landlords and industrialists both exploited mines, though the latter became predominant. Pits were mainly small but some were of sufficient size to employ Newcomen engines. Already, however, the silting of the estuary was producing problems and the coal export trade was consequently giving way to the use of coal in local smelting industries. In the Hawarden district, leases granted to 'immigrant' coal masters in the eighteenth century began the transformation of the industry. An extensive trade developed with Ireland in particular, and tramways were built to facilitate inland transport. By 1740 Flintshire had the highest population density in Wales, an indication of the extent to which its industry had developed; it has been described by K. Lloyd Gruffydd as 'an early tremor'of the industrial revolution.[31]

Industrialisation, 1780–1830

The period of the classic industrial revolution brought widespread industrial growth to north Wales. Much capital was attracted by its abundant water power, cheap labour and its resources, notably minerals and wool. There were instances of spectacular development, such as the Parys Mountain copper mines which came to dominate the world market for copper in the 1790s, and these have formed the basis for attacking Michael Hechter's crude ideas of internal colonialism.[32] For present purposes, however, it is more important to assess the way in which these developments influenced the regional patterning of north and mid-Wales. They did so within the peculiar framework laid down by the 'first Kondratieff cycle' and the way that this was experienced in Britain. It was characterised by major structural change in industry but with a political system still largely in landed control which slowed change in certain areas. Notably, limited free trade policies retarded some industries. Governments retained a commitment to social equilibrium, defined as balancing industry and agriculture, rather than to unlimited industrial development. The crisis which resulted from the disharmony between the political and economic systems came to a head in 1837–42 and was only resolved by Peel's conversion to the belief that, 'Free and universal commerce is more consistent with the wants of a great country' in the 1840s. The application of this policy would contribute mightily to the reorientation of north and mid-Wales.[33]

Overall, Liverpool came to displace Chester as the major city in the wider region and this led to some local adjustments. Liverpool's rivalry with Chester was of long standing and the chronology of its rise and Chester's fall is a matter of much dispute between historians, but there is no doubt about the impact of Liverpool's explosive growth after the Restoration.[34] The city came to be the putative capital of north Wales and its metropolis, with a well-established Welsh and Welsh-speaking community at its heart. Their contribution to building the city was literal and can still be seen in its architectural styles.[35] It was from Liverpool, and behind it Lancashire, that would come the money which produced the north Wales coastal resorts for Lancashire's pleasure seekers, and they have always sat a little uneasily within north Wales, not integrated fully into either north-west or north-east Wales.[36]

Within north Wales the north-west began to increase its orientation to the sea while the north-east began to look towards the English border. The Welsh economy of the nineteenth century has been described as 'imperial' in its overall orientation – that is geared heavily to exports – but north-east Wales emerges as the key exception to this rule. Both these areas emerged as regional complexes – industrial nucleations with associated cultural and social configurations. Mid-Wales, by contrast, was largely left out of this process of regional formation. While much of it had a common economy of upland farming, with limited metal mining and woollen manufacture, it achieved little nucleation and remained culturally diverse.

Very few industries stretched their productive processes – or their wider influences – across the whole of north Wales. Copper was the industry which more than most expressed the dynamics of the wider region. The productive mines of Ynys Môn were linked to smelters on both Deeside and Merseyside, though they also sent their ores for smelting in Swansea and were shaped by their rivalry with and domination of the Cornish producers. Thomas Williams, the copper King, placed the focus of the industry in Anglesey and bestrode the western coasts of the island in the process.[37]

Most industries fitted into narrower geographical ranges. Slate drew in capital from Liverpool and found crucial markets in Lancashire and other industrial areas of England but was largely confined to north-west Wales. Its transformation began on the Penrhyn estate in the 1780s when wage labour replaced a kind of petty commodity production and soon a new industrial village began to emerge at Bethesda. Investments in tramways and Port Penrhyn made the transition to an industry run on a capitalist basis complete. Where the Penrhyn estate led, the neighbouring Faenol estate soon followed. Here, at Llanberis, settlement pushed up the mountainside into areas which had been merely common, and holdings were carved out for quarrymen who were initially seen as part-time or seasonal workers. Their small holdings provided a measure of security – including freedom from the attentions of the poor law relieving officer – and this may be seen as the equivalent of proto-industrialisation in slate.[38] The Ffestiniog district, the last of the three major slate-producing areas to develop, was more handicapped by transport problems than were either Bethesda or Llanberis. The difficulties of transport from locations up to 1,900 feet above sea-level added huge costs and the problem was not really resolved until the construction of the Ffestiniog Railway in 1836. Ffestiniog would be the district most dependent on overseas markets when it finally took off and it was especially retarded by the tax on coastal slate which was imposed from 1794 to 1831. In this period it barely moved beyond the stage of sporadic exploitation by local petty producers working open quarries, though the foundations for more extensive developments were laid in the 1820s by immigrant entrepreneurs from Lancashire, the area's axis point of industrialisation. The underground mines which characterised the full development of the district would follow soon afterwards. Transport remained in the hands of farmers who provided carts and the quaintly named 'Philistines' who plied a dangerous trade in boating slate along the River Dwyryd. In 1810 the price of slate from the more developed quarries was raised by 50 per cent by the short but difficult overland trip to the quays where it was loaded on to barges for transfer to sailing ships. This statistic sums up the early problems of the district. Slate had become a significant industry by 1830 when it employed over 2,000 people in Gwynedd but it had not reached the peak of development which would lead it to make its impress over a whole region. It was yet too weak and there remained rivals for the dominance of the north-west.[39]

The woollen industry was extensive throughout the area but it retained its foci along the River Mawddach, which links Barmouth and Dolgellau, and in the Severn Valley around Newtown and Llanidloes. Liverpool merchants came to dominate the Merioneth industry in the 1790s and the product was increasingly sent out by sea. Slowly and reluctantly machinery was introduced in the first two decades of the nineteenth century. Dolgellau's population grew from just under 3,000 to over 4,000 in the period. Yet by then the area's time of industrial glory was slipping beyond the horizon. The Napoleonic Wars were fatal to its seaborne trade and the escape from the monopoly of the Shrewsbury drapers provided only a brief respite of freedom. Outside the sheltered market was the competition of Yorkshire and Lancashire. Under its impact wool began to be exported to Yorkshire rather than manufactured locally. Machinery was brought in from Yorkshire but there was insufficient investment in it for the district to begin to compete. Decline set in rapidly in the 1820s and by 1831 production was far less than it had been in 1800.[40]

The border areas had a rather different experience. Their flannel was distinctive and quite different from the webs of Merioneth. Local markets emerged for the product and along with improvements in roads and canals these broke the stranglehold of Shrewsbury. Welshpool's market was created in 1782 while others at Newtown and Llanidloes followed in 1832 and 1836 respectively. Limited mechanisation was associated with these developments. Carding engines began to appear, followed at a respectful distance by spinning jennies. There were 40 carding engines in Montgomeryshire by the end of the eighteenth century, though it was 1810 before the first spinning jenny appeared. The technology was imported from Yorkshire. Newtown became the centre of the factory industry, aided by the construction of the Montgomeryshire Canal and, in an ultimately futile exercise in self-promotion, the town was dubbed the 'Leeds of Wales'. The area had always suffered from the volatility of the flannel markets, especially when they were disrupted by the wars against America and France. As Humphreys expresses it: 'its brief flashes of prosperity were often shadowed by remorseless slumps'. Enclosure undermined the cottager economy on which wool production depended and its workers became proletarianised. The growth in population strained resources in the corn-importing upland parishes. In the end this uneven struggle ended with the collapse of the industry from the 1830s. The transport links which had given access to markets across the border now brought in cloth from Lancashire and Yorkshire. By 1913 Newtown was in a such a precarious position that, on losing a few office jobs in the Welsh National Memorial Association when it moved to Cardiff, it mounted a campaign of vilification against 'Chinatown', as it dubbed the Welsh metropolis.[41]

Orientation across the border was even more marked in the north-east Wales coalfield. The early prominence of Flintshire in the coal export trade was undercut by the silting of the Dee estuary. The problem was a natural one, exacerbated by human action. The river's power to scour its estuary was too feeble in relation to the width of the outlet, and the construction of a new channel to Chester in the 1730s was associated with land reclamation which reduced the flow further. The channel was diverted on to the Welsh shore of the Dee by these actions but progressive silting remained as a long-term and continuing problem.[42] This did not prevent the development and extension of industries based on the estuary. Lower Deeside, from Point of Air to the end of the estuary, was based on the relative cheapness of transporting ores from the lead mining areas of the interior to the coast. Brass manufacture, lead, copper and silver smelting were basic, and Holywell's abundant water power, harnessed through a series of dams in the Greenfield Valley was a valuable additional resource. In 1849 Flintshire was responsible for a quarter of Britain's lead smelting. The Upper Deeside from the estuary towards Chester became more oriented to inland ventures. Bricks and earthenware were manufactured at Buckley and some ironworks also appeared in this zone.

Most ironworking was, however, across the county border in Denbighshire rather than Flintshire. Iron took the coalfield from scratching away in the cause of domestic usage to more commercial exploitation. This focused on Wilkinson's ventures at Bersham which specialised in the manufacture of cannon, and cylinders for Boulton and Watt steam engines. In the early nineteenth century the exposed portion of the Denbighshire coalfield was worked quite extensively, largely in the cause of iron production. The older Flintshire coalfield had higher densities of population than did Denbighshire (with the exception of Wrexham) in the early nineteenth century. This was especially marked in northern Flintshire where lead mining added to the density.[43]

Outcomes, 1830–1914

The period of the classic industrial revolution saw significant shifts in the industrial structure of north-east Wales. An industrial belt centred on the Lower Dee estuary, depending on the sea for much of its activity, was supplemented and gradually had leadership wrested from it by an inland coalfield which manufactured iron and earthenware products. Capital came from Merseyside (in the case of the outliers of the Lancashire cotton industry established at Holywell) and from the Midlands (in the case of Wilkinson's ventures in Denbighshire).

This change in the orientation of the regions within north Wales was to be completed during the second part of the first Kondratieff cycle and the subsequent period of the 'second industrial revolution' or second Kondratieff. After 1830 Britain became definitively a free trade economy and the growing importance of steam power meant a closer correlation between industrialisation and coalfields. The innovations which completed this phase of growth were introduced during a period of prolonged political and social crisis. Part of it was a wholesale restructuring of north Wales.

In the north-west there was widespread decline. The Parys Mountain copper mines were an early indicator. Around the turn of the century the large lodes were worked out and the great opencasts gave way to mineshafts. This deprived it of its cost advantage over Cornwall and the ores had always been of lower grade. The mines remained significant ventures but they lost their dominance of the copper market. Merioneth's woollen industry followed on this downward path a little later with rapid decline in the 1820s. Most industries in the north-west showed all too clearly the symptoms of what Cyril Erlich has called 'fragile industrialisation'.[44] Water power, limited mineral resources and cheap labour had enabled them to prosper and grow extensively but by the end of the Napoleonic Wars the writing was on the wall. Now the requirements were coal, labour which was skilled rather than just cheap, and abundant resources in which a region held a comparative advantage.

In north-west Wales only slate – and to a much lesser extent granite – could expand and prosper in this new economic environment. Slate had the advantage of the best British resources and once the slate tax was repealed in 1831, after hard lobbying by north Wales interests, it could take off into the stratosphere. As a heavy commodity it was particularly dependent on improvements in transport and the increased skill of the quarrymen in splitting, both of which reduced the cost of the finished product. It was oriented to the sea. Barmouth the port and shipbuilding centre of the woollen industry gave way to Porthmadog, Port Dinorwic, Caernarfon and Bangor, the slate ports and shipbuilding centres of the central decades of the nineteenth century. The Ffestiniog district with Porthmadog as its outlet came to depend especially on a European and international trade once its internal transport difficulties were resolved by the Ffestiniog railway. In this area slate was mined in underground caverns rather than in the open quarries of Caernarfonshire. Slate became part of the 'imperial economy' of exports which characterised much of Wales and was its component in the free trade system created after 1830. Granite quarrying was much smaller in scale and confined to coastal locations for reasons of transport.[45]

In the second half of the nineteenth century slate came to place its impress over the whole of the north-west of Wales. The mines and quarries became minor tourist attractions because of their size. At the peak of production there were 16,000 quarrymen and the economy revolved around them. Railway workers and dockers were dependent on their trade and the slate areas sustained population growth in Merioneth up to 1881 and in Caernarfonshire right up to the First World War. Slate reached out from the mountainous interior to dominate the coast at the ports which it had created or enlarged.

Some idea of the counterfactual – north-west Wales without slate – can be seen in the history of Anglesey which was not endowed with the rock. Its rural depopulation started on the course of decline in 1851 and some of its population weekly crossed the Menai Straits to work in the Caernarfonshire quarries. They acquired a reputation as strikebreakers who were not fully integrated into the values of the industrial world in which they were something like *gästarbeiter*. The unionised quarry workers of Caernarfonshire dismissed them as 'moch Ynys Môn' (Anglesey pigs). The quarry workers showed a similar contempt for their benighted brethren who remained on the land and adopted a distinctive form of dress to distinguish themselves from them. The quarry workers created a union which was regionally based, reflecting the dynamics of their industry which had 80 per cent of British production and a distinctive set of skills which made them more-or-less immune to external strikebreakers. They had little need of outside allies and remained separate until they formed part of the original amalgamation which created the Transport and General Workers Union in 1922. Their communities had all the badges of an industrial society – billiard halls, few gardens and football teams, along with the chapels which proclaimed their Welshness.[46] What had been created by the boom after 1830 was a region based on slate which was economically, socially and culturally distinct from the rest of north Wales.

A similar process took place on the north Wales coalfield. After the mid-1820s the iron industry experienced a protracted period of depression and decline. The same was true of the Deeside metalworking industries by the 1880s. They suffered competition from south Wales and imported ores from

America and Australia. The mining of cannel coal, from which oil was derived, gave this sub-region a burst of energy in the mid-nineteenth century but it was quickly destroyed by the growing exploitation of natural oils in the world. The region revived with the exploitation of the concealed coalfield of Denbighshire from the 1850s. Very large pits were sunk into this area, and the balance of population was shifted eastwards by this and by the expansion of the towns through which the Shrewsbury to Chester railway ran. Wrexham grew more rapidly than did Chester under the impact of these developments. Railway construction added to the accessibility of Denbighshire's coal and Ruabon fireclay gave it a prosperity not achieved by iron. Gas production also formed a market for local coal and some ironworking survived at Brymbo to be transformed into steel production in the late nineteenth century. Deeside also saw new developments. There was a limited amount of shipbuilding and engineering from the mid-nineteenth century and in 1896 the John Summers steelworks was erected on reclaimed marshland. Coal was in decline and by 1922 only the Point of Air mine survived in Flintshire while chemicals, a spin-off from metal industries, were also declining. Connors Quay became the principal port and the focus of the sub-region, though by the time of the First World War it was experiencing problems with silting and in the twentieth century iron ore for the steelworks at Shotton would be imported through Merseyside ports, symbolising the influences which were coming to dominate north-east Wales. Shotton's connection with the Dee was rather tenuous and it was bound into the Mersey rather than the local waterway.[47]

The same link was revealed by the development of trade unionism amongst the coalminers of north-east Wales. After making many attempts, throughout the nineteenth century, to form localised unions, they joined the Miners Federation of Great Britain (MFGB) in 1893. Originally the MFGB was a federation of inland coalfields and the export coalfields of Durham and south Wales remained aloof from it. North Wales, orientated inland, was part of it from the beginning.[48] Nor could it create the viable regional union which characterised the slate district; it was too much part of a wider British market and society for this to be the case. This orientation would help preserve north-east Wales from the devastation visited upon the outlying industrial areas of Britain in the interwar period. Its experience was different from that of south Wales, and also from Gwynedd where the precipitous decline of slate started in the 1880s rather than the interwar period.[49] Despite the smallness of the coalfield it had achieved some kind of critical mass in its development. Coal was employed for a range of manufactured products, including steel and brick. A certain continuity in development was achieved. Copper smelting had produced a limited amount of chemical production and this was sufficient to give it the basis for its later excursions into rayon manufacture. Slate was far less fertile of economic growth; its by-products and manufacturing potential were very limited and the slate districts rapidly lost population once the industry went into decline.

What had emerged in north Wales by 1914 was two industrial regions, each centred on an extractive industry; the slate communities which straggled through Snowdonia and Wrexham provided foci for them. This was a marked contrast to the tiny pockets of industry in a pastoral setting which had characterised the pre-industrial period, or to the patterns created by the widespread 'fragile industrialisation' of the late eighteenth and early nineteenth centuries. It provided a limited end point for the industrial revolution in north Wales. Dodd's classic study has, rightly, been accused of not providing this and of leaving the story with 'frayed ends'. The backwash, which Dodd was a pioneer in describing, and the subsequent consolidation of coal and its subsidiaries in the east and slate in the west provides the hemming.

Some sense of the overall scale of the industrialisation of the regions of north Wales can be gained from a brief look at its population vital statistics. North Wales after 1851 was an area which failed to retain its whole natural increase, far less to experience net gains through migration. Only occasionally did a coalmining or quarrying area buck this trend, and they did so less markedly than those areas which contained holiday resorts. Population growth in north-east Wales did vary with the distribution of mining but these areas were restricted in their extent and impact on the wider region.[50] They did not save the counties in which they were located from net out-migration. Even areas close to the coalfield like the Vale of Clwyd felt only a limited effect from its development. Great hopes were engendered by the coming of the railway, but its impact proved to be decidedly limited.[51] Within that area, the town of Rhuthun remained stuck at a population of around three thousand, sustained merely by providing marketing services and by the local demands created by the two public institutions which balanced each other at each end of its west–east axis – the prison and the workhouse. The feeling that the modern world was passing it by was palpable in public discussion but, despite vigorous efforts, its citizens proved unable to benefit from many of the wider social changes of the period.[52] Whatever the limits of the reach of the narrow industrial bands of north Wales, they did draw some of the surrounding population into their bounds.

Cultural patterns

Locked into the structure of regions in north Wales was a pattern of cultural differentiation. The Caernarfonshire slate belt had a particularly narrow area from which it drew its population, almost entirely from the surrounding Welsh-speaking rural communities.[53] North-east Wales, by contrast, drew a larger proportion of its population from across the border. The consequence of this was the westward movement of its linguistic frontier. Industrialisation became associated with bilingualism and subsequent anglicisation in a way which never happened in the industrial centres of Gwynedd.[54] In south Flintshire the attraction of migrants from Staffordshire was sufficient to give the area a distinctive local dialect. The general cultural divisions within the area can be seen from tables 10.1–10.4. The Anglican Church was strong nowhere in Wales; Gwynedd had levels of communion which clustered around the Welsh average while north-east Wales was significantly above this. The difference was even more marked in regard of Nonconformity. Gwynedd was a solid bastion of Dissent with over 40 per cent of its population (and over 50 per cent in Merioneth) seeking an alternative to the Established Church. It had held out against the Methodists for fifty years but then rapidly from the 1780s became a bastion of Calvinistic Methodism, the distinctively Welsh brand of the creed, under the leadership of Thomas Charles.[55] North-east Wales never found that level of enthusiasm for Nonconformity expressed in Gwynedd, however late its start. Denbighshire merely hugged the Welsh average while Flintshire fell well below it.

Similar patterns obtained in respect of language. North-east Wales had levels of monoglot Welsh-speaking at the turn of the century which approximated to the Welsh average, while Gwynedd soared above this with half its population unable to speak English. This meant that Welsh was used in many areas of public life, such as political debate and campaigning.[56] Around half the population of north-east Wales was able to speak Welsh, compared with a consistent 90 per cent plus in Gwynedd. Conversely English monoglots were thin on the ground in Gwynedd while they were between a third and a half of the population in the north-east (see tables 10.1–10.4).

These patterns had been created by the migratory flows associated with industrialisation. The regional nature of north Wales is revealed by the poles of attraction and repulsion of population within it. In the north-east the exposed coalfield was the frontier between two cultures. At the beginning of our period it was already a bilingual zone, with Welsh dominant to the west of it and English to the east. In the next century the English area encroached on the bilingual one, shifting bilingual areas to English-speaking ones and Welsh ones to bilingual. The migrants to north-east Wales came predominantly from Cheshire and Lancashire, rather than from Merioneth and Anglesey. Furthermore, migration from north-west Wales was diffused through north-east Wales, while that from England concentrated in the coalfield, amplifying its effects. The coalfield was a religious frontier as much as a linguistic one. Calvinistic Methodists, a distinctively Welsh denomination, dominated the west of the region while the Wesleyan Methodists, a denomination weak in Wales in general, dominated the east. They met on the coalfield.[57]

The bilingual zone was sharply defined both north and south of Brymbo,

Table 10.1 **Denominational communicants, 1905, by county (%)**

County	C of E	Nonconformist	Neither
GWYNEDD			
Anglesey	9.49	41.99	48.52
Caernarfon	10.53	42.52	46.95
Merioneth	8.57	50.32	41.11
CLWYD			
Denbigh	13.02	27.19	59.79
Flint	14.22	17.21	68.57
MID-WALES			
Cardigan	15.22	46.55	38.23
Montgomery	14.07	29.24	56.69
Radnor	16.68	20.87	62.45
Brecon	12.03	25.70	62.27
WALES	9.56	27.40	63.04

Source: calculated from data in Kenneth O. Morgan, *Wales in British Politics, 1868–1922* (Cardiff, 1963) p. 313.

Table 10.2 **Percentage of population (aged 3+) monoglot Welsh speakers, 1901, 1911, by county**

County	Welsh only 1901	Welsh only 1911
WALES	15.1	8.7
Flint	7.5	3.5
Denbigh	18.3	10.2
Merioneth	50.6	37.5
Caernarfon	47.6	36.4
Anglesey	48.0	37.3
Cardigan	50.5	34.8
Brecon	9.3	5.5
Radnor	0.2	0.1
Montgomery	15.6	11.0

often the result of selective migration. Rhosllanerchrugog and Johnstown are contiguous but were citadels of the respective languages which one would expect from their names. Rhos grew in the nineteenth century on the exposed coalfield and its chaotic layout reflected the manner of its development. A cultural world away was Llay growing in the early twentieth century on the con-

Table 10.3 **Percentage of population (aged 3+) able to speak Welsh, 1901, 1911, by county**

County	able to speak Welsh 1901	able to speak Welsh 1911
WALES	49.9	44.6
Flint	49.2	43.3
Denbigh	61.9	57.6
Merioneth	93.8	92.1
Caernarfon	89.6	87.5
Anglesey	91.8	91.2
Cardigan	93.2	91.1
Brecon	45.9	42.1
Radnor	6.3	5.4
Montgomery	47.5	44.7

Table 10.4 **Percentage of population (aged 3+) speaking English only, 1901, 1911, by county**

County	English only 1901	English only 1911
WALES	50.1	55.4
Flint	50.8	56.7
Denbigh	38.1	42.4
Merioneth	6.2	7.9
Caernarfon	10.4	12.5
Anglesey	8.2	8.8
Cardigan	6.8	8.9
Brecon	54.1	57.9
Radnor	93.7	94.6
Montgomery	52.5	55.3

Source for Tables 10.2–10.4: calculated from the Censuses of 1901 and 1911 by Dot Jones.

cealed coalfield, thoroughly Anglicised and planned. This bilingual zone has been seen as easing the tensions of Anglicisation but other evidence might lead us to question this.[58] North-east Wales was the one area of Wales where an English presence quite frequently led to the outbreak of ethnic tensions. In 1754 there had been an attack by the Welsh-speaking inhabitants of Henllan on the English-speaking 'strangers' of Denbigh and a Welsh blacksmith was killed in the disturbances. In the next century the coalfield was frequently a site of tension between English and Welsh miners. In 1869, after Welsh miners were brought to court in Mold for running the English out of the area, a riot ensued and troops killed four people in putting it down.[59]

Mid-Wales illustrates the failure to achieve a regional identity. Wool had failed in Montgomeryshire by the mid-nineteenth century and though there was a new development of factory industry in Cardiganshire in the last quarter of the century it was of insufficient scale to provide a focus for a socially disparate area. Metal mining gradually faded away, even the Van Lead Mine outside Llanidloes which employed some 500 people as late as the 1870s. Most metal mines were so small that they only lightly marked the distribution of population. By 1914 the sense of desperate social crisis was intense. One inhabitant of Cardiganshire remarked that they were 'mugs to stay around here' when the social facilities of the Rhondda Valleys beckoned. Levels of rural depopulation were the highest in England and Wales and palliative measures to stem the flow by providing village institutes and promoting local crafts had little impact.[60] At least one man, Stuart Rendel, the MP for Montgomeryshire from 1880 to 1894, tried to engender a sense of regional consciousness by his promotion of the University College of Wales, Aberystwyth and by the creation of a separate Liberal Party organisation for mid-Wales. He was outmanoeuvred by those who wanted a single organisation for north Wales in order to provide some counterweight to the burgeoning population of the south. Their expedient was simple: they offered him the chairmanship and he was flattered enough to accept.[61]

The religious and cultural diversity of the four counties of mid-Wales showed what a forlorn hope a regional identity was. It included Radnorshire which had been Anglicised since the eighteenth century and contained minimal numbers of monoglot Welsh speakers and, by the turn of the century, few able to speak Welsh at all. Related to this it had a higher than Welsh average percentage of Anglican communicants and a lower than average percentage of Nonconformists. By contrast, in Cardiganshire in 1901, over 90 per cent of the population was able to speak Welsh and just over half were unable to speak English. While its adherence to the Church of England was above average, so was its commitment to Nonconformity. The other two counties ranged between these extremes, each recording lower than average proportions of monoglots and close to average proportions of Welsh speakers. Internal divisions rather mocked these county averages in Montgomeryshire, and serve to emphasise the cultural diversity of the area. (tables 10.1–10.4).

Comparisons

'Relative failure during industrialisation, like success, is probably best tackled by means of comparative analysis.'[62] How did the experience of north Wales compare with that of other areas of western, upland Britain in the period? Generally that area played a part in the industrial revolution but most of it was, at varying dates, affected by backwash. The 'fragile industrialisation' of *c.* 1760–1820 was disproportionately located there. Only a few areas, all of them coalfields, more permanently escaped the limitations upon development imposed by a harsh physical environment and poor soils. Collins has picked out the period 1850–75 as the watershed in the upland zone. The hopes entertained for railways were finally dashed, and competition from the lowlands and from abroad sapped their industrial bases. The one-sided free trade of the late nineteenth century hit the zone hard, and the earlier potential offered by water power and minerals had largely been exhausted. Only areas which had unique advantages like slate and stone deposits continued to attract large scale capital investments. In some areas hydroelectricity offered the hope of another new boom period, in sectors like aluminium smelting, but it proved to be limited and 'the multiplier effect of capital intensive industry in the raw materials sector is not uncommonly weak'.[63]

In order to move beyond generalities about the upland zone we need to make more specific comparisons within it. Two regions have been selected for that purpose – John Marshall's Cumbria and Cornwall.

Cumbria had been an important industrial centre in the middle ages – one which provided a deal of the justification for the now outmoded idea of an industrial revolution of the thirteenth century. This textile industry was, from the Tudor period, supplemented by metal extraction. More importantly, expansion began in the late seventeenth century with the Lowthers's development of Whitehaven which had a cross-channel coal trade with Ireland and a cross-oceanic one in tobacco. It emerged as one of two regional sub-centres, with Kendal, dominating the cloth trade, as the other. The market towns were the growth points of this period rather than the coalfield areas. Metal mining and slate working expanded in scope. As in north Wales in the period up to 1820, this phase was characterised by extensive activity. In the nineteenth century a different pattern emerged. In the place of two sub-regional economies came a unity created by railways. They also produced a real and spectacular industrial revolution on the coast in west Cumbria and in Furness. This had concentrated 60 per cent of the region's population in the coastal strips and main towns by 1881. Yet this proved to be the peak of success and massive de-industrialisation took effect from this time, slower in iron and steel than in bobbin-making, but real nonetheless. Shipbuilding funnelled back into Barrow, where it concentrated. Like north Wales, though with a different timing, it had produced a brief but important flurry of industrial activity and a residue which concentrated in distinct zones. Equally this was not enough to save the region from a net outflow of population. In the course of the nineteenth century 100,000 people left to seek opportunities elsewhere.[64]

The region evolved an identity which transcended county boundaries. It revolved around its mountainous core and drew sustenance from topographical studies and guides which covered the Lake District as a unit rather than its constituent counties. These were read within the area as well as by tourists, and so was the proliferating regional press and the work of dialect versifiers. Exiles from the area contributed to its regional consciousness by indulging their nostalgia in cultural societies established in distant cities.[65]

Cornwall became a major industrial region in Britain in the period 1700–1850. Growth accelerated from the 1740s based on copper extraction with the older tin industry as a subsidiary. After fighting off the challenge from Anglesey between the 1770s and 1790s, it continued to expand into the early nineteenth century. By 1851 its economy relied heavily on copper extraction, with 29 per cent of men in quarrying and mining, a concentration greater than north-west England's 27 per cent in textiles. Cornish deep mining produced an expertise which proved exportable and much of the identity of the area came to be invested in this industrial prowess and the beam engines which symbolised it. A set of institutions emerged which expressed this scientific and technical identity. It is not, perhaps, too fanciful to see this as some compensation for the withering of the Cornish language by the eighteenth century.[66]

This was added to by the development of a distinctive religious culture in which Methodism became almost as dominant as it was in north Wales, and in which the Church of England catered only for a fraction of the population. In 1851 their respective shares of the attendances were 60 per cent and 27 per cent. Two decades earlier, an Anglican minister had admitted: 'We have lost the people'. Methodism absorbed an older *mentalité*, stressing non-human intervention in the world, arising from the role of luck in its key occupations of fishing and mining. This success was rooted in the dispersed habitat of an under-urbanised industrial complex: 'The tightness of the mining villages with those disproportionately large Methodist chapels which are still the visible reminders of a great culture influence suited the hold as well as the spread of religious movements.'[67] Cornish dominance in metal extraction was a fairly brief glory. In 1850 Cornwall had a third of the world's tin and copper production; by 1880 its share of a rapidly growing market was negligible. In the 1830s Chile and Cuba between them produced 36 per cent as much as Cornwall but a decade later they outstripped Cornwall. In the next decade major producers like South Australia (benefiting from cheap freights whereby copper ore was effectively ballast in ships used to transport wool) and Michigan came on stream. In these circumstances, free trade in ores proved to be disastrous. The American Civil War may have delayed the inevitable but the real collapse came in the 1860s and was accelerated by speculation and the financial failure of the banking house of Overend and Gurney. In 1865 Cornwall produced 160,000 tons of lead; this had halved to 80,000 tons by 1870 and halved again to 40,000 tons by 1880. Within 15 years production had fallen by 75 per cent. Growing tin production and china clay quarrying produced but little respite from this decline. Population levels plummeted. Cornish miners and engineers began a great diaspora in the 1830s. Initially the movement was of single roving miners but after the collapse of the 1860s whole families moved. This began to benefit the region's rivals and reinforced the local decline.

Industrial decline produced a new regional geography. Industrial Cornwall had been almost an island, with sea on three sides and the formidable barrier of the River Tamar on the fourth. Its connections with its markets were largely maritime ones. It had been an early pioneer of the railways but these merely connected the inland mining areas with the sea. At the point when its industry collapsed, the main line railway arrived to bridge the Tamar and link it with England more firmly than had ever been the case before. Tourists arrived in numbers, helping to repair some of the damage done by rapid de-industrialisation. Along the Tamar, Plymouth emerged as a regional metropolis drawing migrants, and even a suburban fringe of commuters, from Cornwall. It became the focal point for an emerging south-west region which linked Devon and Cornwall. Their histories had been divergent in the era of industrialisation: de-industrialisation yoked them together.[68]

Comparisons within the highland zone show both the similarities in the basic processes involved and differences in the trajectories of development and timing. The idea of a highland zone is a static one, difficult to disentangle from geographical determinism, and it is of only limited usefulness as a device for understanding the development of the regional societies in which people sought to live out their lives in the era of the long industrial revolution. Dynamic forces reshaped each of them from within and without, creating new social and economic geographies and new patterns of relationships with the wider world. It is a challenge to historians to capture and analyse the shifting formations that were created by this dynamism. John Marshall has done more than most to pose questions about the nature of regions and their identities. In doing so he has provided the means to illuminate crucial processes in modern history.

Notes

Thanks to my colleague Allan Parfitt, a former Shotton steelworks instrument mechanic, for some useful discussions which helped to formulate some of my ideas Dot Jones kindly made available census figures which she has painstakingly extracted and which will be published in G. H. Jenkins (ed.), *Social History of the Welsh Language* (Cardiff, University of Wales Press, 1998). Bernard Deacon kindly sent me his valuable and extensive unpublished work on Cornwall. Thanks also to Ieuan Gwynedd Jones and Pam Michael for discussing a draft with me.

1 This essay continues and extends an analysis begun in my lecture '*The industrial revolution in north Wales* revisited', *Transactions of the Caernarfonshire Historical Society*, forthcoming
2 The analogy is, of course, with Eric Hobsbawm's 'long nineteenth century' in his great trilogy on nineteenth-century Europe – and beyond, *The Age of Revolution, 1789–1848*, *The Age of Capital, 1848–1875*; *The Age of Empire, 1875–1914* (London, 1962, 1975, 1987).
3 H. Perkin, *The Origins of Modern English Society, 1780–1880* (London, 1969) ch. 1.
4 D. W. Meunig, 'The continuous shaping of America: a prospectus for geographers and historians', *American Historical Review*, 83 (1978), 1186–205, esp. 1202.
5 *Ibid*, pp. 1202–3.
6 *Ibid*, p. 1205.
7 H. Carter, 'The urban hierarchy and historical geography: a consideration with reference to north east Wales', in A. R. H. Baker, J. D. Hamshere and J. Langton (eds), *Geographical Interpretations of Historical Sources: Readings in Historical Geography* (Newton Abbot, 1970).
8 A. H. Dodd, 'Welsh and English in east Denbighshire: a historical retrospect', *Transactions of the Honourable Society of Cymmrodorion* (1940), 34–65.
9 B. Deacon, 'A "failed" early industrial region: the case of Cornwall, 1740–1860', (unpublished paper).
10 E. J. T. Collins, 'The economy of upland Britain, 1750–1950', in R. B. Tranter (ed.), *The Future of Upland Britain*. Centre for Agricultural Strategy, University of Reading (Reading, 1978).
11 F. J. North, 'The background of history in north-eastern Wales', *Archaeologia Cambrensis*, 87:1 (1932), 1–47.
12 J. D. Marshall, 'Proving ground or the creation of regional identity? The origins and problems of regional history in Britain', in P. Swan and D. Forster (eds), *Essays in Regional and Local History: In Honour of Eric M. Sigsworth* (Hull, Humberside Polytechnic, 1991, reprinted Beverley, 1992), pp. 22–3.
13 The term 'pastoralisation' is from F. Crouzet, 'Wars, blockade and economic change in Europe, 1792–1815', *Journal of Economic History*, 24:4 (1964), 567–88, esp. 580–1; 'backwash' comes from Gynnar Myrdal via Immanuel Wallerstein who has popularised it in his multi-volume *The Origins of the Modern World System* (New York and London, 1974ff.).
14 Evans, 'Revisited'.
15 M. Roberts, 'Another letter from a far country: the prehistory of labour, or the history of work in preindustrial Wales', *Llafur: The Journal of Welsh Labour History*, 5:2 (1989), 93–106.
16 R. A. N. Jones, 'Women, community and collective action: the *ceffyl pren* tradition', in A. V. John (ed.), *Our Mothers' Land: Chapters in Welsh Women's History, 1830–1939* (Cardiff, 1991). I am also indebted to conversations with Rosemary Jones and to reading her unpublished work.
17 Marshall, 'Proving ground', pp. 13, 23.
18 J. D. Marshall, *Furness and the Industrial Revolution: An Economic History of Furness*, (Barrow in Furness, 1958).
19 Marshall, 'Proving ground', p. 13.
20 Roberts, 'Another letter'; E. Countryman, *Americans: Collisions of Histories* (New York, 1996).
21 N. Evans, 'Two paths to economic development: Wales and the north east of England' in P. Hudson (ed.), *Regions and Industries: A Perspective on the Industrial Revolution in Britain* (Cambridge, 1989).
22 L. Colley, *Britons: Forging the Nation, 1707–1837*, (New Haven and London, 1992), p. 15.

23 W. E. Minchinton, 'Bristol: metropolis of the west in the eighteenth century', *Transactions of the Royal Historical Society*, 5th series, 4 (1954), 69–85.

24 R. C. Jarvis, 'The head port of Chester; and Liverpool, its creek and member', *Transactions of the Historic Society of Lancashire and Cheshire,* 102 (1950), 69–84.

25 M. I. Williams, 'Glimpses of life in seventeenth-century Cardiganshire', *Ceredigion* 12:4 (1996), 3–20.

26 D. Defoe, *A Tour through the Whole Island of Great Britain* [1727], limited facsimile ed. G. D. H. Cole (London, 1927), p. 458; M. Roberts, 'The empty ladder: work and its meanings in early modern Cardiganshire', *Llafur,* 6:4 (1995), 9–29.

27 T. C. Mendenhall, *The Shrewsbury Drapers and the Welsh Wool Trade in the XVI and XVII Centuries* (Oxford, 1953), pp. 120, 210–13.

28 M. J. Jones, 'The Merioneth woollen industry from 1750 to 1820', *Transactions of the Honourable Society of Cymmrodorion* (1939), 181–208. The quotation is on p. 190.

29 M. Humphreys, *The Crisis of Community: Montgomeryshire, 1680–1815* (Cardiff, 1996), pp. 16, 21–3, 47–8, 85–7.

30 D. Thomas, 'The seashore industries and trade of Caernarfonshire', in *NUT Conference Souvenir, Llandudno, 1939* (Cardiff and Wrexham, 1939); J. Lindsay, *The North Wales Slate Industry* (Newton Abbot, 1974) ch. 1; G. H. Williams, 'Masnach forwol Arfon, 1630–1690' ['Maritime Trade of Arfon'], *Cymru a'r Môr / Maritime Wales,* 3 (1978), 9–24.

31 K. Lloyd Gruffydd, 'The development of the coal industry in Flintshire to 1740' (unpublished M.A. thesis, University of Wales, 1981), quotation on p. 166; Gruffydd, 'The export of Flintshire coal before the industrial revolution', *Flintshire Historical Society Journal*, 34 (1996), 53–88; I. M. Evans, 'The geography of Flintshire in the eighteenth century' (B.A. Honours thesis, apparently in Geography, University of Manchester, 1961 [copy in Flintshire Record Office, Hawarden]); Adrian Teale, 'The economy and society of north Flintshire, 1660–1714', (unpublished M.A. thesis, University of Wales, 1979), quotation from Blome on p. 123; R. Rees Rawson, 'The coalmining industry of the Hawarden district on the eve of the industrial revolution', *Archaeologia Cambrensis,* 96:2 (1941), 109–35.

32 M. Hechter, *Internal Colonialism: The Celtic Fringe in British National Development, 1536–1966* (London, 1975); R. M. Jones, 'Notes from the margin: class and society in nineteenth-century Gwynedd', in D. Smith (ed.), *A People and a Proletariat: Essays in the Social History of Wales, 1780–1980* (London, 1980).

33 R. Lloyd Jones, 'The first Kondratieff: the long wave and the British industrial revolution' *Journal of Interdisciplinary History*, 20:4 (1990), 581–605. The quotation is on p. 603. The Russian economist Nikolai Kondratieff (1892–1938?) argued that market economies were subject to broad 50–year cycles of expansion and contraction.

34 P. G. E. Clements, 'The rise of Liverpool, 1665–1750', *EcHR*, 29:2 (1976), 211–25.

35 T. A. Roberts, 'The Welsh influence on the building industry in Victorian Liverpool', in M. Doughty (ed.), *Building the Industrial City* (Leicester, 1986).

36 A full study of their development is badly needed; in the meantime see A. H. Dodd, 'The rise of the north Wales coastal resorts', in *NUT, 1939;* and A. Fletcher, 'Rhyl: the evolution of a resort', *Flintshire Historical Society Journal,* 33 (1992), 119–49; and his 'The role of landowners, entrepreneurs and railways in the urban development of the north Wales coast during the nineteenth century', *Welsh History Review*, 16:4 (1993), 514–41.

37 J. R. Harris, *The Copper King* (Liverpool, 1964); J. Rowlands, *Copper Mountain*, Anglesey, Antiquarian Society (Llangefni, 1966).

38 F. A. Barnes, 'Settlement and landscape changes in a Caernarfonshire slate quarrying parish', in P. Osborne *et al.* (eds), *Geographical Essays in Honour of K. C. Edwards* (Nottingham, 1970).

39 J. G. Jones, 'The Ffestiniog slate industry: the industrial pattern to 1831', *Journal of the Merioneth Historical and Record Society*, 6 (1969), 50–65; M. J. T. Lewis and M. C. Williams, *Pioneers of Ffestiniog Slate*, Snowdonia National Park Study Centre (Maentwrog, 1987); M. J. T. Lewis, *Sails along the Dwyryd*, Snowdonia National Park Study Centre (Maentwrog, 1989); M. J. T. Lewis, *How Ffestiniog got its Railway*, Railway and Canal Historical Society, 2nd edn. (Caterham, 1968) .

40 Jones, 'Merioneth woollen industry'

41 J. G. Jenkins, 'The woollen industry in Montgomeryshire', *Montgomeryshire Collections*, 58:1 (1963), 50–69, esp. 57; Jenkins, 'The woollen industry', in D. Moore (ed.), *Wales in the Eighteenth Century* (Swansea, 1976), pp. 97–103; Dodd, *Industrial Revolution*, ch. 7; Humphreys, *Crisis of Community*, pp. 66–7, 85–7, 152–5, quotation on p. 257; N. Evans, 'Gogs, Cardis and Hwntws: region, nation and state in Wales, 1840–1940', in Evans (ed.), *National Identity in the British Isles*, Coleg Harlech Occasional Papers in Welsh Studies, 3 (Harlech, 1989).

42 M. E. Marker, 'The Dee estuary: its progressive silting and salt marsh development', *Transactions of the Institute of British Geographers*, 41 (1967), 65–71; T. S. Willan, 'Chester and the navigation of the Dee, 1600–1750', *Journal of the Chester Archaeological and Historical Society*, new series, 32 (1937–38), 64–7; H. Robinson, 'Cheshire river navigations with special reference to the River Dee', *Journal of the Chester Archaeological Society*, 55 (1968), 63–87; R. Craig, 'Some aspects of the trade and shipping of the River Dee in the eighteenth Century', *Transactions of the Historic Society of Lancashire and Cheshire*, 114 (1963), 99–128.

43 J. A. Taylor, 'The northern borderland and the Vale of Clwyd', in E. G. Bowen (ed.), *Wales: A Physical, Historical and Regional Geography* (London, 1957); R. Lawton and W. Smith, 'The north Wales coalfield and Chester', in Smith *et al.* (eds), *A Scientific Survey of Merseyside*, British Association (Liverpool, 1953).

44 Quoted in E. Richards, 'Regional imbalance and poverty in early nineteenth-century Britain', in R. Mitchison and P. Roebuck (eds), *Economy and Society in Scotland and Ireland, 1500–1938* (Edinburgh, 1988).

45 I. E. Davies, 'A history of the Penmaenmawr quarries', *Transactions of the Caernarfonshire Historical Society*, 35 (1974), 27–72.

46 R. M. Jones, *The North Wales Quarrymen, 1874–1922* (Cardiff, 1981).

47 Taylor, 'Northern borderland'; Lawton and Smith, 'North Wales coalfield'

48 E. Rogers, 'The history of trade unionism in the north Wales coalfield' (M.A. thesis, University of Wales, 1928), ed. R. O. Roberts in *Transactions of the Denbighshire Historical Society*, 12–23 (1963–74).

49 F. Holloway, 'The interwar depression in the Wrexham coalfield', *Transactions of the Denbighshire Historical Society*, 27 (1978), 49–88; F. Holloway, 'Industrial Flintshire in the interwar years' (unpublished M.A. thesis, University of Wales, 1978).

50 Net migration figures by registration district 1851–1911 supplied by Dot Jones; Lawton and Smith, 'North Wales coalfield'; North, 'Background of history'

51 A. Fletcher, 'Social and economic changes in the Vale of Clwyd during the railway era' (unpublished M.Phil. thesis, University of Wales, 1991).

52 This is based on intensive, but as yet unpublished, research on the town, *c.* 1850– 1930. It is impossible to document this here, but I intend to publish an article on it in due course.

53 P. E. Jones, 'Migration and the slate belt of Caernarfonshire in the nineteenth century', *Welsh History Review*, 14:4 (December 1989), 610–29.

54 The former quarry towns remain bastions of the Welsh language.

55 I. G. Jones, 'Thomas Charles (1755–1814)', *Pioneers of Welsh Education*, University College of Swansea, Faculty of Education (Swansea, 1964).

56 N. Evans and K. Sullivan, '"Yn llawn o dân Cymreig" ["Full of Welsh fire"]: the lan-

guage of politics in Wales, 1880–1914', in Jenkins (ed.), *A Social History of the Welsh Language*.

57 W. T. R. Pryce, 'Migration and the evolution of cultural areas: cultural and linguistic frontiers in north-east Wales, 1750–1851', *Transactions of the Institute of British Geographers*, 65 (1975), 79–107; and 'Industrialism, urbanization and the maintenance of industrial areas: north-east Wales in the mid-nineteenth century', *Welsh History Review*, 7:3 (1975), 307–40.

58 Pryce, 'Migration' and 'Industrialism'; R. Laidlaw, 'Community, work and religion: mentalities in the villages of the north Wales coalfield, *c*. 1930–*c*. 1960' (unpublished Ph.D. thesis, University of Warwick, 1995).

59 D. Howell, 'Welsh agricultural neighbourhoods in the eighteenth-century' in C. Richmond and I. Harvey (eds), *Recognitions: Essays Presented to Edmund Fryde* (Aberystwyth, 1996); Rogers, 'History of trade unionism'; A. Burge, 'The Mold riots of 1869', *Llafur*, 3:3 (1982), 42–57.

60 T. A. Morrison, 'Some notes on the Van mine, Llanidloes, Montgomeryshire', *Industrial Archaeology*, 8:1 (1971), 35–50; Morrison, 'The initiation of mining settlement in the north Cardiganshire orefield', *Industrial Archaeology*, 10:2 (1973), 161–96; G. Williams, 'The disenchantment of the world: innovation, crisis and change in Cardiganshire, 1880–1914', *Ceredigion*, 9 (1983), 303–21; Evans, 'Gogs, Cardis'.

61 K. O. Morgan, *Modern Wales: Politics, Places and People* (Cardiff, 1995) ch. 18.

62 Richards, 'Regional imbalance', p. 204.

63 Collins, 'Economy of upland Britain', quotation on p. 598; Richards, 'Regional imbalance'.

64 J. D. Marshall, 'Stages of industrialisation in Cumbria', in Hudson (ed.), *Regions and Industries*, pp. 132–55.

65 J. D. Marshall and J. K. Walton, *The Lake Counties: From 1830 to the mid twentieth Century* (Manchester, 1981) pp. 14–16, 156, 159, 221–2.

66 Deacon, '"Failed" early industrial region'; P. Payton, *The Making of Modern Cornwall: Historical Experience and the Persistence of 'Difference'* (Redruth, 1992); J. Rowe, *Cornwall in the Age of the Industrial Revolution*, 2nd enlarged edn. (St Austell, 1993); Rowe, *The Hard Rock Men: Cornish Immigrants and the North American Mining Frontier* (Liverpool, 1974) ch. 1; G. Burke, 'The Cornish diaspora of the nineteenth century', in S. Marks and P. Richardson (eds), *International Labour Migration: Historical Perspectives* (London, 1984).

67 Payton, *Making of Modern Cornwall*; J. Rule, 'Methodism, popular beliefs and village culture in Cornwall, 1800–50', in R. D. Storch (ed.), *Popular Culture and Custom in Nineteenth-Century England* (London, 1982), quotations on pp. 48–9 and 58–9.

68 J. Simmons, 'The railway in Cornwall, 1835–1914', *Journal of the Royal Institution of Cornwall*, new series 9:1 (1982), 11–29; Deacon, '"Failed" early industrial region'.

J. D. Marshall: the making of the identity of a regional historian

It is impossible to have a casual meeting with John Marshall. As he comes towards you on campus or at a conference he radiates purpose and energy. John always has some scheme or idea bubbling away that he is eager to share. Short in stature, with a shock of vigorous hair, his physical vitality reflects the intense intellectual and emotional activity within. He is a man who has always lived a life that has been engaged, at the edge. His mind and heart have combined in an attempt to make sense of the past and the present, to empathise with the experience of men and women then and now, and to join with others to make a better future. These activities have never been clearly distinct, for they never could be in such an integrated, focused man. History has helped him to understand how society operates and this has formed the direction of his personal involvement in social and political action. At the same time, his life of extraordinarily wide experience and activity has shaped and deepened the questioning of the past which is, for him, the essence of historical study and research. All this has made him a distinctive, sometimes difficult, always challenging figure in the world of academic history, that has become increasingly bland, professional and detached over the course of his career.

For these reasons John's work can only be understood through his life.[1] He has not studied history simply for the delight of scholarship and discovery (though these he has certainly enjoyed). He has never seen his work as a congenial way to earn a reasonable living or build a career. For him ideas have always been a basis for commitment and involvement. He came into history to clarify his understanding of economic and social life, so that he and others could have a more informed basis for action. And while the directions this has taken him in have changed over the years, the fundamental approach has not. John's life has, to a greater extent than is perhaps usual, taken a form that he consciously shaped for himself, often against the prevailing wind. Of course, chance has played its part, but just as he has gratefully seized such good fortune as has come his way, he has stuck to his course with determination in less happy times.

John was born in Ilkeston, a Derbyshire colliery town, in 1919, where his father, a Yorkshireman, had been posted to manage an employment exchange. After attending local schools, he went to Nottingham High School in 1932. He enjoyed reading (his home was well supplied with books), cycling and cricket (in which he made his mark at school and discovered a life-long passion) more than academic work. But he recollects a school that was 'A rather superior forcing house for the boys of Nottingham middle class families . . . obsessed with Oxford and Cambridge exhibitions'. His cycling took him to the Derbyshire valleys, where he was intrigued by the mills that provided physical evidence of the early stages of factory development. And he was thunderstruck by a friendly schoolmaster who, despite his apparent lack of academic ability, told him out of the blue, that he should read history at university.

He did not stay long enough at school to be able to realise this suggestion, leaving in 1936 to become a copy runner and junior reporter on the *Derby Evening Telegraph.* Court reporting provided a rich introduction to the underside of east Midlands society. His cricketing prowess suggested that he should specialise on the sports side, so along with the usual routine, he pasted up the racing cards for the compositors and reported on 'all-in' wrestling. The latter led to a chance meeting with an adult education tutor who introduced him to the *New Statesman* and invited him to attend his modern literature evening class in Ilkeston. Thus began John's real academic education. Reading Aldous Huxley, he learned the importance of detached observation and thought. William Cobbett became a hero. Penguin books and the Left Book Club provided his library. Friends introduced him to jazz, art and amateur drama. He began to flex his muscles as a writer of both short stories and verse at a writers' club in Derby, where he found new friends prepared to encourage his efforts.

Meanwhile, he lost his job at the newspaper after a row with an assistant editor. Eventually he was employed by a solicitor who chased up debts on commission. This took John into some of the poorest and most blighted parts of the Midlands, providing a further education in the social pathology of the period that made a deep impression on an observant and intelligent young man. When John later wrote about the problems of the poor, he was commenting from an understanding that was founded on very direct personal experience and observation.

Given his reading, his friendships and his disenchanted view of society, it is scarcely surprising that John moved towards the Independent Labour Party pacifism that was the response of many young people to the international tension and domestic social problems of the late 1930s. For him, these views were sufficiently consolidated to require him to become a conscientious objector when war came. And this took him to the town, and the experience of social life and political activity, that was to become so important a part of his later life. He went to work in forestry in the Lake District and found comradeship in the local communist party in Barrow, where he learnt about political activism and working-class life in a shipyard town. This led him to begin to see an individual witness to pacifism as ineffectual. The party provided a framework for energetic work that offered the promise of being effective. Even more importantly, he found (perhaps for the first time) acceptance and self-respect among the kind, straightforward and idealistic working-class party members – who contrasted so sharply with the more self-regarding middle-class membership he was to meet after the war. He discovered himself in action and commitment and this remained an important aspect of his character and life long after he finally left the party. For the rest of his life he has retained a passionate and deeply romantic view of Furness, the southern Lakes and especially its coast, sometimes expressed in verse. It was, perhaps, a conjunction of the happiness and fulfilment that came from his friendships and commitments in industrial Barrow and the beauty of the fells and the subtle lights and shades of Morecambe Bay. In the two following post-war decades his life was spent in less congenial settings and the southern Lakes became a home of the spirit, providing an escape from less promising circumstances. We may imagine that this fuelled his commitment to later historical work on the area.

Contact with the harder edge of life in Barrow and those who sought to change it, modified his views. Full pacifism seemed too simplistic, especially after the Soviet Union entered the war. He volunteered for military service in 1941. As for many of his generation, the experience of war broadened his outlook. Serving in the Royal Signals, he was able to explore London when stationed in the Surrey-Berkshire borderlands. During the invasion of Europe, he passed through France, Belgium and Holland, gaining confidence in languages. Finally, he spent nearly a year in Berlin, where he came to know Germans on a relaxed basis and where his duties were sufficiently undemanding to allow him to do a good deal of reading. This gave him a European perspective that permanently freed him from the Anglo-centrism that marks some British historical writing. True to form, he remained close to the centre of action, finishing the war as a radio operator in Montgomery's operational headquarters, and was present when the first German emissaries arrived to negotiate the surrender.

During the war, John's mind turned to reading for a degree with a view to a career in teaching. His literary interests inclined him to focus on English literature, but, in a comment deeply redolent of the highly charged political atmosphere of the time, an Army Education Corps officer suggested that this was 'fiddling while Rome burns' and that economics would be more useful in helping to change the world. As a result, John entered the University College in Nottingham to read for an external London degree in that subject. As many ex-servicemen found, return to an institution used to educating those who had no experience of life beyond school did not prove as liberating as he had anticipated. Economics as a theoretical discipline was of little interest to him, and his political views and their associated energetic activities brought him into conflict with influential members of the college. But he was exceedingly fortunate in one respect. His degree included a substantial element of economic history, largely taught by J. D. Chambers, a scholar of the highest quality and a man of great wit, sensitivity and professional commitment. His background and interests were well designed to catch John's imagination and contribute valuably to his academic formation. Chambers was a brother of the young D. H. Lawrence's close friend Jessie, brought up on a farm near to John's childhood home near Ilkeston, linking familiar territory with his literary interests. Chambers's scholarly interests concentrated on Nottinghamshire and he discussed the industrial revolution in terms of the early Midland mills that had intrigued John during his boyhood cycling expeditions. Of greatest significance, he had pioneered a regional approach to the real sources of economic and social change, in a series of important publications, that provided a foundation on which John could build his own distinctive approach.[2]

This enabled John to see formal study as providing a means to fulfilling a commitment he had entered into with himself during the war. During a brief leave spent in Barrow, his close friend Jack Mowat had shared his excitement at reading some volumes on local history recently bought at a sale. The subtitle of Fisher's *Popular History of Barrow-in-Furness: The English Chicago* made his pulse race.[3] For the first time he began to see the revolutionary character of the town's development in the nineteenth century. Studying an 1886 surveyor's map of the town, he saw how it was possible to recreate the past imaginatively from such evidence, and from what he saw about him. At once he determined to collaborate with Jack to write a history of Barrow from the point of view of its people. His motive was initially political, seeing history as an important way of understanding the reality of social and economic relations. He wrote at the time 'we would be writing *about* people *for* the people; in other words, describing the effects of economic relations *upon* people'. Through the war years, he had begun to read all he could about the history of the town and its industries and to quarry more general works that would illuminate a local study.

Chambers's teaching and example provided an ideal introduction to a more formal and structured approach to this task and John's historical studies became far more serious, committed and adventurous than those of the conventional undergraduate. In order to understand better the character of working lives in Barrow he took a job as a fitter's mate in the shipyard. He thus became a temporary member of the Amalgamated Engineering Union and carried the main bolts on a propeller shaft of the *Orcades* to where they had to be fitted. He made friends among the small group of local amateur historians of Furness and used their knowledge, along with the union connections of some of his political associates, to open up archives in the local library, the London School of Economics special collections, the Public Record Office, and in trade union headquarters in London. For him there was no easy advice from supervisors or the provision of a pre-packaged collection of papers to work on. Each new archive had to be traced and approached with none of the introductions that sometimes come with an established position as a research student or university academic.

After graduation in 1949 John proceeded to a teaching certificate course. In the last year of his degree he had married Audrey Pullinger, an LSE graduate and social worker he had met through the communist group in Nottingham. Celia's birth in 1950 required him to obtain a position to support this new family. There was talk of a position in adult education in his university. This fell through and an interview in which he was closely questioned about his political views made it clear that these had not helped. His first post was in a small school based in an art college in Mansfield, where he was wholly responsible for the education of about fifty teenagers. In 1953 he moved to a more bracing further education institution, teaching Coal Board apprentices at Hucknall in South Nottinghamshire.

It was against this apparently unpromising background, and partly as an escape from its limitations, that John brought the work on Barrow that he had first mapped out in the war years to fruition. It took the form of the external London doctoral thesis that was to make his academic reputation. The cost was heavy. He had no formal supervision. The research involved was often far removed from Nottinghamshire, in London and Barrow (though the papers of the major Furness proprietors, the Dukes of Devonshire, were nearer to hand at Chatsworth). The writing had to take place in the interstices allowed by arduous teaching, a young family (Alison was born in 1953) and a heavy continuing commitment to local political activism. Nonetheless John broke into print with a paper in more than one reputable journal before completing the thesis.

His sense of embattlement was exacerbated by the continuing implications of his political connections. He remained an active communist and a member of the CP Historians' Group, which provided his most important contact with other academic historians. They were, of course, a distinguished group. In 1956 he presented a paper at a seminar chaired by Maurice Dobb with Eric Hobsbawm, Christopher Hill, Edward Thompson, John Saville and Rodney Hilton in the audience. Sidney Pollard, news of whose foray into Furness history at first disconcerted John, proved a valuable and loyal colleague whose outlook on the world was similar to John's. They shared material and collaborated in publication. At the same time, W. H. Chaloner from Manchester University and G. P. Jones from Sheffield University (who had a home in Furness) encouraged his work and provided important hints on sources and methods of approach. Chaloner, a warm, enthusiastic man who quite transcended his well-known association with the right, proved a particularly valuable friend by accepting John as a colleague so openly, collaborating in writing a paper on John Cartwright and the Revolution Mill.[4] Jones encouraged him to pay attention to the demography of Furness. But it remained the case, as was reported to John at the time, that whenever his name was mentioned in professional circles, the chief thing known about him was that he was a communist. And this did not offer an easy route into a conventional university department in the 1950s when posts were in any event scarce.

The year 1956 provided a turning point. Academically, John was awarded a doctorate. There was a degree of irony that a project that had begun as a people's history of Furness should be examined and approved by two historians often associated with the right, Chaloner and A. H. John. In 1958 a revised version of his thesis was published. The book was well reviewed in the *Manchester Guardian* and Sidney Pollard gave it red carpet treatment in the *Economic History Review*, where he wrote, 'The author, one of the most independent minds engaged in writing economic history today, is quite incapable of writing a dull local chronicle. . . . This is one of the most valuable studies of the industrial revolution in recent years.' The book that had been planned as a popular history had met the highest professional standards as well. For the first time, senior professional colleagues sought him out at conferences. But its original aims were not forgotten. Appropriately, the book was published with the support of Barrow-in-Furness Library Committee. Even the maps, drawn by a local friend, had a distinctive character designed to encourage a popular readership, as those who study the line of vision of the diver appended to the corner of the map in figure 3 will discover.

Politically, after the Soviet invasion of Hungary in 1956, John was involved in a 'rousing row' which led to him leaving the party. In this he followed most of the other members of the Historians' Group, some of whom had spearheaded the attack on the Soviet control of the British Communist Party. It was a sad break with earlier days of hope and action, but it did not mean that John lost any affection for the many real friends he had made in the party, especially in Barrow, or his commitment to a radical political vision. It simply became clear that it had to be pursued by other means.

Professionally, he was successful in applying for a post at the Bolton College which trained teachers for technical colleges. His special teaching experience and understanding of the history of industry made him a valuable recruit for the college. He was rapidly promoted to a principal lectureship, responsible for general studies and the teaching of the history of science and technology. The latter became an absorbing interest. He enjoyed the teaching, for the college's students were mainly mature and provided opportunities for worthwhile discussion. It was an indirect way of realising the ambition he had harboured since the late 1930s of teaching adults, as he had himself been taught.

So the late 1950s were years of hard-won fulfilment. John had established a scholarly reputation with a substantial work of distinction. He had obtained a highly responsible position that offered opportunities for worthwhile and enjoyable work. And this was complemented by a happy family life in a 'leafy' suburb of Bolton, with his wife teaching at the same college. Edward was born in 1963. The new life encouraged a steady flow of scholarly work, with definitive papers on Nottinghamshire and Lancashire labourers and on the New Poor Law, and professional papers on liberal studies in further education, widening the scope of a publication list that was becoming both solid and substantial.

From this firm personal and professional base John began to apply for university posts in the early 1960s. Following an earlier initiative by Chaloner, John had eventually taken on the task of leading a scholarly team in producing an edition of *The Autobiography of William Stout of Lancaster*, an eighteenth-century Quaker merchant. Thus when, in 1965, the new University of Lancaster advertised a post in local history, it could have been designed with him in mind. He could point to the solid achievement of his book on Barrow, visible across the bay from what was to become the new university's campus. There was the prospect of an imminent publication of unimpeachably scholarly character, direct local significance, likely to interest the new university's vice-chancellor, a prominent member of the Society of Friends. For someone who had come to expect that the die was loaded against him, this must have seemed decidedly uncanny. There was an awkward twist. Sidney Pollard offered John a post in economic history at Sheffield. Thus after years of disappointment, two university posts were in his grasp at the same time.

John took the Lancaster post. This enabled him to enjoy the excitement surrounding the creation of a new university, the development of courses from scratch, the stocking of the library, the society of many young staff, 'the long garden party' of relatively easy funding, hard work and the chance to shape one's own professional environment. At the same time he began to develop the connections that were to become so important in the region, teaching evening classes in South Cumbria and talking to local history societies throughout the north-west. The preparation of survey courses on north-west regional history required extensive research in secondary sources. This was supplemented by detailed primary research which nourished a continued commitment to publication, uninterrupted by the other new demands. He acquainted himself with the detail of the industrial history of Cumbria beyond Furness by a study of industrial sites. In *The Industrial Archaeology of the Lake Counties* he tried to show how this approach could be rescued from antiquarianism to contribute to a more widely based understanding of local economic history. A series of papers in the *Transactions of the Cumberland and Westmorland Antiquarian and Archaeological Society* placed the social history of the region on a new basis. His position as a scholar of repute and authority was endorsed by a commission from the Economic History Society to write an account of *The Old Poor Law, 1795–1834* as a guide to the literature for undergraduates. His pioneering of urban history in his work on Barrow was recognised by an invitation to contribute to a collection which was to be a manifesto for the new specialism. He became involved in the affairs of the Cumberland and Westmorland Archaeological and Antiquarian Society, persuading it to take an interest in industrial history, and spent much time helping the local planning authorities to identify sites of value and interest. His energy and scholarship were rewarded by promotion to a Readership in North-West Regional History in 1968.

The emphasis in much of this work was that of social, rather than economic history. That was because John worked closely in the history department with Harold Perkin, who was appointed to the first designated chair in social history in the United Kingdom in 1968. An M.A. by coursework was introduced to exploit the reputation of the two scholars and the popularity of their subject areas. It proved successful, attracting many good students who took courses in both social and regional history. These prepared them to write a dissertation over the summer and it was natural that many chose to explore the stimulating generalisations proffered in Harold Perkin's social history course in the context of the experience of the north-west. Their work created a valuable new library of primary research on regional history that fed back into more richly textured teaching. It was an exciting time.

In this atmosphere of opportunity and expansion, John's ideas about regional study began to take a wider perspective. It was a special and distinctive vision. It drew together his intellectual commitment to multidisciplinary work and the idea that the University of Lancaster should be open to its region, serving it by offering its expertise and increasing opportunities for education for those of all ages. In return, this integration would feed contact with real problems back into the university, stimulating its research and offering new opportunities for teaching of social relevance in practical contexts. For him the idea of the university successfully embedded in and serving its region blended his academic, cultural, social and political interests. It was a radical idea that scouted the professional complacency of the modern university, whose ambitions were more narrowly focused than John was prepared to contemplate. Indeed, few of those with whom John discussed his ideas understood how fundamental they were. While they looked for ways in which a regional commitment could strengthen grant applications or spread teaching loads, John was trying to show them how a university could be at the heart of regional social and economic change.

As always for him, ideas implied action. In 1969 John wrote a paper arguing that the university should encourage 'regionally-oriented study in the university, economic, historical, sociological or archaeological' in a spirit of 'cross disciplinary co-operation of a kind originally envisaged in the university's approach to teaching and education'. A working party set up to investigate these possibilities revealed a good deal of work going on right across the university, including the science departments. A proposal that a centre should be funded to support these activities was at first met by more modest support for a *Regional Bulletin*, edited by John. This spread information about the university's regional activities inside and off the campus. At last in 1973 the university created the Centre for North-West Regional Studies (CNWRS) with John as Director.[5]

The following years should have been filled with achievement, fulfilment and happiness. It was not as simple as that. The earlier productive co-operation he had enjoyed in the history department broke down as different views as to the scope, development and leadership of regional interests emerged. It was a miserable time for all involved, as professional and administrative problems became heavily charged by personal feeling. The strain told. John's health deteriorated and this eventually led to the loss of sight in one eye. His marriage to Audrey broke down. Then, in 1976, against his own wish, he left the history department and became a full-time Director of the CNWRS. He deeply resented the interpretation some placed on this move and the restrictions it imposed on the scope of his teaching activities.

However, out of this phase of what John has called '*Sturm und Drang*' came new good things. In 1976 he married Frances Harland with whom he had discovered the self-confidence to publish the verse he had written intermittently since the years before the war but previously kept private. Between them, with enthusiastic administrative support from Marion McClintock and the patronage of Norman Nicholson, they established the Cumbria Poetry Centre at Charlotte Mason College, Ambleside. This published the work of regional poets and arranged workshops and readings. John became an active poet included in anthologies edited by Ted Hughes and Norman Nicholson. Within the university, the CNWRS created an environment for his work that opened up new opportunities with colleagues who were prepared to think in the broader way that John has always found congenial. Alan Mercer from the Management School, as Chairman of the centre, introduced John to new ways of considering the university's regional role. Marion McClintock provided the administrative backbone for the centre through which she expressed her own committed view of the university's regional role. Elizabeth Roberts, who had begun her Ph.D. research in 1971 with John and Harold Perkin, developed her distinctive and innovative approach to the investigation of women's lives in the twentieth century through oral history. Oliver Westall, from the economics department, enjoyed the opportunity to exercise his entrepreneurial pretensions, commissioning and selling the centre's publication series throughout the north-west. John designed a special course open to undergraduates right across the university, covering a broader spectrum of regional interests and research techniques than would have been possible within the history department. While not what he would have chosen for himself, the eclectic approach and the spread of students across all faculties seemed an arena well suited to his own refusal to box his intellectual and scholarly interests in too narrowly. The release from routine departmental teaching obligations freed John to write some of his most substantial work. The centre's first major project was a *History of Lancashire County Council*, to which John made an important contribution and edited, drawing in the expertise of colleagues from a number of departments. His joint study with John Walton of *The Lake Counties: From 1830 to the mid Twentieth Century: A study in Regional Change* and his pioneering research on 'Agrarian wealth and social structure in pre-industrial Cumbria' were all prepared in these years, along with the now expected regular flow of papers in many journals on a wide variety of topics.

John also found fulfilment through involvement in regional study away from Lancaster. He was an energetic member of the group that established the Conference of Teachers of Regional and Local History in Tertiary Education (CORAL) in 1978, serving as chairman, secretary or convenor for many years. This brought him into closer contact with scholars from many other universities, especially those with regional centres similar to Lancaster, such as the pioneer Centre for East Anglian Studies at the University of East Anglia. The *Journal of Regional and Local Studies* became associated with CORAL and John joined the editorial board. He played an active role in many local historical societies, taking part in their management, helping to ensure that the work they supported and published addressed historical issues of significance.

John's health continued to give him problems. He took formal medical retirement in 1980, but has remained a vigorous and active force in the centre's work. He has taught on its diploma courses since 1981, attended management committee meetings to ensure that his vision of regional work is not lost, and attends seminars, day schools and conferences enthusiastically whenever possible. And he has continued to write with intellectual energy and impressive productivity. He has carved out for himself a role as the philosopher and methodologist of local and regional history, in a stream of papers which he has consolidated into *The Tyranny of the Discrete*, a book that demonstrates that he has lost none of his capacity to challenge convention. With his usual self-deprecating humour, he has written 'Those of us who seriously pursue local and regional history are made empiricist by the nature of our pet studies. The man who puts forward a few theoretical opinions is therefore, the one eyed man (literally in my case) leading the sightless!' Yet these grander thoughts have not been at the expense of a serious engagement at the rock face. In 1995 he published another paper on a characteristic Marshallian theme, 'Out of wedlock: perceptions of a Cumbrian social problem in the Victorian context', in *Northern History*. And his involvement with public life has been more than vigorously maintained. His long engagement with the people of Barrow was dynamised during the late 1980s, when they responded vigorously to drastic changes imposed on their working lives. John celebrated and nourished this activism in a history of *The Barrow Strike, 1988* written with many of his long-standing friends and associates in the town.

In his long and productive retirement, John's health and morale were maintained by Frances. They worked together on a number of projects, including her poetry and a historical project she undertook, to publish an edition of the memoirs of Charlotte Deans (1768–1859) a travelling actress. His life was sadly diminished by her death in 1992. However, he continues to draw enjoyment and fulfilment from his children as they develop their own family and professional lives.

This has been John's life and his colleagues and friends look forward to the further benefits, pleasures and surprises it may grant them. His achievements have been in so many different directions that few have been able to draw all the threads together to take its full measure, though for John the life has been one closely integrated whole. He has been an inspiring teacher in school, college, adult education classes and university, a pioneering scholar, a writer of pungent prose and delicate verse, a political activist and warm, affectionate comrade to his friends in the labour movement in Barrow. In all this, an active and creative mind has worked in tandem with a passionate heart.

Those who write this friendly appreciation are not competent to comment on more than the part of his life that they have seen through his professional work at the University of Lancaster. They would make these claims. He has pioneered important departures in historical research. His work on Barrow helped open up the new field of urban history in the 1950s and showed, in an example that has only rarely been followed, how business and labour history can be successfully synthesised. He was later one of the founders of the Urban History Group in 1966. Under the stimulus of G. P. Jones, his Barrow work was marked by a demographic framework that linked the earlier work of Chambers with those of Armstrong and the Cambridge Population Group whose formation and outreach into the regions he supported in the 1960s. In that decade John moved on to explore new methods of research. His work in industrial archaeology was detailed and careful but always strongly informed and structured by his understanding of the wider history of industry and technology. His investigations here encouraged him to use oral history as an important source for information and understanding otherwise inaccessible and he was a founder member of the Oral History Society in 1971. When Elizabeth Roberts first met John as a nervous postgraduate student, she was told briskly that if she wanted to study women in the twentieth century, she would have to go out with a tape recorder and ask some questions. Initially worried, she followed his instructions, which provided the starting point for all her subsequent work in the field. But it is in the wider field of regional history that John has made his major contribution. The bibliography in this book demonstrates the extraordinary quantity and range of publications he has produced on Cumbrian history. However, it should be noted that all this work is marked by a refusal to see local and regional concerns as of purely parochial interest. John's disenchantment with the fragmentation of history into so many specialist compartments reflects the intellectual conviction, demonstrated in his published work, that the particular, though the crucial building block of history, should always be related to the general. Thus his pioneering work using probate inventories to investigate 'Agrarian wealth and social structure in pre-industrial Cumbria' at once opened up a new phase in the historiography of the region, and contributed to a new understanding of the socio-economic organisation of late seventeenth- and early eighteenth-century English society. It was in this article that he sketched how he saw his role in a few characteristic phrases:

> Professor Holmes's recent critique of Gregory King has splintered that worthy's famous table, or conventional notions of its reliability, beyond apparent hope of repair, even though the critique itself leaves King's more specific local and demographic exercises unblemished. This can only mean that, in future years, an even heavier responsibility will fall upon those hardy but sometimes ill supported frontiersmen, the regional and local historians of economic development and social change.

For some he has been primarily a challenging teacher, full of enthusiasm, his mind stocked with information drawn from an extraordinary range of scientific, cultural, political and social sources, some from wide reading, others from personal experience. While so much of his teaching has been focused on regional and local material, its frame of reference has always been of the very widest. And, contrary to much work in the field that has been essentially antiquarian, it has always been transmitted for a purpose. This has been almost precisely the opposite of the 'heritage' culture by which local and regional history can so easily be fatally infected. John's teaching has been designed to free people from easy and comforting glosses on the past. He has shown them how the past was compounded of problems and tensions much like those of the present, that careful research and creative thought about it can help us understand how society works, and how important the past has been in shaping it. In this way he has helped free his students from the complacency and prejudice that come from intellectual laziness and prepared them for action, for in John's mind understanding and active involvement are necessary concomitants.

As always, John sees himself at the edge, seeking knowledge, change, pressing colleagues to take new scholarly approaches, challenging them to contemplate new roles for themselves and their institutions. His gritty nature has borne tremendous fruit. He has developed his own particular view of history and its role and has worked hard, against the smooth but tight grain of professional academic life, to realise it in his scholarly work and in the creation of institutions to support it. John Marshall has always been an outsider, a man with a different point of view, who cannot be easily categorised, who is unwilling to fit in for the sake of harmony, who has generated strong passions. We are two who have come to value these characteristics, even when we have disagreed with his views or approach and they have tested our patience. For us, it is a test of others whether they value John and his work or not. Universities that do not encourage such independence of mind and commitment to ideas in action will be immeasurably the poorer.

How could such a man walk quiet down lanes?
His passion and his visions stored . . .[6]

Notes

1 The material on which this appreciation is based is necessarily derived from John Marshall, especially for the period before 1970. The authors are two colleagues who have worked closely with him for more than twenty-five years. It is therefore an account of his life seen largely through his own eyes, interpreted sympathetically and affectionately. John has confirmed the accuracy of the factual material but passes no comment on the judgements or opinions expressed. All the references to John's published work can be traced through the appended bibliography and are therefore not referenced directly. The authors are grateful to their colleague Angus Winchester for his helpful comments on an early draft.

2 A survey of Chambers's work and a bibliography of his publications can be found in E. L. Jones and G. E. Mingay (eds), *Land, Labour and Population in the Industrial Revolution* (London, 1967), pp. ix–xvii. The most obvious examples of his regional work are *Nottinghamshire in the Eighteenth Century: A Study of Life and Labour under the Squirearchy* (London, 1932) and 'The Vale of Trent, 1670–1800; a regional study of economic change', *EcHR*, Supplement III (1957).

3 J. Fisher, *Popular History of Barrow-in-Furness: The English Chicago* (Barrow, 1891).

4 On the remarkable Chaloner see 'A Memorial: William Henry Chaloner M.A., Ph.D, 1914–1987', *Transactions of the Lancashire and Cheshire Antiquarian Society*, 85 (1988) which contains J. D. Marshall, 'History and scholarship, the shared pursuits I'. The Cartwright paper was eventually published in N. B. Harte and K. G. Ponting (eds),

Textile History and Economic History: Essays in Honour of Miss Julia de Lacy Mann (Manchester, 1973), pp. 281–303.

5 This account of the early origins of the CNWRS is taken from M. E. McClintock, *University of Lancaster: Quest for Innovation (a history of the first ten years, 1964–1974)* (Lancaster, 1974), pp. 313–15.

6 J. D. Marshall, 'George Fox', in *Poetry Cumbria* 5.

John D. Marshall: a bibliography

Books

Furness and the Industrial Revolution: An Economic History of Furness, 1711–1897 (Barrow in Furness, Library and Museum Committee, 1958; reprinted, Beckermet [Whitehaven], Michael Moon, 1981)

(Edited), *The Autobiography of William Stout of Lancaster, 1665–1752*, Chetham Society, 3rd series, 14 (Manchester, Manchester University Press, 1967)

(With M. Davies-Shiel), *The Industrial Archaeology of the Lake Counties* (Newton Abbot, David and Charles, 1969; and 2nd edition, revised, Beckermet, Michael Moon, 1977)

(With M. Davies-Shiel), *The Lake District at Work: Past and Present* (Newton Abbot, David and Charles, 1971)

Old Lakeland: Some Cumbrian Social History (Newton Abbot, David and Charles, 1971)

(Edited and introduced), Samuel Bamford's, *Walks in South Lancashire and on its Borders: With Letters, Descriptions, Narratives and Observations: Current and Incidental* (Hassocks, Harvester Press, 1972)

The Old Poor Law, 1795–1834 (London, Macmillan, 1973 and 1985)

Lancashire. City and County Histories (Newton Abbot, David and Charles, 1974)

(With M. Davies-Shiel), *Victorian and Edwardian Lake District from Old Photographs* (London, Batsford, 1976; reprinted 1980 and 1987)

(Edited with M. E. McClintock), *The History of Lancashire County Council, 1889–1974* (London, Martin Robertson, 1977)

(With J. K. Walton), *The Lake Counties: From 1830 to the mid-twentieth century: A Study in Regional Change* (Manchester, Manchester University Press, 1981)

Portrait of Cumbria (London, Robert Hale, 1981)

The Tyranny of the Discrete: A Discussion of the Problems of Local History in England (Aldershot, Scolar Press, 1997)

Chapters in books

'Colonisation as a factor in the planting of towns in North-West England', in H. J. Dyos (ed.), *The Study of Urban History* (London, Arnold, 1968), pp. 215–30

'Local and regional history', in H. Perkin (ed.), *History: An Introduction for the Intending Student* (London, Routledge, 1970), pp. 101–14

(With W. H. Chaloner), 'Major John Cartwright and the Revolution Mill, East Retford', in N. B. Harte and K. Ponting (eds), *Textile History and Economic History* (Manchester, Manchester University Press, 1973), pp. 281–303

'Rural society before the Victorians', in O. M. Westall (ed.), *Windermere in the*

Nineteenth Century, Centre for North-West Regional Studies, Occasional Paper No. 1 (Lancaster, University of Lancaster, 1976), pp. 7–17; new edition (Lancaster, 1991)

'North Lancashire ports and the impact of transport upon their development', in E. M. Sigsworth (ed.), *Ports and Resorts in the Regions* (Hull, School of Humanities, Hull College of Higher Education, 1981), pp. 1–12

'Stages of industrialisation in Cumbria', in P. Hudson (ed.), *Regions and Industries: A Perspective on the Industrial Revolution in Britain* (Cambridge, Cambridge University Press, 1989), pp. 132–155

'Proving ground or the creation of regional identity? The origins and problems of regional history in Britain', in P. Swan and D. Foster (eds), *Essays in Regional and Local History* (Hull, Humberside Polytechnic, 1991; reprinted Beverley, 1992)

Pamphlets

The Lancashire Local Historian and his Theme. Presidential Address, May 1977 (Preston, Federation of Local Historians in the County Palatine of Lancaster, 1977)

The Barrow Strike, 1988 (Barrow in Furness, published with the support of members of Barrow Trades Unions, 1989)

Articles

'Corrupt practices at the Lancaster election of 1865', *Transactions of the Lancashire and Cheshire Antiquarian Society* 63 (1952–53), 117–30

(With S. Pollard), 'The Furness railway and the growth of Barrow', *Journal of Transport History* 1:1 (November 1953), 109–26

'The story of People's Hall: a Nottingham social centre', in *Souvenir Programme of the People's Hall Library and Institute* (Nottingham, 1954)

'A history of River Trent flooding', *The Nottinghamshire Countryside* 16:4 (April 1955), 3–6

'Local history in industrial surroundings', *The Amateur Historian* 2:5 (April-May 1955), 146–8

'Early applications of steam power: the cotton mills of the Upper Leen', *Transactions of the Thoroton Society of Nottinghamshire* 40 (1956), 34–43

'The people who left the land', *The Amateur Historian* 3:5 (Autumn 1957), 185–9

'Nottinghamshire labourers in the early nineteenth century', *Transactions of the Thoroton Society of Nottinghamshire* 64 (1960), 56–73

'The Lancashire rural labourer in the early nineteenth century', *Transactions of the Lancashire and Cheshire Antiquarian Society* 71 (1961), 90–128

'The Nottinghamshire Reformers and their contribution to the New Poor Law', *EcHR* 13 (1961), 282–96

(With H. C. Griffiths), 'Liberal studies in north-western technical colleges', *The*

Vocational Aspect of Secondary and Further Education 14:29 (Autumn 1962), 92–101

'The use of local history: some comments', *The Amateur Historian* 6:1 (Autumn 1963), 11–17

'John Henry Reynolds: pioneer of technical education in Manchester', *The Vocational Aspect* 6:35 (Autumn 1964), 176–96

'The use of local history: a brief reply to comments', *The Amateur Historian* 6:7 (Spring 1965), 233–4

(With M. Davies-Shiel), 'Industrial archaeology in the Lake Counties and Furness', *Northern History* 2 (1967), 112–34

'Some aspects of Cumbrian social history (I): migration and literacy', *Transactions of the Cumberland and Westmorland Antiquarian and Archaeological Society* 69 (1969), 280–307

'Some aspects of the social history of nineteenth century Cumbria (II): crime, police, morals and the countryman', *Transactions of the Cumberland and Westmorland Antiquarian and Archaeological Society* 70 (1970), 221–46

'A visit to Lakeland in 1844', *Transactions of the Cumberland and Westmorland Antiquarian and Archaeological Society* 71 (1971), 260–79

'Christian names', *Cumbria* 22 (1972), 327–8

'Statesmen in Cumbria: the vicissitudes of an expression', *Transactions of the Cumberland and Westmorland Antiquarian and Archaeological Society* 72 (1972), 248–73

'The domestic economy of the Lakeland Yeoman, 1660–1749', *Transactions of the Cumberland and Westmorland Antiquarian and Archaeological Society* 73 (1973), 190–219

(With M. Davies-Shiel), 'Industrial archaeology', in *The Lake District National Park*, second edition (London, Countryside Commission, 1975), 72–8

'Kendal 1661–1801: the growth of the modern town (essay)', *Transactions of the Cumberland and Westmorland Antiquarian and Archaeological Society* 75 (1975), 188–257

'The sense of place, past society and the oral historian', *Oral History* 3 (1975), 19–25

(With C. A. Dyhouse), 'Social transition in Kendal and Westmorland, *c.*1760–1860', *Northern History* 12 (1976), 127–57

'A long chapter in education history: the aspirations of the "secondary modern" in Lancashire', *University of Lancaster Regional Bulletin* 6:19 (Summer 1977), 8–10

'Industrial archaeology in the North West', *University of Lancaster Regional Bulletin* 7:21 (Spring 1978), 9–11

'Local or regional history, or both? A dialogue', *The Local Historian* 13:1 (February 1978), 3–11

'Leadership needed to make local history more respectable', *Times Higher Education Supplement* (10 March 1978), 10

'Agrarian wealth and social structure in pre-industrial Cumbria', *EcHR* 23 (1980), 503–52

'Cleator and Cleator Moor: some aspects of the social and urban development in the mid-nineteenth century', *Transactions of the Cumberland and*

Westmorland Antiquarian and Archaeological Society 78 (1978), 163–75, reprinted in *History in the Social Sciences*, Course Guide, Units 1–2 (Milton Keynes, Open University Press, 1981), 65–75

'The study of local and regional communities – some problems and possibilities', *Northern History* 17 (1981), 203–30

'Industrial archaeology: educational force or eclectic's paradise?', *Journal of Local Studies* 2:2 (Autumn 1982), 1–13

'The amateur and local history', *Lancashire Local Historian* 1 (1983), 3–10

'The rise and transformation of the Cumbrian market town, 1660–1900', *Northern History* 19 (1983), 129–209

'The evolution and study of English local history', *The Historian* 1 (Autumn 1983), 12–15

'Teaching local history?', *JORALS* 4:1 (Spring 1984), 61–3

'Cumberland and Westmorland Societies in London, 1734–1914', *Transactions of the Cumberland and Westmorland Antiquarian and Archaeological Society*, new series, 84 (1984), 239–54

'Why study regions? (1)', *JORALS* 5:1 (Spring 1985), 15–27

'Why study regions? (2): some historical considerations', *JORALS* 6:1 (Spring 1986), 1–12

'How did CORAL grow? The story of a view of local history', *Local History* 12 (July/August 1986), 20–2

'History and scholarship, the shared pursuits (I), *Transactions of Lancashire and Cheshire Antiquarian Society* 85 (1988) 39–44. Memorial for W. H. Challoner

'Blue books: and their uses to the Lancashire historian', *Lancashire Local Historian* 5 (1990), 32–9

'Discussion article: regions, regionalism and regional scholarship', *JORALS* 10:1 (Summer 1990), 66–71

'Out of wedlock: perceptions of a Cumbria social problem in the Victorian context', *Northern History* 31 (1995), 194–207

Book reviews (listed alphabetically by author)

Beckett, J. V., *Coal and Tobacco: The Lowthers and the Economic Development of West Cumberland, 1660–1760* (Cambridge University Press, 1981), in *JORALS* 2:1 (Spring 1982), 76–8

Black, A. (ed.), *Community in Historical Perspective, a Translation of Sections from Das Deutsche Gonossenschaftsrecht, by Otto von Gierke* (Cambridge University Press, 1990), in *JORALS* 14:1 (Autumn 1994), 55

Bradbury, J. B., *A History of Cockermouth* (Phillimore, 1981), in *Northern History* 19 (1983), 258

Fell, A., *The Early Iron Industry of Furness and District* (Cassell, 1968), in *Northern History* 5 (1970), 240–1

Fieldhouse, R. and Jennings, B., *A History of Richmond and Swaledale* (Phillimore, 1978), in *EcHR* 32 (1979), 603–4

Fraser, D. (ed.), *The New Poor Law in the Nineteenth Century* (Macmillan, 1976), in *EcHR* 30 (1977), 194–5

Gregory, D., *Regional Transformation and Industrial Revolution* (Macmillan, 1982), in *EcHR* 36 (1983), 455–6

Haigh, E. A. H. (ed.), *Huddersfield: A most handsome Town* (Kirklees Libraries, 1992), in *JORALS* 14:2 (Winter, 1992), 52–3

Hall, P. P., *Dolphinholme: A History of the Dolphinholme Worsted Mill, 1784–1867* (*Transactions of the Fylde Historical Society* 3, 1969), in *The Local Historian* 8:8 (1969), 303.

Harris, A., *Cumberland Iron: The Story of the Hodbarrow Mine, 1855–1967* (Barton, 1971), in *Northern History* 11 (1976), 252–3

Harris, A., *Liverpool and Merseyside* (Cass, 1969), in *History* 54 (1969), 434

Harrop, S., *Old Birkdale and Ainsdale* (Birkdale and Ainsdale Historical Research Society, 1985), in *JORALS* 7:1 (Spring 1987), 78–9

Haythorne, E., *On Earth to Make the Numbers up* (Yorkshire Arts Circus, A People's History of Yorkshire No. 2, 1981), in *JORALS* 5:1 (Spring 1985), 74–5

Heaton, M., *A Tale that is Told* (City of Bradford Metropolitan Council Libraries Division, Occasional Local Publications No. 5, 1983), in *JORALS*, 5:1 (Spring 1985), 74–5

Hills, R. L., *Power in the Industrial Revolution* (Manchester University Press, 1970), in *Northern History* 7 (1972), 149–50

Hodgkiss, N. H., *Two Lives* (Yorkshire Arts Circus, A People's History of Yorkshire No. 3, 1983), in *JORALS* 5:1 (Spring 1985), 74–5

Horn, P., *Education in Rural England* (Gill and Macmillan, 1978), in *Victorian Studies* 23:2 (Winter 1980), 263–5

Hunt, *The Lead Miners of the Northern Pennines* (Manchester University Press, 1970), in *History* 56 (1971), 459–60

Hyde, E., *Liverpool and the Mersey: The Development of a Port, 1700–1970* (David and Charles, 1971), in *Northern History* 8 (1973), 172–3

Johnston, F. R., *Eccles: The Growth of a Lancashire Town* (Eccles and District History Society, 1967), in *Northern History* 4 (1969), 223

Jones, M., *The Hallamshire Historian*, Autumn 1986, Vol. 1, No. 1, in *JORALS* 8:1 (Spring 1988), 84

Joy, D., *A Regional History of the Railways of Great Britain, vol. xiv: The Lake Counties* (David and Charles, 1983), in *Northern History* 22 (1986), 334–5

Lewis, C., *Particular Places: An Introduction to English Local History* (British Library, 1989), in *JORALS* 9:2 (Winter 1989), 62–3

Lindley, K., *Fenland Riots and the English Revolution* (Heinemann, 1982), in *JORALS* 3:1 (Summer 1983), 83–5

Longmate, N., *The Hungry Mills: The Story of the Lancashire Cotton Famine, 1861–5* (Temple-Smith, 1978), in *Northern History* 15 (1979), 252–3

McCord, N., *North East England* (Batsford, 1979), in *EcHR* 33 (1980), 116–17

Mellor, E., *Images of Ilkley in the Nineteenth and Twentieth Centuries* (City of Bradford Metropolitan Council Libraries Division, Occasional Local Publications, 1982), in *JORALS* 5:1 (Spring 1985), 74–5

Millard, R. and Robinson, A., *The Lake Counties* (Eyre and Spottiswood, 1970), in *Northern History* 8 (1973), 161–3

Mills, D. (ed.), *English Rural Communities* (Macmillan, 1973), in *History* 60 (1975), 89

Morgan, N., *Vanished Dwelling: Early Industrial Housing in a Lancashire Cotton Town: Preston* (Mullion Books, 1990), in *JORALS* 10:2 (Winter 1990), 88

Newbert, M., *Reminiscences of a Bradford Mill Girl* (City of Bradford Metropolitan Council Libraries Division, Occasional Local Publications No. 3, 1983), in *JORALS* 5:1 (Spring 1985), 74–5

Oxley, G. W., *Poor Relief in England and Wales, 1601–1834* (David and Charles, 1974), in *EcHR* 28 (1975), 324–5

Phythian-Adams, C., *Rethinking English Local History* (Leicester University Press, 1987), in *EcHR* 41 (1988), 317–18

Rowling, M., *The Folklore of the Lake District* (Batsford, 1976), in *Northern History* 13 (1977), 302–3

Smith, J. H. (ed.), *The Great Human Exploit: Historic Industries of the North West* (Phillimore, 1973), in *Northern History* 11 (1976), 249–50

Stephens, W. B., *Teaching Local History* (Manchester University Press, 1977) in *History* 63 (1978), 96

Williams, L. A., *Road Transport in Cumbria in the Nineteenth Century* (George Allen and Unwin, 1975), in *Northern History* 12 (1976), 271–2

Poetry and literature

Selected poems in:

Common Territory (Walton, Surrey, Outposts Publications, 1978)

Individual poems in:

Poetry Cumbria 5 (Ambleside, Cumbria Poetry Centre, Charlotte Mason College, 1976), p. 16

New Poetry 6, anthology edited by Ted Hughes (London, Arts Council of Great Britain, 1980)

The Lake District: An Anthology, compiled by Norman Nicholson (Harmondsworth, Penguin Books, 1978), pp. 58–9

Between Comets: For Norman Nicholson at 70, edited by William Scammel (Durham, Taxus, 1984), p. 29

Speak to the Hills, edited by H. Brown and M. Berry (Aberdeen, Aberdeen University Press, 1985), p. 56

Selected poem and prose passages in:

Voices of Cumbria: A Miscellany, compiled by C. Arnesen and L. Coope (Kendal, Westmorland Gazette 1987), pp. 84, 125–30

Edited series

(With M. E. McClintock) (eds), *University of Lancaster Regional Bulletin* 5 (1976), 6 (1977), 7 (1978), 8 (1979), Centre for North-West Regional Studies, University of Lancaster

Reports

(With J. E. Blyth), 'Regional seminar on the learning of local history by 11–18 year olds', *The Local Historian* 12:8 (November 1977), 403–7

'A North West Seminar on population history', *University of Lancaster Regional Bulletin* 7:21 (1978), pp. 11–13

'Conference Reports i) CORAL Seminar Report. The uses of hearth tax documents in local history [1983]; ii) Anglo-Scottish conference, University of Newcastle, 7th May 1983; iii) CORAL/LPSS Conference. Population Change in the English Regions [1983]', in *JORALS* 3:2 (Winter 1983), 78–94

'CORAL conference report: tithe records and their uses in local history [1983]', in *JORALS* 4:1 (Spring 1984), 69–71

'CORAL conference reports. The history of religion in its regional context [1984]', in *JORALS* 4:2 (Autumn 1984), 76–84

'The CORAL conference on pro-industrialisation, 1985: industry in the regions: some impressions', in *JORALS* 6:1 (Spring 1986), 75–83

'CORAL seminar on Parliamentary papers, 1987', report in *JORALS* 8:1 (Spring 1988), 46–50

'CORAL seminar on industrial colonies and communities [1988]', in *JORALS* 8:2 (Autumn 1988), 62–6

'Local history qualifications: conference report [1989]', in *JORALS* 9:1 (Summer 1989), 61–8

'The study of suburbia: seminar report [1989]', in *JORALS* 9:2 (Winter 1989), 54–8

'English provincial society and its institutions, *c.* 1250–1650: authority, representation and community. Conference Report [1990]', in *JORALS* 10:1 (Summer 1990), 60–5

(Edited), 'Are British regions neglected? Proceedings of the seminar held at Rewley House, Oxford, 5th May 1990', in *JORALS* 10:2 (Winter 1990), 1–87

Miscellaneous

'Higher degrees in the Open University: theses and dissertations on local and regional topics: work in progress', in *JORALS* 5:1 (Spring 1985), 59–61

'A survey of courses in regional and local history in tertiary education', *JORALS* 6:2 (Autumn 1986), 59–73

'More tertiary courses in regional history', *JORALS* 7:1 (Spring 1987), 65–71

'Courses in local and regional history in higher education', *JORALS* 7:2 (Autumn 1987), 63–6

'Regional and local history in places of tertiary education in Britain: supplement 2', *JORALS* 8:1 (Spring 1988), 52–6

'Courses in local and regional history in higher education: addendum 3', in *JORALS* 8:2 (Autumn 1988), 67

'Current courses and research in regional and local history in tertiary institutions in Great Britain', compiled in *JORALS* 12:2 (Winter 1992), 32–43; 'A second selection', in *JORALS* 14:2 (Winter 1994), 47–51; 'Continued' in *JORALS* 15:1 (Summer 1995), 38–47

'Obituary: Philip Liddle', in *JORALS* 16:2 (Winter 1996), [before p. 1]

List of subscribers

J. V. Beckett
Roger A. Bellingham
Peter Borsay
Centre for North West Regional Studies
Christopher Chalklin
Dr Krista Cowman
D. P. Dymond
G. C. F. Forster
Dr Philip Gooderson
A. J. Heesom
Mollie Hobson
Stephen Jackson
John Langton
Professor Norman McCord
C. B. Phillips
A. J. Pollard
Professor Jeffrey Richards
Dr Paul Richards
Edward Royle
School of Geography, University of Oxford
Robert Speake
Geoffrey Timmins
Dr Simon Townley
Dr John Whyman
Ian Willis
Dr Philip Woodfine
Professor Chris Wrigley

Index

Note: 'n' after a page reference indicates the number of a note on that page; page numbers in *italics* after the other page numbers refer to maps.